U0902402

本书系2018年度重庆师范大学学术专著出版基金资助立项项目

四书白话英语新译

（下）

王方路 著

第四部分 《孟子》(*The Book of Master Meng*)

孟子集注卷一 梁惠王章句上[1]凡七章

【原文】1 孟子见梁惠王[2]。王曰:“叟不远千里而来,亦将有以利吾国乎?”[3]孟子对曰:“王何必曰利? 亦有仁义而已矣。[4]王曰‘何以利吾国’? 大夫曰‘何以利吾家’? 士庶人曰‘何以利吾身’? 上下交征利而国危矣。[5]万乘之国弑其君者[6],必千乘之家[7];千乘之国弑其君者,必百乘之家。万取千焉[8],千取百焉,不为不多矣。苟为后义而先利,不夺不餍[9]。未有仁而遗其亲者也,未有义而后其君者也。王亦曰仁义而已矣[10],何必曰利?”

【白话译文】

孟子觐见梁惠王。梁惠王说:“老先生不远千里来到这儿,将有什么利于我国的呢?”孟子答道:“王呀,为什么一定要说利呢? 只要有仁义就行了。如果王只是说‘怎样才有利于我的国家呢?’大夫只是说‘怎样才有利于我的家呢?’那一般士子和老百姓都说‘怎样才有利于我身呢?’这样,上上下下互相夺取利益,国家便危险了。在有一万辆车的国家里,杀掉国君的一定是有一千辆兵车的大夫;在有一千辆兵车的国家里,杀掉国君的一定是有一百辆兵车的大夫。在一万中取得一千,在一千中取得一百,这不能不说是取得够多了。如果把私利摆在公义前,那不把国君的一切都夺去是不会满足的。从没有行仁德的人遗弃过父母的,也从没有行正义的人怠慢过君上的。王只要讲仁义就可以了,为什么一定要说利呢?”

【英语译文】

Mencius paid a visit to King Hui of Liang State and the latter asked him, “You've come here from thousand *li* afar, and what can you benefit our state?" Mencius responded, "Why do you necessarily mention benefit? It's all right if one is benevolent and righteous. If a king often asks what one can benefit his state, if a minister always asks what one can benefit his family, and if a common man often asks what one can benefit him, then they all strive for benefit. The result is that the state is in danger. In a state of ten thousand fighting carts, the man who murdered the king surely has one thousand carts. And in a state of one thousand fighting carts, the man who murdered the king surely has one hundred carts. It's quite enough if one gets one thousand from ten thousand or one gets one hundred from one thousand. If private benefit honors priority to public righteousness, one cannot get satisfied if he cannot rob all that belong to the king. There was never a filial son who dejects his parents and there never was a righteous man who neglects his king. You, the king just care about benevolence and righteousness. Why do you mention benefit?"

【注释】(1)梁惠王章句上:《孟子》的篇名。是摘取篇头的几个重要字眼做成。“章句”是汉代经学家、训诂家常用的术语,即分析古书章节句读的意思。在这里,用作训解古书的题名。“梁惠王章句上”是东汉赵岐所作《孟子章句》的旧题。他把《孟子》七篇各分为上下两卷,故此题为“章句上”。(2)梁惠王:即魏惠王(公元前400年——公元前319年)战国时魏国君。名罃(yīng)。公元前369年——公元前319年在位。公元前362年从安邑(今山西夏县西北)迁都大梁(今河南开封),僭称王。惠是谥号。史记:“惠王三十五年,卑礼厚币以招贤者,而孟轲至梁。”(3)叟:sǒu,老人。不远千里:不,副词。表示否定。不远千里,谓不以千里为远。亦:语气助词。有以:即“有所以”。意谓有何,有什么。(4)亦有:只有。亦,副词,仅,只。仁义:朱熹四书集注:“仁者,心之德,爱之理。义者,心之制,事之宜也。”(5)交征利:互相夺取利益。征,夺取。万乘之国:乘,读shèng,一辆兵车叫一乘。春秋、战国时,以兵车的多少来衡量国家的大小强弱。(6)万乘之国:有一万辆兵车,是大国。当时有七个大国:秦、楚、齐、燕、韩、赵、魏(梁)。千乘之国只能算小国。(7)千乘之家:古代的执政大夫有一定的封邑,有这种封邑的大夫叫家。公卿的封邑大,可出兵车千乘,大夫的封邑小,可出兵车百乘。(8)万取千焉:一万中取得一千。(9)餍:yàn,饱;满足。(10)亦曰:只说,只谈。

【原文】2 孟子见梁惠王 。王立于沼上,顾鸿雁麋鹿,曰:“贤者亦乐此乎?”[1],孟子对曰:“贤者而后乐此[2],不贤者虽有此,不乐也。诗云:‘经始灵台[3],经之营之[4],庶民攻之[5],不日成之[6],经始勿亟[7],庶民子来[8],王在灵囿[9],麀鹿攸伏[10],麀鹿濯濯[11],白鸟鹤鹤[12],王在灵沼,于牣鱼跃[13]。'文王以民力为台为沼,而民欢乐之,谓其台曰灵台,谓其沼曰灵沼,乐其有麋鹿鱼鳖。古之人与民偕乐,故能乐也。汤誓曰[14]:'时日害丧[15],予及女偕亡[16]。'虽有台池鸟兽,岂能独乐哉?"

【白话译文】

孟子觐见梁惠王。他正站在池塘边,一面欣赏大雁和麋鹿,一面对孟子说:"贤德的人也喜欢这些吗?"孟子回答说:"贤德的人做到了贤德以后也喜欢这些,不贤的人虽有这些,喜欢不起。《诗·大雅·灵台》咏道:'着手规划筑灵台,规划建筑动起来。百姓踊跃一齐努力,不久即成乐开怀,文王本意不急速,百姓如子敬父母。文王来到灵囿里,母鹿安伏格外乖。肥胖圆润还闪亮,对照群鹤一片白。文王站在灵池边,鱼欢跳池水抬。'文王用百姓的劳力筑台挖池,百姓对这事很欢喜,称那个台叫灵台,称那个池叫灵沼,乐意欣赏那些珍奇的鸟兽鱼鳖。古代贤明的国君和百姓同享欢乐,所以能得到真正的快乐。《书·汤誓》中记载着百姓对暴君夏桀的怨歌:'这个太阳啊,你什么时候坠落?我愿意同你一道死亡!'这样的国君,老百姓恨不得与他同归于尽,纵然有高台深池,奇禽异兽,又怎么能独自享受呢?"

【英语译文】

When Mencius visited King Hui of Liang Sate, the latter stood by a pond watching swans and elks, then he asked, "Does an able and moral man also like these?" Mencius responded, "When a man becomes able and moral he will like these. An unable and immoral man cannot like these even if they have these. Lines in *Divine Platform* go as follows: 'Divine Platform was planned to build. The project had been implemented. Ordinary men did jobs voluntarily. Rapid completing made one surprised. The plan originally wasn't urgent. Ordinary men showed their support. King Wen sight-saw among Divine Garden. Female deer behaves peacefully no hurry. Female deer grows fat with shining fur. White birds have their dense white feather. King Wen sight-saw on the Divine Pond, Oh! Fish jumped happily with loud sound.' King Wen of Zhou Dynasty had the people build the platform and they called it divine platform, and called the pond divine one. They loved to appreciate those birds, beasts and turtles. Ancient kings shared pleasure with common people so that they could find real pleasure. *Oath of Tang* in *The Book of History* recorded common people's agony towards dictator King Jie of Xia Dynasty, 'When will this sun fall down? We're willing to perish together with it!' Common people just wanted to perish together with such kind of king. Even though he had such kind of platform and pond, rare beasts and birds, how could he share them alone?"

【注释】(1)鸿雁:大雁。麋鹿:麋,读 mí,哺乳动物。俗名"四不像"。原产中国,是一种稀有的珍贵动物。鹿,哺乳纲鹿科动物的总称。(2)而后:以后,后来。贤者而后乐此,意谓:贤者以贤为先以乐此为后。(3)经始:开始规划营造。灵台:台名,在今陕西西安西北。(4)经之营之:即筹划它营造它。(5)攻:营建。(6)不日:不久。(7)勿亟:不求急速。(8)子来:谓民心归附如子女趋事父母。(9)灵囿:周文王苑囿名。(10)麀鹿:yōu ~,母鹿。攸伏:即"所伏"。栖居处。(11)濯濯:zhuó ~,肥泽的样子。(12)白鸟:白羽的鸟,鹤、鹭之类。鹤鹤:诗经作"翯翯"。音义相同。谓洁白而有光泽。(13)于:wū,叹美词。牣:rèn,盈满;充塞。(14)汤誓:《尚书》篇名。(15)时日:这个太阳。喻指夏桀。时,通"是"。害:hé,通"曷"。疑问代词。什么时候。丧:坠落。(16)偕亡:《书·汤誓》作"皆亡"。皆,谐音近义通。一同死亡。朱熹《四书集注》:"桀尝自言吾有天下,如天之有日,日亡吾乃亡耳。民怨其虐,故引其自言而目之曰,此日何时亡乎?若亡则我宁与之俱亡,盖欲其亡之甚也。孟子引此,以明君独乐而不恤其民,则民怨之而不能保其乐也。"

【原文】3 梁惠王曰:"寡人之于国也[1],尽心焉耳矣[2]。河内凶[3],则移其民于河东[4],移其粟于河内。河东凶亦然。察邻国之政,无如寡人之用心者[5]。邻国之民不加少[6],寡人之民不加多,何也?"孟子对曰:"王好战,请以战喻。填然鼓之[7],兵刃既接,弃甲曳兵而走,或百步而后止[8],或五十步而后止。以五十步笑百步[9],则何如?"曰:"不可,直不百步耳,[10]是亦走也。"曰:"王如知此,则无望民之多于邻国也,[11]不违农时[12],谷不可胜食也[13],数罟不入洿池[14],鱼鳖不可胜食也;斧斤以时入山林[15],材木不可胜用也。榖与鱼鳖不可胜食,材木不可胜用,是使民养生丧死无憾也[16],养生丧死无憾,王道之始也[17]。五亩之宅,树之以桑,五十者可以衣帛矣[18];鸡豚狗彘之畜[19],无失其时[20],七十者可以食肉矣;百亩之田,勿夺其时,数口之家,可以无饥矣;谨庠序之教[21],申之以孝悌之养[22],颁白者不负戴于道路矣[23]。七十者衣帛食肉,黎民不饥不寒,然而不王者未之有也[24]。狗彘食人食而不知检[25],涂有饿殍而不知发[26];人死则曰:'非我也,岁也[27]。'是何异于刺人而杀之[28],曰:'非我也,兵也。'王无罪岁,斯天下之民至焉。"

【白话译文】

梁惠王说:“我对于国家只是竭尽心意罢了。河内灾荒,我就把百姓迁移些到河东,把河东的粮食运些到河内。河东灾荒,也这样处理。我观察邻国的政治,没有像我这样费尽心思的。可是,邻国的百姓不减少,我的百姓不增多,这是为什么呢?”孟子回答道:“王喜欢战争,请让我用战争打个比喻吧。战鼓咚咚震耳响,双方兵器相对,交锋激战,败者丢掉铠甲,拖着兵器逃跑;有的跑了一百步停下,有的跑了五十步停下。跑了五十步的讥笑跑了一百步的,您看这怎么样?”王说:“这不行,讥笑的人也是败逃呀,只不过没跑到一百步罢了。”孟子说:“王如果通晓这个道理,就不要指望老百姓比邻国多。在农忙时,不做违反农活的事,粮食就会多起来吃不完;不用细密的网到水塘里捕鱼,鱼鳖也就吃不完了;不到草木零落时不砍伐树木,木材也就够用了。粮食和鱼鳖吃不完,木材用不尽,这样就使老百姓对生老病死没有什么懊恼了。老百姓对生老病死没有什么懊恼,这就是王道的开端啦。五亩大小的居住地,种植桑树以供养蚕,五十岁以上的人就可以穿丝织品衣服了;鸡狗和各种猪的饲养,不失误繁殖时期,七十岁以上的人就可以有肉吃了。一百亩的耕地,不要侵占它的农活季节,几口人的家庭就可以吃饱了。办好学校教育,伸张孝敬父母、敬爱兄长的教养,须发花白的人就不用背着、顶着重物在路上行走了。七十岁以上的人有丝织品衣服穿有肉吃,一般百姓不受冻挨饿,这样还不能行王道使天下归附,是从来不曾有过的。现在富贵人家的猪狗吃掉了百姓的粮食,还不知道节俭;道路上有饿死的人,却不知道开仓赈济。老百姓死了竟说:‘这不是我的责任,而是年成不好。’这种说法和拿刀子杀了人却说‘这不是我干的呀,是刀子干的呀’有什么不同?王不责怪年成,而完善自己的政治,这样天下的百姓就会投奔而来。”

【英语译文】

King Hui of Liang State said, “I have done my best to my country. When there was famine within Yellow River region, I ordered part of my subjects to migrate to the east region of the River. And when there was famine within the east region of the River, I do the opposite. I observed that the neighbor state’s king didn’t do things that I had done. However, subjects in neighbor country haven’t decreased and those in my country haven’t increased. What is the reason for this?” Mencius responded, “I’ll give you an analogy to war since you like waging war. While drum being beaten the rivalries fight fiercely and the defeated escaped by drawing their weapons. Some run for one hundred paces to stop whereas others do fifty paces to stop. Those who run for fifty paces sneer at those who run for one hundred paces. What do you think about this?" King Hui answered, "It's not OK because they are all the same fleeing away." Mencius said, "If you have known this, then you shall not wish your subjects increase and become more than that of neighbor country. In busy farming seasonthey don't violate the farming rule, and then people will obtain enough food. If they don't use dense woven nets to fish, they will have enough water food. If they don't cut ever-growing trees, they will have enough useful timber. With enough food, water food and timber, the common people don't have to worry about living, aging, diseases or death, which is the beginning of Kingly Way. In a five-*mu* residence, mulberry trees are planted to raise silkworms and people over fifty years old can wear silk clothes. Chicken, dogs, and pigs are reared and people over seventy years old can eat meat. For one hundred *mu* farming field, the farming season is kept in order and then a household with several persons surely have enough food. Schooling is set up to educate children filial to their parents, and then the elder people with gray hair needn't carry loads on the road. There isn't the situation that the Kingly Way can't go smoothly and people hesitate to gather around when seventy-year-old ones can wear silk clothes and eat meat and common people suffer no famine and cold. Nowadays people don't know living shriftly while pigs and dogs in wealthy families ate up common people's food. And people don't relieve those victims of famine when some are dead on the road. On the death of common persons the officials say 'It isn't our fault; it is due to natural calamity'. Such kind of excuse is the same as when someone kills others by a knife and says 'It isn't me but the knife that kills others'. If the king doesn't blame nature but perfect his administration, common people will gather around him."

【注释】(1)寡人:古代诸侯对下的自称。言寡德的人。(2)尽心焉耳矣:尽心,竭尽心意;费尽心思。焉耳矣,同“焉尔矣”。犹如此而已。(3)河内:古代指黄河以北的地区。也专指今河南省黄河以北的地区。凶:灾荒,收成坏。(4)河东:山西省境内黄河以东的地区。河内、河东都是魏地。(5)用心:费心,尽心。(6)加少:犹言增加少的程度。义同“减少”。(7)填然:tián ~,形容鼓声。然,词尾。粘在副词、形容词后,表示声、貌、情、态的样子。没有相应的词可以对译。可以不译或去掉。鼓之:鼓,鼓声。之,语尾助词。(8)弃甲曳兵:丢掉铠甲,拖着兵器。形容战败狼狈逃跑。走:古代慢慢走叫“步”。(9)笑:讥笑;嘲笑。(10)直:副词。只不过;特;但。(11)无:副词。表示禁止。不可、不要。(12)农时:谓春耕、夏耘、秋收之时。(13)胜食:shèng ~(旧读 shēng ~),尽食。(14)数罟:cù gǔ,细密的渔网。洿池:wū ~水塘。(15)斧斤:泛指各种斧子。斤,斧头。(16)养生丧死:yàng shēng sāng sǐ,义同"养生送死""养生送葬"。指子女对父母生前的赡养和死后的殡葬。(17)王道:儒家提出的一种以仁义治天下的政治主张。与"霸道"相对。(18)衣帛:yìbó,穿丝织物。帛,古代丝织物的通称。(19)豚:tún,小猪。亦泛指猪。彘:zhì,猪。亦指野猪。畜:xù,饲养。(20)失其时:失误其繁殖时。(21)谨:谨慎;慎重。庠序之教:庠序,古代的地方学校。后亦泛称学校。庠序之教,犹言学校教育。(22)申:伸展;伸张。孝悌:孝顺父母、敬爱兄长。养:教育;教养。(23)颁白:bān ~,须发半白。颁,同"斑"。负戴:以背负物以头顶物。一种劳作方式。(24)王:实行王道使天下太平百姓归附。(25)检:检束;检约。(26)涂:道路。饿殍:èpiǎo,饿死的人;快饿死的人。莩,通"殍"。发:散发;发给。特指赈济。(27)岁:年岁。义同"年景""年成"。指一年的农业收入。(28)是:代词。此,这。刺人而杀之:用刀剑等锐物刺伤人体使之死亡。

【原文】4 梁惠王曰:"寡人愿安承教[1]。"孟子对曰:"杀人以梃与刃[2],有以异乎[3]?"曰:"无以异也[4]。""以刃与政有以异乎[5]?"曰:"无以异也。"曰:"庖有肥肉[6],廐有肥马[7],民有饥色[8],野有饿莩,此率兽而食人也[9]。兽相食,且人恶之;为民父母,行政,不免于率兽而食人,恶在其为民父母也[10]?仲尼曰[11]:'始作俑者其无后乎![12],为其象人而用之也[13]。如之何其使斯民饥而死也?"

【白话译文】

梁惠王说:"我很乐意接受您的指教。"孟子说:"杀人用棍棒和用刀剑有什么不同吗?"梁惠王说:"没有什么不同。""用刀剑杀人和用政治杀人有什么不同吗?"梁惠王说:"没有什么不同。"孟子说:"那么,厨房里有肥肉,马房里有肥马,百姓脸上有饥饿色,野外有饿死的人,这就是率领着禽兽来吃人啦。禽兽自相吞食的现象,人们还厌恶;做百姓的官,主持政事,却免不了率领禽兽来吃人,那又在哪里去做百姓的官呢?孔子说过:'第一个用木材泥土制造偶人来殉葬的人,该会断绝后代吧!'孔子痛恨这种行为,是由于用木材泥土制造的偶人仿真活人形象而被用来殉葬。用偶人殉葬都还不可,又怎么可以使百姓活活饿死呢?"

【英语译文】

King Hui of Liang State said, "I'm willing to be instructed by you." Mencius asked, "Is there any difference between killing persons by stick and doing so by knife?" King Hui answered, "There is no difference." "Is there any difference between killing persons by knife and doing so by politics?" Mencius said, "Then there are meat in kitchen and horses in stable, and people look thin due to hunger. In wilderness people die from hunger. In that circumstance, beasts are led to eat people. We detest that beasts eat each other while officials lead beasts to eat people. How could they act as parental officials for common people? Confucius ever said 'The first person who used wooden and earthen puppies to bury alive with the dead should have no offspring.' Confucius loathed such kind of action because it imitates the image of person to bury alive with the dead. It is not right to use puppies to bury alive with the dead. How could we let people die from hunger?"

【注释】(1)愿安:情愿,乐意。承教:接受教令。(2)以梃与刃:"以梃与以刃"的省略式。介词短语作状语。用棍棒和用刀剑。梃,读 tǐng,棍棒。刃,读 rèn,刀剑一类的利器。(3)有以:有何,有什么。(4)无以:与"有以"相对。(5)以刃与政:省略了谓语部分,杀人。(6)庖:páo,厨房。(7)厩:jiù,马房。(8)饥色:饥饿的面色。(9)率兽而食人:指统治者为政失职,只图享乐,不关心百姓疾苦。后因以"率兽而食人"比喻虐政害民。(10)恶在:犹"何在""安在"。在何处,在哪里。恶,读 wū,疑问代词。相当于"何""安"。(11)仲尼:孔子字仲尼。(12)俑:yǒng,古时用以殉葬的偶人。一般为木制或陶制。(13)为其象人而用之也:是由于用木材泥土制造的偶人仿真活人形象而被用来殉葬。

【原文】5 梁惠王曰:"晋国,[1]天下莫强焉,[2]叟之所知也。及寡人之身,东败于齐,长子死焉[3];西丧地于秦七百里[4];南辱于楚[5]。寡人耻之,愿比死者壹洒之[6]。如之何则可?"孟子对曰:"地方百里而可以王[7]。王如施仁政于民,省刑罚,薄税敛,深耕易耨[8];壮者以暇日修其孝悌忠信,入以事其父兄,出以事其长上,可使制梃以挞秦、楚之坚甲利兵矣[9]。""彼夺其民时[10],使不得耕耨以养其父母。父母冻饿,兄弟妻子离散。彼陷溺其民[11],王往而征之,夫谁与王敌?故曰:'仁者无敌'王请勿疑!"

【白话译文】

梁惠王说:"我们祖上晋国,天下没有胜过它的。这是您老知道的。到了我来继位,东方败给了齐国,我的大儿子也战死了;西方又败给了秦国,丢掉七百里土地;南方又受到楚国的欺凌。我感到很耻辱。很想为死去的人们雪尽愤恨。请问该怎么样才行呢?”孟子回答说:“纵横各一百里的小国也能实行王道。您如果对百姓施行仁政,减免刑罚,减轻赋税,让百姓勤于农事,精耕细作,让年轻力壮的人,在闲暇时间来讲求孝顺父母、敬爱兄长、为人忠诚守信等道德规范,并遵守这些规范,在家侍奉父母、敬爱兄长,在外尊奉长者和上级。这样,即便让老百姓做些棍棒,也可以抗击装备坚实盔甲、锐利刀枪的秦、楚军队了。秦、楚等国,兵役、徭役繁重,侵占了老百姓正常生产劳动和正常休息的时间。老百姓不能耕田种地来养活父母,父母受冻挨饿,兄、弟、妻、子,分离散失。他们真是让百姓在水深火热中受苦受难。你去征讨这样的国家,还会有谁来与您为敌呢? 所以说:‘仁德的人是无敌于天下的。’请您不要怀疑。”

【英语译文】

King Hui of Liang State said, “There wasn’t a state which ever surpassed Jin State. You know this fact. But when I was in power, it was defeated by Qi State in the east and my eldest son died, and in the west our territory of seven hundred square *li* was ceded to Qin State. In the south, we were bullied by Chu State. I feel ashamed very much and I want to revenge for those who died. How could I do?” Mencius answered, “The Kingly Way can be carried out even in a country of just one hundred square *li*. If you carry out benevolent government, cutdown penalty, lessen tax, let common people focus on intense farming, make the youth obey the moral norms – being filial to parents, respecting elders, being honest and keeping promise. At home they attend parents and brothers and in society they respect elders and leaders. In such circumstance, even if you let your subjects use cudgels, they can defeat those armored soldiers of Qin and Chu states. Because in those states, people suffered so heavy military service and forced labor that they have no time to till their fields or take a rest. Common people cannot till fields to serve their parents who suffer cold and hunger. A man’s brothers, wife, and children fall apart. Those in power really make their subject lead a terrible life. If you decide to attack such kind of state, who can be rival with you? Therefore, ‘a moral and benevolent man has no opponent’. Please believe this.”

【注释】(1)晋国:魏国本晋大夫魏斯与韩氏、赵氏共分晋地而立。号曰三晋(史称三家分晋)。故惠王犹自谓晋国。惠王三十年,齐击魏,破其军,虏太子申。十七年,秦取魏国少梁,后魏又数献地于秦。又与楚将昭阳战败,亡其七邑。(2)天下莫强焉:莫,代词。没有谁,没有哪个。强,超过,胜过。焉,他称代词。在此作宾语。(3)长子死焉:指马陵之战。公元前342年,魏攻韩,韩求救于齐。齐以田忌为大将,孙膑为军师,起兵攻魏。次年齐用孙膑计,以逐日减灶制造齐军大量逃亡的假象,迷惑魏军,引诱其追击。齐军在马陵(今河南省范县西南)设伏,全歼魏军十万。魏将庞涓自杀,魏太子申也被俘杀。魏国势从此衰落。(4)丧地于秦七百里:马陵之役后,魏又屡败于秦,割河西之地及上郡之十五城。(5)南辱于楚:梁惠王后元十一年,楚遣柱国(武官名)昭阳统兵攻魏破之于襄陵(今河南淮阳西),夺得八邑。(6)比:介词。替;为。壹洒:yīxǐ,洗尽耻辱。洒,后作"洗"。洗涤;洗雪。(7)地方百里:指横直各百里之地,相当现今一个不大不小的县的范围。可以王:能够实行王道。(8)深耕易耨:深翻土地,勤除杂草。谓勤于农事。易耨,读yìnòu,易,快,急速。不拖延,不懈怠。耨,小锄;用小锄除草。(9)制梃:制造棍棒。挞:tà,用鞭子或棍子打。引申为攻击;抗击。坚甲利兵:坚实的铠甲和锐利的刀剑。(10)民时:老百姓正常生产劳动和正常休息的时间。(11)陷溺:谓使人处于水深火热之中,祸害人。

【原文】6 孟子见梁襄王[1],出,语人曰[2]:"望之不似人君,就之而不见所畏焉[3]。卒然问曰[4]:'天下恶乎定[5]?'吾对曰:'定于一[6]。''孰能一之?'对曰:'不嗜杀人者能一之[7]''孰能与之[8]?'对曰:'天下莫不与也。王知夫苗[9]乎?七八月之间旱[10],则苗槁矣。天油然作云[11],沛然下雨[12],则苗浡然兴之矣[13]。其如是[14],孰能御之?[15]今夫天下之人牧[16],未有不嗜杀人者也。如有不嗜杀人者,则天下之民皆引领而望之矣[17]。诚如是也,民归之,由水之就下[18],沛然谁能御之?'"

【白话译文】

孟子觐见梁襄王。出来后,对别人说:"远处望见他,不像是国君;走近他身边,不见有威仪。他突然问道:'天下要如何才安定?'我答道:'天下统一了就会安定。'他又问:'谁能统一天下?'我答道:'不爱好杀人的国君,就能统一天下。'他又问:'那有谁跟他在一起呢?'我答道:'天下的人没有不和他在一起的。您认识禾苗吗?七八月间天旱,禾苗就会枯槁。这时,天上一阵乌云涌起,哗哗地下起大雨来,禾苗又继续挺长着。他们这样顺应天时,谁能阻挡?现在天下的国君,没有一个不爱好杀人。如果有一位不爱好杀人的国君,那么天下的百姓都会伸长脖子盼望他了。真的这样,百姓的归附如同水往下流,谁能阻挡得住呢?'"

【英语译文】

Mencius visited King Xiang of Liang State. Upon leaving he said to others, "He didn't appear like a king when you saw him in distance. As you came near him you found nothing dignified in him. And he suddenly asked me, 'How can the world become settled?' I answered, 'After unification the world will be settled.' He asked again, 'Who can unify the world?' I answered, 'The king who doesn't like killing people.' He asked once again, 'Who will stand together with him?' I answered, 'In the world, nobody is unwilling to stand together with him. Have you ever seen grain seedling? During fifth and sixth month, if it's very dry and they will wither. Suddenly clouds gathered and it rained cats and dogs timely. The grain seedling continued growing. They act in accordance with natural law. Who can hinder them? Nowadays kings in the world all love killing people. If there is a king who doesn't love killing people, common people will desire to gather around him. If it is really like this, the common people submit to the authority of him like floating water. Who can hinder this?'"

【注释】(1)梁襄王:梁惠王之子,名嗣(据系本)。朱熹四书集注:"襄王,惠王子,名赫。"(2)语:yù,告诉。(3)所畏焉:所,结构助词。用在动词前组成名词性词组。畏,读 wēi,通"威"。所畏,犹"所威"。威仪;威严的意思。焉,语气助词。用在陈述句末表论断决断或终结的语气,可去掉不译,也可译作"呢""的"。(4)卒然:cù ~,突然;忽然。(5)恶乎定:恶,读 wū,疑问代词。相当于"何""安""怎么"。乎,语气助词。定,安定;平定。(6)定于一:在统一中得到安定。(7)嗜杀人:shì ~ ~,爱好杀人;喜爱杀人。(8)与:yù,亲附;归附;陪从。(9)知夫苗:知,认识。夫,语中助词。苗,禾苗。指尚未开花结实的禾类植物。(10)七八月:这里指周代历法的七八月。周历以夏历(相当于现代农历)的十一月为岁首(正月),其七八月相当于夏历的五六月。这时正是禾苗需要雨水的时候。(11)油然:旺盛兴起的样子。(12)沛然:充满盛大的样子。(13)浡然:bó ~,生长不停的样子;继续生长的样子。(14)其如是:其,他称代词。指上文云、雨、苗。其如是,它们如此;它们这样。(15)御:抗拒;抵挡。(16)人牧:人君,国君。古代指统治人民的人。(17)引领:伸着颈项远望。多形容期望殷切。(18)由:通"犹"。如同;好像。

【原文】7 齐宣王问曰[1]:"齐桓、晋文之事可得闻乎?[2]"孟子对曰:"仲尼之徒无道桓、文之事者,是以后世无传焉,臣未之闻也。[3]无以,[4]则王乎?"[5]曰:"德何如则可以王矣?"曰:"保民而王,莫之能御也。"曰:"若寡人者,可以保民乎哉?"曰:"可。"曰:"何由知吾可也?"曰:"臣闻之胡龁曰,[6]王坐于堂上,有牵牛而过堂下者,王见之,曰:'牛何之?'[7]对曰:'将以衅钟。[8]'王曰:'舍之!吾不忍其觳觫若无罪而就死地。'[9]对曰:'然则废衅钟与?'[10]曰:'何可废也,以羊易之!'不识有诸?"[11]曰:"有之。"曰:"是心足以王矣。百姓皆以王为爱也,臣固知王之不忍也。"王曰:"然。诚有百姓者。齐国虽褊小,[12]吾何爱一牛?即不忍其觳觫,若无罪而就死地,故以羊易之也。"曰:"王无异于百姓之以王为爱也。[13]以小易大,彼恶知之?王若隐其无罪而就死地,[14]则牛羊何择焉?"王笑曰:"是诚何心哉?我非爱其财,而易之以羊也,宜乎百姓之谓我爱也。"曰:"无伤也,是乃仁术也,[15]见牛未见羊也。君子之于禽兽也,见其生不忍见其死;闻其声不忍食其肉。是以君子远庖厨也。"[16]王说曰:[17]"诗云:[18]'他人有心予忖度之'[19]夫子之谓也。[20]夫我乃行之,反而求之,不得吾心。夫子言之,于我心有戚戚焉。[21]此心之所以合于王者,何也?"曰:"有复于王者曰:[22]'吾力足以举百钧'[23],而不足以举一羽;'明足以察秋毫之末',[24]而不见舆薪,[25]则王许之乎?[26]"曰:"否。""今恩足以及禽兽,而功不至于百姓者,独何与?[27]然则一羽之不举,为不用力焉;舆薪之不见,为不用明焉,百姓之不见保,[28]为不用恩焉。故王之不王,不为也,非不能也。"曰:"不为者与不能者之形何以异?[29]"曰:"挟太山以超北海,[30]语人曰'我不能',是诚不能也。为长者折枝,[31]语人曰'我不能',是不为也,非不能也。故王之不王,非挟泰山以超北海之类也;王之不王,是折枝之类也。老吾老以及人之老;[32]幼吾幼以及人之幼。[33]天下可运于掌。[34]诗云:'刑于寡妻至于兄弟,[35]以御于家邦。[36]'言举斯心加诸彼而已。[37]故推恩足以保四海,[38]不推恩无以保妻子。古之人所以大过人者无他焉,善推其所为而已矣。今恩足以及禽兽,而功不至于百姓者,[39]独何与?权,[40]然后知轻重;度,[41]然后知长短。物皆然,心为甚。王请度之!抑王兴甲兵,[42]危士臣,构怨于诸侯,然后快于心与?"王曰:"否。吾何快于是?将以求吾所大欲也。"曰:"王之所大欲可得闻与?"王笑而不言。曰:"为肥甘不足于口与?轻暖不足于体与?抑为采色不足视于目与?[43]声音不足听于耳与?便嬖不足使令于前与?[44]王之诸臣皆足以供之。而王岂为是哉?"曰:"否。吾不为是也。"曰:"然则王之所大欲可知已。欲辟土地,[45]朝秦、楚,[46]莅中国而抚四夷也。[47]以若所为求若所欲,[48]犹缘木而求鱼也。[49]"王曰:"若是其甚与?"曰:"殆有甚焉。[50]缘木求鱼,虽不得鱼,无后灾。以若所为,求若所欲,尽心力而为之,后必有灾。"曰:"可得闻与?"曰:"邹人与楚人战,[51]则王以为孰胜?"曰:"楚人胜。"曰:"然则小固不可以敌大,寡固不可以敌众,弱固不可以敌强。海内之地方千里者九,[52]齐集有其一。[53]以一服八,何以异于邹敌楚哉?盖亦反其本矣。[54]今王发政施仁,[55]是天下仕者皆欲立于王之朝,耕者皆欲耕于王之野,商贾皆欲藏于王之市,行旅皆欲行于王之涂,天下之欲疾其君者皆欲赴愬于王。[56]其若是,孰能御之?"王曰:"吾惛,[57]不能进于是矣。愿夫子辅吾志明以教我。我虽不敏,[58]请尝试之。"曰:"无恒产而有恒心者,[59]惟士为能。若民,则无恒产,因无恒心。[60]苟无恒心,放辟邪侈,[61]无不为已。及陷于罪,然后从而刑之,是罔民也。[62]焉有仁人在位,罔民而可为也?是故明君制民之产,[63]必使仰足以事父母俯足以畜妻子,乐岁终身饱,[64]凶年免于死亡。然后驱而之善,[65]故民之从之也轻。[66]今也制民之产,仰不足以事父母,俯不足以畜妻子,乐岁终身苦,凶年不免于死亡。此惟救死而恐不赡,[67]岂暇治礼义哉?王欲行之,则盍反其本矣。[68]五亩之宅树之以桑,五十者可以衣帛矣;"。鸡豚狗彘之畜,无失其时,七十者可以食肉矣;百亩之田,勿夺其时,八口之家可以无饥矣;谨庠序之教,申之以孝悌之义,颁白者不负戴于道路矣。老者衣帛食肉,黎民不饥不寒,然而不王者,未之有也。"[69]

【白话译文】

齐宣王问孟子:"齐桓公和晋文公的事迹,您可以讲来听听吗?"孟子回答道:"孔子的学生们没有谈到齐桓公和晋文公的事迹的,所以后代没有流传下来,我也没有听说过。您如果一定要我讲有关治国的事,就讲讲用仁义道德安天下的王道吧。"宣王问:"道德要怎样才能安天下?"孟子说:"保证百姓生活稳定而安天下,是没有人能阻挡的。"宣王说:"像我这样的人可以保证百姓生活稳定吗?"孟子说:"可以。"宣王说:"从哪里知道我可以呢?"孟子说:"我曾听胡龁说,您坐在堂上,看见有人牵着牛从堂下经过,便问:'把牛牵到哪儿去?'那人答道:'将要拿它祭钟。'您说:'放了它吧!看他怕得发抖的样子,就这么无罪而被置于死地,我实在不忍心。'那人问道:'那就废掉祭钟吗?'您说:'怎么可以废掉呢?用只羊替换吧!'不知道是否有这回事?"宣王说:"有这事。"孟子说:"凭这种心就够行王道安天下了。百姓都认为您是吝啬,我却早知道您是不忍心。"宣王说:"对呀,确实有这样的百姓。齐国虽然不大,我又何至于舍不得一头牛?只是不忍见它恐惧颤抖着,这么无罪而往死地,才要用羊替换它。"孟子说:"百姓说王舍不得,王也不必奇怪。您用小的换取大的,他们怎么知道王的心意?王若哀怜它无罪而被送往死地,那么牛和羊又凭什么选择呢?"宣王笑着说:"这真是一种什么心呢?我确实不是吝惜钱财去用羊代替牛。百姓说我舍不得也不错。"孟子说:"不要紧。这种不忍心正是仁德之道。因为王只看到了牛的可怜相,却没看见羊也可怜。君子对于飞禽走兽,看见它们活着,便不忍看见他们死去;听见它们悲鸣哀号,便不忍吃它们的肉。因此君子远离厨房。"宣王高兴地说:"《诗经》上说:'别人有心事,我可揣摩到。'说的是先生您这样的了。我只是这样做了,扪心自问,为何这样做,却说不出道理来。经您这么一说,我的心有所感悟了。但我这心合于王道又是为什么呢?"孟子说:"如果向您回话的人说:'我的力气能够举起三千斤,却举不起一根羽毛;我的眼力能够看清楚秋天鸟儿生的细毛的尖端,却看不见面前一车木柴。

这样,您相信他的话吗?'宣王说:"不相信。"孟子立即说道:"现在您的恩德能够施给禽兽,而您所取得的成就不让百姓分享,到底是为什么呢?如此,那么一根羽毛都举不起,只是不肯用力气罢了;一车木柴都看不见,只是不肯用眼睛罢了;百姓得不到生活享受,只是没人施恩罢了。所以您没有实行王道,只是不肯干,不是不能干。"宣王说:"不肯干和不能干在表现上有什么不同?"孟子说:"要把泰山夹在胳膊下跳过北海,告诉别人说:'这个我办不到。'这是真的不能干。替老年人折取草木的丫枝,告诉别人说:'这个我办不到。'这是不肯干,不是不能干。您不实行王道,不是属于把泰山夹在胳膊下跳过北海一类,而是属于替老年人折取草木的丫枝一类。"尊敬自己的长辈延伸到尊敬别人的长辈,爱护自己的小孩延伸到爱护别人的小孩。天下的事,如此办去,就可在自己手掌中运动一样容易。《诗经》上说:'用礼法对待正妻,由此延伸对待兄弟,再用礼法对待封邑国家。'这是说把这仁爱的心如此用到别人身上罢了。所以由近及远地把恩德推广开去就能安定天下;不推广恩德,无法保住妻子。古代的圣贤,他们能够远远超过一般人,没有别的法子,只是他们善于推广自己的好行为罢了。现在您的恩德能够施给禽兽,而您所取得的成就不让百姓分享,到底为什么呢?用秤杆秤一秤,才知道轻重;用尺子量一量,才知道长短。什么东西都是这样,需要检验。人的心更需要检验。请您思量一下吧!""难道要发动全国军队,让将士冒着危险去和别国结仇构怨,这样您心里才快活吗?"宣王说:"不,我怎么会对这样的事感到快活呢?我是想追求我的最大欲望罢了。"孟子说:"您的最大欲望可以讲来听一听吗?"宣王笑着不答。孟子便说:"是求更多的肥美食物才够吃吗?是求更多的轻暖衣服才够穿吗?是求更多的艳丽颜色才够看吗?是求更多的美妙音乐才够听吗?是求更多的近臣才够您使唤吗?这些,王的手下众臣都能够尽量供给,难道您真是为了这些吗?"宣王说:"不是;我不是为了这些呢。"孟子说:"那么,您的大欲可以知道了,想开拓疆土,使秦楚来朝,治理中国,安抚四方异族。用您所做的求您所想要的,就好像爬到树上去捉鱼一样。"宣王说:"像这样严重吗?"孟子说:"当比这更严重呢。爬到树上去捉鱼,虽然捉不到,却没有后患。用您所做的求您所想要的,尽力做去,一定有灾祸在后头。宣王说:"这个道理可以说来听听吗?"孟子说:"假如邹国和楚国打仗,您认为谁会获胜吗?"宣王说:"楚国会获胜。"孟子说:"既然这样,那么,小国本来就不可与大国为敌,人口少的国家本来不可与人口多的国家为敌,弱国本来不可与强国为敌。现在中国的土地,有九个纵横各一千里的地盘那么大,齐国全部土地合起来不过它的九分之一,想以九分之一征服九分之八,这与邹国和楚国为敌有什么分别呢?这也是违反治国安邦的根本的。现在您发布政令,施行仁德。使天下的士大夫都想到齐国来做官,庄稼汉都想到齐国来种地,行商坐贾都想深入齐国的市场,来往的旅客都想经过齐国。各国想批评指责国君的人都想到您这里来上诉。做到了这样,谁能抵挡得住呢?宣王说:"我神志迷糊,不能深入领会这些,希望您老人家辅导我达到目的,明明白白地教导我,我虽不聪明,请让我试试罢。"孟子说:"没有土地田园房屋等不动产却有常存的善心,只有读书人可能做到。一般人如果没有不动产,因此也就没有常存的善心。一旦没有常存的善心,任性胡作非为,什么事都干得出来。等到他犯了法,然后才处以刑罚,这等于陷害他。哪里有仁爱的人坐在朝廷上却做出陷害老百姓的事呢?所以英明的君主制定百姓的产业,一定要使他们上能够赡养父母,下能够抚养妻儿。好年成是一生中丰衣足食的岁月,坏年成也不致饿死。然后再把他们引上善良的道路,这样老百姓也就容易接受治理了。现在呢,制定百姓的产业,上不能够赡养父母,下不能够抚养妻儿。好年成,也是一生中的艰苦岁月,坏年成,只有死路一条。这样,单是拯救自己还怕来不及,哪有闲工夫学习礼仪呢?您如果要施行仁政,为什么不回到根本上来呢?每家给他五亩土地建立宅院,四周遍植桑树,五十岁以上的人就可以穿上丝织物了。鸡狗和猪这类牲畜,不失误繁殖时期,七十岁以上的人就可以有肉吃了。一家人有百亩耕地,不要去妨碍农忙季节,八口之家就可以不饿肚子了。办好各级学校,反复进行孝顺父母敬爱兄长的教育开导,须发半白的人就不至于头顶背负地行路了。老年人穿得好吃得好,一般人不受冻不挨饿,这样还不能使天下归附的,是从来没有的事。"

【英语译文】

King Xuan of Qi State asked Mencius, "Can you tell me the deeds of Duke Huan of Qi State and Duke Wen of Jin State?" Mencius answered, "Since Confucius' disciples didn't record their deeds so they haven't been passed down, I haven't heard about these things. If you wish me to say something about governing a country, I can talk about Kingly Way which employs benevolence and morality to govern one's state." King Xuan asked, "What on earth can I get the world settled?" Mencius said, "Nobody can hinder you if you promise that common people lead a stable life so that the world is settled." King Xuan asked, "Can a person like me make people live stably?" Mencius said, "Of course, you can."

King Xuan asked, "How could you know that I can?" Mencius responded, "I ever heard from Hu He's words that one day you noticed one man lead a bull passing through the hall where you were sitting in your seat, you asked 'Where will you lead the bull?' That man answered 'It will be used to sacrifice the bell.' You said 'Let it go. I can't feel calm when I see it shivers with fear.' That man asked 'Then will the ceremony of sacrificing bell be rid of?' You said 'How can it be rid of? A sheep should be used to replace the bull.' Was there really such kind of thing of you?" King Xuan said, "Yes, there was." Mencius said, "You can carry out Kingly Way to make the world settled with this benevolence. Common people think you are stingy but I know you have a kind heart." King Xuan said, "There are really such kinds of people. Qi State is certainly not big enough, but how can I be unwilling to use a bull to sacrifice the bell? I just can't see a frightened bull die innoceatly. So I ordered a sheep to replace it." Mencius said, "Common people say that you loathe to part with a bull. And you needn't care about it. How could they know your intention when you use a small one to replace a big one? If you pity the bull was sent to death being not guilty, what can the sheep and bull choose?" King Xuan said, smiling, "What is the real feeling? I don't really care about money and use sheep to replace bull. Common people are not wrong saying I'm stingy." Mencius said, "Never mind it. Such pitiful feeling is just a reflection of benevolence and morality. Because you noticed bull was pitiable but you didn't see the sheep was the same. While a moral man sees living birds and beasts he can't see them die. While he hears their tittering and crying he hesitates to eat their meat. Therefore a moral man stays far away from kitchen." King Xuan said smilingly, "Just as *The Book of Songs* say 'I can guess others' happy things'. It tells the same thing as yours. I just did so but when reflecting I didn't know the reason why I did so. After you explained it I began to understand a little bit. But why my feeling is in accordance with the Kingly Way?" Mencius said, "If you told somebody 'I can lift something three thousand *jin* but cannot lift a piece of feather; my eyes can see clearly the tip of hair growing in autumn but cannot see a cart of woodcut.' Do you believe such kind of thing?" King Xuan said, "I cannot believe it." Mencius responded immediately, "Now that you show mercy to birds and beasts but you cannot share your achievements with common people. What's the reason for this? Then, that you cannot lift a piece of feather shows that you're unwilling to use your force, that you cannot see a cart of woodcut shows that you're unwilling to use your eyes, and that common people cannot share happy life shows that nobody shows mercy on them. Therefore, that you haven't carried out the Kingly Way yet shows that you're unwilling to do that, not that you are unable to do that." King Xuan asked, "What is the difference between unwilling to do and being unable to do something?" Mencius answered, "If you are required to cross the North Sea by holding the Taishan Mountain under arm, you tell others that you cannot do that. It really means that you cannot do it. But if you're required to snap a twig for an old man, you tell others that you cannot do that. It means that you are unwilling to do it. That you refuse to carry out the Kingly Way is like to crossing the North Sea not to snapping twigs. One respects his own parents and then extends the respect to others' parents; one loves his own kids and then extends the love to others' kids. World affairs being done like this, it will like acting on one's palms. *The Book of Songs* says 'I treat my wife by rites and laws, and then I extend it to my brothers and fiefs.' That means the kindness is employed to treat other people. Therefore, if you spread your mercy from near to far distant relations, you can bring peace to the whole world. If you don't spread your mercy, you cannot protect your wife and kids. Ancient sages surpassed ordinary men and they just spread their mercy without doing anything more. What is the reason for that you cannot share your achievements with common people while you show mercy on birds and beasts? You can know weight with a scale, and you can know length with a ruler. Everything needs to check like this. People's heart also needs to check. Please think about it. Do you feel happy when you summon your soldiers all over your sate to oppose other states?" King Xuan responded, "How can I feel happy by doing so? I just want to pursue my utmost desire." Mencius asked, "Can you tell me what your utmost desire is?" King Xuan just smiled not answering him. Then Mencius asked, "Do you desire more delicious food to eat? Do you desire more light and warm clothes to wear? Do you desire more bright and shining colors to see? Do you desire more euphonic music to hear? Do you desire more intimate servants to use? But your ministers can do all these for you. And do you really desire all these things?" King Xuan answered, "No. I don't really desire these things." Mencius said, "Then I know that your utmost desire is that you want to expand your state's territory and make Qin State and Chu State surrender and pacify all the minority ethnics. You pursue what you desire by what you have done. That is just like searching fish by climbing in a tree." King Xuan asked, "Is it so serious like that?" Mencius answered, "It's more serious than this. There is no future trouble if you search for fish by climbing a tree and get no fish. But there is certainly future trouble if you pursue what you desire by what you have done." King Xuan asked, "Can you explain this important thing to me?" Mencius said, "If Zou State fights against Chu State, which one do you think will win?" King Xuan answered, "Chu State will surely win." Mencius said, "Now that you think so, therefore, a small state cannot lompete a big one, a less-populous state cannot lompete populous state, a weak state cannot lompete a strong one. Nowadays the whole territory of the Kingdom extends nine thousand square *li*, but the territory of Qi State is less than one ninth of that. That one ninth opposes to eight ninths is the same Zou State opposes to Chu State. Is there any difference? This is violating the fundamentals of bringing peace to the state. Now if you issue edict carrying out benevolence and morality, all scholars want to be officials in Qi State; all farmers want to till fields in Qi State; all peddlers want to trade in Qi State; all travelers want to tour in Qi State; all the men who criticize their monarch want to sue in Qi State. Who can resist you if you have done this?" King Xuan said, "I'm not enlightened and cannot understand the profundity of what you said. Could you please help me and instruct me clearly how to realize the aim? I'm not clever but I will have a try to do that. "Meneias saloy" Only the literati can keep an everlasting kind heart if he has no real estate such as field, house, and orchid. An ordinary man cannot do this. Without an everlasting kind heart one can do any evil things at will. It's harming him that he is punished after his violating laws. Is there a king who sits in imperial court but harms an ordinary man? Therefore a wise monarch should issue enough estate that common men can attend their parents and protect their wife and kids. People have enough food and clothes in a lucky year and they will not suffer hunger to death in an unlucky year. And then they are directed to benevolent way and they are easy to be governed. But nowadays with issued estate, common people cannot attend their parents and protect their wife and kids. A lucky year is also their hard time and unlucky year is the time to die. Thus they have not enough effort to save themselves. How could they learn rites and rituals? Why don't you return to the fundamentals if you carry out benevolent government?" In a five-*mu* residence mulberry trees are planted to raise silkworms and people over fifty years old can wear silk clothes. Chicken, dogs, and pigs are reared and people over seventy years old can eat meat. For one hundred *mu* farming field, the farming season is kept in order and then a household with several persons surely have enough food. Schooling is set up to educate children to be filial to their parents, and then the elder people with gray hair needn't carry loads on the road. There isn't the situation that the Kingly Way can't go smoothly and people hesitate to gather around when seventy-year-old ones can wear silk clothes and eat meat and common people suffer no famine and cold."

【注释】(1)齐宣王:威王之子。姓田氏,名辟疆。约公元前319—公元前301年在位。(2)齐桓、晋文:齐桓公和晋文公。皆霸诸侯者。可得闻乎:得,用在动词前表示能够。闻,有听见,传告,传布,传扬几个相关含义。(3)未之闻也:之,宾语前置的标志。闻的宾语是"桓文之事"已前置。(4)无以:以,通"已"。无以,犹不得已。(5)则:承接连词。用在复句或紧缩句之间,表顺承关系。前此说明原因理由或情况,后此说明相应的措施或结果。译为"就""便"或"于是"。王:以仁义安天下谓之"王"。也叫"王道"。(6)胡龁:~ hé,齐王左右的近臣。(7)之:动词。往。(8)将以衅钟:以后省略了作宾语的代词(指牛的代词"之"或"其")。衅钟,读 xìn ~,古代杀牲取血涂钟行祭。俗称祭钟。(9)觳觫:húsù,恐惧战栗的样子。若:如此;这样的。(10)然则:连词。连接句子表示连贯关系。犹"如此,那么"或"如此"。(11)诸:历来都作"之乎"解释。尹君文言虚词通释中提出诘难:在左传·僖公十三年中两用"予诸乎?"解作兼词,就成了"予之乎乎",如何行通。主张解作代词"之";而且古今汉语里,疑问句或反问句句末不用疑问语气词的不少。(12)褊小:biǎn ~,狭小。指地域、车船等不宽大。(13)无异:不要惊异;不要诧异。(14)隐:哀怜;同情。(15)无伤也,是乃仁术也:无伤,没有伤害。是乃,犹"此乃"。这就是。仁术,仁德之道;行仁政的策略。(16)远庖厨:yuàn páochú,远,离开;避开。庖厨,厨房。(17)说:yuè,后作"悦"。喜悦;高兴。(18)诗云:见《诗经·小雅·巧言》。(19)忖度:cǔnduó,推测。(20)夫子之谓:夫子,指称孟子。之,宾语前置的标志。谓,动词。评论;说。(21)戚戚:qīqī,心动的样子;心里有所触动。(22)有:连词。如果,即使。表示假设。复于王者:向王报告的人,对王回答的人。(23)百钧:三千斤。钧,古代重量单位之一。二十四铢为两,十六两为斤,三十斤为钧。(24)明足以察秋毫之末:明,眼睛;视力。察,明辨;详审。秋毫,亦作"秋豪"。鸟兽在秋天新长出来的细毛。以喻细微之物。秋毫之末,秋天新长出来的细毛的尖端。谓极细。(25)舆薪:满车的柴。比喻大而易见的事物。(26)许:赞同,相信。(27)独:副词。表转折。犹"却"。(28)不见保:不被爱护;受不到爱护。见,用在动词前表示被动,相当于被,受到。(29)形:情况;样子。(30)"挟太山以超北海:挟,读 xíe,夹持;夹在腋下或指间。太山,即"泰山"。北海,指渤海。(31)折枝:zhé ~,折取草茎树枝。喻轻而易举。(32)老吾老:以敬老之道事奉我的父兄。以及人之老:从而延伸到侍奉别人的父兄。(33)幼吾幼:以父母之道爱护我的小孩。以及人之幼:从而延伸到爱护别人的小孩。(34)运于掌:运用在手掌之中。比喻容易。(35)刑于寡妻至于兄弟:"诗云"以下三句,见《诗·大雅·思齐》。刑于,亦作"刑于"。谓以礼法对待。寡妻,嫡妻。至于兄弟,把礼法推行于兄弟。(36)以御于家邦:把礼法应用于采邑和邦国。御,使用;应用。

家,卿大夫及其采邑。邦,古代诸侯的封国。后泛指国家。(37)言举斯心加诸彼而已:言,就是说。举斯心,拿这种好心。加诸,加于,加到。彼,对方,他方。(38)推恩:广施恩惠;移恩。四海:犹言天下,全国各地。(39)功:功绩;成果。(40)权:称量。(41)度:duó,丈;犹量。(42)抑:副词。表示反诘。难道,岂。(43)抑为采色不足视于目与:抑,见注采色,指绚丽的颜色。(44)便嬖:piánbì,亦作"便辟""便僻"。指君王左右受宠幸的小臣。(45)辟土地:pí ~ ~,开拓疆土。(46)朝:cháo,使动用法。使来朝见。(47)莅中国:lì ~ ~,治理中国。莅,临视;治理。抚四夷:安抚四方少数民族。(48)以若所为求若所欲:句中两个"若"字的意义都是"你的"。所为,行为。所欲,欲望。(49)缘木而求鱼:爬上树去捉鱼。比喻行动和目的相反,劳而无所得。缘,读 yuán,攀缘。(50)殆有:dàiyòu,殆,副词。当;必。有,通"又"。还;更加。(51)邹人:邹国人。邹国土地面积极小,在今山东邹县。(52)海内之地方千里者九:全中国的地盘纵横各千里的有九大块。(53)齐集有其一:齐人的土地,集合起来占有全中国土地的九分之一。(54)盖亦反其本矣:盖,连词。承接上文,表示原因或理由。亦反其本矣,意谓以一服八和邹人敌楚人一样也是违反了治国安邦之本。(55)发政:发布政令;施行政治措施。施仁:施行仁政。(56)欲:想。疾:非难,批评指责。赴愬:即"赴诉"。谓奔走求告;上诉。(57)惛:hūn,神志不清,迷迷糊糊。(58)请尝试之:请,敬辞。具体意义随文而异。这里是表示自己愿意干,请对方允许。尝试,犹试行;试验。(59)恒产:指土地、田园、房屋等不动产。恒心:常存的善心。(60)因:连词。因而;因此。(61)放辟邪侈:肆意为非作歹。(62)罔民:欺骗陷害百姓。(63)制民之产:制定百姓的产业。(64)乐岁:lè ~,丰年。终身饱:一生不挨饿。(65)而:代词,他;他的。(66)轻:轻易;容易。(67)赡:足够;满足。(68)盍:hé,副词。表示反诘,犹何不。反其本:复归根本;复归农业。(69)未之有也:没有这样的事。之,代词。这,这个。

孟子集注卷二　梁惠王章句下 凡十六章

【原文】1 庄暴见孟子,[1]曰:"暴见于王[2],王语暴以好乐[3],暴未有以对也。"曰[4]:"好乐何如?"孟子曰:"王之好乐甚,则齐国其庶几乎[5]!"他日,见于王曰:"王尝语庄子以好乐,有诸?"王变乎色,曰:"寡人未能好先王之乐也,直好世俗之乐耳。"曰:"王之好乐甚,则齐其庶几乎!今之乐由古之乐"也[6]。曰:"可得闻与?"曰:"独乐乐,[7]与人乐乐,孰乐?"曰:"不若与人。"曰:"与少乐乐,与众乐乐,孰乐?"曰:"不若与众。"臣请为王言乐。今王鼓乐于此,[8]百姓闻王钟鼓之声,管钥之音,[9]

举疾首蹙頞而相告曰:[10]‘吾王之好鼓乐,夫何使我至于此极也?[11]父子不相见,兄弟妻子离散。’今王田猎于此,百姓闻王车马之音,见羽旄之美,[12]举疾首蹙頞而相告曰:‘吾王之好田猎,夫何使我至于此极也?父子不相见,兄弟妻子离散。’此无他,不与民同乐也。今王鼓乐于此,百姓闻王钟鼓之声,管钥之音,举欣欣然有喜色而相告曰:‘吾王庶几无疾病与?何以能鼓乐也?’今王田猎于此,百姓闻王车马之音,见羽旄之美,举欣欣然有喜色而相告曰:‘吾王庶几无疾病与?何以能田猎也?’此无他,与民同乐也。今王与百姓同乐,则王矣。”

【白话译文】

齐宣王的臣子庄暴来见孟子,说道:“我应君王召见,君王告诉我他爱好音乐,我无话可答。”接着又说:“爱好音乐怎么样?”孟子说:“王爱好音乐很深,那么齐国就相当不错了!”几天过后,孟子应君王召见,说:“您曾经告诉庄暴您爱好音乐,有这事吗?”宣王脸色骤然显红,不好意思地说:“我并不是爱好古代的严肃音乐,只是爱好流行乐曲罢了。”孟子说:“王爱好音乐很深,那么齐国就相当不错了!今天的流行乐曲同古代的严肃音乐都能引诱、教化人。”宣王说:“这道理我可以听听吗?”孟子说:“一个人欣赏音乐快乐,与别人一块欣赏音乐也快乐,两种情况,哪一种更快乐?”宣王说:“跟别人一块欣赏更快乐些。”孟子说:“跟少数人欣赏音乐快乐,跟多数人欣赏音乐也快乐,到底哪种更快乐?”宣王说:“跟多数人一块欣赏更快乐些。”“那么,让我跟您谈谈乐道吧。如果今天您在这儿击鼓奏乐,老百姓听见您的钟鼓声,箫笛声,全都焦头烂额,相互议论,说:‘我们国王这样爱好音乐,为何使我们苦到这个地步,父子不能相见,兄弟妻儿东逃西散。’如果今天您在这儿打猎,百姓听到车马的声音,看到旌旗的华丽,全都焦头烂额,相互议论,说:‘我们国王这样爱好打猎,为何使我们苦到这个地步,父子不能相见,兄弟妻儿东逃西散。’这没有别的原因,就是因为没与百姓一同娱乐。假使您在这里奏乐,百姓听到钟鼓声,箫笛声,全都高高兴兴地说:‘我们国王大概很健康吧,要不然怎么能奏乐呢?’假使您在这里打猎,百姓听到车马的声音,看到旌旗的华丽,全都高高兴兴地说:‘我们国王大概很健康吧,要不然怎么能打猎呢?’这没有别的原因,就是因为与百姓一同娱乐。如果您和百姓一同娱乐,就可以使天下归附了。”

【英语译文】

Zhuang Bao, a minister of King Xuan of Qi State, paid a visit to Mencius, saying, “I was called in by King Xuan and he told me he loved music, but I had nothing to say.” He asked again, “How about loving music?” Mencius said, “If the King loves music deeply, it's very good for Qi State." After several days, being called by King Xuan, Mencius asked, "You ever told Zhuang Bao that you loved music, didn't you?" King Xuan flushed immediately, replying shyly, "I don't like ancient music but like popular one." Mencius replied, "If you love music deeply, it's very good for Qi State. Both serious music in ancient time and popular music in present days can attract and educate common people." King Xuan asked, "Could I listen to your explanation about this?" Mencius asked, "One person enjoys music alone and becomes happy, and or he enjoys music with others and becomes happy, and on what circumstance is the person happier?" King Xuan answered, "He is happier when he enjoys music with others." Mencius asked, "One person enjoys music with a few people and becomes happy, or he enjoys music with many people and becomes happy, on what circumstance is the person happier?" King Xuan answered, "He is happier when he enjoys music with many people." "I will discuss the way of being happy," said Mencius, "If you play music instruments here and common people hear it and become overwhelmed arguing 'Our king loves music so much. But how could he make us so unfortunate that parents cannot see their kids, while wife, brothers and kids flee away without whereabouts?' If you go out hunting here and common people hear tottering of your carts, see your carts' banners and become overwhelmed arguing 'Our king loves music so much. But how could he make us so unfortunate that parents cannot see their kids, while wife, brothers and kids flee away without whereabouts, There is no other reason for this. It's only because you haven't enjoyed music or things together with common people. If you play music instruments here and common people hear it and all become happy saying 'Our king is very healthy, if not, how can he play music here?' If you go out hunting here and common people here tattering of your carts, see your carts' banners and all become happy, saying, 'Our king is very healthy, if not, how can he hunt here?' There is no other reason for this. It's only because you haven't enjoyed music or things together with common people. If you can enjoy music and things together with common people, they will all submit to the authority of you."

【注释】(1)庄暴见孟子:庄暴,齐国的大臣。见孟子,犹言来看孟子。(2)见于王:意为“被王接见”。(3)语:yù,告诉。好乐:hàoyuè,爱好音乐。(4)曰:一个人的话中间加一“曰”字,表示讲话人有所停顿。(5)庶几乎:“庶几”加语气助词“乎”。差不多;大概可以。(6)由:通“犹”。如同;好像。(7)独乐乐:dú yuèlè,

独,谓独自一人。乐乐 ,谓欣赏音乐而快乐。(8)鼓乐:击鼓和奏乐。(9)管钥:~yuè ,两种管乐器名。常泛指乐器或音乐。(10)举疾首蹙頞:举,皆;全。疾首,头痛。指忧苦至极。蹙頞,读 cù'è,皱缩鼻梁。愁苦的样子。(11)极:困窘;疲困。(12)羽旄之美:古时常用鸟羽和旄牛尾作旗帜的装饰;这里的"羽旄"是"旌旗"的代称。

【原文】2 齐宣王问曰:"文王之囿方七十里[1],有诸?"孟子对曰:"于传有之[2]。"曰:"若是其大乎?"曰:"民犹以为小也。"曰:"寡人之囿方四十里,民犹以为大,何也?"曰:"文王之囿方七十里,刍荛者往焉[3],雉兔者往焉[4],与民同之。民以为小不亦宜乎? 臣始至于[5]问国之大禁,然后敢入。臣闻郊关之内有囿方四十里[6]杀其麋鹿者如杀人之罪,则是方四十里为阱于国中[7]民以为大,不亦宜乎?"

【白话译文】

齐宣王问孟子,说道:"周文王那个蓄养鸟兽的园林,纵横各七十里,有这么大吗?"孟子回答说:"古书上有这样的记载。"齐宣王说:"真是这么大吗?"孟子说:"老百姓还以为太小呢。"齐宣王说:"我的园林,纵横各四十里,老百姓还以为太大了,这是为什么呢?"孟子说:"周文王的园林,纵横各七十里,割草、打柴的人进去,捕捉鸟兽的人进去,文王和老百姓一同享受。老百姓认为太小,不是很自然的吗?我刚到齐国边境时,问明了齐国最大的禁令后才敢入境。我听说在齐国首都的郊区,有一个纵横各四十里的园林,谁杀了里面的麋鹿,其罪责等于杀人。那么,这纵横各四十里的园林,就是在国内给老百姓布置了一个大陷阱,他们认为太大了,不也是很自然的吗?"

【英语译文】

King Xuan of Qi State asked Mencius, "Does the garden of King Wen of Zhou Dynasty extend seventy *li* in width and length respectively?" Mencius replied, "It's recorded so in classics." King Xuan asked, "Is it really so spacious?" Mencius answered, "But the common people thought that it was too narrow." King Xuan asked, "My garden extends forty *li* in width and length and common people think it's too spacious. Why?" Mencius said, "For the garden of King Wen of Zhou Dynasty, common people could go into it and cut wood and grasses or hunt beasts and birds. King Wen enjoyed these with them. Wasn't it natural that they thought it was too narrow? Whereas, on my arriving the border of Qi State, I dared to enter your territory only after I had known the great prohibition. I have heard that in the suburb of your capital, there is a garden extending forty *li* in width and length. If a man kills an elk in it, his guilt is the same as killing a man. Then this garden is just like a big pitfall for common people. Isn't it natural that they think it is too spacious?"

【注释】(1)囿:yòu,古代帝王繁育鸟兽的园林。(2)传:zhuàn 著作;书传。(3)刍荛者:chúráo zhě,割草、打柴的人。(4)雉兔者:zhìtù zhě,捕捉鸟兽的人。(5)境:疆界;边界。(6)郊关:四郊之门。古代城邑四郊用作拱卫防御的关门。(7)阱:jǐng,捕野兽的陷坑;泛指深坑;喻指陷害人的圈套。

【原文】3 齐宣王问曰:"交邻国有道乎?[1]"孟子对曰:"有。惟仁者为能以大事小,是故汤事葛,[2]文王事昆夷。[3]惟智者为能以小事大,故太王事獯鬻,[4]勾践事吴。[5]以大事小者,乐天者也;以小事大者,畏天者也。乐天者保天下,畏天者保其国。诗云:'畏天之威,于时保之。[6]'"王曰:"大哉言矣!寡人有疾,[7]寡人好勇。"对曰:"王请无好小勇。夫抚剑疾视曰,'彼恶敢当我哉!'此匹夫之勇,敌一人者也。王请大之!诗云:'王赫斯怒,[8]爰整其旅,[9]以遏徂莒,[10]以笃周祜[11],以对于天下。'此文王之勇也。文王一怒而安天下之民。书曰:[12]'天降下民,作之君,作之师,惟曰其助上帝宠之。四方有罪无罪惟我在,[13]天下曷敢有越厥志[14]?'一人衡行于天下,[15]武王耻之。此武王之勇也。而武王亦一怒而安天下之民。今王亦一怒而安天下之民,民惟恐王之不好勇也。[16]

【白话译文】

齐宣王问道:"和邻国打交道有什么窍门吗?"孟子答道:"有啊。只是仁爱的人才能够以大国服侍小国,所以商汤服侍葛国,文王服侍昆夷。只是聪明的人,才能够以小国服侍大国,所以太王服侍獯鬻,勾践服侍吴国。以大国服侍小国的,是乐意顺应天命的人;以小国服侍大国的,是畏惧天命的人。乐意顺应天命的人安定天下,畏惧天命的人保护自己的国家。《诗经》上说;'怕上帝威力灵验,在此保护民安全。'"齐宣王说:"说得真好!但我有个小毛病,我爱勇武。"孟子答道:"请您不要爱小勇。拿着剑瞪着眼睛说:'他怎么敢抵挡我呢?'这只是普通人的勇武,只能抵挡一个人。请王把勇武扩大。《诗经》上说;'我王勃然大发怒,整肃军队如猛虎;阻止强暴侵莒国,增添周室的福禄,回报天下的相助。'这是文王的勇武;文王一发怒便安定天下。书经上说:'上天降生下民,为他们安排了君主、安排了师傅,就是叫他们协助上天宠爱下民。现在诸侯各国有罪无罪,责任在我身上。天下怎么敢违背上天的意志呢?'当时有一个纣王在世上横行霸道,武王引以为奇耻大辱。这是武王的勇武;武王也一发怒安定了天下。如今您若一怒而安定天下,人民还生怕您不爱勇武呢。"

【英语译文】

King Xuan of Qi State asked, "Is there any knack to deal with neighbor country?" Mencius answered, "Yes, there is. Only benevolent and righteous man can make a big country serve a small one, therefore Tang of Shang Dynasty served Ge State and King Wen of Zhou Dynasty served Kunyi State. Only clever man can make a small country serve a big one, therefore Tan Fu served Xun Yu and Gou Jian served Wu State. Those who willingly made big country serve small one were someone who followed the Mandate of the Heaven, and those who willingly made small country serve big one were someone who feared the Mandate of the Heaven. Those who willingly followed the Mandate of the Heaven settle down the world, and those feared the Mandate of the Heaven settle down his country. Lines in *Cooking* of *Zhou Hymns* of *the Book of Songs* go like this 'Worshipping heaven's power and ways, I'll protect people in coming days.'" King Xuan of Qi State said, "You are right there. But I have a drawback that I love valiant force." Mencius answered, "Please don't love small valiant force. Holding sword and staring you say to others 'Who can hinder me?' This is just average valiant force which can frighten one person. You, please expand your valiant force. Lines in *The Great God* of *Greater Ode* of *the Book of Songs* go like this 'Upon this into big rage King Wen's bursting. He summons his royal troops to march on, Troops intend to defend state from invasion. He tries to consolidate happiness of Zhou. Let common people see bright future glow.' This is King Wen's valiant force and as he bursted into rage he could settled down the whole world." As it goes in *The Book of History*, 'The Heaven produced human beings and provided monarch and teachers for them. Monarch and teachers aided him to show mercy on human beings. Now whether kings of vassal states are guilty or not is attributed to myself. How can people in the world violate the Mandate of the Heaven?' King Wen of Zhou felt ashamed at King Zhou of Shang and bursted into great rage, finally he brought peace to the world. Nowadays if you burst into rage and bring peace to the world, people will fear that you're not valiant enough."

【注释】(1)道:道的释义,不可拘泥。齐宣王于此是在寻找门路、方法。他之所谓"道",实谓窍门、秘诀、权术之类。(2)汤事葛:参阅《滕文公下》第五章;论文较详。(3)昆夷:kūn~,一作"混夷"。周朝初年的西戎国名。(4)太王:亦作"大王"。即古公亶父。獯鬻:xūnyù,亦作"熏育",即猃狁(xiǎnyǔn)。当时北方的少数民族。第十四章、十五章之"狄人",所指同此。(5)勾践事吴:越王勾践惨败于吴,卑辞厚礼求和,给吴王夫差当马前卒。后返国,十年生聚,十年教训,终于兴国灭吴。(6)于时:于是,在此。见《诗・周颂・我将》。(7)疾:缺点,毛病。(8)赫斯:犹"赫然"。勃然大怒的样子。语出《诗・大雅・皇矣》。后用以指帝王盛怒的样子。(9)爰:yuán,语气助词。用在句首或句中补凑音节,没有实在意义。旅:军队编制单位;这里泛指军队。(10)以遏徂莒:遏,止。徂,往。莒,国名。(11)以笃周祜:笃,厚。周,指周朝。祜,福。(12)书曰:书经上说。这里引用的是尚书逸文,文辞与现存尚书略异。(13)四方:指四方诸侯之国。(14)曷:副词。表反问,岂、难道。有越:离开;违背。有,在此作为"词头"。厥志:其志。这里指上天的意志。(15)一人:一个人;这里指殷纣王。衡行:同"横行"。(16)惟恐:只怕。

【原文】4 齐宣王见孟子于雪宫。[1]王曰:"贤者亦有此乐乎?"孟子对曰:"有。人不得,[2]则非其上矣。不得而非其上者,非也;[3]为民上而不与民同乐者,亦非也。乐民之乐者,民亦乐其乐;忧民之忧者,民亦忧其忧,乐以天下,忧以天下,然而不王者,未之有也。昔者齐景公问于晏子曰:[4]'吾欲观于转附、朝儛,遵海而南,放于琅邪,[5]吾何修而可以比于先王观也?[6]晏子对曰:'善哉问也!天子适诸侯曰巡狩,巡狩者,巡所守也。诸侯朝于天子曰述职,述职者,述所职也。无非事者,春省耕而补不足,秋省敛而助不给,夏谚曰:[7]"吾王不游,吾何以休?吾王不豫,[8]吾何以助?一游一豫,为诸侯度。"今也不然:师行而粮食,[9]饥者弗食,劳者弗息。睊睊胥谗,[10]民乃作慝。[11]方命虐民,[12]饮食若流,[13]流连荒亡,为诸侯忧。从流下而忘返谓之流,从流上而忘返谓之连,从兽无厌谓之荒[14],乐酒无厌谓之亡。先王无流连之乐、荒亡之行。惟君所行也。[15]景公悦,大戒于国,[16]出舍于郊。于是始兴发补不足。[17]召大师曰:[18]'为我作君臣相说之乐!'盖征招、角招是也。[19]其诗曰:'畜君何尤?[20]畜君者,好君也。[21]"

【白话译文】

齐宣王在雪宫里接见孟子。宣王问道:"贤德的人也有这种快乐吗?"孟子回答说:"有啊。人们得不到这种快乐,就埋怨他们的国君说国君的不是。这样埋怨和非议是不对的。可是作为一国之主,不和百姓同乐,也是不对的。国君以百姓的快乐为自己的快乐,百姓也会以国君的快乐为自己的快乐;国君以百姓的忧愁为自己的忧愁,百姓也会以国君的忧愁为自己的忧愁。和天下人同乐,和天下人同忧,这样还不能使天下人归附,是从来没有的。过去齐景公问晏子,说:‘我想到转附、朝儛两座山上去游览,然后沿着海岸往南,在琅琊上纵目观赏。我该怎么办,才能和过去的圣君贤王相比呢?’晏子回答说:‘问得很好!天子到诸侯国去叫巡狩,巡狩就是巡视各诸侯国所守护的疆土的意思。诸侯去朝见天子叫述职,述职就是报告他在职责内的工作的意思。巡狩和述职都没有不和政治工作相关的事。春天巡视耕种情况,对贫穷农户加以补助;秋天考察收获情况,对缺粮农户加以补助。夏代的俗话说:‘我们的王不出游,我们怎么添自由?我们的王不来走,我们怎么提要求?我们王一游一走,立起榜样教诸侯。’现在却不是这样,国王一出巡,兴师动众,到处筹粮运米,饥饿的人得不到吃的,劳苦的人得不到休息,人们无不愤怒埋怨,老百姓就要拿起棍棒造反了。这样出巡违背天命,虐待百姓,浪费粮食如同流水。流连荒亡,使诸侯担忧。顺水下游,乐而忘返叫流;逆水上游,乐而忘返叫连;不厌倦地打猎叫荒;不厌倦地喝酒叫亡。过去的贤君,都没有这种流连的快乐和荒亡的行为。古今两种模式随您自己选择。’景公听了很高兴,先在都城内做好各项准备,然后驻扎郊外,从此开始拿出粮食救济百姓。景公还叫来乐官命他作君臣同乐的乐曲。征招、角招就是君臣同乐的乐曲。歌词说:‘匡正君王的过失有什么不对呢?’匡正君王的过失,就是爱君王。”

【英语译文】

King Xuan of Qi State received Mencius in the Xue Palace and he asked, “Does an able and moral man also enjoy such happiness?” Mencius replied, “Yes, he does. People are inclined to complain about their monarch by pointing out his fault when they can't obtain happiness. But such kind of doings is not correct. However, it's not correct for a monarch not sharing happiness with his subjects. If a monarch regards his subjects' happiness as his own, his subjects will regard his happiness as their own. If a monarch regards his subjects' worries as his own, his subjects will regard his worries as their own. There isn't the situation where a monarch enjoys happiness and worries with his subjects but he isn't still not able to make others submit to his authority. In the old days, Duke Jing of Qi State asked Yan Zi, ‘I want to tour around Mt. Zhuanfu and Mt. Zhaowu and go southward along seashore, to sightsee land-view on Mt. Langya. How can I do like ancient sages and wise kings?’ Yan Zi answered, ‘It's a good question. It's called an imperial inspection tour when a Son of the Heaven goes to a vassal state, which means to inspect the territory guarded by the duke; while it is called report on his work when a duke goes to meet a Son of the Heaven, which means to report his work to His Majesty. Imperial inspection tour and report on one's work both have close relation with administrative affairs. In spring, monarch inspects farming situation and helps the poor men; and in autumn he inspects harvesting situation and helps the men who lack grains. There went the saying in Xia Dynasty 'How can we be free if our king doesn't tour around? How can we require anything if our king doesn't go out? He set an example for dukes when our kings tours round and goes out.' Nowadays, things aren't like this. When our king tours round so many masses are summoned, grains are gathered everywhere but starving men cannot obtain any rice. Toiling men cannot take a rest. All the men burst into rage and they will rebel with their tools. Such kind of inspection violates the Mandate of the Heaven, maltreats common people, and wastes grains like flowing water. Dukes worried about their king's indulgence in pleasure-seeking, hunting and drinking too much. The king just seeks pleasure like floating downstream and upstream. He forgets going homes while he's indulgent in hunting and drinking too much. The old day's sage kings didn't do things like these You are free to choose from the old day's mode and nowadays mode.' Duke Jing felt glad after hearing this. He made preparations within capital and camped in outskirts, and aided common people by giving out grains and rice. Duke Jing also summoned musicians to make music to shae happiness with common people. Notes of Zhi Shao and Jue Shao are such kind of music. Words go like this, 'Is it alright to rectify a king's fault?' If you rectify your king's fault, it means you love your king."

【注释】(1)雪宫:战国时齐国的离宫名。故址在今山东省淄博市东北。宫中有苑囿台池和珍禽异兽。(2)人不得:人,承上文指贤者。人不得,意谓他们(贤者)得不到这种快乐。(3)非其上、非也:反对他们的国君、不对。(4)齐景公、晏子:齐景公,春秋时齐国之君,姓姜名杵臼。晏子,齐国贤臣,名婴。(5)观于转附、朝儛,遵海而南,放于琅邪:观,游览。转附,即今芝罘(fú)山(芝罘岛)。朝儛(wǔ),即今山东荣成东之召石山。遵海而南,沿着海岸往南。放,谓纵目观赏。琅邪,(旧读,lángyé,今读,lángyá。)亦作"琅琊"。山名。在今山东省诸城市东南海滨。(6)先王:前代君王;上古贤明君王。(7)夏谚:相传流行于夏代的俗语。(8)豫:古代专指帝王秋天出巡。(9)粮食:用如动词,谓筹措粮食。(10)睊睊胥谗:睊睊,读 juànjuàn,侧目相视的样子。胥,读 xū,都,皆。谗,读 chán,说别人的坏话;说陷害人的话。(11)慝:tè,邪恶。(12)方命虐民:违抗天命,虐待百姓。

(13)饮食若流:饮食若流水不断消耗。(14)从兽:田猎。(15)惟:听从;随从。(16)大戒于国:大戒,全面做好準备。于国,在国都内。(17)兴发:开仓出粟。(18)大师:tài ~,古代乐师之长。(19)盖征招、角招:盖,语气词。多用于句首。征,读 zhǐ,征和角是古代五音(宫、商、角、征、羽)中的两个。招,读 sháo,通"韶"。(20)畜君:xù ~,匡正君主的过失。尤:过错;罪愆。(21)好君:一解,好,意谓"爱";一解,好,意谓"使(为)……好"。

【原文】5 齐宣王问曰:"人皆谓我毁明堂[1],毁诸?已乎?[2]"孟子对曰:"夫明堂者,王者之堂也。王欲行王政,则勿毁之矣。"王曰:"王政可得闻与[3]?"对曰:"昔者,文王之治岐也,耕者九一,[4]仕者世禄,[5]关市讥而不征,[6]泽梁无禁,[7]罪人不孥。[8]老而无妻曰鳏,老而无夫曰寡,老而无子曰独,幼而无父曰孤。此四者,天下之穷民而无告者。[9]文王发政施仁,[10]必先斯四者。诗云:[11]'哿矣富人,哀此茕独!'"王曰:"善哉言乎!"曰:"王如善之,则何为不行?"王曰:"寡人有疾,寡人好货。[12]"对曰:"昔者公刘好货,[13]诗云[14]:'乃积乃仓,乃裹糇粮,于橐于囊。思戢用光。弓矢斯张,干戈戚扬,爰方启行'故居者有积仓,行者有裹囊也'。王如好货,与百姓同之,于王何有?[15]"王曰:"寡人有疾,寡人好色。[16]"昔者大王好色,爱厥妃。[17]诗云:[18]'古公亶父,来朝走马,率西水浒,至于岐下,爰及姜女,聿来胥宇。'当是时也,内无怨女,[19]外无旷夫。[20]王如好色,与百姓同之,于王何有?"[21]

【白话译文】

齐宣王问道:"别人都对我说拆毁明堂,是拆毁呢还是不拆毁?"孟子答道:"明堂是王者之堂,您如果想实行王道政治,就不要拆毁吧。"宣王说;"可以听你说说王道政治吗?"孟子答道:"从前周文王治理岐周,对农民抽九分之一的税,对做官有功的人实行后代承袭俸禄的制度,在关口和集市上只稽查不征税,设堰捕鱼,没有禁令,惩治罪人不牵连家属。老年无妻叫鳏夫,老年无夫叫寡妇,老年无子叫孤人,幼年无父叫孤儿。这四种人是世上穷苦无靠的人。周文王发布政令实行仁政,必定首先考虑他们。《诗经》上说:'欢乐啊,富有的人,可怜无靠的人吧。'"宣王说:"这话说得真好!"孟子说:"您如果认为这话好,为什么不实行呢?"宣王说:"我有个毛病,我爱钱财。"孟子说:"从前公刘也喜爱钱财《诗经》上说:'谷物成堆装满仓,制作干粮甜又香。装进大袋和小袋,为安民人增荣光。张满弯弓挟直箭,盾戈斧钺肩上扛,一切准备都作好,开始动身向前方。'所以居家有充实的粮仓,行军有充实的行囊,然后才可以开始动身向前方。您如果喜爱钱财,能够与百姓同享,那么实行王道政治有什么困难?宣王说:"我还有个毛病,我爱女人的美色。"

孟子说："从前太王也喜爱女人的美色。他爱自己的妃子。《诗经》上说：'古公亶父心意真，清早骑马向前奔。沿着西边的河岸，一直抵达岐山根。妻子太姜紧相随，一同观察住所情。'在这个时代，既没有老处女也没有单身汉。您如果爱女人的美色，能跟老百姓一道，对您实行王道政治有什么困难？"

【英语译文】

King Xuan of Qi State asked, "Other people told me to demolish the Hall of Brightness. Should I do it or not?" Mencius responded, "The Hall of Brightness belongs to the King and if you want to be a King, don't demolish it." King Xuan asked, "Can I listen to your explanation of Kingly Government?" Mencius answered, "When King Wen of Zhou Dynasty governed the place of Qi, he just gathered tax from one ninth of people's production, and made the offspring of achieved officials inherit their ancestors' position and salary. He didn't tax those who traded on passes and fairs and didn't ban fishing in ponds and didn't spread punishment to criminals' relatives. An old person without wife was called widower; an old person without husband was called widow; an old person without kids was called childless, and a young kid without parents was called orphan. These four kinds of persons were the most unfortunate ones in the world. King Wen would first consider them when he carried out his policy. The *Book of Songs* says 'The rich and fortunate one, please show mercy on those unlucky ones.'" King Xuan said, "It's very good." Mencius asked, "Why don't you carry out Kingly Government if you think it's good?" King Xuan answered, "I have a shortcoming that I love money and wealth." Mencius replied, "In old days, Honest Duke Liu also loved money and wealth. The *Book of Songs* says 'And rice piles full in barn. He wraps food carefully. Bag covers the dry food. He unites people together. All weapons are put in use. Bow, arrows, spears, axes, they set out as being ready.' Therefore, rice piles full in barn and all weapons get ready, and then troops could set off. Is there any difficulty to carry out the Kingly Government if you love money and wealth and share them with your subjects?" King Xuan said, "I still have another shortcoming that I love beauty. Mencius replied, "In the old days, Dan Fu also loved beauty, he loved his imperial concubine. The *Book of Songs* says 'Ancient man Dangong was busy marching forward. At morn, he drove horses Bin State leaving. Along western riverbank of Bin River, finally he reached the place near Qishan Mount. His wife Taijiang was always accompanying him, Exploring sites where they built up new house.' Nowadays there aren't old virgins and single men. Is there any difficulty for you to carry out Kingly Government even if you love beauty but respect common people's preference?"

【注释】(1)明堂:庆赏、选士都在此举行。这里的明堂,在齐国,系指太山明堂。周天子东巡守朝诸侯之处,汉时遗址还在。(2)毁诸、已乎:毁之、止乎。(3)与:语气助词。(4)耕者九一:古井田制,纵横各一里为一井,其田九百亩。中画井字分为九区。一区之中,为田百亩。中央百亩为公田。外围八百亩为私田。八家各受私田百亩,而同养公田,即是九分而税其一。即每家每年所担负的农业税大概相当于收入的九分之一。(5)世禄:指古代有功者世代享受俸禄;也指世代享受俸禄的制度。(6)关市讥而不征:朱熹《四书集注》:"关,谓道路之关。市,谓都邑之市。讥,察也。征,税也。关市之吏,察异服异言之人,而不征商贾之税。(7)泽梁:在水流中用石筑成的拦水捕鱼的堰。(8)罪人不孥:~ ~ ~ nú,治罪止于本人,不累及妻和子女。(9)无告者:无处投诉的人。(10)发政施仁:发布政令施行仁政。(11)诗云哿矣富人,哀此茕独:出自《诗·小雅·正月》。哿,读 gě,欢乐。茕独,读 qióng ~,孤独困苦。(12)货:财物,金钱珠玉布帛的总称。(13)公刘:后稷的曾孙。周朝创业的始祖。(14)诗云以下九句:诗,指《诗·大雅·公刘》。乃,连词。仓,用作动词。裹。包扎;携带。糇粮,读 hóu ~,亦作"糇粮"。干粮;食粮。于,介词。以,用。橐,读 tuó,一种口袋。据说两端有底,中间开口,东西往两头装好后,在中间扎起来。囊,读 náng,一种口袋。据说两端都无底,东西从两端往里装,装好后,把两端捆束起来。《毛传》:"小曰橐大曰囊。"两种说法,大不相同,难定是非。思戢用光:思,按朱熹四书集注解作动词,想。或解作助词,用于句首或句中,无实义。戢,读 jí,通"辑"。安定;和睦。用,介词,以。光,发扬;增光。弓矢斯张:弓矢,即弓箭。弓矢斯张,犹言拿起武器。干,盾牌,古代作战时用来抵御敌人刀箭的兵器。戈,古代的主要攻击兵器,青铜制。盛行于商至战国时期,秦以后逐渐消失。戚,古代兵器名,斧的一种。扬,古兵器名,钺的别称,青铜制,圆刃;形似斧而大。盛行于殷、周时。爰方启行:爰,于是。方,开始。启行,出发,启程。(15)何有:其义随文而异,我们要留意辨别。一般情况作"有什么"解;后面带名词时,作"哪里有,岂有"解;用反问语气时说明没有什么:1)表示不难。本文便是此义。2)表示不怜惜、不爱重。3)表示无关。4)表示不在乎。5)表示无所得。6)表示无所不有。(16)好色:贪爱女子的美色。(17)大王:即太王。大,太的古字。太王,公刘九世孙。古公,太王的本号;亶父,太王的名。厥妃:juéfēi,犹"其妃"。他的妃子。(18)诗云以下六句:见《诗·大雅·绵》。来朝,第二天早晨。走马,骑马疾走;驰逐。率,循,沿着。西,豳之西。浒,读 hǔ,水边。岐下,岐山下。

爰,乃,就。及,跟,同。姜女,即太姜。太王的妃子(妻子)。聿,读 yù,助词。用于句首或句中。无实义。胥,读 xū,观察。宇,房屋;住所。(19)内无怨女:内,犹言室内。怨女,指已到婚龄而长期无配偶的女子。(20)外无旷夫:外,犹言室外。旷夫,无妻的成年男子。

【原文】6 孟子谓齐宣王曰:"王之臣有托其妻子于其友而之楚游者,[1]比其反也,[2]则[3]冻馁其妻子,则如之何?王曰:"弃之。[4]"曰:"士师不能治士,[5]则如之何?"王曰:"已之。[6]"曰:"四境之内不治,[7]则如之何?"王顾左右而言他。[8]

【白话译文】

孟子对齐宣王说:"如果您有一个臣子把妻、儿托付给朋友照顾,自己去游楚国。到他回来的时候,他的妻、儿却在挨饿受冻。对这样的朋友该怎么办呢?"宣王说:"和他绝交。"孟子说:"如果司法长官不能约束他的下级,那该怎么办?"宣王说:"撤他的职!"孟子说:"如果国内治理得不好,那该怎么办?"齐宣王看看侍从,扯来了别处的话题。

【英语译文】

Mencius said to King Xuan of Qi State, "Suppose that you have a minister, and he committed his wife and kids to his friend's care but he himself traveled to Chu State. Upon his coming back, he found that his wife and kids were suffering from hunger and coldn. What do you think that he should do to his friend?" King Xuan answered, "He should break up with his friend." Mencius said, "If an juridical official didn't restrain his subordinates, what should be done?" King Xuan replied, "He should be dismissed from his post." Mencius said, "If your country hasn't been governed well, what should be done?" King Xuan looked at his subordinates and talked about other topics.

【注释】(1)之:往;至。(2)比:介词。待到;等到。反:同"返"。(3)则:转折连词。表转折关系。可译作"然而""但是"或"却"。下文三个"则"是承接连词。表顺承关系。前此说明原因、理由或情况,后此说明措施或结果。可译作"于是","那么"。(4)弃:抛弃;废除。(5)士师、士:士师,古代掌禁令刑狱的官长。士,指其下级官员。(6)已之:yǐ ~,罢免他,黜退他。(7)四境之内:四境,四方疆界;四方边境地区。四境之内,犹言举国,全国。(8)王顾左右而言他:顾,犹视,看。左右,指近臣;侍从。言他,说其他的话。

【原文】7 孟子见齐宣王,曰:“所谓故国者,[1]非谓有乔木之谓也,有世臣之谓也。[2]王无亲臣矣,[3]昔者所进,[4]今日不知其亡也。[5]”王曰:“吾何以识其不才而舍之?[6]”曰:“国君进贤,如不得已,将使卑逾尊,疏逾戚,可不慎与?左右皆曰贤,未可也;[7]诸大夫皆曰贤,未可也;国人皆曰贤,[8]然后察之;见贤焉,然后用之。左右皆曰不可,勿听;诸大夫皆曰不可,勿听;国人皆曰不可,然后察之;见不可焉,然后去之。[9]左右皆曰可杀,勿听;诸大夫皆曰可杀,勿听;国人皆曰可杀,然后察之;见可杀焉,然后杀之。故曰,国人杀之也。[10]如此,然后可以为民父母。[11]”

【白话译文】

孟子觐见齐宣王,说道:“平常所说的历史悠久的国家,不是说它有高大的树木的缘故,是说它有功勋显著的旧臣的缘故。您现在没有亲信的臣子了。昨日进用的人,今天不知跑到哪儿去了。”宣王问道:“我怎样识别那些没有才能的人而不用他们呢?”孟子说:“国君选拔贤才,如果不得已,要把地位低的人放在地位高的人上边,把关系疏远的人放在关系亲密的人上边,可以不审慎吗?身边的人都说某人好,不足同意;大夫们都说某人好,也不足同意;国中的人都说某人好,然后考察了解,发现真的不错,这才任用他。身边的人都说某人不好,不要听从;大夫们都说某人不好,也不要听从;国中的人都说某人不好,然后考察了解,发现真的不好,这才罢免他。身边的人都说某人可以杀掉,不要听从;大夫们都说某人可以杀掉,也不要听从;国中的人都说某人可以杀掉,然后考察了解,发现真的可以杀掉,才杀掉他,所以说,国人把他杀掉了。这样,然后才可以如父母关心爱护儿女一样对待人民。”

【英语译文】

Mencius called on King Xuan of Qi State, saying, “The so-called a country with long history isn't due to the fact that there grew tall trees but due to the fact that there existed distinguished old ministers. Now that you have no intimate ministers and don't know the whereabouts of those who ever sought for posts.” King Xuan asked, “How can I recognize those unable men and stop using them?” Mencius said, “When a monarch choose able men, if he has to do it, then he may place low-posted man before high-posted one and place alienated man before intimate one. Shouldn't he be cautious? If your intimate men said unanimously that someone is good, you should not believe it; if your ministers said unanimously that someone is good , you should not believe it; if people in the country said unanimously that someone is good, you should observe him and if you find he's really good then you may assign him to a post. If your intimate men said unanimously that someone is bad, you should not believe it; if your ministers said unanimously that someone is bad , you should not believe it; if people in the country said unanimously that someone is bad, you should observe him and if you find he's really bad then you may remove him from office. If your intimate men said unanimously that someone can be killed, you should not believe it; if your ministers said unanimously that someone can be killed, you should not believe it; if people in the country said unanimously that someone can be killed, you should observe him and if you find he really can be killed,you may kill him. Therefore, we say countrymen killed him. Consequently, you can deal with your subjects just as parents care about their children."

【注释】(1)所谓:所说的。用于复说、引证等。故国:历史悠久的国家。者:助词,用在名词后面表停顿。非谓:不是说。之谓也:的缘故呢。(2)世臣:谓有功勋的旧臣。(3)亲臣:亲信之臣。(4)昔者:昨天。所进:进用的人。(5)亡:逃跑。(6)舍:舍弃。(7)未可:不足同意。未,不足,还不够。《国语·周语上》:"夫晋侯非嗣也而得其位,亹亹怵惕,保任戒惧,犹曰未也。"可,表示同意,许可。(8)国人:国内的人,全国的人。(9)去:舍弃。(10)国人杀之:孟子之意,凡用人、惩罚人,特别是处以极刑,国君不得专断,必须尊重民意和求真务实,民意与真实相符则行,不符,则继续查考,可行才行,不可行则已。这样,用人、惩罚人,就不致失误;特别是杀人是国人公意,是国人杀之;不是国君独断。(11)为民父母:国君对待人民,要如父母对待儿女一样关心爱护,不得虐待。

【原文】8 齐宣王问曰:"汤放桀,[1]武王伐纣,[2]有诸?"孟子对曰:"于传有之。[3]"曰:"臣弑其君,[4]可乎?"曰:"贼仁者谓之'贼',[5]贼义者谓之'残'。[6]贼残之人谓之'一夫'。[7]闻诛一夫纣矣,[8]未闻弑君也。"

【白话译文】

齐宣王问道:"商汤流放夏桀,周武王讨伐殷纣王,真有这两回事吗?"孟子回答说:"史书上有这样的记载。"宣王说:"做臣子的杀死他的君主可以吗?"孟子说:"破坏仁爱的叫强盗,破坏道义的叫暴徒。这样的强盗、暴徒叫"独夫",众叛亲离,既无百姓也无臣属,我只听说过周武王诛杀了"独夫"殷纣,没听说过周武王杀了自己的国君。"

【英语译文】

King Xuan of Qi State asked, "King Tang of Shang Dynasty exiled King Jie of Xia Dynasty. King Wu of Zhou Dynasty crusaded against King Zhou of Shang Dynasty. Are there the two events?" Mencius replied, "Yes, the history book recorded them." King Xuan said, "Is it alright to murder one's monarch?" Mencius answered, "Those who violate humanity are called thieves and those who violate righteousness are called mobs. These thieves and mobs are called 'autocrats' who have made their relative against himself and have no subject or ministers to support him. I just heard King Wu of Zhou Dynasty killed an autocrat Zhou of Shang Dynasty, but I didn't hear that King Wu of Zhou Dynasty ever murdered his monarch."

【注释】(1)汤放桀:汤,商代开国之君。放,驱逐,流放。桀,夏代最后一个君主,名履癸。相传为暴君。汤兴兵讨伐他,把他流放到南巢(在今安徽省巢县)。(2)武王伐纣:商纣王无道,周武王讨伐他,他兵败自焚而死。(3)传:zhuàn,著作;书传。(4)弑:shì,古代卑幼杀死尊长叫弑。多指臣子杀死君主,子女杀死父母。(5)贼:败坏;毁坏。又指抢劫或偷窃财物的人。(6)残:毁坏;破坏。又指暴虐无道的人。(7)一夫:犹独夫。即残暴无道众叛亲离的统治者。(8)诛:杀戮有罪该死的人。

【原文】9 孟子见齐宣王,曰:"为巨室,[1]则必使工师求大木,[2]工师得大木,则王喜,[3]以为能胜其任也。[4]匠人斫而小之,[5]则王怒,以为不胜其任矣。夫人幼而学之,[6]壮而欲行之,王曰,'姑舍女所学而从我'[7],则何如?[8]今有璞玉于此,[9]虽万镒,[10]必使玉人雕琢之。[11]至于治国家,[12]则曰[13]'姑舍女所学而从我,'则何以异于教玉人雕琢玉哉?[14]"

【白话译文】

孟子觐见齐宣王,说道:"要建筑大房子,那么一定要派工匠去找大木料。工匠得到了大木料,您就高兴,认为他能够担任其事。如果木工把木料砍小了,不合尺寸规格,您就会发怒,认为他不能担任其事。别人从小学习一门技艺,长大了便想运用它。您对他说:'暂时把你所学的放下,听我吩咐!'却是为什么呢?假如这里有块璞玉,重二十四万两,一定会让玉工雕琢它。可是一说到治理国家,您却说:'暂时把你所学的放下,听我吩咐!'这跟教玉工按照您的办法雕琢玉石有什么两样呢?”

【英语译文】

Mencius reported to King Xuan of Qi State, saying, “If you want to build a big house, you surely send craftsman to look for big trees. And you will be happy and think they are qualified for the job when they find big trees. But you'll become angry and think they aren't qualified for the job when the carpenters cut tree into small timbers which are not in a ccordance with the specifications. They learned the skill as a child and they wanted to use it when they grew up. However, you told them, ‘Give up what you'd learnt for a while and listen to what I've said!’ But what's reason for that? Suppose you have a piece of 240-thousand-*liang* jade, you will surely ask lapidary to carve it. But as for governing a country, you said, ‘Give up what you've learnt for a while and listen to what I've said!’ What is the difference between it and the fact you told the lapidary to carve jade according to your idea?”

【注释】(1)为巨室:为,建造。室,房屋。(2)则:承接连词。在承认前面所说的情况下,接过来申说相应的进展。是“既然这样,那么……”的意思。工师:古代官名,主管各种工匠。也指工匠。(3)则王喜:则,因果连词。相当于“因此”“所以”。下文“则王怒”的“则”同此。(4)能胜其任:能担负那个责任。下文“不胜其任”即担负不了那个责任。(5)匠人:木工;工匠。斫:zhuó,砍削。(6)夫人:夫,句首语气助词。人,别人。(7)姑:姑且;暂时。舍:舍弃;放下。女:rǔ,代词。你。通作“汝”。(8)则何如:则,转折连词。视文意,可译为“然而”“但是”或“却”。何如,犹“何故”“什么原因”。(9)今:连词,表示假设关系。相当于“若”、“假如”。璞玉:pú ~,包在石中而尚未雕琢之玉。(10)虽:语首助词,起补凑音节的作用,译时去掉不要。镒:yì,古代重量单位合二十两。一说合二十四两。万镒,即二十万两或二十四万两。这么重的璞玉,价值连城。(11)玉人:雕琢玉器的工人。也称玉工。(12)至于:也作“至于”。转折连词,表示另提一事。现代汉语还常用,可以不译或换用其他转折连词。(13)则曰:却说。则,转折连词。(14)则何以异:则,承接连词,那么。何以,这里用反问语气表示“没有”或“不能”的意思。异,区分;不相同。

【原文】10 齐人伐燕,胜之。[1]宣王问曰:“或谓寡人勿取,[2]或谓寡人取之。以万乘之国伐万乘之国,[3]五旬而举之,[4]人力不至于此。[5]不取,必有天殃。[6]取之,何如?[7]”孟子对曰:“取之而燕民悦,[8]则取之。古之人有行之者,[9]武王是也。[10]取之而燕民不悦,则勿取。古之人有行之者,文王是也。以万乘之国伐万乘之国,箪食壶浆以迎王师,[11]岂有他哉?避水火也。[12]如水益深,如火益热,亦运而已矣。[13]

【白话译文】

齐国攻打燕国,取得了胜利。齐宣王问道:“有人对我说,不要占领燕国;也有人对我说,占领燕国吧。以一个有兵车万乘的国家攻打同样有兵车万乘的国家,只花了五十天就全部攻下,仅靠人力是办不到的,必有天意。如不占领,必有天祸。如果占领燕国,怎么样?”孟子回答道:“如果占领它,燕国人民会觉得高兴,就占领吧。古人有实行占领的,周武王便是。如果占领它,燕国人民会觉得不高兴,就不要占领。古人有实行不占领的,周文王便是。兵车万乘的大国攻打兵车万乘的大国,老百姓用竹筐装着饭食,用瓦壶装着桨汤,欢迎得胜的军队,难道会有别的意思吗?只不过要避开水深火热的苦日子罢了。如果水更深,火更热,也就于此转望他人罢了。”

【英语译文】

Qi State launched a war against Yan State and won the battle. King Xuan of Qi State asked, “Someone told me not to occupy Yan State; but somebody else told me to occupy it. It should be the will of Heaven but not manpower that a country with ten thousand battle carts attacked a country with the same size, and finally it won the battle within fifty days. If I don’t occupy it, there is surely catastrophe. What will happen if I do occupy it?” Mencius replied, “You can occupy it if people in Yan State feel happy after your occupation. There existed ancient example such as King Wu of Zhou Dynasty. You cannot occupy it if people in Yan State feel unhappy after your occupation. There existed ancient example such as King Wen of Zhou Dynasty. Common people provided food and soup with baskets and kettle for troops when a country with ten thousand battle carts attacked a country with the same size. Didn’t they have any strange purpose? They just wanted to get rid of deep distress. If they continued to be in deep distress, they would place their hope on others.”

【注释】(1)齐人伐燕胜之:燕王哙让国于其相子之,国人不服,局势大乱。齐国乘机攻燕,燕士卒不战,城门不闭,齐国因而速胜。(2)勿取:不要拿来;不要占领。(3)万乘之国:能出兵车万乘的大国;大国。(4)五旬:五十天。举:攻克;占领。(5)人力不至于此:人力达不到这个程度,意谓天意如此。(6)天殃:天降的祸殃。这是当时早已流行的观念。(7)何如:怎么样。(8)取之而燕民悦:占领燕国,燕国人民喜悦。(9)古之人:古时的人,即"古人"。有行之者:者字结构。有实行占领的。之,近指代词。指代"取之"。下文"则勿取"后的"古之人有行之者",其中"有行之者"的"之",同样是近指代词。但所指代的是"勿取";因此,这个"古之人有行之者"的意思便是"古人有实行不占领的"。(10)武王是也:武王便是。(11)箪食壶浆:用箪装着饭食,用壶装着浆汤。箪,读 dān,古代用竹或苇编成的盛饭食用的圆筐。壶,读 hú,容器名,深腹敛口,多为圆形也有方形主要用以盛液体,新石器时代已有陶壶,商、周时代的铜壶往往有盖。王师:天子的军队;国家的军队。借指正义的军队。(12)避水火也:逃避水深火热的苦境。(13)亦运而已矣:也就于此转望他人罢了。运,转移,转向。

【原文】11 齐人伐燕,取之。诸侯将谋救燕。宣王曰;"诸侯多谋伐寡人者,何以待之?" 孟子对曰:"臣闻七十里为政于天下者,汤是也。[1]未闻以千里畏人者也。书曰:'汤一征自葛始。[2]'天下信之,东面而征,西夷怨;南面而征,北狄怨,曰:'奚为后我?[3]'民望之,若大旱之望云霓也。[4]归市者不止,[5]耕者不变,诛其君而吊其民,[6]若时雨降。[7]民大悦。书曰:'徯我后,后来其苏。[8]'今燕虐其民,王往而征之,民以为将拯己于水火之中也,箪食壶浆以迎王师。若杀其父兄,系累其子弟,[9]毁其宗庙,迁其重器,[10]如之何其可也? 天下固畏齐之强也,今又倍地而不行仁政,[11]是动天下之兵也。[12]王速出令,反其旄倪[13],止其重器,谋于燕众,置君然后去之,[14]则犹可及止也。"[15]

【白话译文】

齐国讨伐燕国,占领了它。别的国家在打算救助燕国。宣王问道:"不少国家在策划攻打我,该怎样对付呢?"孟子答道:"我听说过,有凭纵横各只七十里的土地来治理天下的,商汤就是。还没听说过,拥有纵横各千里的国土而害怕别国的。书经上说:'商汤初次征讨,从葛国开始。'天下人都相信他是为了百姓。他向东方进军,西方部族的百姓抱怨;他向南方进军,北方部族的百姓抱怨;他们说:'为什么要把我们放在后面呢?'百姓盼望他,好像大旱难受时盼望雨的先兆云霓一样。商汤来了,拥向集市的人不停止,栽田种地照常不变。他惩治无道的昏君,慰问受苦的百姓,如像应时的好雨落下来,老百姓非常高兴。书经上说:'等待我们的君王,君王一来,我们就能从死路上回转来。'现在燕国君主虐待百姓,您去征讨他,百姓认为您是把他们从水火中解救出来,因此都用竹筐装满饭,瓦壶装满酒,来欢迎您的军队。如果杀害他们的父兄,关押他们的子弟,毁坏他们的宗庙祠堂,搬走他们的国家宝器,这怎么可以呢?天下各国本来就害怕齐国的强大,现在国土扩大了一倍,还不行仁政,暴虐无道,这就是在引起天下兴兵动武。您赶快发出命令,放回老老小小的俘虏,不搬迁燕国的宝器,同大众商量,设立一个君主,然后撤军。这样做,还来得及停止各国兴兵。"

【英语译文】

Qi State launched a war against Yan State and occupied it. Other states planned to assist Yan State. King Xuan of Qi State asked, "Many states are planning to attack us, what can I do?" Mencius replied, "I ever heard that King Tang of Shang Dynasty governed his 4,900- square- *li* state. But I never heard monarch of 1,000,000- square- *li* state were afraid of others. As *The Book of History* said 'King Tang of Shang Dynasty started his crusade by attacking Ge State first.' People all over the Chinese land believed that he benefited common people's interest. When his troops marched eastwards, peopk of the western tribes complained; when his troops marched southwards, peopk of the northern tribes complained. They asked 'Why did he place us behind?' Common people yearned for him just as people look forward to rainy clouds in bitter drought. When King Tang of Shang Dynasty came, people kept rushing to fairs and peasants continued farming as usual. He punished the tyrannical ruler, consoled common people who suffered hardship, which was so timely like rain in drought that people were very happy. As *The Book of History* said, 'We're waiting for our king. And we'll return to normal life upon his arriving.' Now people in Yan State are suffering hardships and you launch attack on it. People think that it is you who free them from hardships, and they provide food with baskets and drink in kettles to welcome your troops. How could it be alright if their fathers and brothers are killed, if their sons and younger brothers are imprisoned, if their ancestral temples are demolished, and if their state treasures are removed? All other states are frightened by the strength of Qi State. Now that its territory is enlarged by two times, and if government of humanity isn't carried out but brutal government is practiced, it will cause other states to wage war against it. You should give orders right now that all captives be set free, all treasures be kept there. And then you should discuss with people there to nominate an appropriate ruler. After that you should withdraw your troops. By doing so, you can stop other states waging war against your state."

【注释】(1)七十里:指土地面积纵横各七十里。为政于天下:治理天下。汤:商汤。(2)一征:初次征伐,第一次征伐。自葛始:从葛国开始。(3)奚:xī,疑问词。为何,为什么。(4)大旱:长久无雨,地面过分干涸。农作物枯死,人畜难受。云霓:yúnní,虹。天空中的小水珠经日光照射发生折射和反射作用而形成的圆弧形彩带,呈现红、橙、黄、绿、青、蓝、紫七种颜色。这种圆弧常出现两个,红色在外紫色在内,颜色鲜红的称"虹"也称正(雄)虹;红色在内紫色在外颜色较淡的称"霓"也称副(雌)虹。出现在西方的虹是下雨的先兆。所以"望云霓"是渴望下雨的意思。(5)归市者:从各方拥向市集的人。(6)吊其民:慰问受害的百姓。(7)时雨:应时的雨水,及时雨。(8)徯:xī,等待;期望。后:君主;帝王。下同。其苏:其,副词。苏:苏醒;复活。(9)系累:拘囚;囚禁。(10)宗庙:古代帝王、诸侯祭祀祖宗的庙宇。重器:国家的宝器。(11)倍地:土地成倍增加。(12)动天下之兵:引动(招致)天下的军事(战争)。(13)反:放回,遣返。旄倪:màoní,老年和幼儿。(14)置君:设立一个君主。(15)犹可及止:还来得及止住战事。

【原文】12 邹与鲁哄。[1]穆公问曰:[2]"吾有司死者三十三人,[3]民莫之死也。[4]诛之,[5]则不可胜诛;不诛,则疾视其长上之死而不救,[6]如之何则可也?"孟子对曰:"凶年饥岁,君之民老弱转乎沟壑,[7]壮者散而之四方者,几千人矣;[8]而君之仓廪实,府库充,有司莫以告,是上慢而残下也。曾子曰:[9]'戒之戒之![10]出乎尔者,反乎尔者也。[11]'夫民今而后得反之也。[12]君无尤焉![13]君行仁政,斯民亲其上,[14]死其长矣。"

【白话译文】

邹国和鲁国发生了战斗。邹穆公问孟子:"在这场战斗中,我的官吏死了三十三人,而老百姓却没有一个为他们牺牲自己。把老百姓杀死吧,却杀不了那么多;不杀吧,却又恼恨他们亲眼看着自己的官长被杀都不去营救,怎么办才好呢?"孟子回答说:"在灾荒年,您的百姓,年老体弱的被抛尸于溪沟山野,身强力壮的逃散到四方他国,将近千人。而您的粮仓中堆满了粮食,库房里装满了财宝,您的官吏没有人报告任何实情。这是在上位的人怠慢国事、残害百姓。曾子说过:'警惕啊!警惕啊!你怎样对待别人,别人将同样回报你。'那么百姓现今和以后都能够回报您。您不要怪罪他们。您实行仁政,这样百姓就亲近他们的官长,为他们的官长而死。"

【英语译文】

War broke between Zou State and Lu State. Duke Mu of Zou State asked Mencius, "My thirty three officials lost their lives but none of my common people was willing to die for them. If I kill them, I can't kill so many; but if I don't kill them, I just hate that they just saw the officials die refusing to save them. How can I do for this?" Mencius answered, "In years of famine, elders and youths of your subjects died in valleys and strong men fleed everywhere, which amounted to nearly one thousand. But barns in your state are full of grains and storehouses are full of treasures. None of your officials ever reported the real situation to you. This is the fact that officials cheated their seniors and harmed people. Zeng Zi said 'Be alert! Be alert! People will pay back what you did to them.' Then common people will pay back to you in the future. You needn't blame them. If you practice government of humanity, your subjects will surely be close to their officials and be willing to lose their lives for them."

【注释】(1)邹与鲁哄:邹国与鲁国交战相斗。哄,读 hòng,相斗。赵岐注:"犹构兵而斗也。"(2)穆公:邹穆公。(3)吾:我;我的。有司:官吏。古代设官分职,各有所司,故称。(4)民莫之死:"民莫死之"的倒装。民,老百姓。莫,没有人。之,代词。他们,指"有司"。死,谓为某事或某人而牺牲性命。本句的意思是"老百姓中没有人为他们(有司)而牺牲。"(5)诛之:杀死他们。之,代词。他们,指"老百姓"。(6)则疾视其长上之死而不救:则,转折连词。却又。疾,厌恶;憎恨。"视其长上之死而不救"是疾的宾语。长上,官长、上司。(7)老弱:年老与年轻的人;年老体弱的人。转:弃尸。乎:介词,于。沟壑:gōuhè,山沟;溪谷。引申为野死之处或困厄之境。(8)壮者:身强力壮的人。散而之四方者:离散到四方的。几:jī,将近;接近于。(9)曾子:孔子弟子曾参。(10)戒之:警惕啊。之,语气助词。(11)出乎尔者,反乎尔者也:从你那儿出来的,将是回到你那儿的。意为你怎样对待别人,别人也怎样对待你。在本文中便是这个意思。后简化为"出尔反尔",并引申为言语前后矛盾,反复无常。(12)夫:连词。表承接,和"则"差不多,可以译为"那么"。今而后:现今和以后。得反之:得,用在动词前,表示"能够"。反之,报复你。反,报复。之,对称代词,你。(13)尤焉:尤,责备,怪罪。焉,他称代词,他(们)。(14)斯:承接连词,和"则"差不多。"这么,如此"的意思。亲其上:亲近他们的官长、上司。"上"和下文"长"互文见义。

【原文】13 滕文公问曰:[1]"滕,小国也,间于齐、楚,[2]事齐乎?事楚乎?"孟子对曰:"是谋非吾所能及也。[3]无已,[4]则有一焉:[5]凿斯池也,[6]筑斯城也,与民守之,[7]效死而民弗去,[8]则是可为也。[9]"

【白话译文】

滕文公问道:"滕国是一个弱小的国家,处在齐、楚两个大国中间,是服侍齐国吗,还是服侍楚国呢?"孟子回答说:"这个计策,不是我所能涉及的。您如果定要我说,我就只有一说:把您的护城河挖深,把您的城墙加筑牢固,同百姓一道来守卫它,百姓也跟您一样到死而不离去,这就是当干的事情了。"

【英语译文】

The Duke of Teng State asked, "Teng State is a small and weak one which locates between Qi State and Chu State. Should it serve Qi State or Chu State?" Mencius replied, "I cannot give you such strategy. If you really really denarnd my suggestion, I can only say that you should deepen your city moat, solidify your city walls, and then protect it together with your subjects. Your subjects will stay with you till death and won't leave you. This is what should be done right now."

【注释】(1)滕文公:滕,西周分封的诸侯国。姬姓。开国君主为周文王之子错叔绣。在今山东省滕州市西南。战国初期为越所灭。不久复国。后为宋所灭。滕文公——战国时滕国君,滕定公之子。为世子时路过宋国,曾见孟子。定公死后他又派然友到邹见孟子。孟子教以行"三年之丧",继派毕战向孟子问井田制。(2)间于齐、楚:"于齐、楚间"的倒装。意在强调"间"。于,义同"在":表空间位置。(3)是谋:这个计策。及:涉及;参与。(4)无已:不得已。(5)则有一焉:则,承接连词,就。一焉:一计;一说。焉,代词。指代"谋"。(6)凿斯池:záo ~ ~,凿,挖掘;开凿。斯,这,此。池,护城河。(7)与民:同百姓一起。(8)效死:舍命报效,竭尽忠诚。(9)可为:可,犹所。和动词组合,构成名词词组。可为,即"所干的事"。所,意谓宜,适宜的。

【原文】14 滕文公问曰:"齐人将筑薛,[1]吾甚恐,如之何则可?"孟子对曰:"昔者大王居邠,[2]狄人侵之,[3]去之岐山之下居焉。[4]非择而取之,不得已也。[5]苟为善,[6]后世子孙必有王者矣。[7]君子创业垂统,[8]为可继也。[9]若夫成功,[10]则天也,[11]君如彼何哉?[12]强为善而已矣。[13]"

【白话译文】

滕文公问道:"齐国人要加固薛邑的城池建设,我很害怕,怎么办才好呢?"孟子回答说;"从前太王住在邠地,狄人来侵犯,他搬到了岐山下居住。他不是自愿选取这个地方,而是迫不得已。只要作为一个君主能实行仁政,他的后代子孙必然出现帝王。有德的执政者,开创基业,把它传给子孙,就是要求能代代相传。至于预期的结果如何,自有天意。您能把齐国人怎么办?只有努力实行仁政罢了。"

【英语译文】

The Duke of Teng State asked, "People of Qi State want to consolidate city wall and moat in Xue State and I' m afraid of that so much. What can I do for this?" Mencius replied, "In the old days, Dan Fu lived in the place of Bin and Xun Yu invaded his place. Dan Fu had to move to live at the foot of Mt. Qi. He wasn't willing to live here but had no choice. If only a ruler carries out government of humanity, a King is destined to appear from his descendents. A virtual ruler created a foundation and passed down it to his offspring one generation after another. As for the consequence, it must follow the will of Heaven. How can you deal with Qi State? The only thing you can do is to complement government of humanity."

【注释】(1)筑薛:筑,修建,建造。薛,周初一个小国,故称在今山东省滕州市东南。后为齐所灭,以之封田婴。田婴将筑薛,可能正在孟子从宋国到滕国的时候。(2)居邠:大王,即太王。邠,同"豳"(bīn),在今陕西省旬邑县西。(3)狄人:即獯鬻(xūnyù)。(4)岐山:在今陕西省岐山县东北。居焉——居住在那里。焉,代词。远指代词,指代处所,译为"那里"。(5)非择而取之:不是主动选取这个地方。不得已也:是出于不得不这样。(6)苟:假如;如果;只要。为善:行善。统治者行善,莫大于实行仁政。(7)必:必然;一定。有:产生;出现。王者:帝王,天子。(8)君子:指有德的统治者。创业垂统:开创基业传之子孙。(9)为可继也:为,求取;要求。(10)若夫:至于。成功,成效;事情预期的结果。用于句首或段落的开始,表示另提一事。(11)则天也:则,承接连词。天,天意;命运。(12)君如彼何哉:君,称呼滕文公。译作"您"。彼,指齐人。如彼何哉,谓"您把齐人怎么办呢?""您奈何得了齐人吗?"(13)强:勉力,尽力,努力。

【原文】15 滕文公问曰:"滕,小国也,竭力以事大国,则不得免焉,[1]如之何则可?"孟子对曰:"昔者大王居邠,狄人侵之。事之以皮币,[2]不得免焉;事之以犬马,不得免焉;事之以珠玉,不得免焉。乃属其耆老而告之曰:[3]'狄人之所欲者,吾土地也。吾闻之也:君子不以其所以养人者害人。二三子何患乎无君?[4]我将去之。[5]'去邠,逾梁山。[6]邑于岐山之下居焉。[7]邠人曰:'仁人也,不可失也。'从之者如归市。[8]或曰:'世守也,[9]非身之所能为也。[10]效死勿去。'君将择于斯二者。[11]"

【白话译文】

滕文公问道:"滕是个弱小国家,尽心竭力地服侍大国,却老是不免祸害,怎么办才好呢?孟子回答说:"从前太王住在邠地,狄人来侵犯他,用贵重的毛皮和丝绸去打发,不久又来侵犯;用好狗、名马去打发,不久又来侵犯;用珍珠宝玉去打发,还是又来侵犯。太王便召集邠地的老年人,向他们说:'狄人所想得到的是我们的土地。我听说过:有德行的人不让本来用于养人的东西来害人。各位何必害怕没有君主呢?我将要离开这里。'于是,离开邠地翻过梁山在岐山下筑起城邑住下来。邠地的老百姓说:'他是一位有仁德的人,我们不可失去他。'追随他到岐山下的人像从四面八方进城一样。也有人说:'世世代代守着的土地,不是我能丢掉的,付出生命也不走开。'您姑且在这两个办法中选择。"

【英语译文】

The Duke of Teng State asked, "Teng Sate is a small one and it tried its best to serve the big ones but never dodged disasters. what could we do?" Mencius answered, "In the old days, Dan Fu lived in the place of Bin and Xun Yu invaded his place. He gave them precious fur and silk but the latter invaded soon again. He gave them good dogs and horses but the latter invaded soon again. He gave them jewelry and treasury and the latter invaded soon again. Then Dan Fu summoned people in the place of Bin and told them, 'Xun Yu just wanted to obtain our land. I've ever heard that a virtual man never harmed people by things which are for feeding persons. You needn't worry about there is no a monarch. I will leave here.' Then he left the place of Bin, crossed Mt. Liang and finally settled at the foot of Mt. Qi by building city wall and moat. Common people in the place of Bin said, 'He was a moral and humanistic man and we shouldn't lose him.' People from all directions followed him just like going to towns. Somebody also said, 'We could not give up the land which was inherited for ages. We wouldn't leave it even if we lose our lives.' You just choose one way from these two."

【注释】(1)则:转折连词,却。免焉:幸免侵扰。焉,远指代词作宾语。指代大国的压力。(2)皮币:皮,毛皮。币,缯帛(丝绸的统称)。皮币是古代用作聘享(聘问和宴享)的贵重礼物。(3)属:召集;聚集。耆老:老年人;当地的年长者;后指年老而有地位的绅士。(4)二三子:诸君;各位;几个人。(5)去之:离开这里。去,离开。下文"去邠"即"离开邠"。(6)梁山:在今陕西省干县西北五里。从邠至岐必过梁山。(7)邑:动词。建筑城邑。居焉:定居在这里。焉,近指代词。(8)归市:人们从各方拥向市集。比喻归附者众多。(9)世守:世世代代。守,读 shòu,戍守疆域土地。(10)非身之所能为:身,《尔雅·释诂下》:"身,我也。"非身,即不是我。能为,语出《左传·隐公四年》:"老夫耄矣,无能为也。"后用作"能有所为或有所作为"之意。(11)将:姑且。

【原文】16 鲁平公将出,[1]嬖人臧仓请曰:[2]"他日君出,[3]则必命有司所之。[4]今乘舆已驾矣,[5]有司未知所之,敢请。[6]"公曰:"将见孟子。"曰:"何哉,君所为轻身以先于匹夫者?[7]以为贤乎?礼义由贤者出;而孟子之后丧逾前丧。[8]君无见焉!"公曰:"诺"。[9]乐正子入见,[10]曰:"君奚为不见孟轲也?[11]"曰:"或告寡人曰:[12]'孟子之后丧逾前丧'是以不往见也。"曰:"何哉,君所谓逾者?前以士,后以大夫;前以三鼎,而后以五鼎与?[13]"曰:"否;谓棺椁衣衾之美也。[14]曰:"非所谓逾也,贫富不同也。"乐正子见孟子,曰:"克告于君,[15]君为来见也。[16]嬖人有臧仓者沮君,[17]君是以不果来也。[18]"曰:"行,或使之;止或尼之。[19]行止,非人所能也。[20]吾之不遇鲁侯,天也。臧氏之子焉能使予不遇哉?"

【白话译文】

鲁平公将要外出,他所宠爱的小臣臧仓询问道:"往日您外出,就一定要叫管事人同去。现在车马都预备好了,管事人还不知道去的地方,所以我来问问。"平公说:"我去拜访孟子。"臧仓说:"您不尊重自身,先去拜访一个普通人,是为了什么呀?您以为他是贤德的人吗?礼义是由贤德的人提倡的,而孟子办他母亲的丧事大大超过了办他父亲的丧事。您不要去见他。"平公说:"噢,好吧!"乐正子入宫进见平公,问道:"您为什么不去看孟轲呀?"平公说:"有人告诉我。'孟子办他母亲的丧事大大超过了办他父亲的丧事。'所以不去看了。"乐正子说:"您说的'超过'是什么意思呢?是指父丧用士礼,母丧用大夫礼吗?是指父丧用三只鼎摆放祭品,而母丧用五只鼎摆放祭品吗?"平公说:"不是,我指的是棺椁衣衾的精美。"乐正子说:"那便不能说'超过'了,只是前后贫富不同罢了。"乐正子进见孟子,说道:"我把情况告诉了鲁君,他刚要来看您,一个受宠爱的小臣名叫臧仓阻止了他,因此他不来了。"孟子说:"行动,有使行动的;止定,有阻拦止定的。行动和止定,都有看不见的力量在操纵,不是一般人能够做到的。我不能和鲁侯见面,是由于天命。臧家那小子他怎么能使我和鲁侯见不上面呢?”

【英语译文】

Duke Ping of Lu State was about to go out, and his favored minor official Zang Cang inquired, “You usually go out together with steward, but today he doesn’t know where you go even upon your setting off, therefore, I ask you about this.” Duke Ping said, “I go to visit Mencius.” Zang Cang said, “You don’t respect yourself and intend to pay a visit to an average man. Why? Do you think he is a moral and virtual man? Rites and righteousness are proposed by moral and virtual man but Mencius has made his mother’s funeral ceremony surpass his father’s. You needn’t go to see him.” Duke Ping said, “O, it’s OK! I won’t go to see him.” Yue Zheng went to the palace to visit Duke Ping, asking, “Why didn’t you go to see Mencius?” Duke Ping replied, “Somebody told me that Mencius had made his mother’s funeral ceremony surpass his father’s. Consequently, I didn’t visit him.” Yue Zheng asked, “What do you mean by ‘surpass’? Does it mean that father’s funeral ceremony was carried out according to a scholar’s but mother’s funeral ceremony was done according to a minister’s? Or does it mean that father’s funeral ceremony was provided sacrificial things by three tripods but mother’s funeral ceremony was done by five tripods?” Duke Ping answered, “No. I refer to the fine coffin, outer coffin, clothes, and covers.” Yue Zheng said, “That doesn’t mean ‘surpass’. It just means that there is difference between richness and poverty.” Yue Zheng visited Mencius and said, “I talked with Duke Ping. He was about to go out visiting you but a favored minor official called Zang Cang stopped him, therefore he didn’t come to see you.” Mencius replied, “There is something which causes action and there is also something which causes inaction. Action and inaction are manipulated by invisible powers, and average men cannot manage to do it. That I couldn’t meet Duke Ping is destined by the Mandate of the Heaven. How could the little guy Zang Cang stop our meeting?”

【注释】(1)鲁平公:鲁景公之子,名叔,一说名旅。将出:将要外出。(2)嬖人请曰:嬖人(bì ~)身份卑下而受宠爱的人。这里指亲信的小臣。请曰,犹询问。即询问道。(3)他日:以往;平时;前些日子。(4)则:副词。表相应的动作或情况。可译作“就”“便”。有司:指管具体事务的人。有司所之:所,语气助词。用在主语谓语之间,对谓语有强调作用。现代汉语没有这种用法,译时可以去掉。之,动词。往;至。下文"有司未知所之"的"所"是结构助词,标志它的后附词语是名词性词组(无论其原来是何种性质,而不是别的什么。)所以"有司未知所之"的"所之",意思是去的地方(处所)。(5)今:现在。乘舆:shèngyú,古代特指天子和诸侯所乘坐的车子。(6)敢请:承接上文,敢请,即敢问去的地方。敢,表敬副词。要求语气委婉、恭敬、不粗放。(7)何哉,君所为轻身以先于匹夫者:倒装句。"君所为轻身以先于匹夫者"是主语,"何哉" 是谓语。所,语气助词。用在主语谓语之间。为,谓语动词。做,干。轻身以先于匹夫者,者字结构。意谓:不尊重自身先去拜访普通人的事。下文"何哉,君所谓逾者"句型与此同。(8)后丧逾前丧:后丧,指其母丧。前丧,指其父丧。(9)诺:表示同意、遵命的应答声。可以译作"噢""哦"。(10)乐正子:yuè ~ ~,姓乐正,名克。孟子弟子。仕于鲁。入见:入宫进见;入朝谒见。(11)奚为:xīwèi,为什么。xīwéi,干什么。奚,何,胡。孟轲:孟子名轲。(12)人:古代君主的谦称。(13)三鼎,五鼎:鼎是古代的一种器皿。祭祀时用以盛祭品。祭礼:天子九鼎,诸侯七。卿大夫五,元士三。三鼎,五鼎,体现了士礼和卿大夫礼的差别。(14)棺椁衣衾:guānguǒ yīqīn,古代士以上的人常用两层以上的棺木。内棺叫棺,外棺叫椁。衣衾,死者装殓的衣服和被子。(15)告于:于,语气助词。用在一些单音动词或单音形容词后面补凑音节,由介词转化而来,接近于复音词词尾,可以不译也可去掉不要。(16)为:wéi,将。(17)沮:jǔ,阻止。(18)是以:连词。因此;所以。不果:没有成为事实;终于没有实行。(19)行,或使之;止,或尼之:行动,有使行动的;止定,有阻拦止定的。尼,阻止,阻拦。本句大意是说:行动和止定都有肉眼看不见的力量在操纵。(20)行止,非人所能也:非,不是。人,指一般人。所能,能够做到。

孟子集注卷三　公孙丑章句上 凡九章

【原文】1 公孙丑问曰:[1]"夫子当路于齐,[2]管仲、晏子之功,可复许乎?[3]"孟子曰:"子诚齐人也,[4]知管仲、晏婴而已矣。或问乎曾西曰:[5]'吾子与子路孰贤?[6]'曾西蹴然曰:[7]'吾先子之所畏也。'[8]曰:'然则吾子与管仲孰贤?'曾西艴然不悦,[9]曰:'尔何曾比予于管仲?[10]管仲得君,如彼其专也,行乎国政,如彼其久也;功烈,如彼其卑也。[11]尔何曾比予于是?'"曰:[12]"管仲,曾西之所不为也,[13]而子为我愿之乎?[14]"曰:"管仲以其君霸,晏子以其君显。[15]管仲、晏子犹不足为与?"曰:"以齐王,由反手也。[16]"曰:"若是,则弟子之惑滋甚。[17]且以文王之德[18],百年而后崩,犹未洽于天下；[19]武王周公继之，然后大行[20]。今言王若易然，[21]则文王不足法与？"曰："文王何可当也？[22]由汤至于武丁，贤圣之君六七作，[23]天下归殷久矣，久则难变也。武丁朝诸侯，有天下，犹运之掌也。[24]纣之去武丁未久也。[25]其故家遗俗，流风善政，犹有存者；[26]又有微子、微仲、王子比干、箕子、胶鬲——皆贤人也，相与辅相之，[27]故久而后失之也。尺地，莫非其有也，一民，莫非其臣也，[28]然而文王犹方百里起，是以难也。齐人有言曰：'虽有智慧，不如乘势，虽有镃基，不如待时。[29]'今时则易然也。夏后、殷、周之盛，地未有过千里者也，而齐有其地矣；鸡鸣狗吠相闻，而达乎四境，[30]而齐有其民矣。地不改辟矣，民不改聚矣，[31]行仁政王，莫之能御也。且王者之不作，未有疏于此时者也；民之憔悴于虐政，未有甚于此时者也。饥者易为食，渴者易为饮。[32]孔子曰：'德之流行速于置邮而传命。[33]'当今之时，万乘之国行仁政，民之悦之，犹解倒悬也，[34]故事半古之人，功必倍之，惟此时为然。"

【白话译文】

公孙丑问道："老师，您如果在齐国执政，管仲、晏子的成功事业，可以复兴吗？"孟子说，"你真是一个齐国人，就只知道管仲、晏子。有人曾经问曾西：'您和子路相比谁强？'曾西又惊异又惭愧不安地说：'他是我亡父敬重的人，不可妄谈。'那人又问：'那么，您和管仲相比谁强？'曾西变了脸色生气地说：'你为什么把我和管仲相比？管仲得到国君那样的专任，把持国政那样长久，所谓的成功业绩那样低下；你为什么要把我和这个人相比呢？'"孟子停了停又说："管仲是曾西不屑于相比的人，而你以为我愿同管仲相比吗？"公孙丑说："管仲使齐桓公称霸，晏子使齐景公名扬诸侯，管仲、晏子还不够相比吗？"孟子说："凭齐国推行王政于天下，就像翻转手掌一样不难。"公孙丑说："这样说来，我的疑惑更深了。像文王那样的德行，干到将近一百岁才死，他推行的德政还没有周遍天下；是武王、周公继承了他的事业，然后才大大地推行了王政，现在说推行王政似乎很容易，那么文王也不值得效法了吗？"孟子说："文王谁能够比得上？从汤到武丁，贤明的君主兴起过六七次，天下的人归附殷朝已经很久了，时间一久便很难变动，武丁使诸侯来朝，拥有天下，就像在手掌中运用一样。纣王的年代，上离武丁不太久，世家大族，善良习俗，淳朴风气，好的政令政绩，还存在着一些。又有微子、微仲、王子比干、箕子、胶鬲他们都是贤德的人，共同来辅助他，所以经历了很久才亡了国。当时，没有哪一尺土地不归纣王所有，没有哪一个百姓不归纣王所管，然而文王还是凭方圆一百里的土地来创业，所以是很困难的。齐国有句俗话：'即使有智慧，没有有利形势不行；即使有大锄，没有务农时间不行。'现在的形势要推行王政就容易了：即使在夏商周最兴旺发达的时候,土地也没有超过方圆一千里的,现在齐国却有这么广阔的国土了,鸡鸣狗叫的声音,彼此相闻,人烟密集,这种景象,直到四方边境,全国一样。国土不必再开拓了,民众不必再招来了,只要实行仁政治理天下,没有谁阻止得了。而且统一天下的王者不出现的时间,从来没有这样长久过。老百姓困顿于暴虐的苛政,也从来没有这么厉害。饥饿的人不挑剔食物吃得快,口渴的人不挑剔饮水喝得快。孔子说过:'德政的广泛传布,快于用车马传达命令。'现在这个时代,拥有万驾兵车的大国实行仁政,老百姓的高兴,就好像被倒吊着受折磨的人得到了解救一样。所以花古人一半的精力和时间取得超过古人一倍的功效,只有这个时代能做到。"

【英语译文】

Gongsun Chou asked, "Master, if you hold power in Qi State, can you revive Guan Zhong and Yan Zi's successful causes? " Mencius said, "You are really a man of Qi State and know only about Guan Zhong and Yan Ying. Someone ever asked Zeng Xi, 'You and Zi Lu, who is stronger?' Zeng Xi, being surprised, ashamed and uneasy, answered, 'Zi Lu was the one whom my deceased father respected and I cannot talk boldly about him. ' Then the man asked again, 'You and Guan Zhong, who is stronger?' Zeng Xi got angry and answered, 'Why do you compare me with Guan Zhong? Guan Zhong was exclusively favored by the monarch and held power for a very long time but achieved so little in administration. Why do you compare me with such a person?' " Mencius paused for a while and then said again, "Guan Zhong was a person whom Zeng Zi disdained to be compared with, and do you think I am willing to be compared with Guan Zhong?" Gongsun Chou asked, "Guan Zhong made Duke Huan of Qi State dominate in all states, and Yan Zi made Duke Jing of Qi State famous. Weren't they good enough to be compared?" Mencius replied, "It is as easy as turning over one's palms to implement kingly government in Qi State. " Gongsun Chou said, "My confusion deepens upon your explanation. King Wen of Zhou Dynasty didn't succeed in implementing his virtual government until his death when he was almost one hundred years old. It were King Wen and Duke Zhou who followed his cause and carried kingly government successfully. Now you say it's easy to implement kingly government. Does it mean that we can learn nothing from King Wen?" Mencius said, "Who can match King Wen? There arose wise and able monarchs for six to seven times from Tang to Wu Ding in Shang Dynasty, and people submit to the authority of it for ages. It was difficult for any change and Wu Ding made princes follow just as easy as turning his palms. In the age of King Zhou, there still existed big families, good custom, simple living-way, and fine policies since it was not long after Wu Ding's time. There were also Wei Zi, Wei Zhong, Prince Bi Gan, Ji Zi, and Jiao Ge who assisted him so that Shang Dynasty lasted for a little long time before its perishing. At that time, all land belonged to King Zhou and all people were controlled by him but King Wen of Zhou Dynasty laid the foundations by just one- hundred- square- *li* land. So it was quite difficult. In Qi State, there is a saying ' It isn't alright without advantageous situation even if you are wise; it isn't alright without proper farming season even if you have big hoe. ' It is quite easy to implement government of humanity today. There wasn't an area without one thousand square *li* even in most prosperous Xia, Shang, and Zhou dynasties. But nowadays Qi State has so spacious land where people live peacefully and crowdedly with their cock-crow and dog- bark heard. There is no need to expand land and to increase population. No one can hinder it even if it carries out government of humanity. There wasn't so long a period when a king unifying the land under heaven didn't appear. Common people never suffered so brutal government before. A hungry man isn't picky for food but eats fast and a thirsty man isn't picky for water but drinks fast. Confucius said, ' Virtual government spreads faster than carts spread order. ' Nowadays it is just like saving a person from being hanged upside down if a big state with ten thousand carts and soldiers implements government of humanity. Therefore it is in this age that we can get double the result of ancient people by making half effort and time. "

【注释】(1)公孙丑:孟子弟子。齐人也。(2)当路:执政;掌权。(3)管仲:齐桓公之相。晏子:即晏婴。齐景公之相。功:事业。复许:复兴。许,犹兴起,进行。(4)子:代词,表示第二人称。相当于"您"。诚:真是;真实。(5)曾西:曾申,字子西。鲁人曾参之子。(6)吾子:对对方敬爱之称。一般用于男子之间。可译作"您"。注意:吾子,另有"我的儿子"一义和读作 yázǐ, 即"小孩子" 一义。子路:孔子弟子,即仲由。(7)蹴然:cù ~,惊惭不安的样子。(另读:蹴然 zú ~,恭敬的样子。)(8)先子:亡父;祖先。所畏:名词性词组。敬重的人,心服的人。(9)艴然:bó ~,恼怒的样子。(10)何曾: ~ zēng,为何,何故。(11)功烈:亦作"功列"。功业勋绩。(12)曰:此曰,仍是孟子曰。在记录一个人的谈话中添一个"曰"字,表示有较长停顿。(13)之所不为也:之所,同义复用。为:作,做。承上文训"比"。(14)子:代词,表示第二人称,相当于"您"。为:以为,认为。(15)以其君:使他的君主。(16)由反手:由,同“犹”。反手,翻转手掌。比喻事情极容易办。(17)滋甚:愈益;更加;更甚。表一种状态或程度的扩展。相当于加大;加深;加多;更厉害;更严重等。(18)且以文王之德:且,进层连词。“而且”“并且”。以,介词。表示论事的对象、依据及标准。相当于“以……而论、就……而论”。文王,商末周族领袖。姓姬,名昌,商纣王时为西伯,亦称伯昌。在位五十年。(19)百年而后崩:百岁而后死。(据传文王活了九十七岁。言百年,是可接受的概数。)意谓一生老长时间。洽:周遍。(20)武王周公继之,后然大行:武王,(?——公元前1041年)西周王朝的建立者,文王之子)。公元前1046年——公元前1043年在位(从灭商之年起算)。名发。继承文王遗志,联合庸、蜀、羌、髳、微、卢、彭、濮等族,于公元前1046年率军攻商。牧野(今河南淇县西南)之战大胜。灭商建立西周王朝,都于镐(今陕西西安市长安区沣河以东),分封诸侯。后病卒。周公,西周初起重要政治家。姓姬,名旦,也称叔旦。文王之子,武王之弟,成王之叔。因采邑在周(今陕西岐山北),故称周公。辅武王灭商。武王死,成王幼,周公摄政。管叔、蔡叔、霍叔等不服,联合武庚和东方夷族反叛,他出师东征。叛乱评定后,大规模分封诸侯,并营建洛邑(今河南洛阳市)为东都。又制礼作乐,建立典章制度。主张明德慎罚。大行,指全面推行王道。(21)王若易然:王,称王;行王政。若易然,似乎很容易一样。(22)何可当:何可,谁能够。当,对等;相当;抵敌;比得上。(23)由汤至于武丁,贤圣之君六七作:作,量词。表示动量。相当于“次”。贤圣之君六七作,意谓贤圣的君王兴起过六七次。据《史记·殷本纪》,汤至武丁有汤、太甲、太戊、祖乙、盘庚、武丁是贤圣之君。(24)朝诸侯,有天下,犹运之掌也:朝诸侯,使诸侯来朝。有天下,拥有天下;治理天下。运之掌,运用在手掌之中。比喻容易。省作“运掌”。(25)纣之去武丁未久也:由武丁至纣,其间历祖庚、祖甲、廪辛、庚丁、武乙、太丁、帝乙七帝。但廪辛至帝乙五帝,在位年数都极短。(26)其故家遗俗:指世家大族和前代留传下来的风俗习惯。流风善政:指前代流传下来的风气(多指好风气)和良善的政令政绩。(27)又有微子、微仲、王子比干、箕子、胶鬲……相与辅相之:微子,名启。纣的庶兄。微仲 ,微子之弟,名衍。王子比干,纣的叔父。屡次向纣进谏,纣说:“吾闻圣人心有七窍。”于是剖之以观其心。箕子,也是纣的叔父 ,比干被杀,箕子装疯为奴,还是被囚;武王灭商后,他得到了释放。胶鬲,纣王之臣。鬲,读gě。相与,共同;一道。辅相,读fǔxiàng,辅助;帮助。(28)尺地:极言地之小。莫非:没有一个不是。一民,一个百姓。(29)虽:表让步,犹“虽然”。表假设,相当于“纵然”“即使”。乘势:趁势。谓凭借有利形势;乘机。镃基:zī~,农具名,大锄。待时:等待时机,指把握农时。(30)鸡鸣狗吠相闻:形容百姓安居乐业。达乎四境:到达四方边境;遍及全国。(31)不改辟矣:土地不另行开拓,民不改聚矣:民众不另行增加。改,意谓重新,再;另。辟,亦作“辟”。开拓;开辟。聚,聚集;积聚。引申为增多。(32)为食,易为饮:饥、渴者不挑剔饮食,吃喝得快。(33)流行:广泛传布;盛行。置邮:用车马传递文书信息。亦谓传递文书信息的驿站。古制,置为马递,邮为步递,原有区别,后即混用。传命:传达命令。(34)倒悬:人体被倒吊,头向下,脚朝上,十分难受。比喻极其困苦或危急。

【原文】2 公孙丑问曰:“夫子加齐之卿相,[1]得行道焉,虽由此霸王,不异矣。[2]如此,则动心否乎?[3]”孟子曰:“否。我四十不动心。”曰:“若是,则夫子过孟贲远矣。[4]”曰:“是不难,告子先我不动心。[5]”曰:“不动心有道乎?[6]”曰:“有。北宫黝之养勇也,[7]不肤挠,不目逃,[8]思以一豪挫于人,若挞之于市朝。[9]不受于褐宽博,亦不受于万乘之君。[10]视刺万乘之君,若刺褐夫。[11]无严诸侯,恶声至,必反之。[12]孟施舍之所养勇也,[13]曰:‘视不胜犹胜也。量敌而后进,虑胜而后会,是畏三军者也。[14]舍岂能为必胜哉?能无惧而已矣。’孟施舍似曾子,北宫黝似子夏。[15]夫二子之勇,未知其孰贤,然而孟施舍守约也。[16]昔者曾子谓子襄曰:[17]‘子好勇乎?吾尝闻大勇于夫子矣;[18]自反而不缩,[19]虽褐宽博,吾不惴焉[20],自反而缩,虽千万人,吾往矣。’孟施舍之守气,[21]又不如曾子之守约也。”曰:“敢问夫子之不动心,与告子之不动心,可得闻与?”“告子曰:‘不得于言,[22]勿求于心;[23]不得于心,勿求于气。[24]’不得于心,勿求于气,可;不得于言,勿求于心,不可。夫志,气之帅也;气,体之充也。[25]夫志至焉,气次焉。[26]故曰:‘持其志[27],无暴其气。[28]’”“既曰志至焉,气次焉’,又曰‘持其志,无暴其气’何也?”曰:“志壹则动气,[29]气壹则动志也。今夫蹶者趋者,[30]是气也,而反动其心。”“敢问夫子恶乎长?[31]”曰:“我知言,[32]我善养吾浩然之气。[33]”“敢问何谓浩然之气?”曰:“难言也。其为气也,[34]至大至刚,以直养而无害,[35]则塞于天地之间。其为气也,配义与道;[36]无是,馁也。[37]是集义所生者,[38]非义袭而取之也。[39]行有不慊于心,[40]则馁矣。我故曰告子未尝知义,以其外之也。[41]必有事焉,[42]而无正;[43]心无忘,无助长也,[44]无若宋人然。宋人有闵其苗之不长而揠之者,[45]芒芒然归,[46]谓其人曰:‘[47]今日病矣![48]予助苗长矣!’其子趋而往视之,苗则槁矣。天下之不助苗长者寡矣。以为无益而舍之者,不耘苗者也[49];助之长者,揠苗者也,非徒无益而又害之。”“何谓知言?”“诐辞知其所蔽,[50]淫辞知其所陷,[51]邪辞知其所离,[52]遁辞知其所穷。[53]生于其心,害于其政;发于其政,害于其事。圣人复起,必从吾言矣。”“宰我、子贡善为说辞,[54]冉牛、闵子、颜渊善言德行。[55]孔子兼之,[56]‘我于辞命,则不能也。’然则夫子既圣矣乎?[57]”曰:“恶![58]是何言也?昔者子贡问于孔子曰:‘夫子圣矣乎?’孔子曰:‘圣则吾不能,我学不厌而教不倦也。’子贡曰:‘学不厌智也,教不倦仁也。仁且智,夫子既圣矣。’夫圣,[59]孔子不居[60]是何言也?""昔者窃闻之[61]:子夏、子游、子张皆有圣人之一体,[62]闵子、颜渊则具体而微,[63]敢问所安?[64]"曰:"姑舍是。[65]"曰:"伯夷、伊尹何如?"曰:"不同道,非其君不事,非其民不使;治则进,乱则退,[66]伯夷也。何事非君,何使非民;[67]治亦进,乱亦进,伊尹也。可以仕则仕。可以止则止,[68]可以久则久,可以速则速,[69]孔子也。皆古圣人也,吾未能有行焉;[70]乃所愿,[71]则学孔子也。""伯夷、伊尹于孔子,若是班乎"[72]曰:"否;自有生民以来,[73]未有孔子也。"曰:"然则有同与?"曰:"有。得百里之地而君之,[74]皆能以朝诸侯,有天下;行一不义,杀一不辜而得天下,皆不为也。是则同。[75]曰:"敢问其所以异。"曰:"宰我、子贡、有若,[76]智足以知圣人,污不至阿其所好。[77]宰我曰:'以予观于夫子,贤于尧、舜远矣。[78]'子贡曰:'见其礼而知其政,闻其乐而知其德,由百世之后,[79]等百世之,[80]莫之能违也。[81]自生民以来,未有夫子也。'[82]有若曰:'岂惟民哉?麒麟之于走兽,凤凰之于飞鸟,泰山之于丘垤,河海之于行潦,[83]类也。圣人之于民,亦类也。出于其类拔乎其萃,[84]自生民以来未有盛于孔子也。'"

【白话译文】

公孙丑问道:"老师,您若做了齐国的执政大臣,能够实行自己的主张了,即使从此建立霸业和王业,也是不奇怪的。这样,您的心情会不会有波动?"孟子说:"不会,我从四十岁起,心情就不波动了。"公孙丑说:"像这样,老师,您那就远远超过孟贲了。"孟子说:"这个不难,告子心情不波动比我还早。"公孙丑说:"心情不波动有方法吗?"孟子说:"有。北宫黝他自己培养勇气:肌肤被刺戳,不颤抖;眼睛被刺激,不避开。他觉得输给别人一丝一毫,就像在大庭广众中挨了棍棒鞭子一样。既不容忍卑贱人的行为,也不容忍大国君主的行为;把刺杀大国君主看成刺杀卑贱人一样;对各国的君主,毫不畏惧,对于不恭不敬的话,一定回击。孟施舍自己培养勇气的方法呢,他说:'我看待不能胜,心气同看待能胜一样。如果先估量了敌人势力才前进,先考虑了胜败才与敌人交战,这是畏惧强大军队的表现。我怎么能取得必胜呢?能够无所畏惧罢了。'孟施舍类似曾子,北宫黝类似子夏。这两个人的勇气,我也不知谁更强,但是孟施舍的方法简单易行。从前曾子对子襄说:'你喜欢勇敢吗?我曾经在老师那里听到过大勇的理论:扪心自问,自己不占理,对方即使是最下贱的人,我也不使他恐惧;扪心自问,自己占理,即使是千军万马来临,我也勇往直前。'孟施舍的坚持勇气又不如曾子的方法简明易行。"公孙丑说:"我冲口问问,老师,您的心不波动,与告子的心不波动,我可以领教吗?"孟子说:"告子曾说:'言语上没有收获,不要求助于心思;心思上没有收获,不要求助于意气。'心思上没有收获,不要求助于意气,是对的。言语上没有收获,不要求助于心思,是不对的。因为心思意志是意气感情的统帅,意气感情是充满体内的力量。心思意志到了哪里,意气感情也就充满哪里。所以我说:'要坚持心思意志,不要滥用意气感情。'"公孙丑说:"您既然说,'心思意志到了哪里,意气感情也就充满哪里。'却又说,'要坚持心思意志,不要滥用意气感情。'这是为什么呢?"孟子说:"专心致志于某一点,意气感情也就随着去了;意气感情专缠于某一点,心思意志也就随着去缠。跌倒和奔跑,主要是体气和意气的投入,但必然引起心思意志的波动。不会像稻草人那样随风动静。"公孙丑说:"请问老师,您擅长哪一方面?"孟子说:"我能了解别人说的话,还能好好地培养我的正大刚直的气。""请问什么叫正大刚直的气?"孟子说:"几句话说不清。这种气呀,最伟大,最坚强,用正义去培养它,毫不污染它,就会充满在天地之间。这种气呀,要与行道和行义相配合,缺乏这种配合,就空虚无力了。它是由正义的日积月累生成的,不是用一两次行义的行为夺取来的。只要做一次于心有愧的事,他就软弱了。所以我说还不懂义,因为它把义看作心外之物。一定要从内心培养义,但不要有预定的目的要求。时刻记住培养义,但不要催促它生长,不要像那个宋国人一样。宋国有个担心禾苗长不快,而去把它拔高的人,迷迷糊糊,疲困地回到家里,对家里人说:'今天累了,我帮助禾苗长高了!'他儿子赶快跑去一看,禾苗都枯萎了。天下不帮助禾苗长高的人是很少的。认为无益而放弃培养禾苗的,是种庄稼不除草松蔸的懒汉;帮助禾苗长高的人,用提拔禾苗的方法,不但没有好处,反而伤害了它。"公孙丑说:"怎样才算了解别人说的话呢?"孟子说:"偏斜不正的话,知道它哪里闭塞不通;邪僻荒诞的话,知道它哪里有缺陷或沉溺;不合正道的话,知道它哪里背离了正路;支吾搪塞的话,知道它哪里隐瞒了真实。这四种话,从心里产生,必然危害政事;从政事上散发开去,必然危害国家的各项事业。圣人再出现时,他一定会赞成我这话。"公孙丑说:"宰我、子贡,善于讲话,冉牛、闵子、颜渊,修养很好,善于德行;孔子具有这两个方面的强项,但是他还说:'我对于说话,不流畅。'如此,那么老师您,已经是圣人了罢?"孟子说:"哎呀!这叫什么话!从前子贡问孔子:'老师,您已经是圣人了罢?'孔子说:'圣人,我算不上;我只不过学习不知厌倦,教人不嫌疲劳罢了。'子贡说:'学习不知厌倦,是智;教人不嫌疲劳,是仁。既仁且智,老师已经是圣人了。'圣人,孔子都不肯自信,你刚说的叫什么话呢!"公孙丑说:"从前我听说过,子夏、子游、子张都各学得孔子的一部分;冉牛、闵子、颜渊,都大概学得了孔子的全部,但规模小,境界未到。请问老师,您怎样定位自己?"孟子说:"暂且不谈这个。"公孙丑说:"伯夷和伊尹怎么样?"孟子说:"他们的主张不相同。不是理想的君主不去服侍,不是理想的百姓不去使唤,天下太平就出来做官,天下昏乱就居家不出门,伯夷就是这样的。是君都可服侍,是民都可使唤,太平也做官,不太平也做官,伊尹就是这样的。该做官就做官,辞职就辞职,该继续干就继续干,马上离开就马上离开。孔子就是这样的。他们都是古代的圣人。我没能像他们那样做;至于我的愿望,便是学习孔子。”公孙丑问:“伯夷、伊尹与孔子不相上下吗?”孟子说:“不是;从有人类以来,没有比得上孔子的。”公孙丑又问:“那么这三位圣人有相同的地方吗?”孟子说:“有。治理方圆百里的地盘,他们都能使诸侯来朝而统一天下;做一件不合道义的事,杀一个无罪的人而取得天下,他们都不会干。这就是他们相同的地方。”公孙丑又问:“请问他们不同的地方是什么?”孟子说:“宰我、子贡、有若三人,他们的智慧能够了解圣人,不会坏到偏袒自己喜欢的人。宰我说:‘用我的眼光看老师,比尧、舜强多了。’子贡说:‘看见一个国家的礼制,就了解它的政治;听到一个国家的音乐,就知道它的世风。所以我在这百代之后,评比百代以来的帝王,没有谁能够违背礼乐的检查。从产生人类以来,未有孔子这么高尚的人。’有若说:‘难道仅仅人类有高下不同吗?麒麟与走兽,凤凰与飞鸟,泰山与土堆,河海与水沟,各自为同类。圣人与百姓,也是同类。麒麟、凤凰、泰山、河海和圣人,都远远超出了各自的同类,都大大高出了各自的一群。从产生人类以来,未有比孔子更伟大的。’”

【英语译文】

Gongsun Chou asked, “It isn't strange for you to carry out your political ideal and establish dictatorship or kingly way if you hold power as a minister. Will your mood swing?” Mencius said, “No, it won't. My mood hasn't swung since I was forty.” Gongsun Chou said, “If so, you've surpassed Meng Ben quite a lot.” Mencius said, “It wasn't difficult. Gao Zi's mood didn't swing when he was under forty.” Gongsun Chou asked, “Is there any method for one's mood not swinging?” Mencius said, “Yes, there is. Beigong You nurtured courage like this: he didn't shiver when his skin was stabbed; he didn't dodge when his eyes were stirred. He felt like being beaten by cudgel in public when he got lost a little bit. He didn't bear not only any humble men's action but also any monarch's action of big country. He regarded murdering monarch as the same as killing humble men. He never feared any monarch and counter-attacked any disrespectful words and actions. As for method of nurturing courage, Meng Shishe said, ‘I regard being unable to win as the same as being able to win. It was the manifestation of fear when you considered enemy's strength before you start out, or took victory or failure into consideration before fighting with enemy. How could I surely win? It was because that I feared nothing.’ Meng Shishe was something like Zeng Zi and Beigong You was something like Zi Xia. As for the two men's courage, I don't know which was superior. But I think Meng Shishe's method is simple and practical. In old days, Zeng Zi told Zi Xiang, 'Do you like courage? I've heard my master's theory of great courage: ask yourself, if you are unreasonable, you won't make the rival fear even if he is the humblest man; ask yourself, if you are reasonable, you will head forward even if troops of thousand men approach'. Meng Shishe's method wasn't as simple and practical as Zeng Zi's method." Gongsun Chou asked boldly, "Could you explain your method and Gao Zi's method of keeping mood not swinging?" Mencius said, "Gao Zi ever said, 'Don't rely on your mood if you haven't obtained from words; don't rely on will if you haven't obtained from mood.' It's correct not to rely on will if you haven't obtained from mood. But it's not correct not to rely on your mood if you haven't obtained from words. Because one's will commands one's mood and mood is the strength filled in one's body. Mood fills the place where will goes. So I said, 'One must stick to will but not abuse mood.'" Gongsun Chou said, "What do you mean by saying that 'Mood fills the place where will goes' and 'One must stick to will but not abuse mood'?" Mencius said, "If you are focused on a point, then your mood goes there; if your mood intertwines a point, then your will goes there. Stumbling and running are due to one's energy but surely cause mood's swinging. But it doesn't do as straw swings with wind." Gongsun Chou asked, "Master, which aspect are you good at?" Mencius said, "I can understand what others say, and I can nurture my upright and vast energy." "What is your upright and vast energy?" Mencius said, "I cannot make it clear easily. It is greatest and strongest. If it is nurtured by righteousness and not contaminated, it will fill the Heaven and the Earth. It should accompany with Way and Righteousness. If not, it will become weak and empty. It is accumulated by righteousness day after day but not obtained by one or two righteous actions. It becomes weak on just one action which is against righteousness. Therefore I say we don't understand righteousness because it is regarded as something outside of one's heart. We must nurture righteousness within our heart without any goal or requirement. We should bear in mind to nurture righteousness but should not promote its growing as the person in Song State did. In Song State, there was a person. He worried about growth of rice-shoots and pulled them upwards. Tired and confused, he went home telling his family, 'I'm tired because I helped rice-shoots to grow.' His son hurried out to look at the rice-shoots and found that they had already withered. There are seldom persons who don't help rice-shoots to grow up. Those who think it useless and give up nurturing rice-shoots are lazybones who plant grain without weeding. However, the person who helped them to grow up by pulling them upward did harm to them." Gongsun Chou asked, "How can I understand what others say?" Mencius answered, "For skewed words, we know where it was blocked; for absurd words, we know where it had drawbacks; for words against the right path, we know where it went against the Way; for hedge and dodge words, we know where it evaded the issue. These four kinds of words surely harm governmental affairs if they arose from inner hearts; in turn, they certainly do harm to all causes of a country. When a sage appears, he will surely agree with me." Gongsun Chou asked, "Zai Wo and Zi Gong were good at speaking. Ran Niu, Min Zi and Yan Yuan were virtual and well cultivated. Confucius was superior in all these respects but he still said 'I'm not eloquent.' Master, you are already a sage." Mencius said, "Oh, do not say so. Zi Gong ever asked Confucius 'Master, are you already a sage?' Confucius answered, 'I'm not qualified as a sage. I just don't feel bored while learning and don't feel tired while teaching.' Zi Gong said, 'It's wise not to feel bored while learning and it's humanistic not to feel tired while teaching. You are already a sage since you are both wise and humanistic.' Confucius was still not confident in being a sage. Therefore, don't say that I'm a sage." Gongsun Chou said, "I've ever heard that Zi Xia, Zi You and Zi Zhang learned a part of Confucius' teachings respectively; Ran Niu, Min Zi and Yan Yuan learned all teachings of his but didn't reach his state. What state have you reached, Master?" Mencius said, "Put it aside just now." Gongsun Chou asked, "What do you think about Bo Yi and Yi Yin?" Mencius said, "They had different ideals. Bo Yi held that he wouldn't serve monarch who didn't have the same ideal with him, and he wouldn't summon common people who didn't cherish ideal. And when the world was peaceful he would be in office but when it was chaotic he would not. On the contrary, Yi Yin held that he would serve any monarch and summon any common people. And he could be in office in both peaceful and chaotic world. It was all right to be an official at any time, to continue doing administrative things at any time, and to leave the post at any time. Confucius was a man who did the same. They were all ancient sages. I didn't do things like they had done. As for my hope, I just want to learn from Confucius." Gongsun Chou asked, "Were Bo Yi and Yi Yin almost on a par with Confucius?" Mencius answered, "No. They weren't. No one could match Confucius since human beings existed." Gongsun Chou asked, "Then, is there any similarity among these three sages?" Mencius said, "Yes, there is. Even if they ruled an area of one hundred square *li*, they could make princes pay tribute to the court; they refused to do one thing which wasn't righteous or kill one innocent person to win the sovereignty over all states. That is the similarity." Gongsun Chou asked again, "What is the difference among them?" Mencius said, "Zai Wo, Zi Gong and You Ruo were so wise that they could understand others but weren't partial to and side with those whom they liked. Zai Wo said, 'From my point of view, Master is superior to sages Yao and Shun.' Zi Gong said, 'When he noticed one state's rites he knew its politics and when he heard one state's music he knew its custom. Therefore, after one hundred generations, if all monarchs are commented none of them can be escaped from ritual check. There wasn't anyone who was as noble as Confucius since human beings existed.' You Ruo said, 'Don't human being have inferiority and superiority? Unicorns and beasts, phoenix and birds, Mt. Tai and mound, seas- rivers and brooks all belong to the same kinds of things respectively. Sages and common people also belong to the same kind. Unicorns, phoenix, Mt. Tai, seas, rivers all surpass other members of the same kind, and are greater than the same species. There was no one who was greater than Confucius ever since human beings existed.'"

【注释】(1)加齐之卿相:加,使居其位,担任。卿相,执政大臣。(2)虽:假设连词,纵然、即使。不异:不奇怪。(3)动心:为外物所诱心情发生波动;心志动摇。(4)孟贲:~bēn,古之勇士。卫国人;一说齐国人。(5)告子:墨子的弟子。比孟子年长三四十岁。(6)有道乎:道,方法。(7)北宫黝:~~yōu,姓北宫,名黝。其人不详。(8)肤挠:谓肌肤被刺而挠屈(屈服),犹示人以弱。目逃:眼睛受到突然刺激而避开。形容心存怯懦。(9)思以一豪挫于人:思,助词。用于句首或句中。以,认为。一豪,豪通"毫"。一豪,即一根毫毛,比喻极小或很少。挫,败。挞,读tà,用鞭子或棍子打。市朝,市场和朝廷,也用来偏指市场或偏指朝廷。(10)受:容纳。此受义同易·咸:"君子以虚受人。"的"受"。于:助词。褐宽博:古代贫贱者所穿的宽大粗布衣服,也借指贫贱者。万乘之君:拥有万驾兵车的大国君主。(11)褐夫:穿粗布衣服的人;贫贱者。(12)严:畏惧。恶声:粗鲁的声气;怨恨的声气。(13)孟施舍:勇士,事迹不详。(14)视不胜犹胜也:看待不胜,心气同看待胜一样。量敌而后进:估量敌人势力后才前进。虑胜而后会:考虑胜败后才与敌交战。三军:周制诸侯大国三军;《周礼·官·司马》:"凡治军万有二千五百人为军。王六军,大国三军,次国二军,小国一军。"古代指步、车、骑三军;现代指海、陆、空三军。引申为强大的敌人。(15)曾子、子夏:孔子弟子曾参和卜商。(16)守约:简易可行。(17)子襄:曾子的弟子。(18)大勇:超乎寻常的勇敢;极为勇敢的人。夫子:指孔子。(19)自反:反躬自问;自己反省。缩:直。(20)不惴焉:~zhuì~,不使他恐惧。惴,恐惧。使动用法,意谓使恐惧。焉,他称代词作宾语。译为"他"。(21)守气:谓保持勇气。(22)不得于言:言语没有收获。得,获得;成功。言,言语;论辩;指责。(23)勿求于心:不求助于心思。(24)不得于心,勿求于气:参考注(22)、(23)。(25)气体之充也:气是身体的充实物。没有气,人就死去。活着的人才有:体气、生气、力气、志气、意气、勇气、骨气等。(26)至:到。次:止,停留。(27)持其志:保持意志。(28)暴:乱。(29)壹:专一。(30)今夫:发语词。与单用"今"或"夫",作用差不多,表示下面要提出问题或设想一种情况来予以议论。现代汉语没有这种用法,可以去掉不译。蹶、趋:jué,qū,跌倒、奔跑。(31)恶:wū,疑问代词。相当于"何""安""怎么"。恶乎长,擅长什么。(32)知言:善于辨析他人的言辞。(33)浩然之气:正气;正大刚直的气。(34)其为气也:这气的特点。(35)以直养而无害:用正义培养不可歪曲。(36)配义与道:同仁义和大道相匹配。(37)馁也:丧失勇气;害怕。(38)集义所生者:由多次不断行义生成的。(39)非义袭而取之也:不是以义为名夺来的。(40)慊:qiè,满足;满意。(41)外:动词,意动用法。告子持"仁内义外"之说。参看告子上第四章。(42)必有事焉:服侍,帮助。(43)正:期必;预定。(44)助长:帮助生长。(45)闵:mǐn,忧虑;担心。后多作"悯"。揠:yà,拔起;提高。(46)芒芒然:疲倦的样子。一说匆忙的样子。(47)其人:家人。(48)病:疲惫。(49)耘苗:给禾类植物除草松蔸。(50)诐辞:bì~,偏邪不正的言论。诐,偏颇;不正。所蔽:隐蔽;遮隔。(51)淫辞:邪僻荒诞的言论。所陷:缺陷;沉溺。(52)邪辞:不合正道的言论。所离:背离;偏离。(53)遁辞:理屈词穷或不愿吐露真意而话。所穷:没有道理;不说真话。(54)宰我、子贡善为说辞:宰我,孔子弟子。姓宰名予,字子我,亦称宰我。子贡,孔子弟子。姓端木,名赐,字子贡,善为说辞,善于讲话。(55)冉牛、闵子、颜渊善言德行:冉牛,孔子弟子。姓冉,名耕,字伯牛。闵子,孔子弟子。姓闵,名损,字子骞。颜渊,孔子最得意的弟子。姓颜,名回,字渊,亦作子渊。善言德行,谓善于德行。言,犹"于"。(56)兼之,曰:兼,同时具有或涉及几种事物或若干方面。之,指代上文"善为说辞,善言德行"。曰,是孔子曰。(57)然则夫子既圣矣乎:然则,连词。连接句子,表示连贯关系。犹"如此那么"或"那么"。夫子,这里是公孙丑称呼孟子。既圣,已经是圣人。(58)恶:wū,一说古音同今日的"ɑ"。叹词。(59)夫圣:fú~,犹言论圣人。(60)不居:不占有;不自认为。(61)昔者窃闻之:昔者,从前。窃,表自谦的表敬副词。可译作"我"或说话人的"名"。(62)子夏、子游、子张皆有圣人之一体:子夏即卜商。子游、即言偃。子张即颛孙师。都是孔子弟子。一体,四肢之一。比喻一部分。(63)具体而微:各部分大体具备,而形状或规模较小。(64)所安:犹"所处"。公孙丑因孟子既不敢比孔子则问他对于子夏等数子来说所处的位置。(65)姑舍是:姑,暂且。舍,放下。是,代词,此,这。孟子的抱负不小,志在效法孔子,不愿与其他人相比。(66)伯夷、伊尹:伯夷,和弟叔齐是孤竹国君的两个儿子。他俩互相让位,终于逃走。周武王伐纣,两人叩马而谏。周既一统,义不食周粟,饿死于首阳山。伊尹,商汤的贤相。(67)何事非君,何使非民:犹言是君都可事,是民都可使。(68)仕、止:仕,谓为官;任职。止,谓辞官;退职。(69)久、速:长久、短暂。(70)有行:有所作为。(71)乃所愿:乃,转折连词。用在句子之间表他转关系。把话头从甲引向乙。通常译作"至于"。所愿,愿望。(72)伯夷、伊尹于孔子,若是班乎:于,义同"与""和"。若,他们。班,等同;并列。(73)生民:指人类。亦谓人类诞生。(74)得百里之地而君之:治理方圆百里的地盘,他们都能使诸侯来朝而统一天下。(75)是:此;这。(76)有若:孔子晚年弟子。姓有,名若,字子有。春秋末鲁国人。少孔子三十三岁。(77)污不至阿其所好:污,"污"的异体字。这里是"鄙陋;卑下"的意思。阿,偏袒。所好,读 ~hào,名词性词组,这里指喜爱的人。(78)以:介词。依,凭。予:宰我的名。观于:观察;看。于,语助词。夫子:指孔子。贤于:比……贤。于,介词。表比较。(79)由:经由;经过。百世:百代。(80)等:比较;衡量。(81)莫之能违也:之,代词。指代孔子之道。(82)自生民以来:生民,谓人类诞生。(83)泰山之于丘垤:太山,即泰山。之,语助词。于,连词。义同"与""和"。丘垤,读 qiūdié ,小土山和小土堆。(丘,指自然形成的小土山;垤,本指蚁冢:蚂蚁做窝时堆积在洞口的小土堆。后泛指小土堆。)行潦:xínglǎo,沟中的流水。说文:"潦,雨水也。从水寮声,卢皓切。《段玉裁》注:"各本作雨水大貌。今依《诗·采苹正义》,文选《陆机赠顾彦先诗》注,众经音义卷一订。《曲礼释文》亦曰:"雨水谓之潦。"雨水,谓雨下之水也。《左传》曰:"水潦将降。"召南:"于彼行潦"传曰:"行潦,流潦也。"按,传以流释行。服注《左传乃云道路之水赵注孟子乃云道旁流潦》。以道释行,似非。潦水流而聚焉,故曰行潦,不必在道旁也。(84)出于其类,拔乎其萃:卓越出众,不同一般。"出""拔"是同义词,超出、高出的意思。"类""萃"是同义词,"类""群"。

【原文】3 孟子曰:"以力假仁者霸,[1]霸必有大国;以德行仁政者王,王不待大,[2]汤以七十里,文王以百里。[3]以力服人者,非心服也,力不赡也[4];以德服人者,中心悦而诚服也,如七十子之服孔子也。[5]诗云:'自西至东,自南至北,无思不服'。[6]"

【白话译文】

孟子说:"仗恃强力冒充仁义的,实行霸道,行霸道,必须拥有强大的国力;依靠道德实行仁义的,实行王道。行王道,不等候强大的国力。汤用方圆七十里的土地、文王用方圆百里的土地实行了仁政,天下民心归附。仗恃强力使人服从的,那不是内心服从,是因为实力不够,不服从走不脱;依靠道德使人服从的,那是心悦诚服,是因为深受感动,出于内心。好像七十二位大弟子归附孔子一样。《诗经》上说:'从东从西,从南从北,无不心悦诚服。'正是这个意思。"

【英语译文】

Mencius said, "Those who rely on strength and carry out false humanity and righteousness implement dictatorship. Dictatorship requires strong state capabilities. Those who rely on virtue and carry out real humanity and righteousness implement Kingly Way. Kingly Way doesn't await strong state capabilities. King Tang of Shang Dynasty ruled land of forty nine hundred square *li*, and King Wen of Zhou Dynasty ruled land of ten thousand square *li*. However, they both made people all around submit to the authority of them . It was not inner-heart obedience when people were made obedient by force because they weren't strong to counteratt ack others. It was inner-heart obedience when people were made obedient by morality because they were moved from deep heart. This was the same as seventy two disciples submitted to the authority of Confucius. *The Book of Songs* say, 'From west to east. From north to south. People in all places come over to him. '"

【注释】(1)假:借。霸:做诸侯联盟的首领,称霸。(2)王:行王道;不待:不等候;不依靠。大:强大的国力。(3)七十里、百里:言国土面积小。这两句都损略了谓语动词"王"。(4)赡:shàn,足够。(5)七十子:《史记·孔子世家》:"孔子以诗书礼乐教弟子,盖三千焉,身通六艺者七十有二人。"这"七十有二人"通称"七十子"。(6)诗云:引自《诗·大雅·文王有声》。思:助词,用于句首或句中。

【原文】4 孟子曰:"仁则荣,不仁则辱;今恶辱而居不仁,是犹恶湿而居下也。[1]如恶之,[2]莫如贵德而尊士,贤者在位,能者在职;国家闲暇,及是时,明其政刑。[3]虽大国,必畏之矣。[4]诗云:[5]'迨天之未阴雨,[6]彻彼桑土,[7]绸缪牖户。[8]今此下民,[9]或敢侮予?"[10]孔子曰:'为此诗者,其知道乎!能治其国家,谁敢侮之?'今国家闲暇,及是时,般乐怠敖,[11]是自求祸也。祸福无不自己求之者。诗云:[12]'永言配命,[13]自求多福。'太甲曰：[14]'天作孽，犹可违；[15]自作孽，不可活。[16]此之谓也。"

【白话译文】

孟子说："如果实行仁政，就会得到荣誉；如果不行仁政，就会遭受屈辱。现在一些人厌恶屈辱却又居处于不仁的地位，这就像厌恶潮湿却又居处于低洼地点一样。若真厌恶受屈辱，最好是崇尚道德而尊敬有见识的人，让贤人居于高位，让能人担任要职；国家既无内忧也无外患，抓住这时，完善政治法度，即使是大国，必然畏惧你了。《诗经》上说：'趁着天没阴也没下雨，桑树根上剥些皮。紧密缠好门和窗，不问下面人好多，哪个敢来把我欺？'孔子说：'这诗的作者真懂道理呀！能治好自己的国家，谁敢欺侮自己？'现在国家没有内忧外患，趁这时，任意作乐，懒惰游逛，是自己寻找祸害。祸害和幸福没有不是自己找来的。《诗经》上说：'要永远配合天命，自己找更多幸福。'《太甲》说：'天降的灾祸，还可躲避；自造的灾祸，不能甩脱。'正是这个意思。"

【英语译文】

Mencius said, "If you carry out government of humanity, you will be honored; but if you don't do that, you will be humiliated. Nowadays there are people who hate humiliation but hold post without humanity. It is just the same as you hate humidity but live in low-lying land. If you really hate humiliation, you should cherish morality and respect insightful men, and make virtual men in high posts and able men in critical posts. There aren't domestic troubles or foreign invasions. You should take the opportunity to perfect regulations and laws. In that case even a big state will fear you. *The Book of Songs* says, 'I should be hurry doing thing before it rains. And I will peel the mulberry root. I will repair door and window. You human beings under tree, /Today who could ever bully me?' Confucius said, 'The author of this poem was really reasonable. If you can rule your country well, who then dare to bully you?' Nowadays, there aren't domestic troubles and foreign invasions, but if you take this opportunity to seek pleasure and indulge in laziness and sightseeing you are inviting disasters yourself. Disaster and happiness had never fallen on you. *The Book of Songs* says, 'Obeying heaven's order they never violate, they'd be self-reliant pursuing happiness.' *The Book of History* says, 'People can dodge scourges bestowed by the Heaven, but they cannot escape catastrophes created by themselves.' This means all the same."

【注释】(1)下:低处;底部。(2)如恶之:之,代“辱”。(3)及是时明其政刑:及,乘;趁。明,修明;完善。政刑,政治法度。(4)必畏之矣:之,代词,用于对称,译为“你”。(5)诗云:见《诗·豳风·鸱鸮》。(6)迨:趁着。(7)彻彼桑土:彻,剥;取。彼,远指代词,那(个、些、种、样)。桑土,读 sāngdù,桑树根的皮。(8)绸缪牖户:chóumóu yǒuhù,意谓用桑根皮紧紧密密地把门窗缠缚好。(9)下民:指居室下面的人。(10)或敢:谁敢。(11)般乐怠敖:pánlè dàiáo,大肆作乐,怠惰遨游。般,大。(12)诗云:见《诗·大雅·文王》。(13)永言配命:永,长久。言,语助词,调和音节。配命,配合天命,犹言顺从天的命令。(14)太甲:《尚书》篇名。据说原文已佚,今本三篇是伪古文。(15)违:避开。(16)不可活:活,生。《尚书》今本作“逭”,读 huàn,逃避。

【原文】5 孟子曰:“尊贤使能,俊杰在位,[1]则天下之士皆悦,而愿立于其朝矣;市,廛而不征,[2]法而不廛,则天下之商皆悦,而愿藏于其市;关,讥而不征,[3]则天下之旅皆悦,[4]而愿出于其路矣;耕者,助而不税,[5]则天下之农皆悦,而愿耕于其野矣;廛,[6]无夫里之布,[7]则天下之民皆悦,而愿为之氓矣。[8]信能行此五者,则邻国之民仰之若父母矣。[9]率其子弟攻其父母,自有生民以来未有能济者也。[10]如此,则无敌于天下。无敌于天下者,天吏也。[11]然而不王者,未之有也。”

【白话译文】

孟子说:“尊重有道德的人,任用有才能的人,杰出的人物都有职位,那么天下的学子都会高兴,都愿意到那朝廷去任职做官了。在集市上,或只收取储藏、堆积货物的房舍用费,不收取货物税,或房舍用费也不收,只按法令维护市场秩序。那么天下的商人都会很高兴,都愿意把货物藏在那市场上了。在关卡上,只盘问检查,不收税。那么天下的旅客、过路人,都会很高兴,都愿意经过那里的道路了。对于耕田的人,只要他出力助耕公田而不收私田的税。那么天下的农夫都会很高兴,都愿意在那田野上种庄稼了。在人们居住的地方,不交额外的劳役钱和地税。那么天下的百姓,都愿意做那里的侨民了。真正能做到这五项,那么周边国家的老百姓会像仰望父母一样仰望那里。把父母的子弟率领起来攻击父母,从有人类以来没有成了功的。像这样,就是无敌于天下。天下无敌的人就是奉天命治民的人。奉天命治民而不能统一天下的,是从来不曾有过的。”

【英语译文】

Mencius said, "When moral men are respected, able and prominent men are assigned to a post, then all scholars everywhere become happy and are willing to be officials in the court. In fairs, fees of storing goods and warehouses are charged, or fees of warehouses won't be charged, and order of fairs is maintained according to law. In that case all peddlers and businessmen will become happy and are willing to store their goods in fairs. In all passes, people are inspected but not taxed. In that case, all people are willing to walk on the roads on the passes. Peasants aren't taxed for their private fields if they are willing to toiling public fields. In that case, all peasants will become happy and are willing to toil fields there. People needn't pay extra tax of corvée and field. In that case all people are willing to be emigrants there. If the five things are carried out well, people in neighboring areas will look up there just like respecting their parents. There wasn't one successful example that parents' sons and younger brothers gathered to attack themselves since human beings existed. A monarch ruling a country like this has no rival and he is ruling land under heaven on the mandate of the Heaven. There hasn't been one ruler on the mandate of the Heaven who cannot unify the land under heaven."

【注释】(1)俊杰:才能出众的人。(2)廛而不征:廛,读chán,市场中储藏或堆积货物的栈房。征,征税。(3)讥:读jī,稽查;盘问。(4)旅:寄居外地或旅行于途的人;旅客。(5)助:古代的一种劳役租赋制度,但使出力以助耕公田,而不税其私田。(6)廛:泛指民居、住宅。(7)夫里之布:即夫布、里布。都是古代赋税的一种。布,古代的币、钱。夫布,指以货币形式支付的代替力役的人口税。里布,指以货币形式支付的土地税。(8)氓:máng,指外地迁来之民。(9)仰:仰望;敬慕;依赖。(10)济:成功;成就。(11)天吏:奉天命治民的人。

【原文】6 孟子曰:"人皆有不忍人之心。[1]先王有不忍人之心,斯有不忍人之政矣。[2]以不忍人之心,行不忍人之政,治天下,可运之掌上。谓人皆有不忍人之心者,[3]今人乍见孺子将入于井,[4]皆有怵惕恻隐之心[5]——非所以内交于孺子之父母也,[6]非所以要誉于乡党朋友也,[7]非恶其声而然也。[8]由是观之,无恻隐之心,非人也;无羞恶之心,[9]非人也;无辞让之心,非人也;无是非之心,非人也。恻隐之心,仁之端也;羞恶之心,义之端也;辞让之心,礼之端也;[10]是非之心,智之端也。人之有是四端也,犹其有四体也。有是四端而自谓不能者,自贼者也;[11]谓其君不能者,贼其君者也。凡有四端于我者,[12]知皆扩而充之矣,[13]若火之始然,[14]泉之始达。苟能充之,足以保四海;[15]苟不充之,不足以事父母。"

【白话译文】

孟子说:"人人都有怜悯心,先王有怜悯心,于是有怜悯别人的政治了。用怜悯心实行怜悯别人的政治来治理天下,不难,能够运用在手掌之中。我说人人都有怜悯心,原因在于:假如忽然看见一个小孩就要掉进井里了,是人都会产生惊惧怜悯的同情心。这种心情的产生,不是为了要和小孩的父母攀交情,不是为了要在乡亲、朋友间讨声誉,也不是被那小孩的哭声惊动而产生的。从这里来看,没有怜悯心,不算是人;没有羞恶心,不算是人;没有推让心,不算是人;没有是非心,不算是人。怜悯心是仁的萌芽,羞恶心是义的萌芽,推让心是礼的萌芽,是非心是智的萌芽。人有这四种萌芽,好比有手足四肢一样,运用自如。有这四种萌芽,自己却说这也不行那也不行的人,是自暴自弃。认为他的君主不行的人,是残害他君主的人。凡是自己拥有这四种萌芽的人都把它们扩大充实了,那就像火开始燃烧,像泉水开始涌出。如果能继续扩充,能够安定天下;如果不继续扩充,连赡养爹妈都办不到。"

【英语译文】

Mencius said, "Everyone has the feeling of compassion. The deceased king had feeling of compassion and sympathized with other's governance. It's not difficult and it's just like playing game in one's palm to sympathize with other's governance and rule the land under the heaven with feeling of compassion. I say everyone has feeling of compassion for the reason that anyone will have the feeling of surprise and compassion at a kid who is falling down into a well. This kind of feeling isn't aroused by the desire for friendship with his parents, or the honor got among friends and neighbors, or the bitter cry of the kid. From this point, one is not a man who lacks the feeling of compassion; one is not a man who lacks the feeling of shame; one is not a man who lacks of the feeling of modesty; one is not a man who lacks feeling of the distinction between the right and the wrong. The feeling of compassion is the beginning of humanity; the feeling of shame is the beginning of righteousness; the feeling of modesty is the beginning of rites, and the feeling of the distinction between the right and the wrong is the beginning of wisdom. These four beginnings but are like the four limbs which can move flexibly. A person with the four beginnings but claims that he cannot do this or that abandons himself. Those who think their monarch is not capable do harms to him. All those who have the four beginnings want to expand them just like fire flaming and water swelling. If he continues expanding he can rule the land under the heaven; but if he doesn't, he cannot support his parents."

【注释】(1)不忍人之心:不狠心对人的心。即同情心。(2)斯:承接连词。可译作"便""就"。(3)所以:原因;情由。(4)今:连词。表假设关系。相当于"若""假如"。乍:zhà,突然;忽然。孺子:rú ~,幼儿、儿童。将入于井:就要沉落于井中。(5)怵惕恻隐:chùtì cèyǐn,惊惧怜悯;戒惧同情。(6)内交:nà ~,内,纳的古字。内交,即"纳交"。义同"结交"。谓与人交往建立情谊。(7)要誉于乡党:要誉,读 yāoyù,求取声誉;讨好。乡党,同乡;乡亲。(8)恶:wù,畏惧。其声:指啼哭声。文中但就乍见这一瞬间视觉反应,绝无其他因素,就能窥见人的固有怜悯心。所以把听觉反应也除开;当然听觉同样能触动人的固有怜悯心。(9)羞恶:xiūwù,对自己或别人的坏处感到羞耻厌恶。(10)端:开始;开始之点。(11)贼:杀害;毁坏;伤害。(12)我:自己。(13)知:助词,犹"夫"。表议论的开始。(14)然:"燃"的本字。(15)保四海:安定天下。保,安定。四海,犹言天下,全国各处。

【原文】7 孟子曰:"矢人岂不仁于函人哉?[1]矢人唯恐不伤人,函人唯恐伤人。巫匠亦然。[2]故术不可不慎也。[3]孔子曰:'里仁为美。择不处仁,焉得智?[4]'夫仁,天之尊爵也,人之安宅也。莫之御而不仁,是不智也。不仁、不智、无礼、无义,人役也。[5]人役而耻为役,由弓人而耻为弓,[6]矢人而耻为矢也。如耻之,莫如为仁。仁者如射;射者正己而后发;发而不中,不怨胜己者,反求诸己而已矣。"

【白话译文】

孟子说:"造箭的人难道比造铠甲的人本性要残忍些吗?造箭的人生怕他的箭不能伤人,造铠甲的人生怕他的铠甲不能保护人体而遭杀伤。为人祈福治病的巫医和为人做棺材的木匠也是这样对着干。可见选择谋生的技艺不能不审慎。孔子说:'与仁德的人共处是美好的,选择住处不与仁人为邻,怎么算是聪明呢?'仁是上天赐予的最尊贵的爵位,是人最安心的住宅。没有人阻拦你,你却不仁,是不明智的。不仁、不智、无礼、无义,这种人只能做别人的仆役。作为一个仆役而以听人使唤为耻,好比造弓的人以造弓为耻,造箭的人以造箭为耻一样。如果真以为耻,不如好好行仁。行仁 ,如比赛射技一样:射箭的人先必须端正自己的心态和姿势,然后放箭,如果没有射中,不能埋怨那些胜过自己的人,只能回头寻找自身的原因罢了。”

【英语译文】

Mencius said, “Isn’t a person who makes arrows more brutal than a person who makes armors? An arrow-maker works hard for fear that his arrows cannot hurt people but an armor-maker works hard for fear that his armors cannot protect human body. A witch doctor who prays for patients and a carpenter who makes coffins for people always do the opposite. Therefore we should be cautious to choose job for living. Confucius said, ‘A dwelling place with humanity is ideally beautiful. It’s unwise not to live as neighbor of humane people.’ Humanity is blessed by the Heaven and a resting place for one’s heart. You are not wise if no one is in your way but you don’t implement humanity. A person who lacks humanity, wisdom, rites, and righteousness can only be a servant. That as a servant one feels ashamed to be ordered about is the same as that a armor-maker feels ashamed to make bows and an arrow-maker feels ashamed to make arrows. If they really feel ashamed, they would rather carry out humanity. Carrying out humanity is just like archery: a shooter must at first correct his position and mentality and then shoot out. Do not complain about those who win the game, but find out your own factors leading to failure.”

【注释】(1)矢人、函人:造箭的工匠,叫矢人。造铠甲的工匠,叫函人。(2)巫匠:巫,指为人祈祷治病的巫或医。匠,指为人做棺椁的木匠。(3)术:技艺;从业手艺。(4)焉得智:以上所引孔子的话见《论语·里仁篇》第一章。(5)人役:仆役,奴婢。(6)由:同“犹”。

【原文】8 孟子曰:“子路,人告之以有过,则喜。禹闻善言,[1]则拜。大舜有大焉,[2]善与人同,[3]舍己从人,乐取于人以为善。自耕稼、陶、渔以至为帝,[4]无非取于人者。取诸人以为善,是与人为善者也。[5]故君子莫大乎与人为善。”

【白话译文】

孟子说:“子路,别人指点他的错误,他就高兴。禹听到了正确无误的言论,就给人敬礼。大舜更伟大,他对为善没有什么别人和自己的区分,抛弃自己的不足,接受人家的长处,快乐地学习别人的善行。从他种庄稼、做瓦器、打鱼直到当天子,没有一样不是采取了别人的优点的。采取别人的优点而行善,就是同别人一起做好事。所以君子最高的德行就是同别人一起做好事。”

【英语译文】

Mencius said, “Zi Lu became happy when someone picked out his fault. Great Yu saluted to a person who made him hear correct words. Great Shun was greater in that he made no difference between himself and others when carrying out humanity, and he gave up his own shortcomings and learnt from others' strong points, and from other's humanistic actions. From farming to fishing, from doing pottery to being a king, he adopted all advantages of other people. Adopting others' advantages and carrying out humanity is doing good deeds together with others. The most morality of a moral man is doing good deeds together with other people.”

【注释】(1)禹闻善言:—禹,姒姓,名文命。鲧之子。又称大禹、夏禹、戎禹。原为夏后氏部落领袖,奉舜命治理洪水,领导人民疏通江河,兴修沟渠,发展农业。据传治水十三年中,三过家门不入。后被选为舜的继承人,舜死后即位,建立夏代。后世视为圣王。善言,《尚书·皋陶谟》:“禹拜昌言”。《史记·夏本纪》:“禹拜美言”从此知道“昌、善、美”字不同义同。(2)有:同“又”。(3)善与人同:犹言同别人相互交流自己之善。(4)耕稼、陶、渔:《史记·五帝本纪》:“舜耕历山,历山之人皆让畔;渔雷泽,雷泽之人皆让居;陶河滨,河滨器不苦窳(yǔ)。一年所居成聚二年成邑三年成都。”(舜在历山做庄稼,历山的人都在田界上让对方多占有土地,不争边界;在雷泽做渔夫,雷泽的人都让出居住地;在河滨烧制陶器,河滨的陶器质量不粗糙低劣。经过一年,他的居住地,成了村落;经过两年,他的居住地,成了县城;经过三年,他的居住地,成了大都市。)(5)是与人为善者:同别人一起做好事。

【原文】9 孟子曰:“伯夷,非其君,不事;非其友,不友。不立于恶人之朝,[1]与恶人言,如以朝衣朝冠坐于涂炭。推恶恶人之心,[2]思与乡人立,[3]其冠不正,望望然去之,[4]若将浼焉。[5]是故诸侯虽有善其辞命而至者不受也,不受也者,[6]是亦不屑就已。[7]柳下惠不羞污君,[8]不卑小官;进不隐贤,必以其道;遗佚而不怨;[9]阨穷而不悯。[10]故曰,‘尔为尔,我为我,虽袒裼裸裎于我侧,[11]尔焉能浼我哉?’故由由然与之偕而不自失焉,[12]援而止之而止。援而止之而止者,是亦不屑去已。”孟子曰:“伯夷隘,柳下惠不恭。隘与不恭,君子不由也。[13]”

【白话译文】

孟子说:“伯夷,不是他理想的君主,不去服侍;不是他理想的朋友,不去结交;不站在坏人的朝廷里;在坏人的朝廷上,不同坏人说话;站在坏人的朝廷上,同坏人说话,就像穿戴着礼服礼帽坐在稀泥炭渣上。这种厌恶坏人的心情延伸到与乡下人站在一块,如果对方帽子没戴正,就扫兴地走开,好像会被玷污一样。所以当时的各国君主虽然有好言好语相邀,他却不接受。他之所以不接受,也是他怕弄脏自己。柳下惠不以侍奉无道之君为耻,不以官小为卑下;入朝做官,不隐藏自己的才能,一定按自己的方式办事;不被起用,也不怨恨,艰难困苦,也不忧伤。所以他说:‘你是你,我是我,你纵然在我身边赤身露体,你怎能玷污我呢?’所以他愉愉快快与人相处,不失常态。牵住他叫他留下,他就留下。叫他留下就留下,也是他不以为会弄脏自己。”孟子又说:“伯夷太狭隘,柳下惠太油滑。狭隘和油滑,都是君子所不取的。”

【英语译文】

Mencius said, “Bo Yi refused to serve monarch who wasn't his ideal one; he refused to befriend those who weren't his ideal ones; he refused to stand in scoundrels' court; he refused to talk with others while standing in scoundrels' court, and he thought it like sitting on mud and breeze in ritual hat and gown to talk with scoundrels. Such kind of feeling extends to staying with villagers. When the villagers didn't correctly wear their hats, he would leave away unhappily and felt being stained. Even though many monarchs invited him with good will, he refused them all because he was afraid to be stained. Liu Xiahui didn't feel ashamed when he served tyrannical monarch; he didn't feel humble when he was a low official; he didn't hide his capability and did things at his will while he was an official in court. He didn't complain about anything while not being promoted and didn't feel sad while things not going smoothly. Therefore he said, “You are yourself and I am myself. Even if you are naked before me you cannot stain me.” He got well along with other people, and he never mal-practiced himself. On inviting to stay he would stay. He would stay because he thought no one can stain him.” Mencius said again, “Bo Yi was too narrow-minded and Liu Xiahui was too foxy. Narrow-mindedness and being foxy are all rejected by moral men.”

【注释】(1)不立于恶人之朝:意谓不在恶人之朝为官。古代诸侯、卿大夫处理政务的地方皆称朝。(2)推:推广。(3)思与立:思,助词。用于句首或句中。乡人,乡下人;俗人。(4)望望然:失望的样子,扫兴的样子。(5)浼:měi,沾污;玷污。(6)也者:语气助词,这里表示提示。(7)不屑:不值得。表示轻视。就:受,接受。已:语气助词。(8)柳下惠:春秋鲁大夫展获,字季,又字禽,曾为士师官食邑柳下谥惠故称其为展禽,柳下季,柳士师,柳下惠等,以柳下惠之名最为著称。相传他与一女子共坐一夜,不曾淫乱。后用借指有操行的男子。污君:亦作"污君"。无道之君。(9)遗佚:亦作"遗逸""遗轶"。遗漏;遗弃而不用。(10)阨穷:è~,困厄穷迫。悯:忧愁;忧伤。(11)袒裼裸裎:tǎnxī luǒchéng,赤身露体。谓粗野无礼。(12)由由然:愉悦高兴的样子。(13)不由:不为,不从事。

孟子集注卷四 公孙丑章句下 凡十四章,自第二章以下,记孟子出处行实为详

【原文】1 子曰:"天时不如地利,地利不如人和。[1]三里之城,七里之郭,[2]环而攻之而不胜。[3]夫环而攻之,必有得天时者矣;然而不胜者,是天时不如地利也。城非不高也,池非不深也,兵革非不坚利也,[4]米粟非不多也;委而去之,[5]是地利不如人和也。故曰域民不以封疆之界,[6]固国不以山溪之险,威天下不以兵革之利。[7]得道者多助,失道者寡助。寡助之至,亲戚畔之;[8]多助之至,天下顺之。以天下之所顺,攻亲戚之所畔;故君子有不战,[9]战必胜矣。"

【白话译文】

孟子说:"天时不如地利,地利不如人和。一座小城,内城墙每边长只有三里,外城墙每边长只有七里。敌人却围攻不下它。能够围攻,一定得到了适合作战的自然气候条件。然而围攻不下,这就说明得天时不如占地理优势。城墙不是不高,兵器甲胄不是不锐利坚固,粮食不是不多;弃城逃跑,这就说明占地理优势不如得人和。所以说划分居民区域,不必用国家疆界,巩固国防不必靠山川的险阻,使天下畏惧屈服不必凭兵器的锐利。行仁政得治国之道的,帮他的人就多;不行仁政失去治国之道的,帮他的人就少。帮他的人少到了顶点,连亲戚也背叛他;帮他的人多到了顶点,普天下都顺从他。以全天下顺从的力量去攻击连亲戚也背叛的人,那么,仁君圣主,也许不会发动战争,发动取战争必然胜利。"

【英语译文】

Mencius said, "Natural climate is inferior to geographical advantage, which in turn is inferior to human harmony. There was a small town. Each side of its inner walls extends three *li* and each side of its outer walls extends seven *li*. But the enemy could not capture it. The enemy surely took some natural advantage to fight. However, they couldn't capture it because natural climate is inferior to geographical advantage. People in a town fled on a battle even though walls were high enough, and armors were thick enough and weapons were sharp enough and foods were plenty enough. This means that taking geographical advantage is inferior to harmonizing common people. Therefore, it's unnecessary to divide civil community according to state border; it's unnecessary to solidify state defense relying on precipitous mountains and rivers, and it's unnecessary to make others submit to your authority depending on weapon's sharpness. Those who carry out government of humanity and gain the Way of governance obtain more help and those who don't do so obtain less help. Relatives betray him when he obtains the least help whereas common people submit to him when he obtains the most help. If a humanistic monarch with his all submitted men attacks another whose relatives have betrayed him, then war may not be launched. Even a war was launched, he was destined to win."

【注释】(1)天时、地利、人和:天时,指宜于做某事的自然气候条件。地利,指地理优势。人和:人事和谐;民心和乐。(2)三里之城,七里之郭:内城墙边长三里,外城墙边长七里围成的小城。◎城,指都邑四周的墙垣。一般分两重,里面的叫城,外面的叫郭。城字单用时,多包含城与郭。城、郭对举时只指城。郭,古代城外加筑的城墙叫"郭",即外城墙。(3)环:包围。(4)兵革:兵器和甲胄的总称。泛指武器军备。坚利:坚固和锐利。(5)委:舍弃。(6)域民:划分居民区域。不以:不用。封疆之界:国家界限。(7)威:威慑。用声势或威力使之恐惧屈服。(8)畔:通"叛"。(9)有不战:有,用同"或"。或许;也许。

【原文】2 孟子将朝王,王使人来曰:"寡人如就见者也[1]不可以风。[2]朝,将视朝,[3]不识可使寡人得见乎?"对曰:"不幸而有疾不能造朝。[4]"明日,出吊于东郭氏。[5]公孙丑曰:"昔者辞以病,今日吊,或者不可乎?"曰:"昔者疾,今日愈,如之何不吊?"王使人问疾,医来。孟仲子对曰:"昔者有王命,[6]有采薪之忧,[7]不能造朝。今病小愈,趋造于朝,我不识能至否乎?"使数人要于路,[8]曰:"请必无归,而造于朝!"不得已而之景丑氏宿焉。[9]景子曰:"内则父子,外则君臣,人之大伦也。[10]父子主恩,君臣主敬。丑见王之敬子也,未见所以敬王也。"曰:"恶!是何言也!齐人无以仁义与王言者,岂以仁义为不美也?其心曰'是何足与言仁义也'云尔,[11]则疾不敬莫大于是。我非尧舜之道,不敢以陈于王前,故齐人莫如我敬王也。"景子曰:"否,非此之谓也。礼曰:'父召无诺;[12]君命召,不俟駕。[13]故将朝也,闻王命而遂不果,[14]宜与夫礼若不相似然。[15]"曰:"岂谓是与?曾子曰:'晋楚之富,不可及也。彼以其富,我以吾仁;彼以其爵,我以吾义,[16]吾何慊乎哉?'[17]夫岂不义而曾子言之?是或一道也。[18]寒天下有达尊三:[19]爵一齿一德一。朝廷莫如爵,乡党莫如齿,辅世长民莫如德,[20]有恶得有其一,以慢其二哉?故将大有为之君,必有所不召之臣。欲有谋焉则就之。其尊德乐道,不如是不足与有为也。故汤之于伊尹,学焉而后臣之,故不劳而王;桓公之于管仲,学焉而后臣之,故不劳而霸。今天下地丑德齐,[21]莫能相尚。无他,好臣其所教,[22]而不好臣其所受教。[23]汤之于伊尹,桓公之于管仲,则不敢召。管仲且犹不,[24]可召,而况不为管仲者乎?"

【白话译文】

孟子正准备去朝见齐王时,齐王派人来传话说道:"我本应该来拜见你,但是感冒了,不能吹风。早晨,我要临朝议事,不知是否能让我在那时见到你?"孟子的回答是:"抱歉啊,我也病了,不能上朝。"第二天,孟子出门到东郭大夫家去吊丧,公孙丑说:"昨天说有病,谢绝齐王召见,今天去吊丧,也许不可以吧?"孟子说:"昨天生了病,今天病好了,为什么不去吊丧呢?"齐王派人探病,还有医生同来。孟仲子对他们说:"昨天王有召见令,他得了小病,说不能奉命上朝;今天稍好一点,已经上朝去了,但我不晓得他能走得到不?"接着孟仲子派了几个人在几条路上阻拦孟子,说:"请一定不要回去,快上朝廷去!"孟子只好去景丑家过夜。景丑说:"在家庭内,父是父,子是子,在家庭外,君是君,臣是臣;这是人间最重要的关系。父子间以慈爱为主,君臣间以恭敬为主。我只看见了王对你很尊敬,没看到你对王是如何尊敬的。"孟子说:"哎!这算什么话呀!在齐国人中,没有一个拿仁义的道理向王进言的,难道他们以为仁义不好吗?不,他们心里想的是'这个王哪里值得同他谈仁义'而已;没有比这更大的不敬王了。我呢,不是尧舜之道不敢向王陈述;所以说,在齐国人中间没有谁有我这么恭敬王的。"景丑说:"不,我指的不是这个,古礼有,父亲召唤,应一声'唯'就起身,不说'诺';君主召唤,不等车马驾好就先走。你呢,本来准备朝见王,一听到王召见,反而不应召。这好像于礼不相合吧。"孟子说:"难道你是说这个么?曾子说过:'晋国和楚国的财富,我们是赶不上的;他们运用财富,我们运用仁;他们运用爵位,我们运用义,我们遗憾什么呢?'难道曾子说的这些话不合道义吗?这又是一条大道。天下公认为尊贵的东西有三样:爵位是一样,年龄是一样,道德是一样。在朝廷中,先论爵位;在乡党中,先论年龄;感化世人,治理百姓,当然以道德为上。怎么能拿爵位一样来侮慢年龄和道德这两样呢?所以大有作为的君主,一定有他不能召唤的臣子,如果有事要商量,就亲自到臣子那儿去。他要尊崇道德,乐于仁政,不这样做,便不能有所作为。所以,商汤对于伊尹,先向他学习然后以他为臣,所以不太费力统一了天下;桓公对于管仲,也是先向他学习然后以他为臣,所以不太费力而称霸诸侯。现在天下各个大国,土地大小相当,行为作风也不相上下,谁也不能超过谁,没有别的缘故,只是这些国家的君主,喜欢用他教的人为臣,不喜欢用教他的人为臣。商汤对于伊尹,桓公对于管仲,不敢召唤。连管仲也还不可以召唤,何况不屑于做管仲的人呢?"

【英语译文】

Mencius was about to be presented at court of King of Qi State. At that time, King of Qi State dispatched a man telling him, "I should visit you myself but I caught a cold and was afraid of wind-blowing. In the morning, I will discuss things with ministers at court. I'd like to see you there." Mencius replied, "I am sorry that I'm also ill and can't be presented at court." The next day, Mencius went to Minister Dongguo's family to pay a condolence call and Gongsun Chou said, "Yesterday you refused to see the King by saying that you're ill, but today you go to pay a condolence call. It seems to me that it's not alright." Mencius said, "Yesterday I was ill and today I am better. Why not do this?" The King sent someone to visit Mencius with a physician. Meng Zhong Zi told them, "Yesterday he was ill and couldn't be presented at the court and this morning he was recovered a little bit and went to the court. But I don't know whether or not he could get there." After that Meng Zhong Zi dispatched several groups of persons to several crossroads to interfere and tell him, "Don't go home and hurry up to the court!" Mencius had no choice but stay overnight at Jing Chou's house. Jing Chou said, "In one's family, father is father and son is son; outside of the family, King is King and minister is minister. This is the most important human relationship. Love exists mainly between a father and his sons and respect exists mainly between a king and his ministers. I just noticed the King respects you but I didn't notice that you respect him." Mencius said, "Oh, how could you say so? Among people of Qi State, there isn't one person who gives advice to the King with humanity and righteousness. Don't they think that humanity and righteousness aren't good? No! They just think that this King isn't qualified to discuss humanity and righteousness with them. There isn't anything beyond this which means not respecting the King. I only state the Ways of Sages Yao and Shun before him. Therefore, among persons in Qi State, nobody respects the King like me." Jing Chou said, "I don't refer to this point. According to ancient rites, on one's father summoning, the son stands up by uttering '*wei*', not '*nuo*'; on one's monarch summoning, one walks forward while cart isn't ready. But you refused to visit him when the King summoned you. It seems that it wasn't in accordance with the rite." Mencius said, "Don't you mean this? Zeng Zi ever said, 'People in Jin State and Chu State had wealth and we don't. They used wealth and we used humanity. They used titles of nobility and we used righteousness. What could we regret for?' Didn't Zeng Zi's words fit for the rites? This is another Great Way. There are three honorable things commonly recognized by all people, i. e. title of nobility, age, and morality. In the court, title of nobility goes first; among villagers, age goes first; and as for moving and governing people, morality goes first. How could one use title of nobility to treat age and morality disrespectfully? So the greatly achieved monarch has minister who cannot be summoned. If the monarch has something to discuss with his minister he will go himself. He should respect morality and happily implement government of humanity. If he doesn't do these, he is doomed to achieve nothing. Therefore King Tang of Shang Dynasty learned from Yi Yin and then made him his minister. After that he made little effort to unite the land under Heaven; Duke Huan of Qi State learned from Guan Zhong and then made him his minister, after that he managed to dominate among the bing. Nowadays, all states have the same size. They do things in the same way, and no one can surpass others. There isn't other reason. It's just because each monarch makes one his minister whom he educates, but doesn't make one his minister who educates himself. King Tang of Shang Dynasty daren't summon Yi Yin and Duke Huan of Qi State daren't summon Guan Zhong. Guan Zhong couldn't be summoned, let alone someone who refuses to be a man like him."

【注释】(1)如:应当。就见:前往拜访。(2)有寒疾:感受了寒邪生病了。风:fèng,被吹,受风。(3)朝:zhāo,早晨。下文诸"朝"字皆读"cháo"。视朝:~cháo,临朝议事。(4)不幸而有疾不能造朝:不幸,表示不希望发生而竟然发生。义近"抱歉"。有疾:生病了。造朝:上朝,晋谒,朝觐。(5)东郭氏:齐国大夫。(6)孟仲子:赵岐认为是孟子的堂兄弟。昔者:昨天。古人用以指说话时之前的间不论长短。(7)采薪之忧:自称患病的谦辞。朱熹《四书集注》:"采薪之忧,言病不能采薪,谦辞也。”(8)要:yāo,阻拦。(9)景丑氏:朱熹《四书集注》:“景丑氏,齐大夫家也。景子,景丑也。”(10)大伦:人间的基本伦理道德;人间关系的常道。(11)云尔:亦作“云耳”。用于语尾,表示如此而已。(12)父召无诺:《礼记·曲礼上》说:“父召无诺,先生召无诺,唯而起。”(父亲召唤,不要答应“诺”,先生召唤不要答应“诺”,都要答应“唯”,而且随着应声立即行动。)郑玄注:“应声‘唯’恭于‘诺’。”(13)不俟駕:《论语·乡党》:“君命召,不俟駕行矣。”(14)不果:没有成为事实;终于没有实行。(15)宜:犹大概;似乎;恐怕。表示不十分肯定。(16)我以吾义:此句以上四句的“以”意谓使用;运用。(17)慊:qiǎn,又读 qiàn,不满足;遗憾;恨。(18)是或:是,代词,此,这。或,副词,又。(19)达尊:谓天下众所共尊。(20)辅世长民:辅佐世人,为民之长。(21)丑:相同。(22)好臣其所教:hào,喜好。臣,动词使动用法。使之为臣;以……为臣。其所教,他教的人。(23)其所受教:教他的人。(24)且犹:尚且,也还。表示进一层的意思。提出程度更甚的事例作为衬托,下文常用“况”“何况”等词相呼应。

【原文】3 陈臻问曰:[1]“前日于齐,[2]王馈兼金一百而不受;[3]于宋馈七十镒而受;于薛,[4]馈五十镒而受。前日之不受是,则今日之受非也;今日之受是,则前日之不受非也;夫子必居一于此矣。”孟子曰:“皆是也。当在宋也,予将有远行,行者必以赆;[5]辞曰:‘馈赆。[6]予何为不受?当在薛也,予有戒心,[7]辞曰:‘闻戒,故为兵馈之’[8]予何不受?若于齐,则未有处也。[9]无处而馈之,是货之也。[10]焉有君子而可以货取乎?[11]”

【白话译文】

陈臻问道:“往日在齐国,齐王送您上等好金一百镒,您不接受;在宋国,宋君送您七十镒,您受了;在薛,田家送您五十镒,您也受了。如果过去的不接受是正确的,那么后来的接受便是错了;如果后来的接受是正确的,那么过去的不接受便是错了。两种行为中,老师一定有一种是错误的。”孟子说:“都是正确的。当在宋国时,我准备远行,对远行人一定要送些盘费或其他礼物,因此宋君说:‘送上一点盘费吧!’我为什么不受?当在薛时,我有自我防卫的心。薛君说:‘听说您需要自我防卫,送点钱给您置办兵器吧!’我为什么不受?说到在齐国时,我没有要耗费钱财之处;没有要耗费钱财之处,却要送一些钱给我,实际是贿赂我。哪里有正人君子能够被用钱财收买的呢?”

【英语译文】

Chen Zhen asked, “In the other day, when you were in Qi State, the King presented you the copper of two thousand *liang* but you didn't accept it. In Song State, the King presented you the copper of one thousand and four hundred *liang* and you accepted it. In the City of Xue, Tian Ying presented you the copper of one thousand *liang* and you accepted. If rejection was right, then acceptance should be wrong. If acceptance was right, then rejection was wrong. One of your two actions should be wrong." Mencius replied, "They were both right. When I was in Song State, I was about to go for a long journey. For a man who was about to go for a long journey, people usually give him some traveling expenses or other things as gift, therefore, the King of Song State said, 'I will present you some traveling expenses!' Why didn't I accept it? When I was in the City of Xue, I had sense of self-defense. The head of Xue said, 'I heard that you want to defend yourself, and then I will present you some money to prepare some weapon.' Why didn't I accept it? When I was in Qi State, I needn't use any money. It was bribing me that the King of Qi State presented me money when I needn't use any money. How could a moral man be bribed by money?"

【注释】(1)陈臻:孟子弟子。(2)前日:前些日子,往日。(3)兼金一百:兼金,价倍于常金的好金。古之所谓金实际是铜。一百,是一百镒或一百金的省文。镒,古重量单位,战国和秦代以一镒为一金。金,是货币单位。一镒,即言"重二十两";一金即言"金二十两"。(4)薛:指古薛国亡于齐国所遗之薛城。时为齐靖郭君田婴的采邑。(5)赆:jìn,送行时赠送的财物。行者必以赆,是"必以赆行者"的倒装。意谓一定要送一些礼物给远行的人。(6)馈赆 kuìjìn:赠送行资;赠送财物。(7)戒心:戒备、警惕之心。(8)为兵:设置兵器。(9)处:chù,"未有处"与下文"无处"同义。在句中作状语,句中的谓语承上文省略了。(10)货:贿赂。(11)货取:用货财收买。

【原文】4 孟子之平陆,[1]谓其大夫曰:[2]"子之持戟之士,[3]一日而三失伍,[4]则去之否乎?[5]"曰:"不待三。[6]""然则子之失伍也亦多矣。凶年饥岁,子之民,老羸转于沟壑,壮者散而之四方者,几千人矣。"曰;"此非距心之所得为也。"曰;"今有受人之牛羊而为之牧之者,[7]则必为之求牧与刍矣。求牧与刍而不得,则反诸其人乎?抑亦立而视其死与?[8]"曰;"此则距心之罪也。"他日,见于王曰:"王之为都者,[9]臣知五人焉。知其罪者,惟孔距心。"为王诵之。[10]王曰:"此乃寡人之罪也。"

【白话译文】

孟子到达平陆,对那里的长官孔距心说:"假如你的战士一天三次掉队,你会开除他吗?"回答道:"用不着三次。"孟子说:"那么你自己掉队的地方也很多了。灾荒年间,你的百姓,年老体弱饿死在山沟的,和正当年轻逃亡四方的,已接近一千人了。"回答道:"这种事情不是我能够办好的。"孟子说:"假如有人接受别人的牛羊而代替牧放,那就必须寻找牧场和草料。寻找不到牧场和草料,就把牛羊还给原主呢?还是只站起看着牛羊一个个饿死吗?"回答道:"这就是距心——我的罪过了。"过后有一天,孟子朝见齐王,说:"王的地方长官,我认得五位。明白自己的罪过的,只有孔距心一个人。"于是把同孔距心的交谈复述了一遍。王说:"这个也是我的罪过呢!"

【英语译文】

Mencius arrived at Pinglu and asked the local official Kong Juxin, "If your soldier broke the ranks thrice one day, will you dismiss him?" Kong answered, "It needn't to be thrice." Mencius said, "You yourself have fallen behind in many things. In year of famine, the old and the weak of your subjects starved to death in the ravines, and the strong men fled from home. These almost amounted to one thousand." Kong answered, "I cannot manage to do these things." Mencius said, "Supposing a man accepts others' goats and ox and put them out to pasture, then he should look for pasture and fodder. Will he return the animals to the original owner, or will he stand by while the animals starve to death when he has failed in finding pasture and fodder?" Kong answered, "This is my sin." One day after that Mencius appeared before the King of Qi State, saying, "I have known five local officials of yours. But only one of them has known his sin. That is Kong Juxin." And then he repeated their conversation to the King. The King said, "This is also my sin!"

【注释】(1)平陆:齐边境邑名。今山东汶上县北是其遗地。(2)大夫:古代有不同级别的大夫,并非都是高官。战国时的邑宰也称大夫,相当于今之县长。(3)持戟之士:战士。戟,读 jǐ,古代兵器名。合戈、矛为一体,兼有戈之横击、矛之直刺两种作用,杀伤力比戈矛为强。(4)三失伍:三次落伍(掉队)。(5)去之:使之离去,开除。(6)不待:用不着;不用。(7)牧:放牧的场地。(8)抑,连词,"或者","还是"。亦:副词,只,只是,仅,仅仅。(9)为都者:指在都城为官的人。都,古称建有宗庙的城邑。《左传·庄公二十八年》:"凡邑有宗庙先君之主曰都,无曰邑。”(10)诵之:复述已往的言语、事情。

【原文】5 孟子谓蚳蛙曰:[1]“子之辞灵丘而请士师,[2]似也,为其可以言也。今既数月矣,未可以言与?”蚳蛙谏于王而不用,致为臣而去。[3]齐人曰:“所以为蚳蛙则善矣;所以自为,则吾不知也。”公都子以告。[4]曰:“吾闻之也:有官守者不得其职则去;[5]有言责者,[6]不得其言则去。我无官守,我无言责也则吾进退岂不绰绰然有余裕哉?[7]”

【白话译文】

孟子对蚳蛙说:“你之所以辞去灵丘县官而要求做掌禁令刑狱的法官,好像是这样吧,这样可以向王进言。到现在你已经上任好几个月了,还不能向王进言吗?”蚳蛙向王进谏而不被采纳,辞去了做臣子的责任远走了。齐国有人说:“孟子替蚳蛙的考虑是不错的,他对自己的考虑如何,我还不知道。”公都子把这话转告了孟子。孟子说:“我听说过:在册的行政官吏,得不到职权,就可离去;在册的谏官,进言不被采纳,也可离去。我既没有官位职守,也没有进言的责任,那么,我的进退不是有很宽松的空间吗?”

【英语译文】

Mencius told Chi Wa, “The reason why you resigned the Magistrate of Lingqiu County and asked to be judicial officer seems to me that you can remonstrate to the King. Till now, you've been empowered for several months. Couldn't you make remonstration to the King?” Chi Wa made some suggestion to the King but he was refused and then he gave up his post. Somebody in Qi State said, “It's alright for Mencius considering Chi Wa's situation, but I don't know how he considered his own situation.” GongDu Zi reported this to Mencius. Mencius replied, “I heard that those registered officials who couldn't get post may leave; and those registered remonstrators whose advice were rejected may also leave. I not only have no post but also have no responsibility to remonstrate. Then am I free enough to be promoted or to withdraw?”

【注释】(1)蚳蛙:chí ~,齐国大夫。蚳姓,蛙名。(2)灵丘:齐国边境邑名。其地即今山西省灵丘县。士师,古代掌禁令刑狱之官。(3)致:归还;交还。(4)公都子:孟子弟子。(5)官守:官位职守;官吏的职责。有官守者,指在册的行政官吏。(6)言责:进言的责任。有言责者,指在册的谏官。(7)绰绰:宽松的样子。余裕:

宽绰,宽裕。

【原文】6 孟子为卿于齐,出吊于滕,[1]王使盖大夫王驩为辅行。[2]王驩朝暮见,反齐滕之路,未尝与之言行事也。[3]公孙丑曰:“齐卿之位,[4]为小矣;齐滕之路,不为近矣,反之而未尝与言行事,[5]不何也?”曰:“夫既或治之[6],予何言哉?”

【白话译文】

孟子在齐国当卿,奉命到滕国去吊丧,齐王还派盖邑县长王驩作为副使同行。王驩同孟子朝夕相见,往返在齐藤两国的旅途上,孟子没有和他一起谈过出使的事。公孙丑说:“齐国卿的官位,不算小了;齐滕之间的路程,也不算短了,往返一趟,却没和王驩谈过一回关于出使的事,这是为什么呢?”孟子说:“他既然包揽这事,我还谈什么呢?”

【英语译文】

Mencius was ordered to pay a condolence call in Teng State when he was a minister in Qi State, and the King of Qi State dispatched Wang Huan, the magistrate of Ge County to accompany him as the vice envoy. Wang Huan stayed together with Mencius all day long but Mencius didn't mention one word on the journey to Teng State and that back to Qi State. Gongsun Chou said, “ A minister in Qi is a high post and the journey to and back from Teng State is a long one. Why didn't you talk about the journey as an envoy with Wang Huan ?” Mencius said, “I needn't speak anything since he had done all the things. ”

【注释】(1)出吊于滕:出,义同“去”,“到”。吊,吊丧(吊滕文公之丧)。于,义同“往”“去”。滕,西周分封的诸侯国。在今山东省藤县一带。(2)盖大夫王驩为辅行:盖,读 gě,齐国邑名。古城在今山东沂水县西北八十里。大夫,这里是任官职者的通称。盖大夫,即盖邑县长。王驩(huān),齐王的嬖(bì)臣。辅行,副使。辅助正使行事,故称。(3)行事:出使之事,行人之事。(4)齐卿之位:齐卿,这里指王驩。其人受齐王宠幸以县官充列卿位出使。位,爵位,官位。(5)反之:反,同返。之,往。(6)夫既或治之:夫,代词,他。既,连词,既然。或,语助词。治,办理;主管。之,代词。代上文“行事”。

【原文】7 孟子自齐葬于鲁,[1]反于齐,止于嬴。[2]充虞请曰:[3]“前日不知虞之不肖，[4]使虞敦匠事。[5]严，予不敢请。[6]今愿窃有请也：[7]木若以美然。[8]"曰："古者棺椁无度，[9]中古棺七寸，[10]椁称之。自天子达于庶人，非直为观美也，[11]然后尽于人心。[12]不得，[13]不可以为悦；[14]财，不可以为悦；得之为有财，[15]无古之人皆用之，[16]吾何为独不然？[17]且比化者无使土亲肤，[18]于人心独无恔乎？[19]吾闻之也：君子不以天下俭其亲。[20]"

【白话译文】

孟子从齐国运送母亲的遗体到鲁国埋葬后返回齐国，到了嬴县停留下来。充虞请问道："前些日子，承老师不弃，派我管理木匠制造棺椁；当时都很忙，不敢请教。今天我私自希望能得到请教时间：棺木似乎太好了。"孟子说："上古对于棺椁的尺寸，没有一定的规矩。到了中古，才规定棺厚七寸，椁的厚度与棺相称。从天子一直到老百姓，对棺椁不仅是讲美观而是要尽孝心。法制有所不允许，在棺椁上做不到尽孝称心；没有钱财，在棺椁上做不到尽孝称心；法制允许又有钱财，古来的人都在棺椁上做到尽孝称心，我为什么独自不这样做呢？而且，用上等棺椁替死者不让泥土接触肌肤，在孝子心中难道没有快意吗？我听说过，在任何地方，君子都不应该在父母身上俭省钱。"

【英语译文】

Mencius returned Qi State after he escorted his mother's body and buried her in Lu State. During the trip, he stopped in Ying County. Chong Yu asked him, "The other days I was honored to be responsible for making coffin and outer coffin and had no time to ask your opinion. Today I personally want you to teach me that I thought the coffin seemed too fine." Mencius answered, "There wasn't fixed rule for coffin in ancient times. And till the middle ancient times, it was stipulated that coffin was seven *cun* thick and the outer coffin was the same. From the king to common people, they all concerned about not only the coffin pleasing to the eye but also the filial piety of kids. If there was forbidden rubes in laws, then filial piety couldn't be expressed through coffins; if people had no money, then they couldn't express their filial piety; if there wasn't forbidden rubes in laws and people had enough money, people from ancient times could fully express their filial piety. Why didn't I alone do things like this? Furthermore, we use fine wood to make coffin and keep the dead body from earth harming. Aren't we filial offspring feeling relaxed? I have heard that a moral man should not save money concerning things of his parents."

【注释】(1)自齐葬于鲁:孟子仕于齐,母随之,丧,归葬于鲁。(2)嬴:yíng,齐国南部地名。故城在今山东省莱芜市西北。(3)充虞:孟子弟子。(4)不知虞之不肖:谦辞。句意谓您不了解我不材。不肖,读~xiào,本义子不似父。引申为无财,不成器。(5)敦匠事:指经管木匠做棺椁。敦,读 duī,治理,管理。匠事,木匠制造事务。(6)严:急,紧急。不敢请:不敢请教。(7)今愿窃有请也:今,现在。愿,希望。窃(qiè),敬辞。有,取得,得到。请,请教。(8)木若以美然:木,棺木。若,如,像。以,通"已",相当于"太""甚"。美然,美好。(9)度:指棺木的厚薄尺寸规矩。(10)中古:指周公制礼时。(11)非直:不但,不仅。观美:外观美,表面好看。(12)然后:表示接着某一动作或情况之后。尽于人心:尽量施展善心孝心。(13)不得:谓"法制所不允"。(14)为悦:做到称心。(15)得之为有财:得之,与"不得"之义相对;犹言为"法制所允"。为,相当于"与""和"。有财,有金钱物资。(16)用:采用;听从。(17)不然:不如此,不是这样。(18)且比化者无使土亲肤:且,进层连词。比,介词。为;替。化者,死者。无使,不让。土,泥土。亲,接触;挨着。肤,体肤,体表。(19)独无:犹言难道,没有。恔:xiào,快慰,满。(20)俭:薄;少。

【原文】8 沈同以其私问曰:[1]"燕可伐与?[2]"孟子曰:"可;子哙不得与人燕,[3]子之不得受燕于子哙。[4]有仕于此,[5]而子悦之,不告于王而私与之吾子之禄爵;夫士也,[6]亦无王命而私受之于子,则可乎?——何以异于是?"齐人伐燕。或问曰:"劝齐伐燕,有诸?"曰:"未也。沈同问'燕可伐与?吾应之曰'可'彼然而伐之也。[7]彼如曰'孰可以伐之?'则将应之曰:'为天吏,[8]则可以伐之。今有杀人者,'或问之曰'人可杀与'?则应之曰'可'。彼如曰'孰可以杀之'?则将应之曰:'为士师,[9]则可以杀之。'今以燕伐燕,[10]何为劝之哉?"

【白话译文】

沈同以私人身份问孟子:"燕国可以讨伐吗?"孟子说:"可以,燕王子哙不可任意把燕国交给别人,他的相国子之也不可随便从子哙那里接过燕国。比如有个要求做官的人在这儿,你喜欢他,便不向国王报告就把你的俸禄、官位都送给他;他也没有国王的任命就从你手里接过俸禄和官位,这样可以吗?子哙和子之的行为与这有什么不同?"齐国讨伐燕国后,有人问到孟子:"你劝说过齐国伐燕,有这事吗?"孟子回答道:"没有,沈同凭私交曾经问我道:'燕国可以讨伐吗?'我答应道:'可以';他们认为对,就去讨伐燕国了。如果他再问:'谁可以去讨伐它?'那我便会说:'是天吏的才有资格去讨伐。'比如有个杀人犯,有人问道:'这犯人该杀吗?'那我会说:'该杀'。如果他再问:'谁可以杀他?'那我就会说:'只有执法官才可以杀他'。如今是一个同燕国一样暴虐的齐国攻打燕国。我为什么要去劝说他呢?"

【英语译文】

Shen Tong, in his private time, asked Mencius, "Can Yan State be attacked?" Mencius answered, "Yes, it can be. The King of Yan State Zi Kuai cannot give Yan to any other people at his will. His prime minister Zi Zhi also cannot take over Yan from him at will. For example, suppose there is a person who wants to be an official and whom you like very much, and you give your post and salary to him without reporting to the king. Then without king's commission, the person accepts your post and salary. Is it ok? Is there any difference between Zi Kuai and Zi Zhi's actions and this?" After Qi State attacking Yan State someone asked Mencius, "You ever persuaded Qi State to attack Yan State, didn't you?" Mencius replied, "No, I didn't do that. But Shen Tong privately asked me 'Can Yan State be attacked?' I answered, 'Yes, it can be.' They thought I was right and then went on attacking it. If he asked again, 'Who can attacked it?' Then I would say, 'Those who were ordered by heaven were qualified to attack.' For example, suppose there is a murderer and someone asks, 'Should this criminal be killed?' Then I will say, 'Yes.' If he asks again, 'Who has the right to kill the criminal?' Then I will say, 'Only sheriff has the right.' Nowadays a tyrannical Qi State crusaded against the same tyrannical Yan State. Why do I persuade it?"

【注释】(1)沈同:齐国之臣。以其私:以私人关系、私人名义;不代表王命。(2)燕可伐与:参阅梁惠王下,第十、第十一两章及本篇第九章经文和注。(3)子哙(kuài):燕之昏君。(4)子之:燕王哙之臣。(5)仕:通"士"。谓以道艺武勇谋求仕进的人。(6)夫士也:此"士",指从仕的人。(7)然:相当于"认为对"。(8)天吏:奉天命而治民的人。(9)夫士师:执掌刑狱的法官。(10)以燕伐燕:指如燕一样暴虐的齐国讨伐燕国。喻同样暴虐的国家之间的征讨。

【原文】9 燕人畔。[1]王曰:"吾甚惭于孟子。[2]"陈贾曰:[3]"王无患焉。王自以为与周公孰仁且智?"王曰:"恶!是何言也!"曰:"周公使管叔监殷,[4]管叔以殷畔;[5]知而使之,是不仁也;不知而使之,是不智也。仁智,周公未之尽也,而况于王乎?贾请见而解之。[6]"见孟子问曰:"周公何人也?"曰:"古圣人也。"曰:"使管叔监殷,管叔以殷畔也,有诸?”曰:“然。”曰:“周公知其将畔而使之与?”曰:“不知也。”“然则圣人且有过与?[7]”曰:“周公弟也,管叔兄也。周公之过不亦宜乎!且古之君子,[8]过则改之;今之君子,过则顺改之。古之君子,其过也如日月之食,[9]民皆见之;及其更也,民皆仰之。[10]今之君子,岂徒顺之,[11]又从为之辞。[12]”

【白话译文】

燕国人反抗齐国占领;齐国说燕人反叛。齐王说:“我对孟子感到很惭愧。”陈贾说:“王不要难过,您自己认为和周公相比谁更仁更智?”齐王说:“哎!这是什么话呀?”陈贾说:“周公让管叔监督殷国遗民,管叔却率领殷国遗民叛乱;如果周公知道他会如此,竟然派给他这份差事,那便是不仁;如果不知道他会如此,才派给了他这份差事,那便是不智。仁和智,周公也未能完全做到,何况于您呢?我请求您让我去见孟子做个解释。”陈贾来见孟子,问道:“周公是个怎样的人?”回答:“古代的圣人。”陈贾说:“他让管叔监督殷朝遗民,管叔却率领他们来叛乱,有这回事吗?”回答:“是这样。”问道:“周公知道他将会叛乱而派遣他的吗?”回答:“不知道。”陈贾说:“这样看来,圣人也还有过错吗?”孟子回答:“周公是弟弟,管叔是哥哥,周公的这种错误,不也是合乎情理的吗?而且,古代的君子,有了错误,随即改正;今天的君子,有了错误,便将错就错。古代的君子,他的错误就像日食月食一样,老百姓个个都看得到;当他改正时个个都欣喜地抬头望着。今天的君子,何止将错就错,还要紧随着编些话来辩解。”

【英语译文】

People in Yan State resisted the occupation of Qi State but the authority of Qi State criticized that Yan people led uprising. King of Qi State said, “I am abashed at Mencius.” Chen Jia said, “You needn’t worry about that. Duke Zhou and you, who do you think is wiser and more kindhearted?” King said, “Oh, why did you say like that?” Chen Jia said, “Duke Zhou asked Guan Zhong supervise the survivors of Yin (Shang) Dynasty but he led them revolt. Duke Zhou wasn’t a humanistic man if he knew that Guan Zhong would lead uprising but still assigned him this task; Duke Zhou wasn’t a wise man if he didn’t know that Guan Zhong would lead uprising and still assigned him this task. Duke Zhou couldn’t be both humane and wise, let alone you. Please permit me to give an explanation to Mencius.” Chen Jia went to visit Mencius, asking, “What kind of man was Duke Zhou?” Mencius replied, “A sage in ancient times.” Chen Jia said, “He let Guan Zhong supervise the survivors of Yin (Shang) Dynasty but the latter led them take uprising. Is it true?” Mencius answered, “Yes, it is." Chen Jia asked, "Did Duke Zhou know that he would revolt and still assigned him this task?" Mencius replied, "No, he didn't." Chen Jia asked, "So, did sages still make mistake?" Mencius said, "Duke Zhou was younger than Guan Zhong. Wasn't it reasonable that he made such mistake? Moreover, the ancient monarch would correct it at once when he made any mistake. But today's monarch will make the best of a mistake. In ancient times common people could see their monarch' mistakes which were like eclipses. When he corrected people look up at him. But today's monarch, besides making the best of his mistake, he will make up more lies to deceive his people."

【注释】(1)燕人畔:齐破燕,意在吞燕。燕王哙死,子之亡。赵武灵王派人将燕王哙之庶子职送归燕国收破局即位,志在复仇。齐国视为燕人叛。(2)吾甚惭于孟子:孟子曾劝齐王"速出令,反其旄倪,止其重器,谋于燕众,置君然后去之。"(见《梁惠王下》十一章)。齐宣王不听。(3)陈贾:齐大夫。(4)周公使管叔监殷:武王既克纣,封叔鲜于管是谓管叔封叔度于蔡是谓蔡叔;使二人监纣子武庚,治殷遗民。(5)管叔以殷畔:《史记·管蔡世家》:"武王既崩,成王少,周公旦专王室。管叔、蔡叔疑周公之为不利于成王,乃挟武庚以作乱。周公旦承成王命伐诛武庚,杀管叔,而放蔡叔,迁之。"(6)请见而解之:请准向孟子解释。(7)且:副词。也,还。(8)且:进层连词,而且。(9)日月之食:即日食和月食。食亦作"蚀"。(10)仰之:抬头望着。(11)岂徒:难道只是;何止。(12)又从为之辞:又从,还随即。为之辞,编话辩解。

【原文】10 孟子致为臣而归。[1]王就见孟子,[2]曰:"前日愿见,而不可得,得侍同朝甚喜。[3]今又弃寡人而归,不识可以继此而得见乎?[4]"对曰:"不敢请耳,固所愿也。[5]"他日,王谓时子曰:[6]"我欲中国而授孟子室,养弟子以万钟,[7]使诸大夫国人皆有所矜式,[8]子盍为我言之?[9]"时子因陈子而以告孟子。[10]陈子以时子之言告孟子。[11]孟子曰:"然。[12]夫时子恶知其不可也?如使予欲富,辞十万而受万,是为欲富乎?季孙曰:[13]'异哉子叔疑![14]使己为政,不用,则亦已矣,又使其子弟为卿。人亦孰不欲富贵?[15]而独于富贵之中,[16]有私龙断焉。[17]'古之为市也,[18]以其所有易其所无者,有司者治之耳。[19]有贱丈夫焉,[20]必求龙断而登之,以左右望而罔市利。[21]皆以为贱,故从而征之。征商自此贱丈夫始矣。[22]"

【白话译文】

孟子辞去齐国的官职就回老家。齐王亲自来见孟子,说道:"起初想见到您没能如愿;后来才得相随同朝,我真高兴;现在您又将抛弃我回家乡去,不知我们今后还可以相见不?”回答说:“只是不敢请求罢了,这本来是我的愿望。”过了几天,齐王对时子说:“我想在都城中给孟子一幢房子,用万钟粮食来供养他的弟子,让我国的官吏和百姓都有个榜样。你何不替我去向孟子谈谈!”时子托陈臻把齐王的话转告孟子。陈臻便把时子的话告诉了孟子。孟子说:“嗯。那时子他哪晓得这么干是不行的呢?假使我想发财,辞去十万钟的俸禄来接受这一万钟的赠予,有这种发财经吗?季孙说过:‘奇怪呀,子叔疑!自己要做官,人家不用,也就算了吧,又使儿子兄弟来做卿大夫。一般人谁不想升官发财?他独自在升官发财中私心太重,想把一切都垄断起来。’古代做买卖,都是以货易货,用其所有的东西换其所无的东西,有关部门只是管理秩序罢了。却有个卑鄙汉子一定要找个高坡登上去,左边望望右边望望,巴不得把一切买卖的好处一口吞下去。别人都认为他太低劣,要征他的税。向商人征税就从这里开始。”

【英语译文】

Mencius resigned his post in Qi State and returned to his home. The king of Qi State came to visit him personally and said, “Originally I didn’t manage to see you; later on, you and I were in the same court so that I was very happy; now you reject me and return to your home and I wonder whether or not we can meet in the future?” Mencius answered, “I dare not ask your permission but this is my original hope.” Several days later the King said to Shi Zi, “I want to award Mencius a mansion and support his disciples with very much grain so to set an example for our country and people. Why don’t you talk to Mencius about this on behalf of me?” Shi Zi entrusted Chen Zhen to pass this information to Mencius by somebody else. Mencius said, “Shi Zi didn’t know that it wasn’t fine to do so. If I wanted to make fortune, how could I resign a post being worthy of one hundred thousand peck to receive a mansion of ten- thousand- peck? Is there such way to make fortune? Ji sun ever said, ‘It was strange for Zi Shu Yi. He himself wanted to be an official but he was refused. Then he made his son and brother become ministers. Ordinary men all wanted to be official and make fortune. He was so selfish in doing these that he wanted to monopolize all things in this field.’ In ancient trade, people usually exchanged goods with goods and got what they didn’t have by what they owned. Some authorities just kept things in order. However, there was a mean man who wished to climb up the steep slope and swallow all benefits after watching all directions. All others thought that he was too low-graded that he was taxed.

Taxing the merchants just began from him."

【注释】(1)致为臣而归:致,归还;交还。为臣,指臣位,官职。而归,然后归老家。而,进层连词。(2)就见:亲自来见;主动来见。用于从上位到下位。(3)侍:陪从或伺候尊长。(4)不识:不知道。继此:此后。(5)不敢请耳,固所愿也:为了强调"不敢",颠倒了句子的主从位置。(6)时子:齐国之臣。(7)中国:在国都之中。中,谓居于其中,在其中。国,指国都;即临淄城。钟:古容量单位。春秋时齐国公室的公量合六斛四斗。之后亦有合八斛及十斛之制。(8)矜式:jīn ~,敬重和取法。有所矜式,即"有敬重、取法的楷模"。(9)盍:hé,副词,表示反诘,犹何不。(10)因:依托。陈子:陈臻。(11)以:介词,用,拿。(12)然:表示肯定的答语,犹言"嗯""是的"。(13)、(14)季孙、子叔疑:朱熹《四书集注》:"季孙、子叔疑,不知何时人。"(15)人亦:人,众人;一般人。亦,语气助词没有实在意义。(16)而:代词,他。(17)有私龙断焉:有私,有私心。龙断,即垄断。冈垄,高地。朱熹《四书集注》:"龙音垄。垄断,冈垄之断而高也。"引申为把持,独断。焉,代词,相当于"之""此"。(18)为市:交易,做买卖。(19)有司者:管理部门。(20)丈夫:成年男子。(21)罔市利:搜括贸易之利。(22)征:征税。

【原文】11 孟子去齐,宿于昼。[1]有欲为王留行者,坐而言。[2]不应,隐几而卧。[3]客不悦曰:"弟子齐宿而后敢言,[4]夫子卧而不听,请勿复敢见矣。[5]"曰:"坐!我明语子。昔者鲁缪公无人乎子思之侧则不能安子思;[6]泄柳、申详无人乎缪公之侧,则不能安其身。[7]子为长者虑,[8]而不及子思;[9]子绝长者乎?长者绝子乎?"

【白话译文】

孟子离开齐国,在昼县过夜。有一位想为齐王挽留孟子的人,恭敬地坐着同孟子说话。孟子没有回应,伏在靠几上休息。那人不高兴地说:"小辈我昨天就斋戒沐浴了,才敢来和您说话,老先生休息不听,请了,以后再也不敢和您相见了。"孟子说:"坐下吧!我明白地告诉你,过去,鲁缪公如果没有人在子思身边那就不能安定子思;如果泄柳、申详没有人在缪公身边,也就不能使自己安身。你为老头儿考虑,却不晓得子思的情况,是你对老头儿做得绝呢?还是老头儿对你做得绝呢?"

【英语译文】

Mencius left Qi State and stayed overnight at Zhouxian County. A man who wanted to persuade Mencius to stay sat modestly and said to Mencius. The latter didn't respond and just took a rest by a table. The man said unhappily, "I fasted and took bath yesterday and then I was encouraged to talk with you, however, you master refused to listen to me and just take a rest. Thank you and I have no courage to see you again." Mencius said, "Please sit down. I can tell you plainly that in the old days Duke Mu of Lu State couldn't calm down Zi Si if there wasn't anyone beside Zi Si. If Xie Liu and Shen Xiang didn't accompany him, Duke Mu couldn't calm down himself. You considered me the old one but you didn't know Zi Si' situation, therefore, did you get things into an impasse to me, or I got things into an impasse to you?"

【注释】(1)昼:zhòu,春秋齐邑名。其地在今山东省淄博市境。为孟子自齐反邹必经之地。(2)坐:古人铺席于地,两膝着席,臀部压在脚后跟上,谓之"坐"。后来把臀部平放在椅子、凳子或其他物体上以支持身体称为"坐"。(3)隐几而卧:靠着几案伏着休息。(4)弟子:客人自谦辞。齐宿:同"斋宿"。先一日斋戒。朱熹四书集注:"斋宿,斋戒越宿也。"(5)请:敬辞,表示随即离开。(6)昔者鲁缪公句:缪,同"穆"。鲁缪公,名显在位三十三年。子思,孔子孙。名伋。缪公尊敬子思,经常派人向子思表达他的诚意。子思,于是能安心留下。(7)泄柳申详句:泄柳,即《告子下》第六章的子柳。鲁缪公时的贤人。申详,孔子学生子张之子,子游之婿。朱熹四书集注:"〔泄柳申详〕缪公尊之不如子思,然二子义不苟容,非有贤者在其君之左右维持调护之亦不能安其身矣。"(8)长者:孟子年老,比来客大,故自谓长者。(9)而不及:而,转折连词,却。不及,不识,不知。

【原文】12 孟子去齐,尹士语人曰:[1]"不识王之不可以为汤、武,则是不明也;识其不可,然且至,则是干泽也。[2]千里而见王,不遇故去,三宿而后出昼是何濡滞也?[3]士则兹不悦。[4]"高子以告。[5]曰:"夫尹士恶知予哉?千里而见王,是予所欲也;不遇故去,岂予所欲哉?予不得已也。予三宿而出昼,于予心犹以为速,王庶几改之![6]王如改诸,[7]则必反予。[8]夫出昼,而王不予追也,[9]予然后浩然有归志。[10]予虽然,岂舍王哉!王由足用为善;[11]王如用予,则岂徒齐民安,天下之民举安。王庶几改之!予日望之!予岂若是小丈夫然哉?[12]谏于其君而不受,则怒,悻悻然见于其面,[13]去则穷日之力而后宿哉?[14]"尹士闻之曰:[15]"士诚小人也。"

【白话译文】

孟子离开齐国,尹士对别人说:"不晓得齐王不能做商汤、周武,那便是孟子的糊涂;晓得他不行,然而又来了,那便是贪求富贵了。老远地跑来见齐王,不相融洽又走人,在昼县歇了三夜才离开,行动为什么这样缓慢呢?我就不喜欢这么干。"高子把这话告诉了孟子。孟子:"那尹士哪能了解我呢?大老远地跑来见齐王,是我的希望,不相融洽又走人,难道也是我所希望的吗?我只是不得已罢了。在昼县歇了三夜才离开,我心里还认为太快了,齐王也许会改变态度的;他如果改变了态度,一定会召我返回。我出了昼县,他还没来追回我,我才无所留恋地坚定了回乡的念头。即便这样,我难道肯抛弃齐王吗?他也还是可以行仁政的;他如果用我,又何止齐国的百姓得到太平,天下的百姓都将得到太平。他或许会改变态度的!我天天都盼望!我难道要像这小家子一样吗?向王进见不被接受就怨恨失意气色破脸,一旦离去就整日奔走不到气尽力竭不落脚吗?"尹士知道了这些话后说:"我真是一个小人。"

【英语译文】

After Mencius left Qi State, Yin Shi told others, "Mencius was muddled if he didn't know that King of Qi State couldn't become a king like Tang of Shang Dynasty and King Wu of Zhou Dynasty. He was thirsty for richness and nobility if he did know this. He came here from a place far away and left because he couldn't get well along with the King, and stayed at Zhouxian County for three nights after his leaving. Why did he act so slowly? I don't like him doing so." Gao Zi told Mencius what Yin Shi had said. Mencius responded, "How could Yin Shi understand me? It's my hope to come here to see the king from a place far away. Don't I wish that I left because I didn't get well along with the king? I thought it was too fast for staying at Zhouxian County for three nights because I thought the King of Qi State would change his attitude. If he changed his attitude he would certainly summon me back. After I went out of Zhouxian County, he didn't run after me, therefore I firmly determined to go back hometown. Even it went like this, wasn't I willing to reject the king? He could also carry out government of humanity. If he employed me, common people of other states as well as those of Qi State could lead peaceful life. Every day I hope he will change his attitude. Don't I act myself just like this young man? He would get enraged and disappointed if his remonstrance was rejected by the king. Once leaving he would hurry for other places without rest." After he heard these words of Mencius, Yin Shi sighed, "I am just a mean man."

【注释】(1)尹士:一个齐国人。(2)干泽:gān ~,犹干禄。求禄位,求仕进。(3)濡滞:迟延;久留。(4)则兹不悦:则,副词,乃,就是。兹不悦,“不悦兹”的倒装,谓不悦此(不喜欢这一个)。(5)高子:孟子弟子。(6)庶几:或许,也许。(7)诸:代词,同“之”。(8)反予:反,归,回。后作“返”。使动用法。谓使归,使回。反予,使我返回。(9)予追:“追予”的倒装。意谓追赶使我返回。(10)归志:同“归心”。返回的念头,回家的念头。(11)王由足用为善:由,通“犹”。足用,足以,可以。为善,行善;行仁政。(12)然:助词。用于句末与“若”“如”等配合,表比拟。犹言“那样”“似的”“一般”。(13)悻悻然:xìng xìng ~,怨恨失意的样子。见:同“现”。(14)穷日:尽一整天的时间。终日。(15)闻:听说,知道。

【原文】13 孟子去齐,充虞路问曰:[1]“夫子若有不豫色然。[2]前日虞闻诸夫子曰:[3]‘君子不怨天,不尤人。’”曰:“彼一时也,此一时也。五百年必有王者兴,其间必有名世者。[4]由周而来,七百有余岁矣。以其数则过矣;以其时考之,[5]则可矣。夫天未欲平治天下也;如欲平治天下,当今之世,舍我其谁也!吾何为不豫哉?”

【白话译文】

孟子离开齐国,充虞在路上问道:“老师的脸色显示出心中有什么不高兴似的。以前我听您讲过:‘有德行的人不怨恨命运,不责怪别人。’”孟子说:“以前是一个时候,现在又是一个时候。历史上,每过五百年,一定有圣君兴起。这期间也一定有名显于世的治国能人。从周文武以来,现在已经七百多年了。论年数,已超过了五百,论时势,应该是圣君贤臣出现的时候了。大概上苍还没想平治天下,如果想平治天下,当今这个时代,除了我,又有谁愿担待呢!我为什么不高兴呢?”

【英语译文】

Mencius left Qi State and Chong Yu asked him on the road, “You master seem to have something unhappy. I' ve heard in other days that you said, ‘A man with integrity should not complain about his destiny and not blame others.’” Mencius replied, “It was a certain situation in other days and it is a new situation nowadays. Every five hundred years in history, there was a sage king. during this period, during there were surely many able ministers. It was seven hundred years from the time of King Wen and King Wu of Zhou Dynasty. As for time duration it has exceeded five hundred years and as for current situation it's time for a sage king to appear. Maybe the Heaven doesn't want to bring peace and tranquility to the world under heaven. If the Heaven does, nowadays who will be willing to shoulder the responsibility except me? Why don't I feel happy?"

【注释】(1)路问:在路上问。(2)豫:喜悦;欢快。(3)诸:代词。同"之"。一说,代词"之"和介词"于"的合音。(4)名世者:名显于世的人。多用于称誉有治国才能的人。"名世"同"命世"。(5)时:指时势,时局。

【原文】14 孟子去齐,居休。[1]公孙丑问曰:"仕而不受禄,古之道乎?[2]曰:"非也。于崇,[3]吾得见王,退而有去志;不欲变,故不受也。继而有师命,[4]不可以请。久于齐,非我志也。"

【白话译文】

孟子离开齐国,居于休地。公孙丑问道:"做官却不受俸禄,是古道吗?"孟子说:"不是。在崇那里,我见到了齐王,退场下来,便有离开的意思;不想改变,所以不接受俸禄。不久,齐国有战事,不可以请求离去。长久滞留在齐国,不是我的心愿。"

【英语译文】

Mencius left Qi State and lived in the place of Xiu. Gongsun Chou asked, "Is it the ancient way not to receive payment while you are an official?" Mencius said, "No. In the place of Chong, I met the King of Qi State and after I retreated from the meeting, I cherished the hope to leave. And I didn't want to change my hope, so I didn't receive payment. In the future war will break in Qi State and I cannot request to leave. It's not my wish to stay in Qi State for a long time."

【注释】(1)休:故城在今藤县北十五里,距孟子家约百里。(2)古之道:即"古道"。泛指古代的制度、学术、思想、风尚等。(3)崇:地名。现在不详。(4)师命:朱熹《四书集注》:"师命,师旅之命也。国既被兵,难请去也。"有师旅之命,喻有战争。

孟子集注卷五 滕文公章句上 凡五章

【原文】1 滕文公为世子,[1]将之楚,[2]过宋而见孟子。[3]孟子道性善,言必称尧舜。世子自楚反,复见孟子。孟子曰:"世子疑吾言乎? 夫道一而已矣。[4]成覸谓齐景公曰:[5]'彼,丈夫也;我,丈夫也;吾何畏彼哉?'颜渊曰;'舜何人也? 予,何人也? 有为者亦若是。'公明仪曰;[6]'文王,我师也;周公岂欺我哉?'今滕,绝长补短,[7]将五十里也,犹可认为善国。书曰:[8]'若药不瞑眩厥疾不瘳。'

【白话译文】

滕文公做太子的时侯,前往楚国路过宋国,会见了孟子。孟子和他讲了人性本是善良的道理。话题始终不离尧、舜。太子从楚国回来,又会见孟子。孟子说;"太子怀疑我的话吗? 天下的真理就这么一个呀。成覸对齐景公说:'他是个男子汉,我也是个男子汉,我为什么怕他呢?'颜渊说;'舜是什么样的人,我也是什么样的人,有作为的人也会像他那样。'公明仪说:'文王是我的老师,周公难道会欺骗我吗?'现在的滕国,取长补短,也有接近方圆五十里的土地,还可以治理成一个好国家。书经说:'那药吃了如不头晕目眩,那病是好不了的。'"

【英语译文】

Duke Wen of Teng State met Mencius in Song State on his journey to Chu State when he was crown prince. Mencius told him that human nature was originally kind. The discussing always focused on sages Yao and Shun. After returning from Chu State, he met Mencius again. Mencius asked, "Do you doubt my words? The truth in the world is just this one. Cheng Jian ever told Duke Jing of Qi State, 'He is a man, and I am a man. Why am I afraid of him?' Yan Yuan said, 'I am the kind of man what Shun was and a competent man will be also like him.' Gongming Yi said, 'King Wen of Zhou Dynasty was my teacher. Didn't Duke Zhou cheat me?' Nowadays Teng State owns an area of two hundred and fifty square kilometers and it can become a fine state. *The Book of History* says 'One's illness won't be cured if he doesn't feel dizzy after taking medicine'."

【注释】(1)世子:即"太子"。帝王或诸侯的嫡长子。在古籍中世与太以音相近常通用。(2)将之楚:前往到楚国。将,行进(向前行走)。之,往;至。(3)过宋:经过宋国。宋都彭城(今徐州市)在滕国南约二百里,是从滕国至楚国的必经之地。(4)道一而已:谓从尧、舜、文、武、周公、孔子直到孟子本人,都是从人性本善出发讲仁义道德,别无二致。(5)成覸: ~jiàn,齐国的勇臣。(6)公明仪:姓公明,名仪。曾子弟子。(7)绝长补短:计量国土纵广的用语。从长的地方截取一部分补在短的地方。(8)书曰句:瞑眩,读 miánxuàn,指用药后产生的头晕目眩的强烈反应。厥疾,读 jué ~,那种病。厥,远指代词,犹"其",可译为"那"。瘳,读 chōu ,病愈。

【原文】2 滕定公薨,[1]世子谓然友曰:[2]"昔者孟子尝与我言于宋,于心终不忘。今也不幸至于大故,[3]吾欲使子问于孟子,然后行事。[4]"然友之邹问于孟子[5],孟子曰:"不亦善乎!亲丧固所自尽也。[6]曾子曰:"生,事之以礼,死,葬之以礼,祭之以礼,可谓孝矣。[7]侯之礼,吾未之学也;虽然,吾尝闻之矣。三年之丧,齐疏之服,[8]飦粥之食,[9]自天子达于庶人,三代共之。"然友反命,[10]定为三年之丧。父兄百官皆不欲,曰:"吾宗国鲁先君莫之行,[11]吾先君亦莫之行也,至于子之身而反之,不可。且志曰:[12]'丧祭从先祖。'"曰:"吾有所受之也。"谓然友曰:"吾他日未尝学问,好驰马试剑。[13]今父兄百官不我足也,[14]恐其不能尽于大事,[15]子为我问孟子!"然友复之邹问孟子。孟子曰:"然,不可以他求者也。孔子曰:'君薨,听于冢宰,[16]歠粥,[17]面深墨,即位而哭,百官有司莫敢不哀,先之也。'[18]上有好者,下必有甚焉者矣。君子之德,风也;小人之德,草也。草尚之风,[19]必偃。[20]是在世子。"然友反命,世子曰:"然,是诚在我。"五月居庐,[21]未有命戒。[22]百官族人可,谓曰知。及至葬,四方来观之,颜色之戚,哭泣之哀,吊者大悦。

【白话译文】

滕定公去世,太子对他的师傅然友说:"过去在宋国,孟子对我谈得不少,我心中一直没忘。现在不幸父亲去世,我想请您去请问孟子,然后才办丧事。"然友到邹去问孟子。孟子说:"好啊!父亲去世,本来就该尽心竭力办丧事。曾子说:'父母在生时,依礼奉侍,去世了,依礼埋葬,依礼祭祀,这样,算是尽到孝心了。'诸侯的礼节我虽然没有学过,但也听说过。守丧三年,穿粗麻布的缝边孝衣,喝稀饭,从天子一直到老百姓,夏、商、周三代都是这样。"然友回国交差,回报了孟子的话。太子决定实行三年的丧礼。滕国的父老官吏都不愿意,说道:"我们的同宗国家历代先君没有实行过,我国历代先君更没有实行过,到你这里却来改变祖先的做法,是不可以的。而且志上说:'丧事祭事都照祖先的做法办。'"太子说:"我的做法是有传承的。"他又对然友说:"我过去未曾做过学问,只喜欢跑马练剑,现在父老官吏都对我不满,恐怕这个丧礼不能让我尽心竭力;您再为我去请问孟子吧!"然友又到邹去请问孟子。孟子说:"嗯!这种事不可以求别人。孔子说:'君主去世,太子把政务交给首相,自己喝稀饭,脸色灰暗无光,到孝子的位置上哀哭,大小官吏没有人敢不悲哀,这是因为太子带了头。'在上位的有什么爱好,在下面的人一定有更加爱好的。君子的德行,好像风;小人的德行,好像草。风向哪边吹,草向哪边倒。这件事完全决定于太子。"然友回来转述了孟子的话。太子说:"对!这件事真是应该取决于我。"

【英语译文】

Duke Ding of Teng State passed away and the crown prince told his master Ran You, "In the old days in Song State, Mencius talked much with me and I have always kept it in my mind. Now it's unfortunate that my father passed away and I want you to consult Mencius. After that, we shall conduct a funeral." Ran You went to Zou County to consult Mencius. Mencius said, "It's good. Upon father's death, the son should try his best to hold a funeral. Zeng Zi said, 'It was one's filial piety that he serves his parents when they are alive and buries them and sacrifices them according to rites after they are dead.' I have heard of princes' rites although I haven't learnt them. In Xia, Shang and Zhou dynasties, from king to common people, when one's parents were dead, he kept vigil beside the dead for three years, during which he dressed in coarse linen, and ate porridge." Ran You went back and reported to the crown prince what Mencius had said. The crown prince decided to hold funeral for three years. But people and officials in Teng State weren't willing to do like that and complained, "The passed kings of the-same-clan states didn't hold funeral for three years, and those of our state didn't do so either. But you came here and change our ancestors' conducts. It isn't right for you to do that. Furthermore, annals say, 'Funeral and sacrifice should be conducted according to what ancestors had done.'" The crown prince said, "My conduct does inherit from ancient doings." And then he said to Ran You, "In the past, I did not learn alot but loved sword and horse race. And now people and officials are not satisfied with me so that I'm afraid I can't hold the funeral with way utmost copacity. Could you please go and consult Mencius?" Once again Ran You went to Zou County to consult Mencius. Mencius replied, "You cannot depend on others when you do such kind of thing. Confucius said, 'After the king was dead the crown prince entrust administrative affairs to prime minister and he himself ate porridge and cried sadly beside the coffin in green complexion. Other ministers all cried sadly because the prince took a lead.' The subordinates love even more when the superior love anything. The virtue of the superior is like wind and that of the subordinates is like grass. The grass will bow towards the direction to which the wind blows. Therefore, this totally depends on the crown prince himself." Ran You came back and reported to him what Mencius had said. The crown prince said, "Yes, it should depend on me."

【注释】(1)滕定公:文公之父。薨:hōng,死的别称。自周代始,人之死亡有尊卑之分。"薨"以称诸侯之死。妇人之死则从夫称。《礼记·曲礼下》:"天子死曰崩,诸侯曰薨,大夫曰卒,士曰不禄,庶人曰死。"(2)然友:世子的师傅。(3)大故:重大的事故。指对国家社会或个人有重大影响的祸患,如灾害、兵寇、国丧、亲死等。(4)行事:举行丧礼;办丧事。(5)之邹:邹,孟子家乡。在今山东邹县一带。邹距滕仅四十余里,一日之内,可以往返。(6)亲丧固所自尽也:《论语·子张篇》:"曾子曰,吾闻诸夫子:人未有自致者,必也丧亲乎!"孟子所言本此。"自尽"与"自致"都有竭尽自己的心力的意思。(7)曾子曰:以下几句话是孔子的话。见《论语·为政篇》。(8)三年之丧,齐疏之服:子生三年,然后免于父母之怀。故父母之丧,必以三年。齐疏,读 zīshū ,旧时丧服名。即"齐衰"。旧时丧服(亦称孝服)用粗麻布做,下部左右的边和下边都不缝的叫"斩衰";下部左右的边和下边都缝的叫"齐疏"或"齐衰"。疏、衰即粗麻布。(9)飦粥:zhānzhōu,同"饘粥"。今称"稀饭"。(10)反命:同"复命"。完成使命后回报情况。(11)宗国:同姓诸侯国。因与天子同宗为其支庶故称。赵岐注:"滕鲁同姓,俱出文王。鲁,周公之后。滕,绣公之后。"周公封鲁行辈较长,其余姬姓诸国,均以鲁为宗国。(12)志:史家记事之书。(13)试剑:练剑;击剑。(14)不我足:"不足我"的倒装。足,满足;满意。(15)其:代词,第一人称,世子自指。尽于大事:尽,尽力。大事,指实行三年丧礼。(16)冢宰:亦称太宰。周代官名。六卿之首。后亦用于称吏部尚书。(17)歠粥:chuò zhōu,喝稀饭。(18)先之:带头。先,引导,倡导。(19)草尚之风:拿风吹草。尚,动词。增加;施加。之,介词。相当于"以"。(20)偃:yǎn,倒伏。(21)五月居庐:诸侯薨五月而葬,未葬时(长达五个月),孝子居倚庐于中门之外,非丧事不言。倚庐,古人为父母守丧时居住的简陋棚屋。(22)命戒:命令与禁令。朱熹《四书集注》:"居丧不言,故未有命令教戒也。"太子住在守丧的棚屋里五个月,不曾颁布过任何命令和禁令。官吏和族人都很赞成,认为知礼。到举行葬礼时,四方的人都来观看,太子悲戚的面容、哀痛的哭泣,来吊丧的人都被感动了。

【原文】3 滕文公问为国。孟子曰:"民事不可缓也。[1]诗云:[2]'昼尔于茅,[3]宵尔索绹;[4]亟其乘屋,[5]其始播百谷。[6]'民之为道也,[7]有恒产者有恒心,[8]无恒产者无恒心。苟无恒心,放辟邪侈,[9]无不为已。[10]及陷乎罪,然后从而刑之,是罔民也。[11]焉有仁人在位罔民而可为也?是故贤者必恭俭礼下,取于民有制。阳虎曰:[12]'为富不仁矣,为仁不富矣。'夏后氏五十而贡,[13]殷人七十而助,周人百亩而彻,其实皆什一也。彻者,彻也;助者,藉也。[14]龙子曰:'治地莫善于助,莫不善于贡。[15]'贡者挍数岁之中以为常。[16]乐岁,粒米狼戾,[17]多取之而不为虐,则寡取之;凶年,[18]粪其田而不足,[19]则必取盈焉。[20]为民父母,使民盻盻然将终岁勤动,[21]不得以养其父母,又称贷而益之,[22]使老稚转乎沟壑,恶在其为民父母也?夫世禄,[23]滕固行之矣。诗云:'雨我公田,遂及我私。[24]惟助为有公田。由此观之,虽周亦助也。设为庠序学校以教之;庠者,养也;校者,教也;序者,射也。夏曰校,殷曰序,周曰庠,学则三代共之,皆所以明人伦也。[25]人伦明于上,小民亲于下。有王者起,必来取法,是为王者师也。诗云:'周虽旧邦其命惟新[26]'文王之谓也。子力行之,亦以新子之国!"使毕战问井地。[27]孟子曰:"子之君将行仁政,选择而使子,子必勉之!夫仁政必自经界始。[28]经界不正,井地不钧,[29]谷禄不平。[30]是故暴君污吏必慢其经界。经界既正,分田制禄,可坐而定也。夫滕,壤地褊小,将为君子焉,将为野人焉。[31]无君子莫治野人,无野人莫养君子。请野九一而助,[32]国中什一使自赋。卿以下必有圭田,[33]圭田五十亩;馀夫二十五亩。[34]死徙无出乡,乡田同井,[35]出入相友,守望相助,疾病相扶持,则百姓亲睦。方里而井,[36]井九百亩,其中为公田。八家皆私百亩,同养公田;公事毕,然后敢治私事,所以别野人也。此其大略也;若夫润泽之,[37]则在君与子矣。"

【白话译文】

滕文公问孟子怎样治理国家。孟子说:"老百姓的事情是不可拖延的。《诗经》上说:'白天去把茅草割,晚上就把绳索搓。快把房屋检盖好,谷种即将全撒播。'百姓的为人道路是:有固定产业的人才有固定的心思;没有固定产业的人就没有固定的心思。只要没有固定的心思,就会胡作非为,什么事都做得出来。等到犯了罪,然后定罪惩办。这等于陷害。哪有仁人坐在朝廷上却做得出陷害老百姓的事来呢?所以贤明的君主一定要敬业节俭,对待臣子和百姓有礼节。收取民众的人力、财物要遵循一定的制度,不能随意使役,随意摊派。阳虎曾经说过,"求财富的人不顾行仁德,行仁德的人不顾求财富。"夏朝每家五十亩地而实行"贡"法,商朝每家七十亩地而实行'助'法,周朝每家一百亩地而实行'彻'法。这三种税法实际都是十分抽一。‘彻’是通的意思;对不同情况通盘计算,按十分之一收税。‘助’是‘借助’的意思;借民力助耕公田。古代一位贤人龙子说:‘田税最好的是助法,最不好的是贡法。’贡法是比较若干年的收成得出一个常数,年年按常数收税。丰年,粮食多随便堆放,难免抛撒;多收点税不为暴虐,却不多收。荒年,歉收甚至颗粒无收,收到的东西做肥料来肥田都不够用,却要按常数收足税谷。一国的君主号称是百姓的父母,却让百姓整年辛辛苦苦,到头来连自己的生身父母都养不活,还不得不借高利贷来交税;忍心看着老的小的死于荒野。这算在那里给人民当父母呢?在滕国,实行贵族世代享有爵禄。周朝的一篇诗说:‘好雨先下公田里,然后下到我私田。’这样看来,就是周朝,也实行助法。”解决了人民的吃饭问题,就得兴办“庠”“序”“学”“校”来教育他们。“庠”是教养的意思,“校”是教导的意思,“序”是习射的意思,地方学校夏朝叫“校”,商朝叫“序”,周朝叫“庠”。至于大学三个朝代都叫“学”。这些学校都是为了阐明伦理道德而设立的。在上位的人都明白而且遵守伦理道德,老百姓也会和睦亲爱。若有圣王兴起,一定会来学习仿效。这样,滕国便是圣王的老师了。诗经又说:‘岐周虽是旧邦国,国运日新盛事多。’这是赞美文王的诗。要努力做好政事,也使你的国运日新,盛事多吧!”滕文公派毕战向孟子问井田制。孟子说:“你的国君准备实行仁政,经过选择而使用了你,你一定要好好干!实行仁政,一定要从划分和整理田界开始。田界不正确,井田的大小就不均匀,作为俸禄的田租收入也就不会公平合理。所以暴君和贪官污吏一定要打乱田界。田界正确了,人民土地的分配和官吏俸禄的制定处理,就不会受挫而顺利完成了。滕国土地狭小,又有官吏,又有人民。没有官吏,便没有人管理人民;没有人民,便没有人养活官吏。我建议郊野用九分抽一的助法;城市用十分抽一的贡法。公卿以下的官吏一定要有供祭祀用的圭田,每家五十亩,有剩余劳动力的给二十五亩。死亡和搬家,都不离开本乡。同一井田的各家,互相友好来往,互相照看家园,生了疾病互相扶持,这样百姓就普遍和睦成为风俗。每一平方里土地成为一井,每一井九百亩,在当中的一百亩为公田,在外边的八百亩,八家各自拥有一百亩,叫作私田。八家共同种好公田,先公后私,公事未完,不得丢开公事干私事,所以区分了官吏与野人。这不过是一个大概,至于怎么去落实完善,那就在于你的国君和你本人了。”

【英语译文】

Duke Wen of Teng State asked Mencius how to govern a state. Mencius said, “Common people’s things cannot be delayed. *The Book of Songs* says, ‘In daytime we are to cut cogongrasses. At night we make ropes through weaving them. We are hurry to fix the broken roofs. Right away we'll sow different seeds.' Common people have their way of being: One will have perseverance if he has fixed property, but one won't have perseverance if he doesn't have fixed property. They will do anything at their will if they don't have perseverance. When they commit crime they will be sentenced and punished. That equalizes making a false charge against them. Isn't there any humanistic man who sits at the court and does things which make a false charge against common people? Therefore a wise monarch should be devoted to his work and be shrift, he should respect his ministers and subjects according to rites. When he gathers money and wealth from his subjectshe, he should obey regulations. He should not use labor and charge arbitrarily. Yang Hu ever said, 'People who run after wealth never care about virtue and humanity, and people who run after virtue and humanity never care about wealth.' In Xia Dynasty, 'law of tribute' was carried out when each family owned field of fifty *mu*; in Shang Dynasty, 'law of assistance' was carried out when each family owned field of seventy *mu*; and in Zhou Dynasty, 'law of thoroughness' was carried out when each family owned field of one hundred *mu*. In the three method, speople were taxed one tenth. 'Thoroughness' means calculating throughout and taxing one tenth. 'Assistance' means people assist each other to plow the public fields. An ancient sage Long Zi said: The best method is 'law of assistance', and the worst one is 'law of tribute'. 'Law of tribute' is the way where a constant is calculated based on usual harvest and people will be taxed according to the constant. In a bumper harvest year, excessive grains are piled casually, much of which are wasted. It isn't brutal if people are taxed more than usual but they are not. In a famine year, less, even none grain are harvested, and what have been collected aren't enough used as manure. However people will taxed according to the constant. A monarch of a state boasts to be parent of his subjects and makes his people toil for a whole year but cannot keep their parents alive and have to borrow things to pay tax. Their elder and younger family members starve to death in valley. Isn't the monarch the parent of his subjects? In Teng State, generations of aristocrats inherit salaries. *The Book of Songs* says 'Shared fields become very wet. My private ones are watery yet.' From this we can see that in Zhou Dynasty 'law of assistance' was carried out. When common people have food to eat, then *xiang*, *xu* ,*xue* and *xiao* can be set up to educated them. *xiang* means cultivating, *xiao* means educating, *xu* means archery, and local school in Xia Dynasty was called '*xiao*', in Shang Dynasty it was called '*xu*', and in Zhou Dynasty it was called '*xiang*'. The name of great learning was *xue* in three dynasties. All these institutes were all set up to elaborate ethics. The rulers were aware of abiding ethics and common people liked to live harmoniously. If there appears a sage king, he will surely to follow these things. Thus Teng State will become the teacher of the sage king. *The Book of Songs* says again, 'Though Zhou Kingdom is old state, nowadays it's empowered to be a new one.' This was a poem praising King Wen of Zhou Dynasty. You should try your best to govern state in which new things increasingly take place." Duke Teng sent Bi Zhan to consult Mencius about the square-fields system. Mencius said, "Your monarch was ready to carry out government of humanity and Heaven selected you, so you should do utmost. You should begin with dividing field and settling field border when you carry out government of humanity. If the field borders aren't right, then the size of square-fields isn't equal and the income of field tax which is the salary won't be fair. Therefore, the tyrant and the corrupted officials like to make field border in disorder. When the field border is set right, the division of field and salary arrangement will be completed smoothly. Teng State owns a small land area and in it there are officials and common people. If there aren't officials then nobody can administrate people but if there aren't common people then nobody can keep officials alive. I suggest that in suburb the ratio of tax can be one ninth; and in town it can be one tenth. Officials under the rank of ministers must be given fifty *mu* field used for sacrificing and twenty-five *mu* field be given to those families in which there are surplus labors. When people die or are remokede they should not leave their original hometown. Every family living in the same square-fields communicate friendly and look after houses for each other. When someone is ill they support him. Thus it will become a custom for people to live harmoniously. Every square *li* becomes a square-field, nine hundred mu, among which one hundred *mu* in the middle is the public field. And for the periphery eight hundred *mu*, each of the eight households owns one hundred *mu* which is called private field. People in the eight households first farm the public field and then farm their own private field. When public farming hasn't been finished, they cannot farm their own field. Thus you can differentiate officials and selfish man. This is just a general conception. As for implementation, it depends upon your king and yourself."

【注释】(1)民事:犹国政,指农事,民间生活之事。(2)诗云:见《诗·豳风·七月》。(3)昼尔于茅:昼,白天。尔,语助词。于,取。茅,草名。禾本科。(4)宵尔索绹:宵,夜晚。索,动词。铰合使紧;搓。绹,读 tāo,绳索。(5)亟其乘屋:亟,同“急”。赶快。其,语助词。乘屋,指修盖屋顶。(6)其始播百谷:其始,将要开始。播,播种。百谷,谷物的总称。各种谷。(7)民之为道:百姓的生活趋向;百姓的为人道路。(8)有恒产者有恒心:恒产,指土地、田园、房屋等不动产。恒心,常存的善心。(9)放辟邪侈:肆意为非作歹。(10)无不为已:语气词。表确定语气,相当于“了”;表肯定而带感叹语气,相当于“啊”。(11)罔民:欺骗陷害百姓。(12)阳虎:字货。鲁国正卿季氏的总管。事迹参见《论语》。(13)夏后氏:夏后氏,指禹受舜禅而建立的夏王朝。也称“夏氏”“夏后”。五十而贡:夏时一夫授田五十亩,而每夫计其五亩之入以为贡。(14)殷人……藉也:殷人始为井田之制,以六百三十亩之地,划为九区区七十亩。中为公田,其外八家各授一区,但借其力以助耕公田,而不复税其私田。周时一夫授田百亩。乡遂用贡法,十夫有沟;都鄙用助法八家同井。耕则通力而作,收则计亩而分故谓之彻。其实皆什一者,贡法固以十分之一为常数,惟助法乃九一,而商制不可考。周制则公田百亩中以二十亩为庐舍一夫所耕公田实计十亩。通私填百亩,为十一分而取其一,盖又轻于什一也。窃料商制亦当似此,而以十四亩为庐舍,一夫实耕公田七亩,是亦不过什一也。彻,通也,均也。藉,借也。(以上见朱熹《四书集注》。)(15)龙子:上古之贤人。治地:谓管理土地的赋税。(16)挍:jiào,同“校”。比较。(17)粒米狼戾:谷粒撒得满地都是,粮食散乱堆放。形容丰年粮食充盈。(18)凶年:荒年。(19)粪其田而不足:谓荒年田中歉收,甚至颗粒无收,将其秸秆作为肥料肥田还不够用。粪,肥料;肥田,施肥。(20)则必取盈焉:则,转折连词,却,上句的“则”同此。焉,代词,指谷物。(21)盻盻:xìxì,勤苦不歇的样子。将,连词。相当于“而”。勤动:辛勤劳动。(22)称贷:即“举债”。贷款与人;向人请求贷款。(23)世禄:指古代的世禄制。贵族世代享有爵禄。(24)雨我公田,遂及我私:见诗·小雅·大田。雨,读 yù,降雨。遂,副词。于是;随着;就。及,到。(25)人伦:人与人之间的正当关系。(26)其命惟新:见《诗·大雅·文王》。其命,指周的国运。惟新,更新,新进。(27)毕战:滕国大夫。井地:即井田。(28)经界:土地、疆域的分界。(29)钧:通“均”。相同,相等,均衡,均匀。(30)谷禄:即“俸禄”。古代以谷量计俸禄的高下。(31)将为君子焉,将为野人焉:两个“将”同义。连词,表并列;相当于“又”。两个“为”同义,内动词,训“有”。君子,指从政为官的人。野人,指劳动生产的人。两个“焉”同义。语气助词。用在陈述句末表表论断决断或终结语气,一般去掉不译。有时也可译作“呢”“的”。(32)请野九一而助:请,敬辞,训“建议”。野,郊野;边远地方。(33)圭田:古代天子所赐卿、大夫、士供祭祀用的田地。圭,洁,因以养廉,故称。(34)馀夫:古代谓法定的受田人口之外的人。赵岐注:“馀夫者,一家一人受田,其余老小尚有余力者,受二十五亩,半于圭田,谓之馀夫也。”(35)乡田:古谓同井田的各家。(36)方里:一里见方。指长宽各一里的面积。(37)润泽:润色修饰。训“落实完善”。

【原文】4 有为神农之言者许行,[1]自楚之滕,踵门而告文公曰:[2]“远方之人闻君行仁政,愿受一廛而为之氓。[3]”文公与之处。[4]其徒数十人,皆衣褐,[5]捆屦、织席以为食。[6]陈良之徒陈相与其弟辛,[7]负耒耜自宋之滕曰:[8]“闻君行圣人之政,是亦圣人也,愿为圣人氓。”陈相见许行而大悦,尽弃其学而学焉。[9]陈相见孟子,道许行之言曰:[10]“滕君则诚贤君也;虽然,未闻道也。贤者与民并耕而食,饔飧而治。[11]今也滕有仓廪府库,则是厉民而以自养也,[12]恶得贤?”孟子曰:“许子必种粟而后食乎?”曰:“然。”“许子必织布而后衣乎?”曰:“否,许子衣褐。”“许子冠乎?”曰:“冠。”曰:“奚冠?”曰:“冠素。”曰:“自织之与?”曰:“否;以粟易之。”曰:“许子奚为不自织?曰:“害于耕。[13]”曰:“许子以釜甑爨,以铁耕乎?[14]”曰:“然。”“自为之与?”曰:“否;以粟易之。”“以粟易械器者不为厉陶冶;[15]陶冶亦以其械器易粟者,岂为厉农夫哉?且许子何不为陶冶,舍皆取诸其宫中而用之?[16]何为纷纷然与百工交易?何许子之不惮烦?”曰:“百工之事固不可耕且为也”“然则治天下独可耕且为与?有大人之事,[17]有小人之事。且一人之身,[18]而百工之所备;如必自为而后用之,是率天下而路也。[19]故曰或劳心或劳力;劳心者治人,劳力者治于人;治于人者食人,治人者食于人,天下之通义也。[20]当尧之时天下犹未平,洪水横流 ,泛滥于天下,草木畅茂,禽兽繁殖,五谷不登,[21]禽兽偪人,兽蹄鸟迹之道交于中国。[22]尧独忧之,举舜而敷治焉。[23]舜使益掌火,[24]益烈山泽而焚之,[25]禽兽逃匿。禹疏九河,[26]瀹济漯而注诸海,[27]决汝汉,排淮泗而注之江,[28]然后中国可得而食也,当是时也,禹八年于外,三过其门而不入,虽欲耕得乎?后稷教民稼穑,[29]树艺五谷;[30]五谷熟而民人育。[31]人之有道也,[32]饱食、暖衣、逸居而无教,则近于禽兽。圣人有忧之,使契为司徒,[33]教以人伦:父子有亲,君臣有义,夫妇有别,长幼有序,朋友有信。放勋曰:[34]劳之来之,匡之直之,辅之翼之,使自得之,又从而振德之。’圣人之忧民如此,而暇耕乎?尧以不得舜为己忧,舜以不得禹、皋陶为己忧。夫以百亩之不易为己忧者,农夫也。分人以财谓之惠,教人以善谓之忠,为天下得人者谓之仁。[35]‘是故以天下与人易,为天下得人难。孔子曰:‘大哉尧之为君!惟天为大,惟尧则之[36],荡荡乎民无能名焉![37]君哉舜也!巍巍乎有天下而不与焉![38]’尧、舜之治天下,岂无所用其心哉?亦不用于耕耳。[39]”吾闻用夏变夷者,未闻变于夷者也。[40]陈良,楚产也,[41]悦周公、仲尼之道,北学于中国。北方之学者,未能或之先也。[42]彼所谓豪杰之士也。子之兄弟事之数十年,师死而遂倍之![43]昔者孔子没,三年之外,门人治任将归,[44]人揖于子贡,相向而哭,皆失声,然后归。子贡反,筑室于场,[45]独居三年,然后归。他日,子夏、子张、子游以有若似圣人,欲以所事孔子事之,强曾子。[46]曾子曰:'不可;江汉以濯之,秋阳以暴之,[47]皜皜乎不可尚已。[48]'今也南蛮鴃舌之人[49],非先王之道,子倍子之师而学之,亦异于曾子矣。吾闻出于幽谷迁于乔木者,[50]未闻下乔木而入于幽谷者。鲁颂曰:'戎狄是膺,[51]荆舒是惩。[52]'周公方且膺之,子是之学,亦为不善变矣。[53]""从许子之道,则市贾不贰,[54]国中无伪;虽使五尺之童适市,莫之或欺,布帛长短同,则贾相若;麻缕丝絮轻重同,则贾相若;五谷多寡同,则贾相若;屦大小同,则贾相若。[55]"曰:"夫物之不齐,物之情也;或相倍蓰,或相什百,或相千万。子比而同之,[56]是乱天下也。巨屦小屦同贾,[57]人岂为之哉?从许子之道,相率而为伪者也,恶能治国家?"

【白话译文】

有个推衍神农言论的人叫许行,从楚国来到滕国,登门谒见滕文公。他告诉道:"我是远方的人,听说您实行仁政,希望能得到一个住处,来做您的百姓。"文公给了他住房。他的徒弟好几十个,都穿粗麻布衣,靠打草鞋、织席子求生活。陈良的徒弟陈相和弟弟陈辛背着农具,从宋国来到滕国,对文公说:"听说您实行圣人的政治,您也就是圣人了,我们愿意做圣人的百姓。"陈相见了许行,十分高兴,就全丢了自己学得的东西来向许行学习。陈相来看孟子,口里讲着许行的话:"滕君确实是贤明的君主,不过,他还不懂治国大道。贤人要和人民一道耕种,然后吃饭;自己做饭兼治民事。如今滕国有储粮的谷仓,有藏财物的府库,这都是损害别人来奉养自己,怎能叫贤明呢?"孟子说:"许子一定自己种粮食吃吗?"陈相说:"对。""许子一定自己织布做衣裳吗?""不,许子只穿粗麻布衣。""许子戴帽子吗?""戴帽子。""什么帽子?""白绸帽子。""是自己织的吗?""不,用粮食换来的。"孟子说:"为什么不自己织呢?"陈相说:"因为妨碍做农活。""许子用锅甑做饭、用铁器耕田吗?""用。""这些器具都是自己做的吗?""不,都是用粮食换来的。"孟子说:"农夫用粮食换取厨具和农具不能说损害了工匠,那工匠用产品换取粮食能说损害了农夫吗?况且许子为何不当工匠留在家里制作工具、用具供自己使用?为何忙着同各种工匠进行交换?为何许子这样不怕麻烦?"陈相说:"本来就不可能一边种田一边干各种工匠的事。"孟子说:"难道治理天下就能一边种田一边干?有官吏的事,有小民的事。一个人的一辈子,各种工匠都在为他提供产品。如果各种东西都要自己制造才能用,就是率领天下的人疲于奔命,世风衰落。所以说,有的人劳动脑力,有的人劳动体力;劳动脑力的管理人,劳动体力的接受管理。受管理的人养活人,管理人的人受人养活。这是天下的普遍事情。当尧在位时，天下还未平息。洪水成灾，泛滥天下，草木茂密生长，鸟兽成群繁殖。谷物没有收成。飞禽走兽威逼人类，到处都是它们的脚印。尧一个人为天下大事忧虑，于是把舜提拔起来展开治理。舜命令伯益主持火政。伯益把山野沼泽的草木全部烧掉，迫使鸟兽逃跑隐匿。禹疏浚九河，把济水、漯水疏导入海，挖掘汝水、汉水，疏通淮水、泗水，让更多的横流注入长江，这样中国就可以耕种了，人民也才有了饭吃。在这一时期，禹八年在外，好几次经过自己的家门都没进去。即使想亲自耕种，可能吗？后稷教民种庄稼，栽培各种谷物；谷物成熟了，人民就能养育身体了。在人生道路上，只是吃饱、穿暖、居住安逸，却没有教养，那就和禽兽没有区别了。圣人为这种情况很担忧，便让契任司徒官职，主管教育。用人间应有正常关系的大道理来教育人民：父子间有骨肉之亲，君臣间有礼义之道，夫妻间有内外之别，老少间有尊卑之序，朋友间有诚信之德。尧说：‘对勤劳的人与亲附的人要慰问敬重，对有失偏颇的人要纠错扶正。对有所不足的人要帮助提携，要让人人都懂得理性，然后表扬鼓励他们的善行。’圣人为百姓考虑，这样呕心沥血，还有空来耕种吗？尧以得不到舜这样的人而忧虑，舜以得不到禹和皋陶这样的人而忧虑。为自己的百亩田地耕种不好而忧虑的，是农夫。把自己的钱财分给别人的行为，叫作惠；教人行善的行为叫作忠。为天下找到好人才的行为叫作仁。因此把天下让给人家比较容易做到，为天下找到好人才却很难。孔子说：‘尧作为天子真是伟大！只有天最伟大，也只有尧能效法天。尧的圣德广阔无边，老百姓找不到恰当的言辞来形容他！舜也是个好天子，声望崇高如泰山，他却从不享受天子的福威！’尧、舜治理天下，难道不用心思吗？只是不把心思用在自己怎么种庄稼上罢了。我只听说过用华夏的先进去改变少数民族的滞后，没听说过由先进变为滞后的。陈良，出生于楚国，却喜欢周公、孔子的学说，北上中国学习，北方的读书人，还没有超过他的，他是所谓豪杰之士啊！你们兄弟拜他为师，学习了几十年，他一死你们竟背叛了老师！从前，孔子死了，门徒守孝三年后，收拾行李准备回去时，走进子贡住处作揖告别，相对哭泣失声，最后才离开。子贡又回到墓地，重新筑屋，又独自守墓三年，然后回家。过了些时间，子夏、子张、子游以有若像圣人，便想象服侍孔子那样服侍他，勉强曾子同意。曾子说：‘不可以这样；比如曾经用江、汉之水洗涤过，在烈日下曝晒过，真是白得不能再白了。谁可比于夫子？’如今南方来的蛮子，说话如鸟叫，也敢来非议我们祖先圣王之道，而你们却违背师道去向他学习，这就和曾子的态度恰好相反了。我只听说过小鸟飞出幽暗的深谷，搬到高大的树木，没听说过飞下高大的树木进入幽暗的深谷。《诗经·鲁颂·閟宫》说：‘打击西戎和北狄，惩罚楚、舒不迟疑。’蛮邦过分了，周公也要攻击它。你却向它学习，真是不学好而学坏。”陈相说：“如果照许子说的办，市场上的价格就能一致,国中没有欺诈,即使让小孩子上市场去,也没有人来欺骗他。布匹丝绸的长短相同,价钱就一样;麻线丝绵的轻重同,价钱就一样;谷米的多少同,价钱就一样;鞋的大小同,价钱就一样。"孟子说:"各种物品质量不一样,这是自然物的实在情况。有的相差一至五倍,有的相差十至百倍,有的相差千至万倍。你不分质地但就形体勉强比成相同,简直扰乱天下,不分优劣,大鞋小鞋价钱相同,人们能持续干下去吗?照许子说的办,是引领大家走向虚伪,哪里能治理国家?"

【英语译文】

Xu Hang who spread the thought of the School of Agriculturist came to Teng State from the place of Chu State, and he visited Duke Wen of Teng State, saying, "I am a person from distant place. And I want to obtain a dwelling place and become your subject after I have heard that you're carrying out government of humanity." Duke Wen gave him a set of rooms. He had dozens of disciples who all wore coarse linen clothes and made a living by weaving grass shoes and mats. Chen Liang's disciple, Chen Xiang, and his younger brother Chen Xin came to Teng State from the place of Chu State with farming tools on their shoulders. They said to Duke Wen of Teng State, "We have heard that you're carrying sage's government and you are always a sage. We are willing to become subjects of a sage." Chen Xiang was very happy after he met Xu Hang and he dropped what he had learnt and began to learn from Xu Hang. Chen Xiang went to visit Mencius and repeated Xu Hang's words, "Duke Teng is really a wise monarch but he doesn't know about the great way of governing a country. A person of virtue should farm together with other people and then have meal. He should cook himself and at the same time deal with civil affairs. Nowadays, in Teng State there are barns for storing grain and warehouses for keeping wealth. These are collected by harming others and used for keeping himself alive. How could he be a king of virtue ?" Mencius asked, "Do you produce grain yourself?" "Yes." "You weave clothes yourself?" "No. I just wear coarse linen clothes." "Do you wear hat?" "Yes." "What kind of hat?" "White silk hat." "Is it woven by yourself?" "No, it is exchanged with grain." Mencius asked, "Why don't you weave it yourself?" Chen Xiang answered, "Because that will hinder farm work." "Do you use kitchen utensil to cook, and do you use tools to do farm work?" "Yes, I do." "Are these utensil and tools made with yourself?" "No, they are exchanged with grain." Mencius said, "Peasants exchange these tools with grain and we cannot say they've done harm to craftsmen. And can we say craftsmen have done harm to peasants if they exchange grain with tools? Furthermore, why don't you stay at home and make tools for your own use? Why are you busy exchanging things with different craftsmen? Why aren't you afraid of so much trouble?" Chen Xiang said, "It's impossible for somebody to do farm work and crafts work at the same time." Mencius asked, "Isn't it possible for you to do farm work and govern a state at the same time? There are affairs of officials and those of ordinary people. In life time of a person, different craftsmen provide him different products. If all the products must be made by himself, then all people will be busy doing these things and folk custom will be declineed. Therefore some people make their mind work and others make their bodies work. Those who work mind govern other people and those who work bodies are governed by others. Those governed by others raise people and those govern other people are raised by other people, which is an identical law in the world. When the sage Yao was in power, the world wasn't peaceful. There were great and disastrous floods and dense forests where birds and beasts multiplied terribly. People couldn't harvest grain. Birds and beasts threatened mankind leaving prints everywhere. Yao worried very much about this situation, and then he promoted Shun and assigned him tasks to administrate these affairs. Shun ordered Bo Yi to be in charge of fire. Bo Yi burned down dense woods in mountains and swamps, and birds and beast all fled and hid themselveselsewhere. Shun dredged the nine rivers, and he led Ji River and Luo River run towards the sea; he dug Ru and Han rivers; he dredged Huai and Si rivers so that more tributary rivers connected with the Changjiang River. People had more land to toil for growing grain and they could have food to eat. During this period Yu worked in strange places and he passed by his home eight times but never went into it. Could he do farm work even if he wanted to? Hou Ji taught people to grow various crops and grains. When they ripen, people could eat them to be alive. During one's lifetime, if he just eats food, wears clothes, and lives in house comfortably but has no cultivation, then he has no difference from birds and beasts. Sages were worried about the situation and assigned Qi to be schooling head in charge of education. He used the great principle of interpersonal relationship to educate common people: clan intimacy between father and son, ritual law between king and minister, difference between husband and wife, gradable order between the elder and the youth, faithful virtue among friends. Sage Yao said, 'Those diligent men and adherents should be respected, those one-minded men should be corrected, and the men having drawbacks should be helped so that everyone could understand ration. Their kind actions should be praised and encouraged.' The sages made painstaking efforts to worry about common people. Did they have any time to do farm work? Yao became worried when he didn't get Shun, and Shun became worried when he didn't get Yu and Gao Yao. It is a peasant who worries about not farming well his one hundred *mu* field. It is called benefit that somebody gives his money to others; it is called royalty that somebody tells others to act kindly; it is called humanity that somebody looks for talents. Therefore, it's easy to hand over one's land to others but it's hard to look for talents. Confucius said, 'As the Son of Heaven, Yao was really great. Only the Heaven; is the greatest and only Yao could follow the example of the Heaven. Yao was also a good Son of the Heaven and his fame was as noble as Taishan Mountain. However, he never shared his blessing and mightact act as the Son of the Heaven.' When Yao and Shun governed the country, didn't they make use of their intelligence? They only didn't do that to grow crops. I have heard that progress of Huaxia Ethnic Group was used to change backwards minorities but not that progress changed into backwards. Chen Liang was born in Chu State but loved the learning of Duke Zhou and Confucius. He went north to study these learning and none of scholars in the north surpassed him. He could be called a man of heroism. You two regarded him as your teacher and learned from him for decades but you betrayed him after his death. In the old day, after Confucius' death, his disciples observed mourning for three years. When they were to go home by carrying baggage, they went into Zi Gong's room, hugged each other, cried and bade farewell. Zi Gong went back to Confucius' tomb and put up a thatch in which he observed mourning for another three years. After that he went his hometown. After a while, Zi Xia, Zi Zhang and Zi You thought You Ruo was like a sage and they wanted to serve him like Confucius. They went to persuade Zeng Zi. Zeng Zi said, 'We cannot do like that. For example, something was washed by water from Changjiang and Hanshui, and then it was shone under scorching sun. It became no more white. Who could be compared with the Master?' Nowadays barbarian from the south speaks like bird tittering and reproaches the Way of our ancestors and sages but you decide to betray your master and learn from Xu Hang. It is just the opposite to Zeng Zi's attitude. I have only heard that little birds fly from dark valley to big trees but I never heard any birds fly from big trees to dark valley. *Closed Temple*, *Ode of Lu State* in *The Book of Songs* says 'They fought against enemies in frontiers. They punished foes in Jin and Chu States.' If minority states did things excessively Duke Zhou would attack them. You learn from them, and you really learn from the evil not from the good." Chen Xiang said, "If we do things according to what Xu Hang had said, then the price of goods in the fair would be identical. Thus there will be no cheat in the state. Even when a child purchases goods no one will deceive him. The price will be the same if the length of cloth and silk is the same. The price will be the same if the weight of linen cotton and silk wadding is the same. The price will be the same if the quantity of corn and grain is the same. The price will be the same if the size of all shoes is the same." Mencius said, "It is natural that different articles have different quality. Some differentiate one to five times; some differentiate ten to one hundred times, and some even differentiate one thousand to ten thousand times. You are making the world in disorder when you set the same price without considering their different quality. If you give small shoes and big shoes the same price without seeing their superiority or inferiority, who is able to continue doing their jobs? According to what Xu Hang said, the whole country is directed to hypocrisy. How could the country be governed orderly?"

【注释】(1)为神农之言者许行:为,学习。神农,太古帝王名。开始教民为耒耜务农业,故称神农氏。战国时期,反应农业生产和农民思想的学术派别,主张劝耕桑以足衣食。因指这一派为神农或农家;神农之言,即谓神农派的主张。许行,姓许名行。不见于其他古籍。(2)踵门:登门,上门。(3)廛:chán,指市内住宅。氓:指外地迁来的民。(4)与之处:与,给予。之,他(们)。处,处所;居住处。(5)衣褐:衣褐,读 yìhè,穿粗布衣。(6)捆屦:kǔnjù,编织单底鞋;打草鞋。织席:用芦苇、竹篾、蒲草等编织坐卧用的席子。席,席的古字。为食:交易食物。(7)陈良:楚之儒者。(8)耒耜:lěisì,古代翻土耕地的农具。耒是耒耜的柄,耜是耒耜下端起土的部分。一说:耒耜是两种农具。参阅徐中舒《耒耜考》。(9)学焉:焉,代词。指代许行。(10)道许行之言:道,转述。言,话语,言辞。(11)饔飧:yōng sūn,早饭和晚饭;做饭。饔飧而治,谓自己做饭兼治民事。(12)厉民:虐害人民。自养:自奉;自给。(13)害于耕:害,妨碍。于,语气助词。耕,种田。(14)以釜甑爨,以铁耕乎:釜,读 fǔ,古炊器,敛口,圆底,或有二耳。其用如鬲,置于灶口,上置甑以蒸煮,甑,读 zèng,蒸食炊具。其底有孔,古用陶制,殷周时代有用青铜制,后多用木制。俗叫甑子。爨,读 cuàn,烧火煮饭,也泛指烧煮。(15)以铁耕乎:铁,铁中而用之:舍,读 shě,停留;止息。皆,指一切陶器、铁器。诸,介词,和"于"相同。(16)宫:古代对房屋居室的通称;秦汉以来特指帝王之宫。(17)大人:与"君子"之义相近,有时偏指有德者,有时偏指在位者,这里便是后者。(18)一人之身:谓人的毕生,一辈子。(19)路:通“露”,衰败;疲惫;裸露。(20)通义:普遍适用的道理与法则。(21)登:成熟;丰收。(22)偪:bī,同“逼”逼迫;威胁。兽蹄鸟迹之道:禽兽的走道。中国:泛指华夏大地。(23)敷治:治理。(24)掌火:主管用火;管火政。(25)烈山泽:烈,猛火。山泽,山林和川泽。(26)九河:禹时黄河的九条支流:徒骇、太史、马颊、覆釜、胡苏、简、洁、钩盘、鬲津。(27)瀹济漯:瀹,读 yuè,疏通水道;亦泛指疏导。济,读 jǐ,古水名。四渎之一。(28)决汝汉,排淮泗而注之江:决、排,皆去其壅塞之意。汝、汉、淮、泗皆水名。汝、泗入淮,淮自入海,只汉水入江。记者有误。(29)后稷:名弃,周人的始祖,帝尧时为农师。(30)树艺:种植,栽培。五谷:五种谷物。古籍中所指不一。赵岐注:“五谷为稻(水稻)、黍(黄米之黏者)、稷(小米)、麦(小麦)、菽(豆类)。”(31)民人:同“人民”“百姓”。育:育养,育养。(32)人之有道也:之,结构助词。有,动词,相当于“为”。人之有道也,即人之为道也。犹言“(人)在为人的道路上”或“(人)在人生道路上”。(33)契:xiè,殷的祖先。司徒:少昊时官名。唐虞以后因之。周时为六卿之一。(34)放勋:亦作放勛。帝尧之名。(35)得人:得到德才兼备的人。亦谓用人得当。(36)惟天、惟尧、则之:二“惟”,皆副词。“只有”“只是”。则,动词。仿效。之,代词。指代“天”。(37)荡荡:广大、博大、宽广的样子。与下文“巍巍”的崇高伟大同样是用来形容道德崇高,恩泽深广。名焉:名,动词。形容;称说。焉,代词。同“之”,指代“尧”。(38)巍巍乎有天下而不与焉:巍巍,参见前注(37)。有天下,治理天下。与,读 yù,在其中;喜悦;取乐。不与焉,谓不以居高位自我享受。(39)亦:副词,仅仅,只是。(40)变于:变为。夷:我国古代中原地区华夏族对东部各族的总称;亦泛称中原以外的各族。(41)楚产:出生于楚,楚地出生。(42)未能或之先也:“或未能先之也”的倒装。谓(北方的读书人)还没有谁超过他。(43)倍:通“背”,背叛,背弃。(44)治任:整理行装。(45)场:祭坛旁的平地。赵岐注:“场,孔子冢上祭祀坛场也。”(46)所事孔子,强:所事孔子,服侍孔子的礼节。强,读 qiǎng,勉强。使人做不愿做的事。(47)秋阳:烈日,炎热的太阳。(48)皜皜:hàohào,同“皓皓”。洁白的样子;高洁的样子。尚:增加,超过。已:语气词,相当于“了”“啊”。(49)南蛮鴃舌:旧时讥人操难懂的南方方言。南蛮,旧时指南方少数民族。鴃舌,读 jué shé,伯劳弄舌啼聒,比喻语言难懂。(50)出于幽谷迁于乔木者:引自《诗经·小雅·伐木》。是说小鸟从幽暗的深谷里飞出来迁住在高大的树木上。(51)戎狄是膺:此句和下句,引自《诗经·鲁颂·閟宫》。戎,西戎。狄,北狄。膺:伐,击。(52)荆舒是惩:参见前解。荆,楚的旧称。舒,楚的蜀国,在今安徽庐江县。惩:惩罚,处罚。(53)子是之学:子,你。是,认为正确;肯定。之学,这个学派(或学说)。

亦为,确实是。不善变矣,不变为善了。(54)市贾:~jià,同"市价"。市场价格。不贰:同"不二"。无差异,相同。(55)五尺之童:指尚未成年的儿童。古尺短,故称。周尺准今八寸,五尺合今四尺。又,古以两岁半为一尺,五尺,是十二岁半。十五岁则称六尺。适市:到市场去。适,往,去。(56)比:比附。把相差很远的东西拉来勉强相比。而同之:相同看待。(57)巨履小履同贾:大鞋、小鞋价钱相同。

【原文】5 墨者夷之因徐辟而求见孟子。[1]孟子曰:"吾固愿见,今吾尚病,病愈我且往见,[2]夷之不来!"他日,又求见孟子。孟子曰:"吾今则可以见矣。不直,[3]则道不见;[4]我且直之。吾闻夷之墨者,墨之治丧也,以薄为其道也;[5]夷子,[6]岂以为非是而不贵也;[7]然而夷子葬其亲厚,则是以所贱事亲也。"徐子以告夷子。夷子曰:"儒者之道,古之人若保赤子,[8]此言何谓也?之则以为爱无差等,施由亲始。[9]徐子以告孟子。孟子曰:"夫夷子信以为人之亲其兄之子若亲其邻之赤子乎?彼有取尔也。赤子匍匐将入井,非赤子之罪也。且天之生物也,使之一本,[10]而夷子二本故也。盖上世有不葬其亲者,[11]其亲死则举而委之于壑。[12]他日过之,狐狸食之,蝇蚋姑嘬之。[13]其颡有泚,[14]睨而不视。[15]夫泚也非为人泚,中心达于面目。[16]掩之诚是也,则孝子仁人之掩其亲亦必有道矣。"徐子以告夷子。夷子怃然为间曰:[17]"命之矣。[18]"

【白话译文】

墨家信徒夷之靠与徐辟的关系求见孟子。孟子说:"我本来愿意见他,可是现在病还没好,等病好了,我去看他吧,他不必来!"过了一段时间,夷之又求见孟子。孟子说:"现在可以见他了。但是不说直话,思想或主张就不能显现。我就说直话吧。我听说夷子是墨家信徒,墨家办理丧事,主张薄葬;夷子想以此改变天下的风俗。也许他以为不这样不为尊贵;然而他把父母亲的丧事办得很丰厚,这样他便是拿他所轻贱的事来对待父母亲了。"徐子把孟子的话转告夷子。夷子说:"儒家的学说认为,古代的君王爱护百姓就像爱护婴儿一样。这话是什么意思呢?我以为便是人们之间的爱没有亲疏厚薄之分,只是从双亲开始罢了。"徐子又把这话告诉孟子。孟子说:"夷子真正以为人们爱他的侄儿和爱她邻居的婴儿一样吗?夷子只抓住了一点:婴儿在地上爬行快要跌到井里去了,这不是婴儿的罪过。人们看见了都会去救。夷子以为这就是爱无等次。而且,天下的每个动植物,都只有一个根源生出它。人的生身父母只有一对。夷子却认为有两个根源,他和我所以不同。远古时,曾有不埋葬父母的人,父母死了就抬出去丢到山沟里。过了一段时间,发现狐狸在撕咬尸体,苍蝇和蚊子在叮咬尸体,他额头上冒汗,斜着眼睛不忍正视。额头上冒汗,不是给人看的,而是内心的悔恨和愧疚蒸发到了脸面。他回到抛尸地,用铲子和土筐掩埋了尸体。掩埋尸体,固然是对的。那么,孝子仁人的埋葬父母也必定有道理了。"徐子把这话转达给夷子,夷子怅惘地待了一会儿,说:"我得到教诲了。"

【英语译文】

An adherent to Moist, Yi Zhi requested to visit Mencius by means of his relation with Xu Bi, a disciple of Mencius. Mencius said, "I wanted to see him but I'm ill now. I'll go to see him after my recovery and he needn't come here." After a while Yi Zhi wanted to visit Mencius again. Mencius said, "I can see him now. But if I don't express myself directly, then my idea cannot be shown explicitly, so I will express myself straightforward. I've heard that Yi Zhi is an adherent to Moist who hold shrift funeral when they arrange funeral. Yi Zhi wants to change the custom and perhaps he thinks it isn't respectful to hold shrift funeral. And he arranged his parents funeral elaborately, therefore he has done a thing which he disdains his parents." Xu Bi reported to Yi Zhi what Mencius had said. Yi Zhi said, "Confucianism holds that kings in ancient time protected their subjects just as babies. What does it mean? In my opinion, it means that we love people without differing intimacy, isolation, nobility or humbleness. And we begin loving our parents." Xu Bi reported to Mencius what Yi Zhi had said. Mencius said, "Does Yi Zhi really think that someone loves his nephew just like other babies? Yi Zhi has seen one point: a baby is to fall into a well while he is crawling on ground and it isn't his fault. Each person will save him while noticing this. Yi Zhi thought this is non-gradable love. Plant and animal in the world originates from one root or source. A person's birth parents can be only one couple but Yi Zhi thinks a person has two sources, therefore he is different from me. In ancient time, there was a person who didn't bury his parents' bodies. He just threw the bodies into valley. After several days, he noticed that foxes were eating the bodies, that flies and mosquitoes were biting them, therefore he couldn't bare glaring at them and his forehead was wet. His forehead was wet because he felt uneasy and ashamed in deep heart. He returned to the spot where he threw the bodies, and then looked for spade and basket to bury the the bodies. It was right to bury the bodies and then it's reasonable for a filial son and humanistic person to bury parents after they are dead." Xu Bi reported to Yi Zhi what Mencius had said. Yi Zhi stayed for a while being distracted and said, "I have been already educated."

【注释】(1)墨者夷之句:墨者,信奉墨子学说的人。夷之,姓夷,名之,其他不详。徐辟,孟子弟子。(2)病愈我且往见:病愈,谓病好了。愈,异体作"瘉"。往见,去见……。(3)不直:意谓不说直话有所隐晦。(4)道不见:道,政治主张或思想体系。不见,读~xiàn,不显现;不显露。(5)以薄为其道:主张薄葬。墨子有薄葬篇。(6)思以易天下:想改变世风。(7)岂:副词,表示估计、推测。相当于也许、莫非。(8)古之人若保赤子:古之人,指古代君王,若保赤子,谓爱民像保护婴儿一样。见《尚书·康诰》:"若保赤子,惟民其康乂。(要像保护婴儿一样保护臣民,臣民就会康乐安定。)"(9)施由亲始:施,谓施爱。亲,双亲,父母。(10)天之生物也,使之一本:天之生物也,谓天下的动物和植物。使之一本,"一本使之"的倒装。一个本源使其生出。一株树或一株草是由一个根而不是两个根所生出;一个婴儿或一头小牛,是由一对父母而不是两对父母所生出。(11)上世:远古时代。(12)委:放置,舍弃。(13)蝇蚋姑嘬之:yīngruì gūchuài ~,蝇蚋,苍蝇和蚊子。姑,通"盬"。用嘴吸吮。嘬,咬,叮。之,代词。指被弃的亲尸。(14)其颡有泚:颡,读sǎng,额头。泚,读cǐ,冒汗;汗出的样子。(15)睨而不视:nì ~ ~ ~,睨,斜着眼(看);斜视。视,同"睨"对用,意指"正眼看""正视"。(16)归反虆梩而掩之:归反,返回。(指回到弃亲的尸体处。)虆,读léi,古代盛土器。梩,读lí,锹锸一类的起土工具。虆和梩都用作动词。掩之,掩埋尸体。(17)怃然:wǔ ~,怅然失意的样子;惊愕的样子。为间:有顷,一会儿。(18)命之矣:命,教。之,代词。夷之自指。

孟子集注卷六　滕文公章句下 凡十章

【原文】6 陈代曰:[1]"不见诸侯,宜若小然;[2]今一见之,大则以王,小则以霸。[3]且志曰:[4]'枉尺而直寻'[5]宜若可为也。"孟子曰:"昔者齐景公田,[6]招虞人以旌,[7]不至,将杀之。志士不忘在沟壑,[8]勇士不忘丧其元。[9]孔子奚取焉?取非其招不往也。如不待其招而往,何哉?且夫枉尺而直寻者,[10]以利言也。如以利,则枉寻直尺而利。亦可为与?昔者赵简子使王良与嬖奚乘,[11]终日而不获一禽。[12]嬖奚反命曰,[13]'天下之贱工也。[14]'或以告王良。良曰:'请复之。[15]'强而后可,[16]一朝而获十禽。[17]嬖奚反命曰;'天下之良工也。'简子曰:'我使掌与女乘。[18]'谓王良。良不可,曰:'吾为之范我驰驱,[19]终日不获一;为之诡遇,[20]一朝而获十。诗云:"不失其驰,舍矢如破。[21]"我不贯与小人乘,[22]请辞。[23]'御者且羞与射者比;[24]比而得禽兽,虽若丘陵,[25]弗为也。如枉道而从彼,[26]何也?且子过矣;枉己者,未有能直人者也。”

【白话译文】

陈代说:“不去谒见诸侯,似乎过于拘谨不够高大了吧;如今见一见诸侯,收效大可以实行仁政,统一天下;收效小可以富国安民,为诸侯之长。而且志上说:‘弯曲一尺,伸直八尺’,好像可以试一试。”孟子说:“从前齐景公打猎,用旌去召唤山泽管理员,管理员不去,景公要杀他。有志之士坚守节操,不怕抛尸山沟;有勇之士勇于战斗,不怕丢掉脑袋。孔子到底看中管理员的哪一点呢?看中他对于不是自己所应接受的召唤之礼,就是不接受,不应召。如果我不等诸侯相召自动前去,那是为什么呢?况且弯曲一尺伸直八尺,完全是从利的观点考虑的。如果只就利益来说,即使弯曲八尺伸直一尺,也有小利益,不是也可以试一试吗?从前赵简子命令王良给他的宠幸小臣奚驾车去打猎,一整天都没打到一只鸟兽。奚向赵简子回报情况说:‘王良是天底下技艺最坏的驾车人。’有人把这话告诉了王良。王良要求再干一次,奚犹豫再三,勉强同意了。一个早上,打到了十个猎物。奚向赵简子回报情况说:‘王良是天底下技艺最好的驾车人。’赵简子说:‘我叫他专门为你驾车好了。’并且这样吩咐王良,王良不肯,说道:‘我给他按规矩奔驰,整天打不着一件东西;我给他不按规矩奔驰,一个早上就打到十个东西。《诗经》上说:“按照规矩驾车跑,一箭射出猎物倒。”我没习惯同小人打交道,让我辞去这份差事吧。’驾车的人还害羞与坏射手同伙,同伙了,即使打得的禽兽堆成山,也不干。如果我们委屈自己的理想与主张去追随诸侯,那我们又算什么人呢?而且你错了,屈从于人的人,从来没有使对方变正直的。”

【英语译文】

Mencius' disciple Chen Dai said, “It seems overcautious not to pay a formal visit to the prince. Nowadays if we visit him and have good result, then he can carry out government of humanity and unify the world; if the result isn't so good, then he can make the state wealthy and pacify common people, and become the leader of princes. Furthermore, the annals say ‘When you bend one *chi* and you can stretch eight *chi*’. We may have a try.” Mencius said, “In old days, Duke Jing of Qi State went hunt in spring and summon hill-swamp-keeper by colorful banners but the latter didn't go to him. So Duke Jing intended to kill him. A person with lofty ideals sticks to his integrity not fearing to be thrown into valley; a person with courage fights in battle courageously not fearing to be killed. What point of the keeper did Confucius appreciate? He appreciated that the keeper didn't accept the summon which wasn't what he should accept according to rites. If I myself went to a prince without his summon, what does that mean? What's more, it's considered from the point of benefit to say 'When you bend one *chi* and you can stretch eight *chi*'. If we only consider benefit, even if when you bend one *chi* and you can stretch eight *chi*, there is a little benefit. Why don't we have a try? In old days, Zhao Jianzi ordered Wang Liang to drive cart going hunt for his favorite junior minister Bi Xi. But for a whole day Bi Xi didn't get one game. Bi Xi reported to Zhao Jianzi, 'Wang Liang was the worst skilled cart-driver.' Somebody told Wang Liang what Bi Xi had said. Wang Liang requested to drive cart for another time and Bi Xi hesitated for a long time and agreed with reluctance. In just one morning, he got ten games. Bi Xi reported this to Zhao Jianzi, 'Wang Liang was the best-skilled cart-driver.' Zhao Jianzi said, 'I ordered him to drive cart for you only.' And he said the same thing to Wang Liang and the latter refused to do that, saying 'I drove cart according to the rule for a whole day he didn't get one game; but I drove cart violating the rule for one morning he got ten games.' *The Book of Songs* says 'They were driven routine way. One shooting just did its play.' I am not accustomed to get along with a mean man, please permit me to resign this job., The driver was shamed to accompany the shooter. Even if the games piled up he wouldn't do that. If we give up our ideals or ideas to adhere to a prince, what kind of person will we become? What's more, a person who yields to others has never made others become upright."

【注释】(1)陈代:孟子弟子。(2)宜若:表拟测,推断之词。犹言,似乎、好像。小然:过于拘谨,气魄不大。(3)大则以王,小则以霸:大、小,指行为效果的比较程度。王,读 wàng,行王政(行仁政)平天下。霸,做诸侯之长。(4)志:记事著作。(5)枉尺而直寻:朱熹《四书集注》:"枉,屈也。直,伸也。八尺曰寻。枉尺直寻,犹屈己一见诸侯,而可致王霸,所屈者小,所伸者大也。"(6)齐景公田:齐景公,即第十二代齐侯。田,狩猎;亦特指春天打猎。(7)招虞人以旌:招,用言语、手势或其他方式呼唤、使来。虞人,古代掌山泽苑囿之官吏。旌,读 jīng,古代用牦牛尾或兼五彩羽毛装饰竿头的旗子。《左传·昭公二十年》云:"齐侯田于沛,招虞人以弓,不进,公使执之。辞曰:'昔我先君之田也,旃(赤色、无饰、曲柄的旗)以招大夫,弓以招士,皮冠以招虞人。臣不见皮冠,故不敢进。'乃舍之。仲尼曰:'守道不如守官,君子韪(以为是;同意;赞赏。)之。'"《左传》作"弓"与"旌"异。按:事在齐景公二十六年;即鲁昭公二十年。(8)志士不忘在沟壑:犹言,有志之士,不怕穷,时常想到死无棺椁抛弃山沟而不恨。(9)勇士不忘丧其元:犹言,勇敢之士,轻其生,时常想到战斗而死,丢掉脑袋也不顾。丧,读 sàng,失去;丢失。元,头,脑袋。(10)且夫:犹"况且"。承接上文表示更进一层的意思。(11)赵简子使王良与嬖奚乘:赵简子,即赵鞅。春秋末晋国正卿。王良,春秋末善于驾车的人。嬖奚,赵简子的宠臣名奚,嬖读 bì,乘,读 chéng,驾驭。(12)一禽:古籍中"禽"有四种用法,一用作兽的总名;二用指鸟类;三用泛指鸟兽;四用特指鸟兽未孕者。一禽,在本文中应训作"一只飞禽走兽"。(13)反命:复命。谓完成使命后回报情况。(14)贼工:贼,败坏。工,古时对从事各种技艺的劳动者的通称。本文中,"贼工"指称技艺败坏的驾车人。下文"良工"则指称技艺良好的驾车人。(15)请复之:请,要求。复之,再给嬖奚驾车。(16)强而后可:强,读 qiǎng,劝勉;强迫。可,表示同意,许可。(17)一朝、十禽:一朝,一个早晨(天亮至早餐时)。十禽,十只鸟兽。(18)使掌:派……专管。(19)为之范:按照……法度(规范)。(20)为之诡遇:谓违背礼法驱车,以便横射禽兽。(21)诗云句:见《诗·小雅·车工》。不失其驰,谓按照一定的法则驱车,舍矢,放箭。如破,就射中而落倒。(22)不贯:没习惯。"贯"通"惯",习惯。(23)请辞:要求辞去。(24)比:相合。(25)丘陵:比喻高大或多。(26)枉道:违背正道;委屈自己的主张。

【原文】2 景春曰:[1]"公孙衍、张仪岂不诚大夫哉?[2]一怒而诸侯惧,安居而天下熄。[3]"孟子曰:"是焉得为大丈夫乎?[4]子未学礼乎?丈夫之冠也,父命之;[5]女子之嫁也,母命之,往送之门,戒之曰'往之女家,[6]必敬必戒,无违夫子![7]'以顺为正者,妾妇之道也。[8]居天下之广居,立天下之正位,行天下之大道;[9]得志,与民由之;[10]不得志,独行其道。[11]富贵不能淫,贫贱不能移,威武不能屈,[12]此之谓大丈夫。"[13]

【白话译文】

景春说:"公孙衍和张仪难道不是真正的大丈夫吗?他们一发怒,诸侯都害怕。他们安静下来,天下就平息。"孟子说:"这样怎么能算大丈夫呢?你没学过礼吗?男子行加冠礼时,父亲要训导他,女子出嫁时,母亲要训导她。送她到门口时教训说:'到了你的家里,必须恭敬,必须谨慎。不要违背丈夫!'以顺从为正道,是做妇人的基本道理。住在天下最宽广的仁宅里,立在天下最端正的礼位上,走在天下最光明的义路中;能实现志愿时,同百姓一道前进;不能实现志愿时,独自走该走的路。不受富贵诱惑,不为贫贱动摇,不为武力屈服。这样才算大丈夫。"

【英语译文】

Jing Chun said, "Weren't Gongsun Yan and Zhang Yi true men? All princes had been frightened when they got enraged. When they calmed down, the world was peaceful." Mencius replied, "How could they be called true men? Haven't you learnt rites? While the capping ceremony is carried out, the young man will be taught by his father; and when a young girl marries, her mother will teach her. After she is seen off to the outer door, her mother tells her, 'You should be modest and cautious after you get to your husband's family. Don't violate him!' It is the right way for a woman to be obedient. One lives in the most spacious house, works in the most upright post, and walks on the most righteous road. When his ideals can be completed, he heads forward with common people; and when he cannot implements his ideals, he walks alone in the right way. Wealth and nobility cannot entice him; poverty cannot divert his will; might and power cannot make him yield. Such kind of man can be called a true man."

【注释】(1)景春:孟子同时人,属纵横家。(2)公孙衍、张仪:公孙衍,魏人。因担任过魏国的犀首官,人们以官名称谓他犀首。是当时著名的说客。在秦任大良造的官,又曾配五国相印。景春所言之日,正是公孙衍、张仪二人春风得意之时,而且苏秦已死,想必是他没有言及之由。(3)熄:上文"一怒、安居",指公孙衍、张仪二人在政界的动静。诸侯惧、天下熄,夸张二人的动静对于天下的影响。熄,火灭,训"平息"。谓由动乱恢复平常。(4)焉:疑问代词作状语。译为"怎么""哪(里)"。(5)丈夫之冠也,父命之:丈夫,男子。冠,读 guàn,加冠(guān)于首,戴帽子。古时男子到二十岁,算作成年人,要举行冠(戴帽)礼,表示已成年。命,告诫,训导。(6)戒之、女家:戒之,告诫她。女,同"汝"。(7)必戒、夫子:必戒,必须谨慎。夫子,称丈夫,女子的配偶。(8)以顺为正者,妾妇之道也:顺,顺从。正者,者字结构。这里用以指事,义同正道。妾妇,泛指妇女。(9)广居、正位、大道:朱熹《四书集注》:"广居,仁也;正位,礼也;大道,义也。"(10)得志,与民由之:得志,谓能实现志愿。与民由之,同百姓一道实践。(11)不得志,独行其道:不得志,谓不能实现志愿。独行其道,独自走自己的路。(12)富贵不能淫,贫贱不能移,威武不能屈:不受富贵诱惑,不为贫贱动摇,不为武力屈服。(13)之:语气助词。

【原文】3 周霄问曰:[1]"古之君子仕乎?"孟子曰:"仕。传曰:'孔子三月无君,[2]则皇皇如也,[3]出疆必载质。[4]'公明仪曰:[5]'古之人三月无君,则吊。[6]'""三月无君则吊,不以急乎?[7]"曰:"士之失位也,犹诸侯之失国家也。[8]礼曰:'诸侯耕助以供粢盛;[9]夫人蚕缫,以为衣服。[10]牺牲不成,粢盛不絜,衣服不备,不敢以祭。[11]惟士无田,则亦不祭。[12]'牲杀、器皿、衣服不备,不敢以祭,则不敢以宴,[13]亦不足吊乎?[14]""出疆必载质,何也?"曰:"士之仕也,犹农夫之耕也;农夫岂为出疆舍其耒耜哉?"曰:"晋国亦仕国也,[15]未尝闻仕如此其急。仕如此其急也,君子之难仕,何也?"曰:"丈夫生而愿为之有室,女子生而愿为之有家;[16]父母之心,人皆有之。不待父母之命、媒妁之言,[17]钻穴隙相窥[18],逾墙相从[19],则父母国人皆贱之。古之人未尝不欲仕也,又恶不由其道。不由其道而往者,与钻穴隙之类也。"[20]

【白话译文】

周霄问道:"古代的君子做官吗?"孟子说:"做。传记上说:'孔子三个月没有得到君主任用,就焦急不安。出境到另一个国家去一定要带上见面礼。'公明仪说:'古代的人三个月没得君主任用,旁人就会安慰他。'"周霄说:"三个月没得君主任用,就去安慰,不是太急了吗?"孟子说:"士人失掉身份地位,犹如诸侯失掉统治权亡国。礼经说:'诸侯耕籍田,是为了资助祭祀;夫人养蚕缫丝,是为了做祭祀的礼服。用来祭祀的牛羊不合要求,用来祭祀的谷物不干净,祭祀用的礼服不完备,都不敢拿来祭祀。士人没有田,也就不祭祀了。'由于祭品、祭器和祭服不完备,不敢进行祭祀,也不敢设宴聚会,这也不值得慰问吗?"周霄问:"出境到另一个国家去一定要带上见面礼。是什么意思?"孟子说:"士人的做官好像农民的种田;农民难道因出境就舍弃农具吗?"周霄说:"魏国也是一个可以做官的国家,我却未听说过找官做这么急迫。既然急于找官做,却又不轻易做官。是什么道理呢?"孟子说:"男孩一生下来,父母便希望他配个好妻子;女孩一生下来,父母便希望她放个好婆家。天下的父母心都一样。如果不等父母开口,不经媒人介绍,自己挖墙洞、拨门缝互相偷看,翻过墙去,苟且私奔,那么,父母和周围的人都会轻视他。古代的人不是不想做官,但又厌恶不由合礼义的道路去找官做。由不合礼义的道路去找官做的,正像自己挖墙洞、拨门缝互相偷看,翻过墙去,苟且私奔的人。"

【英语译文】

Zhou Xiao asked, "In ancient time, did a moral man want to be an official?" Mencius said, "Yes, he did. Biographies said, 'Confucius felt uneasy when the monarch didn't use him for three months. And when he went out to another state, he surely brought a gift at the first meeting.' Gongming Yi said, 'In ancient time if someone hadn't been empowered for three months, other people would console him.'" Zhou Xiao asked, "He was consoled for not being empowered for three months. Isn't it in a hurry?" Mencius said, "It is the same that a prince loses his control over his state if a scholar loses his identity. *The Book of Rites* says 'A prince plows corvée field in order to assist sacrifice, and his wife raises silkworms in order to weave sacrificial clothes. If the sacrificial animals aren't fitful, if the sacrificial grains aren't clean, and if sacrificial clothes aren't ready, then the ceremony won't be carried out. If a scholar doesn't have field, then it's unnecessary to hold sacrificial ceremony.' People dare not hold sacrificial ceremony and gathering due to the lack of sacrificial animals, grains and clothes. Doesn't it deserve consolation?" Zhou Xiao asked, "What does it mean that when Confucius went out to another state, he surely brought a gift presented to somebody at the first meeting?" Mencius answered, "That a scholar becomes an official is the same as that a peasant plows his field. Doesn't he give up his plowing tools when a peasant goes out of his state?" Zhou Xiao said, "Wei State is a place where people can become an official, but I haven't heard that a person hurries up to be an official. Now that someone hurries up for a post but he refuses to be empowered casually. What does it mean?" Mencius replied, "When a boy is born, his parents wish that he will marry a fine woman in the future; and when a girl is born, her parents wish that she will marry a fine man in the the future. All parents cherish the same wish in the world. If a young man and a young woman peep at each other through a pole in the wall and cross over the wall to make intercourse and then elope together without parents' permission and matchmaker's introduction, then their parents and neighbors will contempt them. People in ancient time did want to become an official but they loathed becoming an official based on rites-violating way. Doing so is the same as those who peep at each other through a pole in the wall and cross over the wall to make intercourse and then elope together without parents' permission and matchmaker's introduction."

【注释】(1)周霄:魏人。(2)无君:朱熹《四书集注》:"无君,谓不得仕而事君也。"(3)皇皇如也:好像惶恐不安的样子。皇皇,今作"惶惶"。(4)出疆:犹出境。古代指离开某一封国疆土,前往他国。载质:载,携带。质,通"贽""挚"。初次相见赠送的礼物;见面礼。士人一般用雉。(5)公明仪:姓公明,名仪。春秋时鲁人。(6)吊:同"吊"。本文中意谓"安慰",不是祭奠。(7)以:通"已"。太;甚。(8)失位:失去身份、地位。失国:丧失国家的统治权;亡国。(9)耕助:指耕种籍田。古代天子、诸侯征用民力耕种的田叫籍田。相传天子籍田千亩、诸侯百亩。每逢春耕将始,由天子、诸侯执耒耜在籍田上躬耕。天子单独三推(扶耜来回三度);以下臣属依次按规定增加推数。称为“籍礼”,表示重视农业亲耕示范。籍田收入,用以补助祭祀。粢盛:zīchéng,古代装在祭器里供祭祀的谷物。(10)夫人蚕缫,以为衣服:夫人,指诸侯正妻。蚕缫,cánsāo,亦作“蚕缲”。饲蚕抽茧丝。衣服,指祭祀时所穿的礼服。(11)牺牲不成、不絜、不备、以祭:牺牲,用作祭祀的牛、羊、猪等都叫牺牲。古代对用来作祭祀品的动物在品种、质量、规格上的要求都很严。不成,犹言不像样,不合要求。不絜,即“不洁”。不干净。絜是“洁”的异体字。不备,不完备;不齐全。以祭,用来祭祀。以,介词。表对事物的处置。相当于“用”“拿”。(12)惟士无田,则亦不祭:惟,语气助词。用在句首句中补凑音节。则,承接连词。在承认前面的叙述后连接相应的叙述。(13)牲杀:畜牧和田猎得来的牺牲。畜牧曰牲,渔猎曰杀。器皿:餐具及覆盖之巾。以宴:用来宴会。参看注(11)。(14)不足:不值得,不必。(15)晋国:实际是魏国。春秋、战国之际,晋国的三卿韩、赵、魏瓜分晋国,并为战国。后魏人还自称晋国。仕国:朱熹《四书集注》:“仕国,君子游宦之国”。谓可以去从政做官的国家。(16)有室:谓男子娶妻。有家:谓女子出嫁。(17)媒妁:méishuò,说合婚姻的人。(18)鑚:穿孔,打眼。穴隙:孔穴;洞孔。窥:从夹缝、小孔或隐蔽处偷看。(19)逾墙相从:指男女跨越墙垣偷情。(20)由其道:谓遵循正道。与:如同;好像。之类:这类;那类。

【原文】4 彭更问曰:[1]“后车数十乘,从者数百人,以传食于诸侯,[2]不亦泰乎?[3]”孟子曰:“非其道,[4]则一箪食不可受于人;[5]如其道,[6]则舜受尧之天下,不以为泰。子以为泰乎?”曰:“否;士无事而食,不可也。”曰:“子不通功易事,[7]以羡补不足,[8]则农有余粟,女有余布;子如通之,[9]则梓匠轮舆皆得食于子。[10]于此有人焉,[11]入则孝,出则悌,守先王之道,以待后之学者。[12]而不得食于子;子何尊梓匠轮舆而轻为仁义者哉?”曰:“梓匠轮舆,其志将以求食也;[13]君子之为道也,其志亦将以求食与?”曰:“子何以其志为哉?其有功于子,可食而食之矣。且子食志乎?[14]食功乎?”曰:“食志。”曰:“有人于此,毁瓦画墁,[15]其念将以求食也,则伟之乎?”曰:“否。”曰:“然则子非食志也,食功也。”

【白话译文】

彭更问道:“跟随的车几十驾,跟随的人几百个,住在诸侯的客馆里接受饮食,这不是过分了吗?”孟子说:“如果不依正路,流逝一筐饭也不接受;如果依正路,那么舜接受了尧的天下,也不觉得过分,你以为过分了吗?”彭更说:“不;士人不干事白吃喝,是不可以的。”孟子说:“你不承认人各有业,互通有无,拿多余的来弥补不够的;那么,农民有多余的米,妇女有多余的布,然而,又缺少别的东西。如果能互通有无,那么,梓人、匠人、轮人、舆人,都能从你那儿得到吃的。假如这里有个人,在家孝顺父母,出外尊敬长辈,严守先王的礼法道义来培养后辈学者,却不能从你那儿得到吃的;那么,你为什么尊敬梓匠轮舆而轻视行仁义的人呢?”彭更说:“梓匠轮舆,他们的动机就是谋饭吃;君子研究学问,推行仁政,他们的动机也是谋饭吃吗?”孟子说:“你为什么要追问动机呢?他们对你有功绩,可以给他们吃的,就给他们吃的罢了。再说,你给他们吃的是凭动机呢?还是凭功绩呢?”彭更说:“凭动机。”孟子说:“假如这里有个人打碎屋瓦给墙画装饰画,他的动机是讨饭吃,你给他吃的吗?”彭更说:“不。”孟子说:“那么,你给吃的,并不是凭动机而是凭功绩了。”

【英语译文】

Peng Geng asked, “Is it excessive for a person to be followed by dozens of carts and hundreds of people, and to be kept alive in prince’s guest house?” Mencius said, “If it doesn’t fit the right way, it’s unacceptable to waste a basket of food. If it fits the right way, then it isn’t excessive for Sage Shun took over the world. Do you think it’s excessive?” Peng Geng said, “No. But it isn’t right for a scholar not to do anything.” Mencius said, “You don’t admit that each person has his own occupation and they can mutually exchange needed products, and peasants have spare grains and women have spare cloth but they lack other things. How to solve this problem? If people can mutually exchange needed products, music craftsman, house builders, wheel makers, carriage makers, bow makers, spear makers and cart makers can get food from you. If there is a man who is filial to parents, respects superior, and educates his disciples according to the rites of late king, but he cannot get food from you. Then why do you respect craftsmen but contempt a humanistic person?” Peng Geng answered, “The motivation of craftsmen doing these things is to make a living; isn’t the motivation of a moral man implementing government of humanity to make a living?” Mencius said, “Why do you ask their motivation? If they have made contribution, you just give them food. Moreover, do you consider their motivation or contribution when you give them food?” Peng Geng answered, “I consider their motivation.” Mencius said, “Suppose a person who breaks tiles to draw decorative picture on the walls in order to make a living, will you give him food?” Peng Geng said, “No, I won’t.” Mencius said, “Then you are considering contribution not motivation when you give people food.”

【注释】(1)彭更:孟子弟子。(2)传食:辗转受人供养。一说传读 zhuàn,客舍的意思。传食,谓止息于诸侯客馆受其饮食。(3)泰:太,过甚。(4)非其道:不是正道;歪道。(5)箪:dān,古时的盛饭器,用竹或苇编成,圆形,有盖。(6)如其道:依正道。(7)通功易事:谓人各有业,互通有无。(8)羡:xiàn,有余;剩余。(9)通之:指互通有无。(10)梓匠轮舆:古代木工分七种:梓、匠、轮、舆、弓、庐、车。梓人,专造乐器悬架、饮器和箭靶等;匠人,主建筑;轮人,制作车轮;舆人,造车厢;弓人,制弓。庐人,制作矛戟的柄;车人,制造车子和农具。(11)有人:泛指有某人。表假设。(12)待:通"持"。扶持。(13)志:目标;动机。(14)食志:sì ~,凭动机给人吃。食功,仿此解。(15)墁:màn,墙壁上的涂饰。按:平常有人用瓦片画临时记号或示意图;绝不能画装饰画。

【原文】5 万章问曰:[1]"宋,小国也;今将行王政,齐、楚恶而伐之,则如之何?"孟子曰:"汤居亳,[2]与葛[3]为邻,葛伯放而不祀,汤使人问之曰:'何为不祀?'曰:'无以供牺牲也。'汤使遗之牛羊。[4]葛伯食之,又不以祀。汤又使人问之曰:'何为不祀?'曰:'无以供粢盛也。'汤使亳众往为之耕,老弱馈食。葛伯率其民,要其有酒食黍稻者夺之[5],不授者杀之。有童子以黍、肉饷,[6]杀而夺之。书曰:'葛伯仇饷。[7]'此之谓也。为其杀是童子而征之,四海之内皆曰:'非富天下也,为匹夫匹妇复仇也。[8]''汤始征,自葛载,[9]' 十一征而无敌于天下。东面而征,西夷怨;南面而征,北狄怨,曰:'奚为后我?'民之望之,若大旱之望雨也。归市者弗止,芸者不变,[10]诛其君,吊其民,如时雨降[11]。民大悦。书曰:'徯我后,后来其无罚![12]''有攸不惟臣,[13]东征,绥厥士女,[14]篚厥玄黄,[15]绍我周王见休,[16]惟臣附于大邑周。[17]'其君子实玄黄于篚以迎其君子,其小人箪食壶浆以迎其小人;救民于水火之中,取其残而已矣。[18]太誓曰:[19]'我武惟扬,侵于之疆,[20]则取于残,杀伐用张,[21]于汤有光。'不行王政云尔,苟行王政,四海之内皆举首而望之,欲以为君;齐、楚虽大,何畏焉?"

【白话译文】

万章问道:"宋是个小国,如今要推行仁政,齐、楚两国因此厌恶,就讨伐它,将怎么办呢?"孟子说:"汤居住亳地,和葛国为邻;葛伯放荡,不祭祀鬼神。汤派人去问:'为什么不祭祀?'答道:'没有法子置办牺牲。'汤便送给他牛和羊。葛伯把牛羊吃了,却不用来祭祀。汤又派人去问:'为什么不祭祀?'答道:'没有法子置办粢盛。'汤便派亳地的民众去替他们耕种;老弱的人去给耕种的人送饭。葛伯却带领他的百姓拦截送饭人,抢夺酒菜好饭,不给的就杀掉。有个小孩去送饭和肉,遭到了抢夺还丢了命。《书经》上说：‘葛伯与送饭人为仇。’就是指这个事件。因为葛伯杀了这个小孩，汤就征讨他。全中国人都说：‘汤不是要富有天下，是要为老百姓报仇雪恨。’‘汤开始征战，从葛国排头。’出征十一次，没打过败仗，没有人能够同他对等。向东方出征，西方的人不高兴；向南方出征，北方的人不高兴；他们说：‘为什么把我们放在后边不理？老百姓盼望他，就像旱灾中盼雨一样，做生意的人照常进城市，做庄稼的人照常干农活。铲除暴虐的君主，安慰受苦的百姓，正像下一场及时雨啊！老百姓十分欢喜。’《书经》上说：‘等候我王，王来他不滥罚！’‘攸国不服做臣下，王东出征讨它，安抚那些老百姓。他们把彩色丝绸装在竹筐里，表示跟随我周王遇到了喜庆福祥，愿做臣民依附于大邦周。’官员们把彩色丝绸装在竹筐里来迎接官员，老百姓提着酒壶饭筐来迎接士兵。征讨是把老百姓从水深火热中解救出来，把残暴的君主抓起来除掉罢了。泰誓上说：‘我们威武要发扬，攻进于国的国疆。捕捉于国的残暴，该死的杀个精光；再现汤王的辉煌。’宋国只是不实行仁政罢了，如果实行仁政，四海以内，都会抬头仰望，拥戴宋君为王；齐、楚两国虽然强大，怕他们什么呢？”

【英语译文】

Wan Zhang asked, “Song State is small but it carries out government of humanity; as a result Qi State and Chu State hate it and attack it. What can it do?” Mencius said, “King Tang of Shang Dynasty lived in the place of Bo and was the neighbor of Ge State. Ge Bo was licentious and didn't sacrifice ghosts. King Tang sent person to ask the reason why he didn't sacrifice ghosts. Ge Bo replied that he couldn't get sacrificial animals. King Tang then gave him ox and goats but he ate them up not using for sacrificing. King Tang sent person again to ask the reason why he didn't sacrifice ghosts. He replied that he couldn't get sacrificial grains. Then King Tang dispatched people in the place of Bo to assist farming, and the elder and the youth to deliver rice. However Ge Bo led his men to interfere persons who delivered rice and killed those who refused to hand out food and drink. A child who delivered rice was robbed and killed. *The Book of History* said ‘Ge Bo revenged on persons who delivered rice’ and it referred to this event. King Tang attacked Ge Bo because he killed this child. People in all states said, ‘King Tang didn't intend to make people wealthy but get revenge for them.’ ‘King Tang started to attack against Ge State to crusade.’ He crusaded for eleven times and succeeded each time with nobody being his rival. When he crusaded to the east, people in the west weren't happy and when he crusaded to the south, people in the north weren't happy. They said, 'Why did he leave us behind and take no notice upon us? Common people are looking forward to him just like rain in drought. Vendors went into town as usual and peasants did farming as usual. It is like timely rain in drought to get rid of tyrant monarch and pacify suffering persons. The common people felt very happy.' *The Book of History* said 'We wait for our king to come, and he doesn't misuse punishment.' 'You State refused to be yielded and King of Zhou dynasty attacked it to pacify people there. People put colorful silk in baskets to show that they have happiness and blessings when meeting the King of Zhou Dynasty, and they were ready to be subjects of great Zhou Dynasty.' Officials put colorful silk in baskets to welcome officials of Zhou, and common people carried wine kettle to welcome soldiers of Zhou. Crusade intended to save people from severe pains and get rid of tyrant monarchs. *Tai Oath* said, 'We are mighty and powerful; we attacked Yu State. We arrested the tyrant monarch of Yu State and killed all those evil men. King Tang's glory was shown completely.' Song State didn't carry our government of humanity. If it implements government of humanity, then people in the world will look up at it and the head of Song State will be elected as King. What would people fear even if Qi State and Chu State are big and strong?"

【注释】(1)万章:孟子的高足弟子。(2)亳:bó,商汤的都城。相传有三处。1)南亳。在今河南商丘市东南。2)北亳。在今河南商丘市北。3)西亳。在今河南偃师县西。为汤攻克夏时所居。(3)葛 :古国名,嬴姓。在今河南宁陵县北。(4)无以:无从,无法。(5)要:阻拦;拦截。(6)饷:xiǎng,与"馈"同义。进食于人,送饭。(7)仇饷:与饷者为仇。(8)富:用作动,匹夫匹妇:平民夫妇。(9)载:zǎi,开始。(10)芸:yún,通"耘"。除草。芸者,泛指做庄稼的人。(11)时雨:应时的雨水。(12)徯我后其无罚:徯,读 xī,等待;期望。后,君主。其,他。无罚,没有惩罚。(13)有攸:有,助词,无义。在古汉语中,可用作名词、动词或形容词词头。攸,国名。惟:为。(14)绥厥士女:绥,安抚。厥,其。士女,青年男女;泛指人民百姓。(15)篚厥玄黄:篚,读 fěi,盛物的竹器。用作动词;谓用篚盛。玄黄,彩色丝织物。(16)绍:继;随后;跟着。见:遇到;接触。休:喜庆;福禄。(17)惟:语气助词。臣附:臣属依附。大邑:犹大邦。殷周时尊称上国之词。亦用于自称。大邑周,即对周的尊称或自称。后世的大汉、大唐、大宋、大明,都是尊称或自称。只是不用邑了。(18)取:捕捉。(19)太誓:即泰誓。尚书篇名。今已亡佚。(20)于:国名。即邘国。周武王之子邘叔的封地。(21)杀伐:杀戮。用:副词,只有。张:

铺开。

【原文】6 孟子谓戴不胜曰:[1]“子欲子之王之善与?[2]我明告子。有楚大夫于此,欲其子之齐语也,则使齐人傅诸?[3]使楚人傅诸?”曰:“使齐人傅之。”曰:“一齐人傅之,众楚人咻之,[4]虽日挞而求其齐也,[5]不可得矣;引而置之庄、岳之间数年,[6]虽日挞而求其楚,亦不可得矣。子谓薛居州善士也,[7]使之居于王所。在于王所者,长幼卑尊,皆薛居州也,王谁与为不善?在王所者,长幼卑尊,皆非薛居州也,王谁与为善?一薛居州,独如宋王何?[8]”

【白话译文】

孟子对戴不胜说:“你想你的君王学好吗?我明白地告诉你。这里有个楚国的大臣,要他儿子会说齐国话,那么,找齐国人教他呢?还是找楚国人教他呢?”答道:“找齐国人教他。”孟子说:“一个齐国人教他,许多楚国人干扰他,即使天天鞭打他,逼他说齐国话,也做不到。如果把它带到临淄城里的庄街、岳里住几年,即使天天鞭打他,逼他说楚国话,那也做不到了。你说薛居州是个好人,要他住在王宫里影响国王。如果住在王宫里的人不论老幼、尊卑、贵贱,都是薛居州一样的好人,那王同谁去干坏事呢?如果住在王宫里的人不论老幼尊卑贵贱都不是薛居州一样的好人,那王同谁去干好事呢?一个薛居州能把宋王怎么样呢?”

【英语译文】

Mencius asked Dai Busheng, a minister of Song State, “Do you wish your king follow good example? I will explain it clearly to you. There is a minister of Chu State who wants his son to speak dialect of Qi State, and then should a person of Qi teach him or a person of Chu do that?” Dai answered, “A person of Qi teaches him.” Mencius said, “While a person of Qi teaches him, many persons of Chu interfere him. In that case, even he is beaten each day and forced to speak Qi dialect he cannot manage to do it. If he is brought to live in Street Zhuang and Lane Yue in Linzi for several years, even if he is beaten and forced to speak Chu dialect, he cannot manage to do it. You say that Xue Juzhou is a good man and you want him to live in the imperial court and influence the king. If people, either elder or younger, either noble or humble, live in the court are all good like Xue Juzhou, with whom can the king do evil things together? If people, either elder or younger, either noble or humble, live in the court aren't all good like Xue Juzhou, with whom can the king do good things together? What can Xue

Juzhou do to King of Song State?"

【注释】(1)戴不胜:宋臣。(2)之善:学好。之,生出,滋长。往;至。(3)傅:辅佐;教导。诸:代词,相当于"之"用作宾语。(4)咻:xiū,喧嚷;扰乱。(5)挞:tà,用鞭子或棍子打。(6)庄、岳:齐国街、里名。(7)薛居州:宋臣。(8)独:将,多用于疑问句,一作"单独,独自"解也通。

【原文】7 公孙丑问曰:"不见诸侯何义?"孟子曰:"古者不为臣不见。段干木逾垣而辟之,[1]泄柳闭门而不纳,[2]是皆已甚;迫,[3]斯可以见矣。阳货欲见孔子而恶无礼,[4]大夫有赐于士,[5]不得受于其家,则往拜其门。阳货瞰孔子之亡也,[6]而馈孔子蒸豚;孔子亦瞰其亡也,而往拜之,当是时,阳货先,岂得不见?[7]曾子曰:'胁肩谄笑,[8]病于夏畦。[9]'子路曰:'未同而言,观其色赧赧然,[10]非由之所知也'[11]由是观之,[12]则君子所养,[13]可知已矣。"

【白话译文】

公孙丑问道:"不去谒见诸侯,是什么道理?"孟子说:"古时,不做诸侯的臣就不谒见诸侯。段干木翻过墙垣避开魏文侯来访。泄柳关闭大门不让鲁缪公进屋看他。他们都做过分了。求见迫切,不得已,是可以见的。阳货想令孔子去见他,又怕有失礼节,按照礼法,大夫有东西赏赐士人,士人当时如不能在家里亲自接受,此后,就得亲自上大夫家去拜谢。阳货窥伺到孔子不在家的日子,派人把蒸熟了的小猪送到孔子家里;孔子也瞅着阳货不在家的日子,上门去拜谢。在那时,阳货率先行动,怎么可以不见呢?曾子说:'耸起两个肩膀,陪着讨好的笑脸,比大热天在田地里干活还累。'子路说:'不情愿的交谈,羞愧得脸上红红的,这不是我仲由所能理解的。'从这些看来,君子所修养的德行,可以知道了。"

【英语译文】

Gongsun Chou asked, "What's the reason for a person not to call to pay respects to a prince?" Mencius answered, "In ancient time, if a minister didn't want to be a prince then he wouldn't visit other prince. Duan Mugan climbed over the wall to avoid Marquis Wen of Wei State visiting. Xie Liu closed his house door, not letting Duke Miu of Lu State in. They all did things excessively. If one wants to see someone else in urgent need, it is alright to do it. Yang Huo wanted Confucius to see him but he feared it would violate rites. According to rites, if a minister wanted to award a scholar but the scholar wasn't at home and couldn't accepted the gift personally, then he should personally acknowledged in the minister's home. Yang Huo privately noticed one day when Confucius wasn't at home and he dispatched a man to bring a baked piglet to Confucius' home. And Confucius privately noticed one day when Yang Huo wasn't at home and he acknowledged personally at Yang Huo's home. At that time, Yang Huo initiated and how couldn't Confucius see him? Zeng Zi said, 'It is more tired to shrug shoulders and flatter others while smiling than to do farm work in the field.' Zi Lu said, 'An unwilling conversation makes one flush, which isn't what I can understand.' From these we can see a moral man's integrity."

【注释】(1)段干木:姓段,名干木。魏文侯时贤者。逾垣:同"逾墙"。翻越墙垣。辟:bì,退避;躲避。(2)泄柳:鲁缪公时人。不纳:不接受;不让进入。按:此二人未为臣。(3)迫:谓求见迫切。(4)阳货欲见孔子而恶无礼:事见《论语·阳货篇》。"见"使动用法。阳货欲令孔子来见。(5)大夫:阳货为鲁正卿季氏之宰(总管)为大夫级。当时孔子在野,称"士"。(6)瞰:kàn,同"瞰",窥伺。亡:外出;出门。(7)岂得:怎能,怎可。(8)胁肩谄笑:胁肩,读 xié ~,耸起肩膀故意表示敬畏。谄笑,谓勉强发笑以求媚。(9)病于:比……还疲惫。夏畦:指夏天在田地里劳动的人。(10)色:脸色。赧赧然:nǎnnǎn ~,惭愧脸红的样子。(11)非由之所知也:"由"是仲由自指。仲由,姓仲,名由,字子路;一字季路。这种"非……所知也"的句法是厌恶的婉转表达。(12)由是:从此。(13)所养:所养的德行。

【原文】8 戴盈之曰:[1]"什一,去关市之征,今兹未能,[2]请轻之,以待来年,然后已,何如?"孟子曰:"今有人日攘其邻之鸡者,[3]或告之曰:'是非君子之道。'曰:'请损之,月攘一鸡,以待来年,然后已。'如知其非义,斯速已矣,何待来年?"

【白话译文】

戴盈之说:"税率定为十分之一,关卡和集市不收税。今年办不到,想减轻一些,等到明年才完全实行,怎么样?"孟子说:"假如有个人,每天偷邻居一只鸡,有人告诉他说:'这不是正派人的行为。'他说:'想减少一些,每一个月偷一只,等到明年才不偷了。'如果晓得自己行为不合道义,就赶快停止,为什么要等到明年呢?"

【英语译文】

Dai Yingzhi, a minister of Song State said, "The ratio of tax is set as one tenth, and passes and fairs aren't taxed. But these cannot be realized. This year tax can be reduced and next year they are completely implemented. How about it?" Mencius answered, "Suppose a person steals one chicken each day from his neighbor. Somebody else tells him 'It isn't upright action.' The person replies, 'I want to reduce the quantity and I will steal one chicken each month. Till next year I will stop stealing.' If someone knows that his action isn't reasonable, he should stop doing so right away. Why does he wait till next year?"

【注释】(1)戴盈之:宋大夫。(2)今兹:今年,表示假设关系,相当于"若""假如"。(3)攘:读 rǎng,盗窃,窃取。

【原文】9 公都子曰:[1]"外人皆称夫子好辩,[2]敢问何也?"孟子曰:"予岂好辩哉?予不得已也。天下之生久矣,[3]一治一乱。当尧之时,水逆行,泛滥于中国,蛇龙居之,民无所定;[4]下者为巢,上者为营窟。[5]书曰:[6]'洚水警余。'洚水者,洪水也。使禹治之。禹掘地而注之海,驱蛇龙而放之菹;[7]水由地中行,江、淮、河、汉是也。险阻既远[8],鸟兽之害人者消,然后人得平土而居之。尧、舜既没,圣人之道衰。暴君代作,[9]坏宫室以为污池,民无所安息;弃田以为园囿,使民不得衣食。邪说暴行又作,园囿、污池、沛泽多而禽兽至[10]。及纣之身[11],天下又大乱。周公相武王,诛纣伐奄,三年讨其君,[12]驱飞廉于海隅而戮之[13]。灭国者五十,[14]驱虎豹犀象而远之。天下大悦。"书曰:'丕显哉,文王谟!丕承者,武王烈!佑启我后人,咸以正无缺。[15]'世衰道微,邪说暴行有作,臣弑其君者有之,子弑其父者有之。[16]孔子惧,作春秋。[17]春秋,天子之事也。是故孔子曰:'知我者其惟春秋乎!罪我者其惟春秋乎![18]'圣王不作,诸侯放恣,处士横议,[19]杨朱、墨翟之言盈天下。[20]天下之言,不归杨,则归墨。杨氏为我,是无君也;墨氏兼爱,是无父也。无父无君,是禽兽也。公明仪曰:[21]'庖有肥肉,厩有肥马,民有饥色,野有饿殍,此率兽而食人也。'杨、墨之道不息,孔子之道不着,是邪说诬民,充塞仁义也。[22]仁义充塞,则率兽食人,人将相食。吾为此惧,闲先圣之道,[23]距杨、墨,[24]放淫辞,[25]邪说者不得作。作于其心害于其事,作于其事,害于其政。圣人复起,不易吾言矣。昔者禹抑洪水而天下平,周公兼夷狄驱猛兽而百姓宁,[26]孔子成春秋而乱臣贼子惧。诗云:'戎狄是膺,荆舒是惩,则莫我敢承。[27]'无父无君,是周公所膺也。我亦欲正人心,息邪说,距诐行[28],放淫辞,以承三圣者;[29]岂好辩哉?予不得已也。能言距杨、墨者,圣人之徒也。"

【白话译文】

公都子说:“别人都说老师您喜欢辩论,请问这是为什么?”孟子说:“我哪里喜欢辩论呢?我是不得已罢了。人间世道的产生已经很久了,平静一段时间又混乱一段时间。当尧治理天下时,大水倒流,泛滥于中国,到处都有蛇和龙居住游腾。人们无处安身。低地的人们只得堆积柴草为窝,高地的人们只得挖地或垒土,做成一个个洞穴。《尚书》说:‘洚水警告我们。’洚水就是洪水。尧令禹治理洪水。禹疏通河道,把水引向大海,把蛇和龙赶回草泽中。水在地沟里流,长江、淮河、黄河、汉水就是这样。艰难困苦已经克服了,害人的鸟兽也不见了。人们这才能够在平地上居住。尧、舜死了以后,圣人的道义逐渐衰落,残暴的君主不断出现。他们毁民房,挖深池,使百姓无处安身,他们毁良田营造游乐园林,使老百姓得不到吃和穿。荒谬的邪说和残暴的恶行又乘机发作。园林、深池、草泽,多了起来,鸟兽也追随而来。到商纣在位的时候,天下又大乱。周公辅佐武王,杀了纣王,又讨伐纣的帮凶奄国,征战三年,杀了奄君。还把纣的幸臣飞廉赶到海边杀了。纣的帮凶国一共被灭掉五十个。老虎、豹子、犀牛、大象也被赶到了远方。天下的百姓都很高兴。《尚书》说:‘文王的谋略多么英明光辉,武王的功绩多么伟大辉煌。帮助启发了我们后代,大家都走正路不缺失。’然而世道又逐渐衰落,邪说和暴行又抬头行动,有臣下杀君主的,有儿子杀父亲的。孔子对此很担忧,写了《春秋》这部史书。写史书,由天子经管;所以孔子说:‘了解我的,也许将由于这部书罢!怪罪我的也许将由于这部书罢!’从此以后,圣王也没出现过,诸侯任意妄为,在野的士人,随意议论,杨朱、墨翟的言论遍及天下,天下的嘴仗,不站在杨朱一边,就站在墨翟一边。杨朱派主张一切为自己,这便是眼中没有君上;墨翟派主张爱要一个样没有差别,这便是眼中没有父母。没有父母和君上,这便成了禽兽。公明仪说过:‘厨房里有肥肉,马房里有肥马,百姓有饥饿的脸色,野外有饿死者的尸体,这就是带领着禽兽来吃人。’杨、墨的主张不消除,孔子的学说不显著,都是由于邪说欺蒙百姓堵塞了仁义。堵塞仁义,就是带领着禽兽来吃人。不讲仁义的人还将互相吞食。我为此担忧,要捍卫古代圣人的学说,抵御杨、墨的谬说,清除邪僻荒诞的错误言论,让持邪说的人不能妄作。妄作于心,危害做事;妄作于做事,危害政治。圣人再次兴起,不会改变我说的这些话。从前大禹制服了洪水,天下太平;周公兼管了少数民族,赶走了猛兽,百姓安宁;孔子写成了《春秋》而乱臣和逆子害怕。诗说:‘攻击作乱的戎、狄,惩罚楚、舒相勾结,达到了所向无敌。’像杨、墨这类无视父母、君上的歹人,正是周公所要攻击的。我也要端正人心,消灭邪说,反对偏邪不正的行为,排斥荒唐的言论,继承大禹、周公、孔子三位圣人的事业。能说我喜欢辩论吗?我实在是迫不得已呀。能够用言论来反对杨、墨的,算是圣人的门徒了。"

【英语译文】

Gongdu Zi, one of Mencius' disciples asked, "The others said that you love debating, would you please tell me why?" Mencius replied, "How could they say that I love debating? I just have to do so. The way of this world has come into being for very long time. This world has existed peacefully for a while and it became chaotic for another period. When the sage Yao was in power, great flood overflowed the land and snakes and dragons grew everywhere leaving no place for human beings. In low land, people made dens from grasses and in high land people dug holes to live in. *The Book of History* said, 'The flood warns us.' And then Yao ordered Yu to control flood. Yu had men dredge rivers and led flood to flow into seas, thus snakes and dragons were forced to go back lakes. Water flowed in trenches so that the Yangtze River, the Yellow River, the Huai River, and the Han River formed. Hardships and difficulties were overcome and ferocious birds and beasts disappeared. As a result, human beings managed to live in plains. After the death of sages Yao and Shun, the sages' Way declined gradually but tyrants kept appearing. They destroyed people's houses and dug deep trenches so that people had no place to live in; they destroyed fertile fields, making them into gardens so that people had no food to eat. Ridiculous heresy and cruel evil doings continued to arise. Gardens, ponds, and swamps multiplied and birds and beasts filed in these places. Till the time of King Zhou of Shang Dynasty's governance, the world became complete riot. Duke Zhou assisted King Wu of Zhou Dynasty to kill King Zhou of Shang Dynasty and to crusade Yan State for three years, which was the accomplice of Shang Dynasty till the killing of its monarch. Furthermore, the favorite minister of Zhou was killed by the sea. Zhou's accomplice State amounted to fifty and they were all completely destroyed. Tigers, jaguars, rhinoceroses, and elephants were also driven away to distant places. People in the world were all very happy. *The Book of History* said, 'How wise were King Wen's strategies and how great were King Wu's achievements. Both of them benefited descending generations and we all went on the right way.' However, the great way gradually declined again, as a result heresy and atrocities began to spread. Someone slain his king and someone slain his father. Confucius worried about this situation and then he finished historic book *The Annals*. The Son of the heaven was in charge of writing historic book. Therefore Confucius said, 'Perhaps people know of me due to this book and people blame me due to this book.' From then on, no sage appeared again; princes did things at will, and men out of power discussed state affairs at will. Words of Yang Zhu and Mo Di prevailed everywhere. The pros and cons were for either Yang Zhu or Mo Di. The school of Yang Zhu argued that men should do things for themselves, and consequently there was no king in their eyes. The school of Mo Di argued that men should love others without difference, and consequently there was no parent in their eyes. If there were no king and parent, men then became the same as birds and beasts. Gongming Yi said, 'In the kitchen there is fat meat; in the stable there is fat horse; in the wilderness there is dead body; in the mean time common people had hungry complexion, thus birds and beasts were led to eat them all.' The reason for that argument of Yang Zhu and Mo Di wasn't rid of and the teachings of Confucius wasn't advocated was that the heresy had deceived common people and blocked humanity and righteousness. Blocking humanity and righteousness is leading the birds and beasts to eat men. Men without humanity and righteousness will eat each other. I worry about this situation and I will defend ancient sage's teaching, resisting the heresy of Yang Zhu and Mo Di, ridding of ridiculous and wrong words and not letting men with heresy act at will. For one's heart, acting at will harms doing things, and for doing things, acting at will harms politics. When sages appear again, they won't change my words. In the old days the great Yu controlled flood so that the world became peaceful; Duke Zhou governed ethnic minorities and drove away beasts so that common people lived calmly, and Confucius wrote *The Annals* so that treacherous ministers and un-filial sons were frightened. *The Book of Songs* said, 'They fought against enemies in frontiers. They punished foes in Jin and Chu States. Who dared hold up great army's/ movement.' The wicked people like Yang Zhu and Mo Di who had no king and parent in their eyes were just the aim attacked by Duke Zhou. I also want to correct men's mind, rid of heresies, fight against evil doings, and exclude ridiculous words so that I can inherit the causes of three sages Great Yu, Duke Zhou and Confucius. Can you say that I love debating? I was really forced to do so. The man who can fight against Yang Zhu and Mo Di with words can be the disciple of sages."

【注释】(1)公都子:孟子弟子。(2)外人:他人,别人,没有亲友关系的人。(3)天下之生:天下,指"中国"。生:产生。(4)无所定:无处安定。(5)下者为巢,上者为营窟:下者、上者,言“低地”“高地”。为巢,堆积薪柴做住处。为营窟,掘地或累土造住所。一说营窟是相连的洞穴。(6)书曰洚水警余:这是《尚书·逸篇》中的文字。洚水,即洪水。(7)菹:jù,水草丛生的沼泽地。(8)阻:险要阻塞之地;艰难困苦。既远:已经胜过。(9)代作:更迭而作。(10)园囿:周围有墙垣布置亭榭石木,间或畜有鸟兽的皇家花园。污池:水池。沛泽:沼泽,水草茂密的低洼地。(11)身:毕生,一辈子。(12)诛纣伐奄,三年讨其君:诛,杀。奄,读 yǎn,古国名。在今山东曲阜市,助纣为虐者。三年讨其君,三年后杀奄君。(13)飞廉:纣的幸臣。戮:杀。(14)灭国者五十:灭国者,灭亡其国家的。五十,五十个。按:这五十个被灭亡的国家,都是助纣为虐的国家。(15)书曰:咸以正无缺:书曰以下六句当为尚书逸篇中文。丕显,英明;大显。谟,计谋;谋略。丕承,谓帝王承天受命。烈,辉煌;显赫。佑启,帮助启发。咸以正无缺,都正确无缺点。其中“以”是助词,补凑音节。(16)有作:又作。臣弑其君者有之:“有臣弑其君者”的倒装。宾语前置是一种强调法,用代词“之”填充宾语本位,免生误会。下句仿此。(17)惧:忧虑,《春秋》:编年体史书名。孔子据鲁修订而成。所记起于鲁隐公元年止于鲁哀公十四年,凡二百四十二年。叙事极简,用字寓褒贬。为其传者,以《左氏》《公羊》《谷梁》最著名。(18)是故:连词,因此;所以。其惟:表推测将来。大概将由,也许将以。(19)不作:不发生,不兴起。放恣:犹“放纵”。任意行为而不受约束。处士:本指有才德而隐居不仕的人。后亦泛指没有做过官的人,横议:hèng ~,恣意议论。(20)杨朱:战国初,魏国人。又称阳子、阳子居、阳生。他主张“贵生”“重己”“全性葆真、不以物累形”;反对墨子的“兼爱”和儒家的伦理思想。墨翟:春秋战国之际晚于孔子早于孟子在世,墨家的创始人,姓墨,名翟,相传原为宋国人,后长期居鲁。曾学习儒术,认为礼太烦琐,反对“天命”和“爱有差等”。(21)公明仪:见“5·1 中注(6)”。(22)诬:欺骗。充塞:堵塞。(23)闲:用于遮拦阻隔的栅栏。引申为“捍卫”“保卫”。(24)距:排斥;抵御。(25)放淫辞:清除邪僻荒诞的言论。(26)兼夷狄:即“兼领夷狄”,谓在管理中华的同时还兼理少数民族的睦邻关系。作“兼并”解,恐非本意。(27)膺:伐,击。荆舒:亦作“荆荼”。指春秋时的楚国和舒国。在今安徽省庐江县境内,时为楚之与国,故连称。承:抵御。(28)息:灭绝。诐行:bì ~,偏邪不正的行为。(29)三圣:指禹、周公、孔子。

【原文】10 匡章曰:[1]“陈仲子岂不诚廉士哉?[2]居于陵,[3]三日不食,耳无闻,目无见也。井上有李,螬食实者过半矣,[4]匍匐往,将食之;[5]三咽,然后耳有闻,目有见。”孟子曰:“于齐国之士,吾必以仲子为巨擘焉。[6]虽然,仲子恶能廉?充仲子之操,则蚓而后可也。夫蚓,上食槁壤,[7]下饮黄泉。[8]仲子所居之室,伯夷之所筑与?

抑亦盗跖之所筑与?[9]所食之粟,伯夷之所树与?抑亦盗跖之所树与?是未可知也。"曰:"是何伤哉?彼身织屦,妻辟纑,[10]以易之也。"曰:"仲子,齐之世家也;兄戴,盖禄万钟;[11]以兄之禄为不义之禄而不食也,以兄之室为不义之室而不居也,辟兄离母,[12]处于於陵。他日归,则有馈其兄生鹅者,己频顣曰:[13]'恶用是鶃鶃者为哉?[14]'他日,其母杀是鹅也,与之食之。其兄自外至,曰:'是鶃鶃之肉也。'出而哇之。以母则不食,以妻则食之;以兄之室则弗居,以於陵则居之,是尚能充其类也乎?若仲子者,蚓而后充其操者也。"

【白话译文】

匡章说:"陈仲子难道不真是一个廉洁的人吗?住在於陵,三天没吃东西,耳朵不能听了,眼睛不能看了。井上有李树,李子被蛴螬一类害虫吃坏了多半,他慢慢地爬起来捡李子吃;吞下了三口,然后,耳朵能听了,眼睛能看了。"孟子说:"在齐国的士人中我必定把仲子看作大拇哥。虽然这样,他怎么能算廉洁呢?要推行他这种操守,只有把人变成蚯蚓才行。蚯蚓,向上吃干土,朝下喝泉水。仲子住的房子是伯夷一样廉洁的人建筑的呢?还是盗跖一样贪婪的人建筑的呢?仲子吃的粮食是伯夷一样廉洁的人栽种的呢?还是盗跖一样贪婪的人栽种的呢?这些都是不可能知道的。"匡章说:"这有什么损伤呢?他亲自打草鞋,妻子绩麻练麻,用自己的成品去换需要的东西。"孟子说:"仲子是齐国的宗族大家,他哥哥陈戴从盖邑收入的俸禄就有几万石;他认为哥哥的俸禄是不义之物,不去吃它;认为哥哥的住宅是不义之产,不去住它。远避哥哥,离开母亲,住在於陵。有一天他回家,恰巧有人给他哥哥送来一只活鹅,他皱着眉头说:'要这种呃呃叫的东西干什么?'过了些时间,他母亲杀了这只鹅做菜给他下饭。正在这时他哥哥从外面回家,说道:'这就是那呃呃叫的东西的肉啊。'他便跑到门外把所吃的东西都呕了出来。对母亲所做的饭菜不吃,却吃妻子同别人所交换得来的食物,对哥哥所有的房屋不住,却远远住在於陵,背兄离母。这能算廉洁到了顶点吗?要把陈仲子这种操守推行开来,只有把人变成蚯蚓才行。"

【英语译文】

Kuang Zhang said, "Wasn't Chen Zhongzi a white-handed man? He lived in Wuling without eating anything for three days and almost became deaf and blind. Beside a well grew plum tree in which the plums were half eaten by scarabs, he crawled there to pick up plums to eat. After he swallowed three times, he could see and hear something." Mencius said, "I surely regard him as an outstanding one among scholars in Qi State. Even so how can he be regarded as a white-handed man? If we spread his integrity, we should change human beings into earthworms. Earthworms eat dry earth and drink underground water. Was the house in which Chen Zhongzi lived built by a white-handed man like Bo Yi? Or was it built by a greedy man like Dao Zhi? Was the grain eaten by Chen Zhongzi planted by a white-handed man like Bo Yi? Or was it planted by a greedy man like Dao Zhi? We cannot know all these things." Kuang Zhang said, "It doesn't matter. He himself wove grass shoes and his wife spun hemp. And he used these things to exchange what they wanted." Mencius said, "Chen Zhongzi belonged to an eminent clan family and his elder brother Chen Dai got several ten thousands of salary grain from Geyi County. He thought that his brother's salary was injustice so that he refused to eat. And he thought that his brother's house was injustice so that he refused to live in. He lived in Wuling after dodging his brother and leaving his mother. One day when he got home, someone sent a goose which was cackling. He asked 'Why do you have this cackling goose?' After a while his mother killed the goose and cooked it for his dinner. At the moment his brother came in and said, 'This is the cackling thing's meat.' He then got out of the door and vomited what he had eaten. He refused to eat what his mother cooked but ate what his wife exchanged. He refused to live in his brother's house but lived in Wuling staying away from his mother and brother. Can we say that he's a most white-handed man? If we spread Chen Zhongzi's integrity we must transform human beings into earthworms."

【注释】(1)匡章:齐人。曾为齐威王将,率兵御秦,大败之。宣王时又曾统兵取燕。(2)陈仲子:又称于陵仲子。齐国高士。(3)于陵:wū ~,地名。在今山东邹平县境。(4)螬:cáo,即"蛴螬"。金龟子的幼虫。(5)匍匐:púfú,爬行。谓手足并行。将:持,取,拿。(6)巨擘:~ bò,大拇指。比喻杰出人物。(7)槁壤:干土。(8)黄泉:地下的泉水。(9)盗跖:~ zhí,一作"盗蹠"。春秋时有名的大盗,柳下惠之弟。(10)身:亲自。织屦:~ jù,用麻、草、丝、革等为材料编织鞋子。辟纑:bìlú,绩麻和练麻。谓治麻的事。(11)盖:gě,地名。战国齐盖邑,陈戴的采邑。参阅《公孙丑下》第六章。钟:古容量单位。春秋时齐国公室的公量,合六斛四斗。之后亦有合八斛,十斛之制。按:十斗曰斛。(12)辟:同"避"。(13)频顣:píncù,亦作"颦蹙""频蹙",皱眉。(14)鶃鶃:yìyì,鹅鸣声。

孟子集注卷七　离娄章句上　凡二十八章

【原文】1 孟子曰："篱娄之明,[1]公输子之巧,[2]不以规矩不能成方员,[3]师旷之聪;[4]不以六律,[5]不能正五音;[6]尧舜之道,不以仁政,不能平治天下。今有仁心仁闻而民不被其泽[7],不可法于后世者,不行先王之道也。故曰:徒善不足以为政,徒法不足以自行。[8]诗云:'不愆不忘,率由旧章。[9]'遵先王之法而过者,未之有也。圣人既竭目力焉,继之以规矩准绳,以为方员平直,不可胜用也;[10]既竭耳力焉,继之以六律正五音,不可胜用也;既竭心思焉,继之以不忍人之政,[11]而仁覆天下矣。故曰,为高必因丘陵[12],为下必因川泽;为政不因先王之道,可谓智乎?是以惟仁者宜在高位。不仁而在高位是播其恶于众也。上无道揆也,下无法守也,朝不信道,工不信度,君子犯义,小人犯刑,国之所存者幸也。[13]故曰,城郭不完,[14]兵甲不多,[15]非国之灾也;田野不辟,货财不聚,非国之害也。[16]上无礼,下无学,贼民兴,丧无日矣。诗曰:'天之方蹶,无然泄泄。[17]'泄泄犹沓沓也。事君无义,进退无礼,言则非先王之道者,[18]犹沓沓也。故曰,责难于君谓之恭,陈善闭邪谓之敬,吾君不能谓之贼。[19]"

【白话译文】

孟子说:"篱娄的视力强,公输般的手艺巧,不用圆规和曲尺,也不能做好方形和圆形。师旷很聪明,不用六律,也不能校正五音。尧、舜之道,如果不行仁政,也不能治理好天下。假如有好心肠、好名声,而老百姓却受不到恩泽,不可以作为后世榜样的,那便是不实行先代圣王之大道的缘故。所以说,只有好心没有好政不能治理好政事;只有好政没有好心,好政等于虚构,不能落实推行。《诗经》上说:'不出错误不忘本,全遵先王的教训。'不反先代圣王法度而犯错误的,是从来没有过的事。圣人用尽了视力,又采用圆规、曲尺、水平仪、墨线等来进行营造方的、圆的、平的、直的东西。于是圣人在这个方面的法度就用不完了。圣人用尽了听力,又采用六律来校正五音,于是圣人在这个方面的法度就用不完了。圣人用尽了听力,又采用仁政,于是圣人的仁德就覆盖天下了。所以说,要求高过丘陵必须依靠丘陵,要求低于川泽必须依靠川泽。进行政治治理,不依靠先代圣王之道,能说是聪明吗?因此,只有仁人应该处于统治地位。不仁的人而处于统治地位,就会把他的罪恶传播给群众。在上的没有准则,在下的就无法履行职守。朝廷不落实准则,官吏不落实法度,有地位的人违反正义,无地位的人触犯刑律,这样的国家还存在的,真是太侥幸了。所以说,城墙不坚固,军备不充足,不是国家的灾难;田野没开辟,经济不富裕,不是国家的祸害;在上的人没有礼义,在下的人没有文化,违法乱纪的人到处都是,到国家灭亡的日子也就没有几天了。《诗经》上说:'上头正处于动乱,切不要自由散漫。'自由散漫就是话多行动慢。服侍君主不正派,前进后退没礼仪,说话就毁谤先王之道,这就是话多行动慢。所以说,用仁政来要求君主,才叫作'恭',向君主宣讲仁义,堵塞异端,才叫作'敬',如果认为君主无能就叫作'伤害'。"

【英语译文】

Mencius said, "Li Lou had strong eyesight. Gongshu Ban had wonderful craft but without compass and carpenter's square, he couldn't make square or circle. Shi Kuang was very smart but without six law, he couldn't adjust five pitches. Without implementing government of humanity, the Way of sages Yao and Shun couldn't administrate the world. He surely hadn't carried out the great way of ancient sages if a monarch had good intention and reputation but the common people couldn't benefit from him and he couldn't set an example for his followers. Therefore, with good intention but without good administration, state affairs cannot be made orderly; with good administration but without good intention it's fictitious to administrate well. *The Book of Songs* said, 'To be so they've made no mistakes. Based on old rules state hasn't perils.' There wasn't the situation where a monarch didn't violate the laws of deceased sages and kings but made mistake. The sages used up their eyesight and employed compass, carpenter's square, level meter, and carpenter's line marker to make square, circle, level and straight things. Thus, sages' laws concerning these things cannot be used up. The sages used up their hearing and employed six law to adjust five pitches. Thus, sages' laws concerning these things cannot be used up. The sages used up their hearing and implemented government of humanity, thus their virtue reaches every corner of the world. Therefore when you want to surpass a mound you should rely on it, and when you want to be below a swamp you should also rely on it. You are not smart when you deal with administrative affairs you don't rely on the ways of deceased sage kings. So only humanistic man can be in the governing post. When a man without humanity is in governing post, he will spread his sins to the masses. If a superior has no rule, the inferior cannot observe his duty. It is fluke for a state to continue to exist, where the court doesn't follow rule, the officials don't follow laws, prestigious people violate justice, and humble people violate the criminal law. It isn't a state's disaster that city walls aren't solid and armaments aren't plentiful and it isn't a state's scourge that fields aren't tilled and economy aren't prosperous. The superior haven't rites and rituals, the inferiors aren't educated, and lots of persons violate laws. Such a state will perish very soon. *The Book of Songs* said, 'The heaven's bringing you chaotic riots. You should not talk about them careless.' Talking about them careless'y means that someone speaks a lot but hesitates to take action. If a person speaks a lot but hesitates to take action, he serves his king in wrong way; he goes in and out of the court without rites and rituals; he slanders the ways of deceased kings when he begins to speak. Therefore, it is respectfulness to require one's king to implement government of humanity and righteousness. It is harm to him if you think your king is incapable."

【注释】(1)离娄:即离朱。黄帝时人。视力特强,能看清百步之外的秋毫之末(一说针锋)。按:秋毫,指鸟兽在秋天新长出的细毛。(2)公输子:姓公输,名班。春秋时鲁国巧匠。亦称鲁班。班,或作"般""盘"。(3)规矩:制作、校正圆形和方形的两种工具。方员:同"方圆"。(4)师旷:春秋时晋平公的太师(乐官之长)。著名的盲人音乐家。(5)六律:中国古代乐律的十二调,从低到高,依次为:1)黄钟、2)大吕、3)太簇、4)夹钟、5)姑洗、6)仲吕、7)蕤宾(ruí bīn)、8)林钟、9)夷则、10)南吕、11)无射、12)应钟。奇数各律称"律",偶数各律称"吕"。六律,即黄钟、太簇、姑洗、蕤宾、夷则、无射。(6)五音:中国音阶之名。即宫、商、角、征、羽。依次相当于 do、re、mi、so、la。(7)今:假设连词。译为"若""假设""如果"。仁心仁闻:仁爱的心和仁爱的名声。(8)徒善、徒法:朱熹《四书集注》:"徒,犹空也。有其心无其政,是谓徒善;有其政无其心是谓徒法。"不足以自行:谓有其政而无其心,其政就是虚设,不能正常推行。(9)诗云:'不愆不忘,率由旧章':见《诗·大雅·假乐》。愆,错误。率由,遵循;沿用。旧章,昔日的典章。(10)准绳:测定物体平直的器具。准,测水平的仪器;绳,量直度的墨线。(11)不忍人之政:犹言"仁政"。(12)为高:要求高过丘陵。下文"为下"与此相反,要求低于沼泽河床。因:依托;利用;凭借。(13)道揆:准则;法度。法守:谓按法度履行自己的职守。朝不信道:朝廷不落实准则。工不信度:官吏不落实法度。君子犯义:有地位的人违反正义。小人犯刑:无地位的人触犯刑律。幸:侥幸,谓意外获得或免除。(14)完:坚固。(15)兵甲:兵器和铠甲。泛指武器、军备。(16)辟:同"辟"。开辟。(17)诗曰:'天之方蹶,无然泄泄:见《诗·大雅·板》。蹶,读 guì,动乱。泄泄,读 yìyì,朱熹《四书集注》:"泄泄,怠缓悦从之貌"。沓沓,读 tàtà,语多貌。按:

凡是话多,行动相应迟缓。(18)非:动词,意动用法,“以为不是”之意。(19)责难:zénán,勉励人作难为的事。(读 zénàn,意谓“指责”“非难”。),陈善闭邪:陈述仁政义举,阻塞异端邪说。吾君:自己的君主。不能:意动用法,认为无能。谓之贼:叫做伤害。

【原文】2 孟子曰:“规矩,方圆之至也;[1]圣人,人伦之至也。[2]欲为君,尽君道;欲为臣,尽臣道。二者皆法尧、舜而已矣,不以舜之所以事尧事君,[3]不敬其君者也;不以尧之所以治民治民,[4]贼其民者也。孔子曰:‘道二,[5]仁与不仁而已矣。’暴其民甚,则身弑国亡;[6]不甚,则身危国削,[7]名之曰“幽”“厉”,[8]虽孝子慈孙,百世不能改也。诗云:‘殷鉴不远,在夏后之世。[9]’此之谓也。”

【白话译文】

孟子说:“圆规和曲尺,是圆形和方形最恰当的准则。圣人是为人处世最恰当的准则。要做君主就要尽君道以义使臣;要做臣子就要尽臣道以忠事君。君和臣只要效法尧和舜就行了。不以舜服侍尧那样的行为服侍君上,便是对君上的不恭敬;不以尧治理百姓那样的行为治理百姓,便是对老百姓的残害。孔子说:‘治理百姓的途径有两条,一条实行仁政,另一条不实行仁政。’暴虐太厉害,本身会遭杀,国家会被灭亡。不太厉害的,本身也很危险,国力会被削弱,死后的谥号叫‘幽’、‘厉’,即使他有孝子贤孙,经历一百代也背着坏名声,不能更改。《诗经》上说:‘殷的镜子并不远,是夏桀所犯罪愆。’说的正是这个意思。”

【英语译文】

Mencius said, “Compass and carpenter's square are the appropriate criterion for a circular and square article respectively. Sages are the most appropriate criterion for being a man and doing things. To be a monarch one should observe the way of monarch and then employ ministers. To be a minister one should observe the way of a minster and then serve the monarch. If someone doesn't serve his monarch in the way that Shun served Yao, he isn't respectful to his monarch. If someone doesn't govern common people in the way that Yao governed his people, he is harming his subjects. Confucius said, ‘There are two ways to govern people, one of which is implementing government of humanity and the other is not implementing it.’ If a tyrant is too brutal, he himself will be killed and his country will perish. If a tyrant isn't so brutal, he himself will be dangerous, and his country power will be weakened. And his posthumous title will be '*you*' which means darkness or '*li*' which means brutality. His notorious reputation cannot be changed for hundred generations even if his offspring are filial. *The Book of Songs* said, 'Mirror for Shang was not so far. You know King Jie's result of Xia.' This exactly means that truth."

【注释】(1)至:极,中正的准则,最恰当的准则。(2)人伦:中国古代指人与人之间的关系和应当遵守的行为准则。(3)舜之所以事尧:舜服侍尧的行为。(4)尧之所以治民:尧治理百姓的行为。(5)道二:道,指治理国家的方法。二,犹言二种,二个。(6)身弑:身,指君主本人。弑,下杀上。(7)国削:国家被削弱。(8)"幽""厉":朱熹《四书集注》:"幽,暗。厉,虐。皆恶也。苟得其实,则虽有孝子慈孙,爱其祖考之甚者,亦不得废公议而改之。言不仁之祸必至于此,可惧之甚也。"《逸周书·谥法解》:"壅遏不通曰幽,动祭乱常曰幽,杀戮无辜曰厉。"按;周朝就有谥为幽之王和谥为厉之王。(9)殷鉴不远:见《诗·大雅·荡》。谓前人失败的教训就在眼前应该引以为戒。赵岐注:"诗·大雅·荡之篇也,殷之所见,视近在夏后之世矣。以前代善恶为明镜也,欲使周亦鉴于殷之所以亡也。"

【原文】3 孟子曰:"三代之得天下也以仁,[1]其失天下也以不仁。[2]国之所以废兴存亡亦然。天子不仁,不保四海;[3]诸侯不仁,不保社稷;[4]大夫不仁,不保宗庙;[5]卿士庶人不仁,不保四体。[6]今恶死亡而乐不仁,[7]是犹恶醉而强酒。[8]"

【白话译文】

孟子说:"夏、商、周三代的获得天下,是由于禹、汤、文、武行仁,他们后来失去了天下,是由于桀、纣、幽、厉不行仁。国家的兴起和衰败,生存和灭亡,也是这样。天子如果不行仁,便不能保有天下;诸侯如果不行仁,便不能保有国家;卿大夫如果不行仁,便不能不保有祖庙;士人和普通百姓如果不行仁,便不能保全躯体。现在有些人怕死却又乐于不仁,这就好像又怕醉又要倾壶干杯。"

【英语译文】

Mencius said, "Xia, Shang, Zhou dynasties got the world successively due to Yu, Tang, Wen, Wu implementing humanity respectively. Later on , the three dynasties lost the world due to Jie, Zhou, You, Li not implementing humanity. The rise, decline, prosperity and perish of a state is also like this. If a king doesn't carry out humanity, he won't keep the world; if a prince doesn't carry out humanity, he won't keep his state; if a minister doesn't carry out humanity, he won't keep his ancestral temple; if a scholar or common person doesn't carry out humanity, he won't keep his limbs. Nowadays someone fears to die but refuses to implement humanity either, which is the same as one fears to be drunk but drinks up all wine in a pot."

【注释】(1)三代:指夏、商、周。禹、汤、文、武,以仁得天下。(2)其失天下:桀、纣、幽、厉,以不仁而失掉天下。(3)四海:犹言天下,全中国。(4)社稷:古代帝王诸侯所祭的土神和谷神。社,土神;稷,谷神。代称国家。(5)宗庙:卿大夫有了采邑后才可能立宗庙祭祖。不保宗庙,犹言失去采邑。(6)士庶人:士人和普通百姓;亦泛指人民百姓。四体:四肢,引申指整个身体。(7)恶死:wù～,怕死。恶,畏惧。下文"恶醉"解同此。(8)强酒:qiǎng～,勉强或过量饮酒。

【原文】4 孟子曰:"爱人不亲,[1]反其仁;[2]治人不治,[3]反其智;[4]礼人不答,[5]反其敬[6]——行有不得者皆反求诸己,[7]其身正而天下归之。[8]诗云:'永言配命,自求多福。[9]'"

【白话译文】

孟子说:"我爱别人,别人却不亲近我,就反省自己的仁德是否深厚。我帮助别人为善,别人却不帮助我为善,就反省自己的智慧是否足够。我以礼对待别人,别人却不以礼对待我,就反省自己的敬意是否不足。——凡是行为没有成效,就反问自己,找自己的原因。若自己正确,天下的人不会不支持我。《诗经》上说:'永远同天命配合,自能求得更多福。'"

【英语译文】

Mencius said, "I will reflect whether my virtue is deepenovgh or not if I love other people but they are not close to me. I will reflect whether my wit is enough or not if I help other people to do kind things but they don't help me to do so. I will reflect whether my respect is enough or not if I deal with other people with rites but they don't do so to me. We should ask and reflect ourselves on condition that our actions aren't effective. If we are correct none doesn't support us. *The Book of Songs* said, 'Obeying heaven's order, they never violate. They'd be self-reliant pursuing happiness.'"

【注释】(1)爱人不亲:紧缩句。省略了"爱人"的主语"我"和"不亲"的主语"人"与宾语"我"。补入被省略的后,即"我爱人人不亲我。"下文"治人不治、礼人不答”两句解同此。(2)反其仁:反,反省。其,我的。仁,仁德,仁术。(3)治人不治:治,整治,修理,使完善。治人,助人为善。(4)智:智慧,智能。(5)礼人不答:礼人,以礼待人。答,报答,回报。(6)敬:敬意。(7)得:成功。反求诸己:犹反躬自问。谓从自己方面找原因。(8)其身正而天下归之:其,假设连词,如果。身正:本身正确,自己正确。(9)诗云:‘永言配命,自求多福’:见《诗·大雅·文王》。言,语气助词。配命,配合天命。一说,天所给予之命。见王国维与友人论诗书中成语书。

【原文】5 孟子曰:“人有恒言,[1]皆曰‘天下国家’。天下之本在国,[2]国之本在家,家之本在身。[3]”

【白话译文】

孟子说:“人间有句俗话,大家常说‘天下国家。’天下的根基在国,国的根基在家,家的根基在每个人。”

【英语译文】

Mencius said, “There is a famous saying that people always say ‘the world and state’. The root of world lies in state, and the root of state lies in family, and the root of family lies in each person.”

【注释】(1)恒言:常言,俗语。(2)本:草木的根。引申为事物的根基或主体。(3)身:个体,自身。

【原文】6 孟子曰:“为政不难,不得罪于巨室。[1]巨室之所慕,[2]一国慕之;一国之所慕,天下慕之;故沛然德教溢乎四海。[3]”

【白话译文】

孟子说:“从事政治并不难,只要不触怒那些有影响实力的世家大族就行了。世家大族所向往的,一国的人都会仿效;一国的人都向往的,天下的人都会仿效。所以运用世家大族,壮阔的道德教化可以在天下流布。”

【英语译文】

Mencius said, “It isn't difficult to engage in politics on condition that those aristocratic families, haven't been offended. People in a whole state will imitate what aristocratic families yearn for; and people in the world will imitate what a whole state yearn for. Therefore, by using the aristocratic families, virtue and education can be spread throughout."

【注释】(1)得罪:冒犯,触怒。巨室:世家大族。战国时诸侯失德,巨室擅权,为患严重。不修其本而遽欲胜之,则未必能胜而取祸,先务修德以服其心为上。(2)慕:mù,向往,仿效。(3)沛然:充盈盛大的样子。德教:道德与教化。溢乎:流布于。乎,介词,同"于"。

【原文】7 孟子曰:"天下有道,[1]小德役大德,[2]小贤役大贤;天下无道,小役大,弱役强。斯二者,天也。[3]顺天者存,逆天者亡。齐景公曰:'既不能令,又不受命,是绝物也。'涕出而女于吴[4]。今也小国师大国而耻受命焉,是犹弟子而耻受命于先师也。如耻之,莫若师文王。师文王,大国五年小国七年,必为政于天下矣。诗云:[5]'商之孙子,其丽不亿。[6]上帝既命,侯于周服。[7]侯服于周,天命靡常。[8]殷士肤敏,[9]裸将于京。[10]'孔子曰:'仁不可为众也。[11]夫国君好仁,天下无敌。'今也欲无敌于天下而不以仁,是犹执热而不以濯也。诗云:'谁能执热,逝不以濯?[12]'"

【白话译文】

孟子说:"天下政治清明,道德较高的人指挥道德较低的人,很贤能的人指挥贤能稍逊的人。天下政治黑暗,大的役使小的,强的役使弱的。这两种情况都取决于天。顺从天的生存,违背天的灭亡。齐景公曾说:'既不能命令别人,又不能接受别人命令,是走绝路。'他流着眼泪把女儿送给了吴王阖庐。如今小国以大国为师,却又以接受命令为耻,这就像学生以听命于老师为耻一样。如果真以为耻,最好以文王为师。大国用五年的工夫,小国用七年的工夫,就可以在天下推行善政了。《诗经》上说:'商朝的后代子孙,超过十万一大群。上天已把命令改,顺服周朝得新生。得到新生顺周朝,天命不常威信高。殷人优美又敏捷,助周裸祭进京镐。'孔子说:'仁没有什么力量能够抗衡,国君如果爱好行仁,就将无敌于天下。'如今一些诸侯心想无敌于天下,却又不行仁政,这就像手捧热物,而不用水来浇凉。《诗经》上说:'谁能捧那烫手物,不用凉水来涤除?'"

【英语译文】

Mencius said, "When politics is clear and bright in the world, more virtuous people instruct less virtuous people and more capable men instruct less capable men. Whereas when politics is dark in the world, the big make the small work and the strong make the weak work. The two situations are decided by the Heaven. Those who are obedient to the Heaven will survive and those who are against the Heaven will perish. Duke Jing of Qi State ever said, ‘It is to head toward disaster if someone refuse to order others and to be ordered.’ He, with tear, presented his daughter to the king of Wu State, He Lu. Nowadays, small states regard big states as teachers but feel ashamed to be ordered by the big one, which is the same as a disciple feel ashamed to be ordered by his master. If someone really feels ashamed, then he'd better regard King Wen of Zhou Dynasty as his teacher. A big state can spread government of humanity in five years and a small state can do this in seven years. *The Book of Songs* said, ‘Offspring of Shang Dynasty come here. The number amounts to hundred million. As soon as the heaven's order is issued. Persons of Shang Dynasty have surrendered. Persons of Shang Dynasty have surrendered. The heaven's order hasn't its fixed method. Old officials in Shang Dynasty are clever. They've all gone to pay respect to the King.’ Confucius said, ‘None can contend with humanity. A monarch will have no rival if he loves to implement humanity.’ Nowadays some princes want to have no rival but hesitates to implement humanity, which is the same as that someone holds hot things but refuse to splash it with cool water. *The Book of Songs* said, ‘Who would be able to get rid of heat, /How could people not take a bath?’”

【注释】(1)有道:~dào,有好的政治局面或政治措施。无道,与此相反。(2)小德役大德:小德,指德行修养较低的人。大德,指德行修养较高的人。役,动词,服役。引申为“服事”,“服侍”。下文仿此。(3)天也:古人长期的一代又一代的观察总结:天地间有一种意志或力量在支配着人。再尽多大的努力也难扭转,只能顺应。这种意志或力量古人概括为“天”。朱熹《四书集注》:‘天者,理势之当然也。’(4)令:发令以使人。受命:听命于人。绝物:犹“绝人”,谓与人世隔绝。物,有“人,众人”一解。女于吴:女,读 nǜ,以女与人;以女嫁人。吴,指吴王阖庐。《说苑·权谋篇》:“齐景公以其子妻阖庐,送诸郊,泣曰:‘余死不汝见矣,’高梦子曰:‘齐负海而县山,纵不能全收天下,谁干我?君爱则勿行。’公曰:‘余有齐国之固,不能以令诸侯,又不能听,是生乱也。寡人闻之,不能令,则莫若从。’遂遣之。”(5)诗云八句——见《诗·大雅·文王》。(6)其丽不亿:丽,读 lǐ,数目。不亿,超过亿数。形容数量极多。按:古以十万为亿。(7)侯于周服:侯服于周的倒文。

侯,乃,于是。服,臣服。(8)靡常:不是固定不变。靡,非,常,固定不变。(9)肤敏:优美敏捷。(10)祼将:guànjiāng,谓助王行祼祭之礼。(祼祭,以香酒灌地而求神。王以圭瓒酌郁鬯之酒以献尸,尸受祭而灌于地。因奠不饮,谓之祼。)于京:于,往。京,指周的京都镐京。遗址在今陕西省西安市。(11)不可为众:朱熹《四书集注》:“不可为众,犹所谓难为兄难为弟云尔。”谓无与伦比;没有什么力量能够抗衡。(12)谁能执热,逝不以濯:见《诗·大雅·桑柔》。朱熹《四书集注》:“言谁能执热物而不以水自濯其手乎?”段玉裁曰:“……此诗谓谁能苦热,而不澡浴以洁其体,以求凉快者乎?”本译文不取。逝,语助词。

【原文】8 孟子曰:“不仁者可与言哉?安其危而利其菑,[1]乐其所以亡者。不仁而可与言,则何亡国败家之有?有孺子歌曰:[2]‘沧浪之水清兮,[3]可以濯我缨,[4]沧浪之水浊兮,可以濯我足。’孔子曰:‘小子听之,清斯濯缨,浊斯濯足矣。自取之也。’夫人必自侮,然后人侮之;家必自毁而后人毁之;国必自伐,而后人伐之。太甲曰:[5]‘天作孽[6]犹可违;自作孽不可活。’此之谓也。”

【白话译文】

孟子说:“不仁的人难道可以同他商谈吗?他对别人的危难不动于心,用别人的灾祸来谋私利,把亡国败家的行为当作快乐。如果不仁的人还可以同他商谈,那么哪里有亡国败家的事了?从前有个小孩歌唱道:‘沧浪河的水清又清啊,正好洗我帽子丝绳;沧浪河的水变浊了啊,也可洗我脚上灰尘。’孔子说:‘同学们,听清楚,水清亮就用来洗帽带,水浑浊就用来洗双脚。这是由水自身的清浊决定的。’人必定先有自我损害名誉或人格的行为,然后别人才来损害他。家必定先有内部败坏自伤的家事,然后别人才来毁坏它。国必定先有内部败坏争夺的国事,然后别人才来讨伐它。《尚书·太甲》说:‘天降的灾祸,还可躲避,自己造的灾祸,不能甩脱。’正是这个意思。”

【英语译文】

Mencius said, “Can we discuss with a man without humanity? He isn’t moved by others’ dangers and difficulties, he make private fortune by means of using others’ disasters and he regards family’s decline and state’s perish as pleasure. If we can discuss with a man without humanity, aren’t there family’s decline and sates’ perish? In old days a child sang, ‘when the water in Canglang River is so clear, it exactly can wash my hat rope; while the water becomes muddy, it still can wash my feet.’ Confucius said, 'Young men, listen clear that clear water can wash hat rope and muddy water can wash feet, which depends on that water is clear or muddy.' A man surely has firstly done things which harm his fame or moral quality, then others harm him. A family surely has firstly some bad things which damage it, and then others will damage it. A state surely has some inner struggles which damages it, and then others will crusade against it. *The Book of History* said, 'People can dodge disasters made by the Heaven but they cannot get rid of disasters created by themselves.' This exactly means that truth."

【注释】(1)菑:同"灾"。(2)孺子:幼儿,儿童。(3)沧浪:古水名。指称不一,有汉水、汉水的别流、汉水的下流、夏水诸说。(4)缨:系帽的丝带。(5)太甲:《尚书》篇名。据说原文已佚,今本三篇是伪古文。(6)孽:灾祸。《太甲》说:'天降的灾祸,还可躲避;自造的灾祸,不能甩脱。'正是这个意思。"

【原文】9 孟子曰:"桀、纣之失天下也,失其民也;失其民者,失其心也。得天下有道:得其民,斯得天下矣;得其民有道:得其心,斯得民矣;得其心有道:所欲与之聚之,[1]所恶勿施尔也。[2]民之归仁也,犹水之就下、兽之走圹也。[3]故为渊驱鱼者,獭也;[4]为丛驱爵者,鹯也;[5]为汤、武驱民者,桀与纣也;今天下之君有好仁者,则诸侯皆为之驱矣。虽欲无王,[6]不可得已。[7]今之欲王者,犹七年之病求三年之艾也。[8]苟为不畜,[9]终身不得。苟不志于仁,终身忧辱,[10]以陷于死亡。[11]诗云:'其何能淑,载胥及溺。[12]'此之谓也。"

【白话译文】

孟子说:"桀和纣的丢掉天下,是由于丢掉了老百姓;丢掉老百姓,就是丢掉老百姓心中的支持。取得天下有正路,只要取得了天下的百姓,就是取得天下了;取得百姓有正路,只要取得百姓心中的支持就取得百姓了;取得百姓心中的支持有正路,只要百姓所想得到的,就为他们积蓄起来,只要百姓所厌恶的,就不甩给他们。老百姓归附仁德仁政,就像水向下流,兽向原野投奔一样生来的规律。所以帮深潭把鱼赶来的,是水獭,帮密林把小雀赶来的,是晨风;帮商汤和周武把老百姓赶来的,是夏桀和殷纣。当今天下的君主中如果有好施行仁政的,那么,其他诸侯都会帮他把老百姓赶来,即使不想称王治理天下,也不得行。当今一些想用仁政来治理天下的,犹如害了七年的顽疾,要用存了三年的老艾来医治,如果是不积蓄,一辈子也得不到。如果无意于仁政,就将终身忧患屈辱而坠入死亡的泥潭。

《诗经》上说;'假如都遭遇恶境,怎样能转危为安?'正是这个意思。"

【英语译文】

Mencius said, "The reason why King Jie of Xia Dynasty and King Zhou of Shang Dynasty lost their world was that they lost their people and the reason why they lost their people was that they lost their people' support. There is the right way to gain the world and when common people are gained then the world is gained. There is the right way to gain common people and when people's support is gained then the people are gained. There is the right way to gain people's support and we should accumulate what they want to get and don't give them what they don't want to obtain. It is the innate law that common people submit to the authority of humanistic governance is the same way that water flows toward low places and beasts run into wilderness. It is otter that drives out fish from deep water, it is falcon that drives out little birds, it is King Jie of Xia Dynasty and King Zhou of Shang Dynasty who drove common people toward King Tang of Shang Dynasty and King Wu of Zhou Dynasty. Nowadays, if a monarch loves to implement government of humanity, other monarchs will surely drive their people to him. He will certainly become a king even if he doesn't want to be a king. Someone wants to administrate his state by means of government of humanity is the same way that seven-year-long illness is cured by three-year-long Ay Tsao. If there isn't allumulation it could not be done in a life time. If someone doesn't like government of humanity, then he will worry about humiliation and death in his life time. *The Book of Songs* said, 'If state affairs couldn't be done well, all of us would be drown to death.' This exactly means that truth."

【注释】(1)所欲与之聚之:所欲,即民之所欲。与之,即为之,替之。聚之,即蓄积之。(2)施,尔,也:施,给予。尔,代词。这,这个。也,语气助词。表论断决断或终结语气时,一般不译,有的也可译作"呢""的"。(3)归仁:归附仁德、仁政。就下:往下。走圹:~kuàng,归附原野。(4)故为渊驱鱼者,獭:为,读 wèi,帮助。驱,同"驱"。驱;赶。獭,读 tǎ,哺乳动物。栖息水边,善游泳,主食鱼类。(5)爵:jué,通"雀",鸟的一种。鹯:zhān,猛禽名,又名晨风。似鹞,羽色青黄,以鸠鸽燕雀为食。(6)虽欲无王:虽,让步连词。虽然,即使,纵使。无,表否定,不。王,读 wàng,动词,统治;称王。下文同。(7)已:yǐ,罢了,算了。(8)七年之病:难愈的老毛病。三年之艾:蓄备很久的陈艾。(9)畜:xù,又读 chù。积蓄;积储。(10)忧辱:忧患和屈辱。(11)以陷于死亡:以,承接连词。和“而”“然后”差不多。陷,坠入;沉入。(12)诗云:‘其何能淑,载胥及溺:见《诗·大雅·桑柔》。淑,善。载,假设连词。胥,都,皆。及,遭遇。溺,陷于危难或某种不良境地。

【原文】10 孟子曰:“自暴者,[1]不可与有言也;[2]自弃者,不可与有为也[3]。言非礼义,[4]谓之自暴也;吾身不能居仁由义,[5]谓之自弃也。仁,人之安宅也;义,人之正路也。旷安宅而弗居,[6]舍正路而不由,哀哉!”

【白话译文】

孟子说:“自己害自己的人,不能同他谈得出有价值的话来;自己抛弃自己的人,不能同他做得出有价值的事来;开口便诋毁礼义,这就叫作自己害自己;自己认为自己不能内心存仁,行事循义,这就叫作自己抛弃自己。仁,人类最安适的住宅;义,是人类最正确的道路。把最安适的住宅空着不去住,把最正确的道路丢开不去走,可悲呀!”

【英语译文】

Mencius said, “We can't discuss anything valuable with those who do harmful things to themselves; we can't do anything valuable with those who deject themselves. It is called doing harmful thing to oneself that one slanders rites while speaking; it is called dejecting oneself that one thinks he himself cannot cherish humanity and cannot act according to righteousness. Humanity is the most comfortable house for human beings, and righteousness is the most correct way for human beings. It is pitiable not to live in the most comfortable house and not to walk on the most correct way!”

【注释】(1)暴:害。(2)有言:有善言。(3)有为:有所作为。(4)非:诋毁。(5)吾身不能:就己而言曰吾,因人而言曰我。身,亲自。所以“吾身不能”即自言自己不能。居仁由义:内心存仁,行事循义。(6)旷安宅:空着安适的住宅。

【原文】11 孟子曰:“道在迩而求诸远,[1]事在易而求诸难;人人亲其亲,长其长,而天下平。”

【白话译文】

孟子说:“道路在近处却往远处去找,事情很容易却往难处做;只要人人都亲爱自己的父母,尊敬自己的长辈,天下就太平了。”

【英语译文】

Mencius said, “While road lies nearby, someone looks for it in the distance; while things are easy, someone complete them in difficult ways. The world will become peaceful when everybody loves his parents and respects his superiors.”

【注释】(1)迩:ěr,近。

【原文】12 孟子曰:“居下位而不获于上,[1]民不可得而治也。获于上有道,不信于友,弗获于上矣。信于友事亲弗悦,弗信于友矣。悦亲有道,反身不诚,[2]不悦于亲矣。诚身有道,不明乎善,[3]不诚其身矣。是故诚者,天之道也;思诚者,[4]人之道也。至诚而不动者,[5]未之有也;不诚,未有能动者也。”[6]

【白话译文】

孟子说:“职位低下,又得不到上级的信任,是不能治理好百姓的。要得到上级的信任,有正路,得不到朋友的信任,也就得不到上级的信任了。要得到朋友的信任,有正路,侍奉父母而不能使他们高兴,朋友也就不信任你了。要使父母高兴,有正路,若是反躬自问,心意有不诚,也就不能使父母高兴了。要使自己诚心诚意,有正路,不真明白什么是善,也就不能使自己诚心诚意了。所以诚实是大自然的正路,追求诚实是人的正路。诚实到顶点,德行极其和顺,却不能感动人的,是从来不曾有过的事;心不诚,没有能感动别人的。”

【英语译文】

Mencius said, “A man in lower post who can't be trusted by his superior cannot administrate people well. There is a right way to be trusted by one's superior, which is if one cannot be trusted by his friend then he can't be trusted by his superior. There is a right way to be trusted by one's friend, which is if one serves his parents but they aren't happy then he can't be trusted by his friend. There is a right way to make one's parents happy, which is if one finds himself not honest while reflecting then he cannot make his parents happy. There is the right way to be honest, which is if one doesn't understand what kindness is then he cannot be honest. Therefore, honesty is the right way of nature and pursuing honesty is the right way for human beings. There never exists the situation that one is the most honest man and his virtue is the most harmonious but he cannot move others. If one isn't honest he can never move others."

【注释】(1)获于上:获得上级信任。(2)反身不诚:反问自己其为善之心有所不实。(3)不明乎善:不真知善之所在。按:要真知善之所在,要能即事以穷理。(4)思诚:要求我持之理都实而无伪。(5)至诚:指极其和顺的德行。(6)动:感动;触动。

【原文】13 孟子曰:"伯夷辟纣,居北海之滨,[1]闻文王作,兴曰:'盍归乎来![2]吾闻西伯善养老者。'[3]太公辟纣,居东海之滨,[4]闻文王作,兴曰:'盍归乎来,吾闻西伯善养老者。'二老者,天下之大老也,而归之,是天下之父归之也。天下之父归之,其子焉往?诸侯有行文王之政者,七年之内,必为政于天下矣。"

【白话译文】

孟子说:"伯夷避开纣王,住在北海边上,听说文王兴起了,高兴地说:'何不到西伯那里去呢?我听说他善于奉养年老的人。'姜太公避开纣王,住在东海边上,听说文王兴起了,高兴地说:'何不到西伯那里去呢?我听说他善于奉养年老的人。'这两位老人,是天下最有声望的老人;他们归于西伯,这等于天下的父亲都归于西伯。天下的父亲都去西伯那里,他们的儿子还会去哪里呢?如果诸侯中有行文王的政治的,最多七年,就一定能全面治理天下了。"

【英语译文】

Mencius said, "Bo Yi fled from King Zhou of Shang Dynasty and lived at the shore of the North Sea. After hearing that King Wen of Zhou Dynasty rose he said happily, 'Why not go to Xi Bo? I hear that he loves serving the elder.' Jiang Shang fled from King Zhou of Shang Dynasty and lived at the shore of the East Sea. After hearing that King Wen of Zhou Dynasty rose he said happily, 'Why not go to Xi Bo? I hear that he loves serving the elder.' These two elders were the most famous ones at that time. They came over Xi Bo and that meant all the fathers in the world came over Xi Bo. Where could their sons go? If a prince can implement the administrative way of King Wen, then he can govern the world in seven years."

【注释】(1)伯夷辟纣,居北海之滨:其具体地址为今河北省昌黎县西北。(2)

盍、来:盍、何不。来,语末助词。(3)西伯:周文王。(4)太公辟纣,居东海之滨:太公,姓姜,名尚。其所居的具体地址为今山东省莒县东。

【原文】14 孟子曰:“求也为季氏宰,无能改于其德,而赋粟倍他日。孔子曰:‘求非我徒也,小子鸣鼓而攻之可也。[1]’由此观之,君子不行仁政而富之,皆弃于孔子者也。况于为之强战?争地以战,杀人盈野;争城以战,杀人盈城,此所谓率土地而食人肉,罪不容于死。[2]故善战者服上刑,[3]诸侯者次之,[4]连辟草莱、任土地者次之。[5]”

【白话译文】

孟子说:“冉求当季康子的总管,不能改变季氏的行为,田赋反而增加了一倍。孔子说:‘冉求不是我的学生,你们可以宣布他的罪状声讨他。’从这里看来,国君不行仁政反而有人帮助搜刮财富,这一伙都是被孔子所唾弃的人。何况于为不仁的君主努力作战的人?为争夺土地而战,杀死的人塞满原野;为争夺城池而战,杀死的人塞满城池;真可叫带领土地来吃人肉,罪恶滔天,一死怎么抵偿得了。所以擅长作战的人处以重刑;煽动诸侯闹事的人,判次一等的刑;驱民开荒备军粮的人,判又次一等的刑。”

【英语译文】

Mencius said, “Ran Qiu acted as the governor of Ji Kang Zi but couldn’t change the latter’s actions. The tax ratio doubled. Confucius said, ‘Ran Qiu isn’t my student and you can announce his guilt to attack him.’ From this we can see that someone will help plunder wealth if a monarch didn’t implement government of humanity. Confucius surely spit in contempt on such kind of persons. Let alone those who fought for inhumane monarch. While fighting for fields, killed men piled up in wilderness; while fighting for cities, killed men piled up in trenches. It is really the situation that fields swallow up human flesh. Such actions are guilty of the most heinous crimes and they can’t be compensated by death. Therefore those who were adept at fight should be sentenced severe punishment, and those who incited princes to riot should be sentenced less severe punishment, and those who drove people till fields and prepare military grain should be sentenced still less severe punishment.”

【注释】(1)求也为季氏宰句:其史实参见《论语·先进》,《左传·哀公十一年》。求,冉求。字子有。孔子弟子。鸣鼓而攻,谓宣布罪状而加以声讨。(2)罪不容于死:义同“罪不容诛”。谓罪大恶极处死犹不足抵偿。(3)善战者,如孙膑、吴起之徒。服,治;治罪。上刑,重刑。(4)连诸侯:联结诸侯。如苏秦、张仪之类。(5)辟草莱、任土地:辟,同“辟”,开垦。草莱,犹草莽,指荒芜之地。任土地,谓分土授民,使任耕稼之责。如李悝尽地力,商鞅开阡陌之类。

【原文】15 孟子曰:“存乎人者,[1]莫良于眸子。[2]眸子不能掩其恶。胸中正,则眸子瞭[3];胸中不正,则眸子眊焉。[4]听其言也,观其眸子,人焉廋哉?[5]”

【白话译文】

孟子说:“观察一个人时,最好是观察他的眼睛。眼睛不能掩盖内心的丑恶。心正无邪,眼睛就明亮;心中不正,眼睛就昏暗失神。听一个人说话时,仔细观察他的眼睛,他怎么隐匿呢?”

【英语译文】

Mencius said, “When you observe a person, it's better to observe his eyes. Eyes can't hide ugliness in one's heart. One's eyes are bright if he has no evil intentions; one's eyes are obscure if he has evil intentions. When you listen to one speaking, observe his eyes carefully. How can he hide anything?”

【注释】(1)存:省察。(2)眸子:móu ~,眼珠。亦称眼睛。(3)瞭:眼珠明亮。(4)眊:眼睛失神,视物不清。(5)廋:sōu,藏匿,隐藏。

【原文】16 孟子曰:“恭者不侮人,俭者不夺人。侮夺人之君,惟恐不顺焉,恶得为恭俭?恭俭岂可以声音笑貌为哉?[1]”

【白话译文】

孟子说:“恭敬的人不会侮辱别人,节俭的人不会掠夺别人。侮辱掠夺成性的君主,生怕别人不顺从自己,怎么能做到恭敬和节俭?恭敬和节俭难道可以用声音和笑脸装扮出来?”

【英语译文】

Mencius said, “A modest man shall not insult others and a shrift man shall not rob others. A monarch who is adept at insulting and robbing others always fears that other people aren't obedient to him. How can he become modest and thrift? Can modesty and thrifty be disguised by voice and smile?"

【注释】(1)为:wéi,做出,装出。

【原文】17 淳于髡曰:[1]"男女授受不亲,[2]礼与?"孟子曰:"礼也。"曰:"嫂溺,则援之以手乎?"曰:"嫂溺不援,是豺狼也。男女授受不亲,礼也;嫂溺援之以手者,权也。[3]"曰:"今天下溺矣,夫子之不援,何也?"曰:"天下溺,援之以道;嫂溺,援之以手。子欲手援天下乎?"

【白话译文】

淳于髡说:"男女之间不亲手交接东西,这是礼制吗?"孟子说:"是礼制。"淳于髡说:"那么嫂嫂掉在水里,用不用手去拉她?"孟子说:"嫂嫂掉在水里,不去拉她,这简直是豺狼。男女之间,不亲手交接东西,这是通常的礼制;嫂嫂掉在水里,用手去拉她,这是应急的变通方法。"淳于髡说:"现在天下的人都掉在水里了,您不去救援,这是为什么?"孟子说:"天下的人都掉在水里了,要用'正确的方法'去救援,嫂嫂掉在水里了,才用手去救援。你难道要我用手去一个一个地救援天下掉在水里的人吗?"

【英语译文】

Chunyu Kun asked, "A man and a woman should not grant and accept anything personally. Is it ritual system?" Mencius answered, "Yes, it is." Chunyu Kun asked, "When your sister-in-law has fallen in to water, will you personally draw her out of water?" Mencius said, "If one doesn't draw his sister-in-law out of water, he is just like a jackal when she falls in to water. It's usual ritual system that a man and a woman should not grant and accept anything personally. It is an emergent action for one to draw his sister-in-law out of water with his hands." Chunyu Kun said, "Now that all people in the world have fallen into water but you don't help them. Why?" Mencius said, "While all people have fallen in water we should use 'correct way' to help them. When one's sister-in-law falls into water one can draw her with his hands. Do you want me to help those fallen in water one by one?"

【注释】(1)淳于髡:chún yú kūn,战国时齐国人。姓淳于,曾受髡刑(截去头发),因称"淳于髡"。以博学强记著称。齐威王在稷下招揽学者被任为大夫,多次讽谏齐威王和相国邹忌,推动改革内政。楚国攻齐他赴赵国求援赵王给以精兵十万革车千乘,楚国因此退兵。后到魏国,魏惠王拟任卿相,他推辞不受。(2)授受:给予和接受。(3)权:权宜,变通。

【原文】18 公孙丑曰:"君子之不教子,[1]何也?"孟子曰:"不行也。[2]教者必以正;以正不行,继之以怒。继之以怒,则反夷矣。[3]'夫子教我以正,夫子未出于正也。[4]'则是父子相夷也。父子相夷,则恶矣。古者易子而教之,父子之间不责善。[5]责善则离,离则不祥莫大焉。[6]"

【白话译文】

公孙丑说:"有地位的人不亲自给孩子有序地传授学业,是为什么呢?"孟子说:"实际情况行不通。传授学业,一定要讲正面的东西,正面的东西行不通时,接下来就容易发怒,一发怒就伤感情了,'您用正理教我,可是你的行为却不出于正理。'这样父子间就相互伤感情了。父子间互相伤感情,不是好事。古时候交换小孩子来进行教育,使父子间不因求好而互相责备。为求好而互相责备,就会变得互相隔离,父子间生疏隔离,是最大的坏事。"

【英语译文】

Gongsun Chou asked, "A distinguished man doesn't personally teach his son. Why?" Mencius answered, "In reality it can't be done smoothly. While teaching one must say positive things. When positive things can't be accepted one must get angry, in turn feelings between son and father are hurt. 'You teach me by positive things but your actions don't arise from them'. As a result, feelings between son and father are mutually hurt, which isn't a good thing. In ancient times people exchange their children to educate in order not to blame each other due to seeking goodness. While father and son blame each other due to seeking goodness they will be isolated psychologically. It is the worst thing for father and son be to isolateed from each other psychologically."

【注释】(1)不教子:教,指有序的学业教育。(2)势:事物之间全方位的相关状况。犹谓"实际情形""实际情况""实际状况"。(3)夷:伤。(4)夫子:夫,句首语气助词。子,您。(5)责善:劝勉从善。是朋友间的道义。(6)祥:善。

【原文】19 孟子曰:“事孰为大?事亲为大;[1]守孰为大?守身为大。[2]不失其身而能事其亲者,吾闻之矣;失其身而能事其亲者,吾未闻之也。孰不为事?[3]事亲,事之本也;孰不为守?守身,守之本也。曾子養曾晳,[4]必有酒肉;将彻,[5]必请所与;[6]余,必曰,‘有。’曾晳死,曾元養曾子,[7]问有必有酒肉;将彻,不请所与;问有余,曰:‘亡矣。’——将以复进也。此所谓养口体者也。若曾子,则可谓养志也。事亲若曾子者,可也。”

【白话译文】

孟子说:“服侍谁放在第一位?服侍父母放在第一位。守护什么放在第一位?守护良心和品德放在第一位。不丢失良心和品德又能够服侍父母的人,我听说过了;丢失了良心和品德还能够服侍父母的人,我没听说过。该服侍的都要服侍;但服侍父母,是服侍的根本。该守护的都要守护,但守护良心和品德,是守护的根本。从前曾子奉养他的父亲曾晳,每餐都一定有酒有肉,餐毕收碗时,一定要请问剩下的给谁。父亲若问是否还有剩余,一定回答还有。曾晳死了,曾元养曾子,每餐也都一定有酒有肉,但是餐毕收碗时,不问剩下的给谁;曾子若问是否还有剩余,曾元便说:‘没有了。’准备下一顿再给曾子吃。这个叫作口体之养,像曾子样称得上奉养心意了。服侍父母像曾子那样的,可以了。”

【英语译文】

Mencius said, “Whom should we serve first? Parents. What should we protect first? Virtue and conscience. I have heard that one could serve his parents without losing his virtue and conscience. But I haven’t hear that one can serve his parents while losing his virtue and conscience. We should serve all those who shall be served but parents are the first. We should protect all that shall be protected but virtue and conscience are the first. In old days Zeng Zi served his father Zeng Xi. In each meal there were meat and wine, and after meal he would always asked to whom should he give the remnant. If his father asked if there was remnant he would answer ‘yes’. After Zeng Xi’s death, Zeng Yuan served his father Zeng Zi. In each meal there were meat and wine, and after meal he wouldn’t ask to whom should he give the remnant. If his father asked if there was remnant he would answer ‘no’. He prepared next meal for his father. This is called physically served and it is alright for Zeng Zi to do like this wholeheartedly.”

【注释】(1)事:服侍。孰:谁,什么。大:排行第一。(2)守:守护;保持。守身:守护良心;保持品德和节操。(3)孰不为事:以反问表示肯定。问:谁不该服侍?意谓该服侍的都要服侍,下文,孰不为守,仿此。(4)曾皙:名点。孔子学生。曾子(曾参)之父。(5)彻:通"撤。食毕撤除剩余食物、餐具和垃圾。(6)必请所与:一定请问剩余的东西给谁。(7)曾元:曾子之子。

【原文】20 孟子曰:"人不足与适也,[1]政不足间也;[2]唯大人为能格君心之非。[3]君仁,莫不仁;君义莫不义;君正,莫不正。一正君而国定矣。"

【白话译文】

孟子说:"那些当政的小人不值得去谴责。他们的政治也不值得去非议。只有大人才能够纠正君主心中的错误。君主仁,没有人不仁;君主义,没有人不义;君主正,没有人不正。一旦把君主端正了,国家也就安定了。"

【英语译文】

Mencius said, "It isn't worthy to blame those empowered mean men. Their administrative affairs aren't worthy to be scolded. Only moral men can correct the fault of monarch. No one cannot be humanistic if the monarch is so. No one cannot be righteous if the monarch is so. No one cannot be upright if the monarch is so. The state will be calmed only if the monarch is upright and his fault is corrected."

【注释】(1)人不足与适也:适,读 zhé,通"谪"。责备,谴责。(2)政不足间也:"人"与"政"对举,犹言"其人","其政"。间,读 jiàn,非难;非议。(3)格:纠正,匡正。

【原文】21 孟子曰:"有不虞之誉,[1]有求全之毁。[2]

【白话译文】

孟子说:"有料想不到的赞扬,有为完美而反遭诋毁。"

【英语译文】

Mencius said, "There is unexpected praise, and there is also slander for seeking perfection."

【注释】(1)虞:猜度;料想。(2)求全:求完美。朱熹《四书集注》:“求免于毁而反致毁是为求全之毁。”

【原文】22 孟子曰:“人之易其言也,[1]无责耳矣。[2]”

【白话译文】
孟子说:“一个人的随意说话,是不值得责备的了。”

【英语译文】
Mencius said, “It isn't worthy to blame what a person has said casually.”

【注释】(1)易:轻易;随便。(2)无责耳矣:不责备算了。

【原文】23 孟子曰:“人之患在好为人师。[1]”

【白话译文】
孟子说:“人的毛病在于喜欢以教导者自居。”

【英语译文】
Mencius said, “The defect of man lies in that they always love to be an instructor of others.”

【注释】(1)患:祸患;毛病。好:hào,喜欢,爱好。

【原文】24 乐正子从于子敖之齐。[1]乐正子见孟子 。孟子曰:“子亦来见我乎?”曰:“先生何为出此言也?”曰:“子来几日矣?”曰:“昔者。”曰:“昔者,[2]则我出此言也,不亦宜乎?”曰:“舍馆未定。[3]”曰:“子闻之也,舍馆定,然后求见长者乎?[4]”曰:“克有罪。[5]”

【白话译文】
乐正子跟随王子敖到齐国去。乐正子去见孟子。孟子说:“你也来看我吗?”乐正子回答道:“老师怎么这样说呢?”孟子问:“你来这里几天了?”乐正子回答道:“昨天。”孟子说:“昨天,那我说的话不也是合适的吗?”乐正子说:“住所没有定下。”孟子说:“你听说过要把住所定下了,才见长辈吗?”乐正子说:“我有罪。”

【英语译文】

Le Zheng Zi followed Wang Ziao to Qi State. Le Zheng Zi went to see Mencius. Mencius asked, “Do you also come to see me?” Le Zheng Zi answered, “Master, why do you say so?” Mencius asked, “How long have you been here?” Le Zheng Zi replied, “Yesterday.” Mencius said, “Yesterday. Then isn't my word appropriate?” Le Zheng Zi answered, “My housing wasn't settled.” Mencius asked, “Have you heard that one visits his elder after he settles his housing?” Le Zheng Zi said, “I'm guilty.”

【注释】(1)子敖:齐国盖(gě)邑大夫王驩的字。参见《公孙丑下》第六章和《离娄下》第二十七章。(2)昔者:昨天。(3)舍馆:住所;客舍。(4)长者:zhěng ~,大概有五个方面的用法:1)指年纪大或辈分高的人,2)指显贵的人,3)指德高望重的人,4)指豪侠,5)旧时对男子的尊称。乐正子是孟子的弟子,孟子自言“长者”不卑不亢,千真万确。(5)克:乐正子的名。有罪:表示失敬赔礼之词。

【原文】25 孟子谓乐正子曰:“子之从于子敖来,徒餔啜也。[1]我不意子学古之道而以餔啜也。[2]”

【白话译文】

孟子对乐正子说:“你跟着王子敖来,只是吃吃喝喝罢了。我没想到你学习古人的大道,竟是为了吃吃喝喝。”

【英语译文】

Mencius said to Le Zheng Zi, “You have followed Wang Zi'ao to here just for wine and dine with others. I never thought that you learn the way of ancient people just for eating and drinking.”

【注释】(1)餔啜:būchuò,吃喝。(2)不意:不料,意想不到。

【原文】26 孟子曰:“不孝有三,[1]无后为大。舜不告而娶,为无后也。[2]君子以为犹告也。”

【白话译文】

孟子说:"不孝的事情有三件,没有后代是最大不孝。舜娶妻没先禀告父母,是因为怕受阻误时,断了后代。德行高尚的人认为他不禀告的心意和禀告的孝心一样。"

【英语译文】

Mencius said, "There are three un-filial behaviors of which having no male heir is the most serious one. Sage Shun got married without reporting to his parents because he feared that he'd have no male heir while being blocked. Virtuous men all think that his intention of not reporting was the same as that of being filial to report."

【注释】(1)不孝有三:赵岐注:"阿意曲从,陷亲不义,一不孝也;家贫亲老,不为禄仕,二不孝也;不娶无子,绝先祖祀,三不孝也。"(2)为无后:因为还没有儿子怕告而误时。

【原文】27 孟子曰:"仁之实,事亲是也;[1]义之实,从兄是也;[2]智之实,知斯二者弗去是也;[3]礼之实,节文斯二者是也;[4]乐之实,乐斯二者,乐则生矣;[5]生则恶可已也?[6]恶可已,则不知足之蹈之手之舞之。[7]"

【白话译文】

孟子说:"仁的基本就是侍奉父母;义的基本就是和顺兄长;智的基本就是明白侍奉父母与和顺兄长这两方面的道理而坚持不弃;礼的基本就是对这两方面进行调节定式;乐的基本就是从这两方面得到快乐;快乐了,就生意盎然,生意盎然了怎么能中止?于是便不自觉地手舞足蹈起来。"

【英语译文】

Mencius said, "The essence of humanity is to serve one's parents; the essence of righteousness is to harmonize with one's elder brother; the essence of wisdom is to understand the reason for serving one's parents and harmonizing one's elder brother and not to give up doing so; the essence of rites is to modulate these two things; the essence of music is to obtain happiness form these two things. While being happy one will be energetic. While being energetic how can one stop doing it? Then he will keep dancing excitedly."

【注释】(1)实:实质,本质,基本。(2)从兄:和顺兄长。(3)二者:指事亲、从兄两方面。弗去:不离开;不丢掉。(4)节文:制定礼仪使行之有度;调节定式。(5)乐之、乐斯、乐则:yuè~,lè~,lè~。(6)恶:wū,疑问代词。相当于"何""安""怎么"。(7)足之蹈之手之舞之:足蹈手舞,插上四个语气助词"之"意义不变,却烘托了形象,渲染了气氛。

【原文】28 孟子曰:"天下大悦而将归己,[1]视天下悦而归己,犹草芥也,[2]惟舜为然。不得乎亲,不可以为人;不顺乎亲,不可以为子。舜尽事亲之道而瞽叟厎豫,[3]瞽叟厎豫而天下化,瞽叟厎豫而天下之为父子者定,此之谓大孝。"

【白话译文】

孟子说:"天底下众人的爱慕将倾向自己。而把天下众人的爱慕倾向自己看得如草芥一样不重要,只有舜是这样。不能得到父母的欢心,不可以做人;不能顺从父母的心意,不能做儿子。舜尽心竭力侍奉父母,终于感动了瞽瞍;瞽瞍高兴了,天下的风俗也开始好转了,瞽瞍高兴了,天下的父子关系也正常确定了。"

【英语译文】

Mencius said, "People under the Heaven all loved themselues. And only sage Shun regarded it as grass that people under the Heaven all loved him. One cannot be a man if he cannot make his parents happy; one cannot be a son if he cannot be obedient to his parents. Shun tried his best to serve his parents, which moved his father Gu Sou. While Gu Sou was happy custom began to change for good, and while Gu Sou was happy the relationship between father and son was set normally."

【注释】(1)大悦:众人的爱慕。归:趋向;归附。(2)草芥:芥是小草。草和芥常用以比喻轻贱 。(3)瞽叟:gǔsǒu,又作"瞽瞍。"舜的父亲 ,心狠手辣。厎:zhǐ,致;至。豫:欢乐。

孟子集注卷八　离娄章句下　凡三十三章

【原文】1 孟子曰:“舜生于诸冯,迁于负夏,卒于鸣条,东夷之人也。[1]文王生于岐周,卒于毕郢,西夷之人也。地之相去也,千有余里;世相后也,[2]千有余岁。得志行乎中国,若合符节。[3]先圣后圣其揆一也。[4]”

【白话译文】

孟子说:“舜出生于诸冯,迁居到负夏,死在鸣条。是中原东方的人。文王出生于岐周,死在毕郢。是中原西方的人。他们生活的地方东西相距一千多里,生活的时代前后相差一千多年。而他们在中国实现自己的志向却像合符节一样相同,前代圣人和后代圣人,道路相同。”

【英语译文】

Mencius said, “Sage Shun was born in Zhufeng, moved to Fuxia and died in Mingtiao. He was a man in the east to Central Plains. King Wen was born in Qishan, and died in Biying. He was a man in the west to Central Plains. The distance between their living places was more than one thousand *li* and the spread between their living times was more than one thousand years. However their ambition to govern the country was the same as a tally. Former sage and latter sage chose the same way.”

【注释】(1)诸冯:地名。传说在今山东省菏泽市南五十里。一说在山西。清顾祖宇《读史方域纪要·山西三·平阳府》:“又诸冯山,在县东北四十里,孟子云舜生诸冯,盖即此。”负夏:地名。不详。鸣条:地名。在今山西运城安邑镇北。东夷:东方民族。下文西夷,仿此。(2)岐周:岐山下的周代旧邑地在今陕西岐山县境,周建国于此故称。毕郢:地名。地近丰镐。有文王墓。世:时代。(3)符节:古代派遣使者或调动兵力用作凭证的东西。用竹木玉或金铜等制成,刻上文字,分成两半。一半存朝廷,一半给外任官员或出征将帅。(4)揆:kuí,道理;准则。

【原文】2 子产听郑国之政[1],以其乘舆济人于溱洧。[2]孟子曰:“惠而不知为政。[3]岁十一月,徒杠成;十二月,舆梁成,[4]民未病涉也。[5]君子平其政,[6]行辟人可也,焉得人人而济之?[7]故为政者,每人而悦之,日亦不足矣。[8]”

【白话译文】

子产主持郑国的行政，用自己所乘之车，帮助别人越过溱水和洧水。孟子说：“这是施小恩惠而不知行大政。如果每年的十一月就检修好走人的小桥，十二月就检修好走车的大桥，百姓就不会为过河发愁了。君子只要修平政治，他外出就清除道路让人回避都可以，哪能用自己坐的车去一个一个地帮人过河呢？所以主持政事的人要一个一个地取悦人们，时间也是不够的。”

【英语译文】

Zi Chan was in charge of governance of Zheng State. He used his carriage to help other people cross Zhen River and Wei River. Mencius said, “This is to show little mercy but not to implement great governance. If little bridges for walk were overhauled in November each year, and big bridges for carts were overhauled in December each year, people would never worry about crossing rivers. Superior men just make administrative affairs in order and while he goes out it’s alright that passersby dodge away. How could he use his own carriage to help others cross rivers? Therefore a man in power had no time to make people happy one by one.”

【注释】(1)子产：郑国大夫，公孙侨的字。(2)乘舆：shèngyú，古代特指天子和诸侯所乘坐的车子。这里泛指车马。溱洧：zhēnwěi，溱水和洧水，在今河南省。(3)惠而不知为政：朱熹《四书集注》：“惠，谓私恩小利。政，则有公平正大之体，纲纪法度之施焉。”(4)岁：年年，每年。徒杠：~ gāng，可供徒步行走的小桥。舆梁：桥梁；可通车舆的桥。(5)病涉：苦于涉水渡川。(6)平其政：同“平政”。修明政治。(7)辟人：pì ~，谓驱除行人使避开。(8)日：时间；光阴。

【原文】3 孟子告齐宣王曰：“君之视臣如手足，[1]则臣视君如腹心；君之视臣如犬马，则臣视君如国人；[2]君之视臣如土芥，[3]则臣视君如寇雠。[4]”王曰：“礼，为旧君有服，[5]何如斯可为服矣？”曰：“谏行言听，膏泽下于民；有故而去，则君使人导之出疆，又先于其所往；[6]去三年不反，然后收其田里。此所谓三有礼焉。如此，则为之服矣。[7]今也为臣，谏则不行，言则不听；膏泽不下于民；有故而去，则君搏执之，又极之于其所往；[8]去之日，遂收其田里。此之谓寇雠。寇雠何服之有？”

【白话译文】

孟子告诉齐宣王说:“君主把臣子当作自己的手脚,臣子就会把君主当作自己的腹心;君主把臣子当作狗马,臣子就会把君主当作路人;君主把臣子当作泥土和小草,臣子就会把君主当作仇敌。”齐宣王说:“礼制规定,已经离职的臣子对过去的君主,还有一定的孝服,君主要怎样对待臣子,臣子才会为他服孝呢?”孟子说:“君主接受臣子的忠告,君主听从臣子的建议,把福利落实到百姓头上,臣子有实情不得不离去,君主一定要派人引导离开国境,而且先派人前去他要去的地方做先行事务。离去了好几年还不回来,才收回他的土地和住房。这样做叫三有礼。这样做臣子就会服孝了。如今做臣子的,忠告,君主不接受;建议,君主不听从;福利,也落实不到百姓头上;有实情要离去,就把他绑起来,还要派人到他要去的地方捣乱,离去那一天就收回他的土地和住房,这样就叫作仇敌。对仇敌般的旧君,臣子为啥要服孝呢?”

【英语译文】

Mencius told King Xuan of Qi State, “When a monarch regards his subjects as his hands and feet, they regard him as their belly and heart; when he regards them as dogs and horses, they regard him as a common fellow; when he regards them as dirt and grass, they regard him as robber and enemy.” King Xuan said, “The ritual system stipulates that ministers should wear funeral clothes for three months after his monarch passed away. How could the monarch do to make his ministers be willing to do so?” Mencius said, “Monarch accepted minister's remonstrance and advice, he benefited common people. When his ministers had to leave him for business he should dispatch some person to lead the minister to the border, furthermore he should dispatch some person to make preparation for his minister to the new place. If the minister has left for several years and cannot come back, he may get back the land and houses of the minister. These called rites of three things. By doing so the ministers would wear funeral clothes. Nowadays the monarch rejected the remonstrance and advice of his ministers. He doesn't benefit his common people. When his ministers have to leave him for business, he arrested them and then dispatched persons to make trouble in the place where the minister will go. As soon as the minister left his land and houses have been got back. Thus he became robber and enemy. Why did ministers wear funeral clothes for their passed monarch who was a robber and enemy?”

【注释】(1)之:结构助词,用在主语“君”和谓语“视”间,使本句失去独立性而成为主从复合句的从句。(2)国人:朱熹《四书集注》:“国人,犹言路人,言无怨无德也。”(3)土芥:泥土草芥,比喻微贱的东西,无足轻重。(4)寇雠:亦作“寇仇”“寇雠”。仇敌;敌人。(5)为:wèi,给;致意。旧君:指曾经服侍过的君主。有服:服孝。仪礼曰:“以道去君而未绝者服齐衰三月。”依规矩离开君主而未破裂情意的臣属,对曾经服侍过的君主去世,要穿三个月缉边孝服。(6)导之出疆:引导离开国境。先于所往:派人先到所去之处接洽过境事务。(7)三有礼:谓对贤臣的三个方面的礼节:一,任用主张;二,尊重去留;三,保留产权希望返归。(8)极之于所往:极,犹穷尽,使动用法。谓使之于所去之国受困穷。

【原文】4 孟子曰:“无罪而杀士,则大夫可以去;[1]罪而戮民,则士可以徙。[2]”

【白话译文】

孟子说:“士人没有犯罪,却被杀掉,那么大夫就可以离开这个朝廷了;群众没有犯罪,却被杀掉,那么士人就可以移居别国了。”

【英语译文】

Mencius said, “If scholars were killed without committing a crime, ministers may leave the court; if masses were killed without committing a crime, scholars may move to live in another state.”

【注释】(1)去:离开。(2)徙:迁移;移居。

【原文】5 孟子曰:“君仁,莫不仁;君义,莫不义。”

【白话译文】

孟子说:“君主如果仁,便没有人不仁;君主如果义,便没有人不义。”

【英语译文】

No one cannot be humanistic if the monarch is so. No one cannot be righteous if the monarch is so.

【注释】(1)本章在上篇(【原文】7·20)中出现过,言人臣当以正君为急,本章是直诫人君。

【原文】6 孟子曰:“非礼之礼,[1]非义之义,[2]大人弗为。”

【白话译文】

孟子说:“违背礼制的任何礼和违背正义的任何义,有道德的人是不会干的。”

【英语译文】

Mencius said, “A virtuous man never observes any etiquette which violates the ritual system or any relationship which violates righteousness.”

【注释】(1)非:违背;不合。礼:礼制;礼法。(2)非:同前解。义:正义;道义。

【原文】7 孟子曰:“中也养不中,[1]才也养不才,[2]故人乐有贤父兄也。[3]如中也弃不中,才也弃不才,则贤不肖之相去,[4]其间不能以寸。[5]”

【白话译文】

孟子说:“善良的教育不善良的,能干的教育不能干的,所以都喜欢有又善良又能干的父母和兄长。如果善良的放弃不善良的,能干的放弃不能干的,那么善良能干与不善良能干之间的距离,就小得不能用尺寸计算。”

【英语译文】

Mencius said, “Kind man educates unkind men and competent men educates incompetent men, therefore people all love kind and competent father and brother. If kind man gives up unkind men and competent man gives up incompetent men, the distance between being kind and competent and being unkind and incompetent cannot be measured.”

【注释】(1)中:zhòng,无过不及之谓中。养:谓涵育熏陶,俟其自化也。(2)才:足以有为之谓才。(3)贤:谓中而才者也。(4)相去:距离。(5)以寸:用尺寸计算。以上见朱熹《四书集注》。

【原文】8 孟子曰:“人有不为也[1],而后可以有为。[2]”

【白话译文】

孟子说:“一个人不要什么都干,然后才可以干出一番事业。”

【英语译文】

Mencius said, “A man should not do everything and then he could accomplish a great cause.”

【注释】(1)不为:~wéi,不做,不干。(2)有为:~wéi,有作为。

【原文】9 孟子曰:“言人之不善,[1]当如后患何?[2]”

【白话译文】

孟子说:“揭露别人的坏处,该怎样对待跟随而来的麻烦?”

【英语译文】

Mencius said, “If you expose other's unkind doings, how can you deal with following troubles?”

【注释】(1)言:说;谈论。说人之不善,等于揭露人之不善,听话人和被说的人会有什么反应难料。(2)当:该,应当。

【原文】10 孟子曰:“仲尼不为已甚者。[1]”

【白话译文】

孟子说:“仲尼不做过头事。”

【英语译文】

Mencius said, “Confucius never overdid things.”

【注释】(1)已甚:过甚,太过。

【原文】11 孟子曰:“大人者,[1]言不必信,[2]行不必果,[3]惟义所在。[4]”

【白话译文】

孟子说:“有德行的人,说话,无须计较信用,行为,无须计较后果,只要牢牢把握着义就行了。”

【英语译文】

Mencius said, “A virtuous man needn't care about credibility while speaking, and he needn't care about consequence while acting only if he firmly sticks to righteousness.”

【注释】(1)者:助词,用在名词后,表示停顿。(2)不必:无须,没有必要。信:信用。(3)果:后果。(4)惟义所在:只要依据义。

【原文】12 孟子曰:“大人者,不失其赤子之心者也。[1]”

【白话译文】

孟子说:“有德行的人,是保持着天真童心不变的人。”

【英语译文】

Mencius said, “A virtuous man is a man who is innocent like a newly-born baby.”

【注释】(1)赤子:初生的婴儿。

【原文】13 孟子曰:“养生者不足以当大事,[1]惟送死可以当大事。[2]”

【白话译文】

孟子说:“奉养父母啊是日常事,算不上大事,只有给他们送终可以算作大事。”

【英语译文】

Mencius said, “It's the usual thing to support and wait upon one's parents, and it can't be the great thing. It is the great thing to attend upon and bury one's parent.”

【注释】(1)养生:奉养父母。者:助词,用在句中,可以表提顿、停顿或舒缓语气,一般去掉不译,有的也可译作“啊”“呀”。当:dàng,当作,算是。(2)送死:送终,为死者办丧事,亦指临终时亲属在身边照料。

【原文】14 孟子曰:“深造之以道,[1]欲其自得之也。[2]自得之,则居之安;[3]居之安,则资之深;[4]资之深,则取之左右逢其原,[5]故君子欲其自得之也。”

【白话译文】

孟子说:“君子循着正路治学而达到高深境界,是想自己有心得体会。自己有心得体会,就把它积储稳固。积储稳固,就依靠深厚。依靠深厚,就在身边得到源头,取用不完。所以君子想自己有心得体会。”

【英语译文】

Mencius said, “A moral man does scholarly research according to right way and reaches advanced state in order to have his own experience and understanding. While he has his own experience and understanding, he will solidify it. Solidifying it relies on deepness. Relying on deepness, he can get sources within his reach without using up. Therefore a moral man wants to have his own experience and understanding.”

【注释】(1)造:学业等达到某种程度或境界。(2)自得:自己有心得体会;自己感到得意或舒适。(3)居之安:将其积储稳固。(4)资之深:依靠深厚。(5)左右:犹言身边。原:本原;来源。

【原文】15 孟子曰:“博学而详说之,[1]将以反说约也。[2]”

【白话译文】

孟子说:“广泛地学习,详细的解释,就是要依据这样的学习和解释回到叙述简要。”

【英语译文】

Mencius said, “The purpose of learning extensively and explaining with detail is to return to brief narration according to such kind of learning and explanation.”

【注释】(1)博学:广泛地学习。详说:详细解释。(2)将:副词,欲,打算。以:介词,表示行为的依据或前提。说约:叙述简要。

【原文】16 孟子曰:“以善服人者,[1]未有能服人者也;以善养人,[2]然后能服天下。天下不心服而王者,未之有也。”

【白话译文】

孟子说:“拿德行来使人顺从的,没有过能使人顺从的;拿德行来培养人,做好培养人的事情,就能得到天下的人顺从。天下的人不心服而能统一天下的,从未有过。”

【英语译文】

Mencius said, “If one makes people obedient by means of virtue, he cannot manage to do it. If we nurture people by means of virtue and do it well, we can make people under the Heaven obedient. There wasn’t the situation where one became a king if people weren’t genuinely convinced.”

【注释】(1)善:指德行。服人:使人顺从。(2)养人:培养人。

【原文】17 孟子曰:“言无实不祥。[1]不祥之实,蔽贤者当之。[2]”

【白话译文】

孟子说:“言语没有实际内容不好;不好的实际内容,要算埋没贤能的话了。”

【英语译文】

Mencius said, “It isn’t good to speak without practical content. A speech without practical content stifles virtuous and competent men.”

【注释】(1)实:真实。不祥:不善,不吉利。(2)蔽贤:埋没贤能的人。当:相当,对等,算是。

【原文】18 徐子曰:[1]“仲尼亟称于水,[2]曰‘水哉,水哉!’何取于水也?”孟子曰:“原泉混混,[3]不舍昼夜,[4]盈科而后进,[5]放乎四海。[6]有本者如是,是之取尔。[7]苟为无本,七八月之间雨集,[8]沟浍皆盈;[9]其涸也,[10]可立而待也。故声闻过情,[11]君子耻之。”

【白话译文】

徐子说:“孔子多次称赞水,说道:‘水啊! 水啊!’他看中了水的哪一点呢?”孟子说:“泉水滚滚向前流,不分昼夜不回头;一坑填满了才前进,如此直到海中游。有源头的水都是这样。孔子所看中的就是这一点罢了。如果没有源头,即使在七八月之间大雨密集,把大小沟渠都灌满了,可是不要等多久,水就枯竭了。所以声誉超过了实际情况,君子认为耻辱。”

【英语译文】

Xu Zi asked, “Confucius praised water many times, saying ‘O, water! O, water!’ Which good point of water did he heed?” Mencius said, “Spring water continues flowing forward and it never flows backward. After filling one pond it starts heading on until it reaches great seas. Water with fountainhead is the same like this. What Confucius heeded is this point. If there isn’t fountainhead, water will dry up even if it fills all brooks in rainy season. Therefore a moral man thinks it shameful if one’s reputation surpasses reality.”

【注释】(1)徐子:徐辟。孟子弟子。参见《滕文公上》第五章。(2)亟:qì,屡次,一再。(3)原泉:同“源泉”。有源之水。混混:gǔn ~,同“滚滚”,水奔流不绝的样子。(4)不舍:不放弃。(5)盈:满。科:坑,地面凹陷处。(6)放乎:至于。(7)是之取尔:之,助词。在本句中作为宾语前置的标志,宾语复位后它就消失了。所以,是之取尔=取是尔。尔,语助词。相当于“耳”。罢了,而已。(8)七八月之间雨集:周历七八月正当夏历五六月,是雨多之季。(9)浍:kuài,田间排水道。(10)涸:hè,水枯竭。(11)闻声过情:名声超过实情。

【原文】19 孟子曰:“人之所以异于禽兽者几希,[1]庶民去之,[2]君子存之。舜明于庶物,[3]察于人伦,[4]由仁义行,非行仁义也。”

【白话译文】

孟子说:“人不同于禽兽之处很少,一般人把它弄丢了,君子却保存了它。舜明白万物的道理,明察人类的常情,沿着仁义之路而行,不是行使仁义。”

【英语译文】

Mencius said, "The difference between man and beasts is quite little. Ordinary people neglect it but moral men cherish it. Sage Shun understood the reason of things, perceived men's ordinary emotions, and walked on the road of humanity and righteousness. He didn't need to carry out humanity and righteousness."

【注释】(1)几希:jī ~,相差甚微,极少。(2)庶民:众民,平民。(3)庶物:众物,万物。(4)察于人伦:明白人间形成的区别于禽兽而普遍的正常关系。

【原文】20 孟子曰:"禹恶旨酒而好善言。[1]汤执中,[2]立贤无方。[3]文王视民如伤,[4]望道而未之见。[5]武王不泄迩,[6]不忘远。周公思兼三王,[7]以施四事;[8]其有不合者,仰而思之,夜以继日;幸而得之,坐以待旦。"

【白话译文】

孟子说:"禹不喜欢美酒,却喜欢金玉良言。汤坚持中道,用人任真贤,不分贵贱地位。文王体谅百姓痛苦,认为个个都像伤员。敬慕有德行的人,如同没了没完。武王不轻慢身边的人,不忘记不在身边的人。周公志在学习夏、商、周三代圣王,实施禹、汤、文、武四王所行之事;若有不合当前情况的,就仰天思考,白天想不好,夜晚继续想;一到想好了,就坐着等天亮,立即施行。"

【英语译文】

Mencius said, "Sage Yu didn't love fine wine but he loved invaluable advice. King Tang of Shang Dynasty stick to the doctrine of mean and employed virtuous men never caring whether they were noble or humble. King Wen of Zhou Dynasty was considerate of masses' pain regarding them as wounded men. He respected virtuous men endlessly. King Wu of Zhou Dynasty never insulted people nearby and never forgot those far away from him. Duke Zhou intended to learn from the three sages in Xia, Shang and Zhou dynasties and he implemented what kings Yu, Tang, Wen and Wu had done. If there was anything inappropriate to present situation he would think it over day after night. Once coming up an idea he would sit up till daybreak and carried it right away."

【注释】(1)旨酒:美酒。(2)执中:谓持中庸之道无过与不及。(3)立贤无方:朱熹《四书集注》:“方,犹类也。立贤无方,惟贤则立之于位,不问其类也。”清焦循《孟子正义》:“方,常也……惟贤则立,而无常法,乃申上执中之有权。”(4)如伤:像有伤痛的样子。(5)望道:敬慕有道的人。而:rú,如同。(6)泄:通“媟”,狎侮;轻慢。(7)三王:指夏、商、周三代圣王。(8)四事:指禹、汤、文、武四王所行之事。

【原文】21 孟子曰:“王者之迹熄而诗亡,[1]诗亡然后春秋作。[2]晋之乘[3],楚之梼杌,[4]鲁之春秋,一也;[5]其事则齐桓晋文,[6]其文则史。[7]孔子曰:‘其义则丘窃取之矣。[8]’”

【白话译文】

孟子说:“圣王的功业停止了,诗也就随着消亡了;诗消亡了,孔子便创作了《春秋》。晋国的《乘》,楚国的《梼杌》,鲁国的《春秋》,一样都是史书。书中记载的事情,都是齐桓晋文一类人物的活动,书中的文字记载,都是史官之言。孔子说:‘《春秋》书中的含义便是我私自采取的了。’”

【英语译文】

Mencius said, “Poetry disappeared when sage kings’ causes stopped; Confucius wrote *The Spring and Autumn Annals* when poetry disappeared. *Sheng of Jin State*, *Tao Wu of Chu State*, and *The Spring and Autumn Annals of Lu State* were all historic books. What was recorded in them were the activities of Duke Huan of Qi State and Duke Wen of Jin State, and what historians commented. Confucius said, ‘What *The Spring and Autumn Annals* has conveyed is what I privately adopt.’”

【注释】(1)王者之迹:省文曰“王迹”,亦作“王迹”,谓帝王的功业。熄:火灭,引申为“消亡”“停止”。朱熹《四书集注》:“王者之迹熄,谓周平王东迁,而政教号令不及于天下也。”诗亡:朱熹《四书集注》:“谓黍离降为国风而雅亡。”(2)春秋作:《春秋》,春秋时代编年体简史。相传孔子依据鲁国史官所编鲁史加以整理修订而成。起于鲁隐公元年(公元前722年),止于鲁哀公十四年(公元前481年),计二百四十二年。“以纪元年,正时日月”而成为编年史的始祖。《春秋》文字简短,寓有褒贬之意,后世称为春秋笔法。(3)乘:shèng,春秋时晋国的史书。(4)梼杌:táowù,楚国史书名。(5)一也:谓都是史书之名。(6)其事:指书中所记之事。

齐桓晋文:春秋之时,五霸迭兴,而齐桓晋文为盛。(春秋五霸所指,有三种版本:一,指齐桓公、晋文公、宋襄公、楚庄公、秦穆公。见《吕氏春秋·当务》;二,指齐桓公、晋文公、楚庄王、吴王阖庐、越王勾践。见《荀子·王霸》。三,指齐桓公、晋文公、宋襄公、秦穆公、吴王夫差。见《汉书·诸侯王表》)。(7)其文:指书中的文字记载。则史:就是历史。(8)其义:指书中的含义。窃取:谦辞,谓私自采取。

【原文】22 孟子曰:“君子之泽,五世而斩,[1]小人之泽,五世而斩。予未得为孔子徒也,予私淑诸人也。[2]”

【白话译文】

孟子说:“君子的影响五代过后就断绝了,小人的影响五代过后也断绝了。我出生太晚没能做孔子的学生,我私下敬仰从诸贤人那里获得了圣人遗教。”

【英语译文】

Mencius said, “The influence of moral men was broken after five generations and that of mean men was also broken after five generations. I was born too late and couldn’t become his confucius disciple, but I privately respect many sages and have got teachings from them.”

【注释】(1)泽:影响。朱熹《四书集注》:“泽,流风余韵也。”(2)私淑:私自敬仰而未得到直接的传授。诸人:指子思之徒。

【原文】23 孟子曰:“可以取,可以无取,取伤廉[1];可以与,可以无与,与伤惠;[2]可以死,可以无死,死伤勇。[3]”

【白话译文】

孟子说:“可以取来,可以不取来,取来了有损廉洁;可以给予,可以不给予,给予了,有损恩惠本义。可以死去,可以不死去,死去了,有损勇德。”

【英语译文】

Mencius said, “It may be obtained or it may not be obtained, but it will harm probity upon being obtained. It may be given or it may not be given, but it will harm mercy upon giving. One may die or may not die, to be dead will harm courage.”

【注释】(1)可以……可以:“两可”之间,以“不为”为上。不为,无触犯;为,有所触犯。(2)伤:损害。(3)廉、惠、勇:廉洁;恩惠;勇德。

【原文】24 逢蒙学射于羿,[1]尽羿之道,思天下惟羿为愈己,[2]于是杀羿。孟子曰:“是亦羿有罪焉。[3]”公明仪曰:“宜若无罪焉。”曰:“薄乎云尔,[4]恶得无罪?郑人使子濯孺子侵卫之,[5]子濯孺子曰:‘今日我疾作,不可以执弓,吾死矣乎!’问其仆曰:‘追我者谁也?’其仆曰:‘庾公之斯也。[6]’曰:‘吾生矣。’其仆曰:‘庾公之斯,卫之善射者也,夫子曰“吾生”,何谓也?’曰:‘庾公之斯学射于尹公之他,尹公之他学射于我,夫尹公之他,端人也,[7]其取友必端矣。’庾公之斯至,曰:‘夫子何为不执弓?’曰:‘今日我疾作,不可以执弓,’曰:‘小人学射于尹公之他,尹公之他学射于夫子。我不忍以夫子之道反害夫子。虽然,今日之事,君事也,我不敢废。’抽矢,扣轮,[8]去其金,[9]发乘矢而后反。[10]”

【白话译文】

逢蒙跟羿学射箭,完全学会了羿的本领。他想到天下只有羿比自己强了,便杀害了羿。孟子说:“这件事,羿也有过错。”公明仪说:“好像没有什么错误吧。”孟子说:“错误不大罢了,怎么可以说没有错误?从前郑国派子濯孺子侵犯卫国,卫国派庾公之斯追击子濯孺子。子濯孺子说:‘今天我的病发作了,拿不了弓,我算死定了。’他向仆从问道:‘追我的是谁呀?’仆从说:‘庾公之斯。’他便说:‘我可以活命了。’仆从说:‘庾公之斯是卫国有名的射手,您反说可以活命了,这是什么道理呀?’子濯孺子说:‘庾公之斯的射技,是跟尹公之他学的,而尹公之他又是跟我学的;尹公之他是个正派人,他选取的学生或朋友,一定也是正派的。’庾公之斯追上来了,问道:‘老师为何不拿弓?’子濯孺子说:‘今天我的病发作了,拿不了弓。’庾公之斯说:‘我跟尹公之他学射,尹公之他跟您学射。我不忍用您的本领反过来伤害您;虽然如此,今天的事是国家的公事,我又不敢废弃。’便抽出箭在车轮上敲了几下,去掉了箭头,发射了四箭后回去了。”

【英语译文】

Pang Meng learned archery from Yi, and he got all the skills of Yi. Then he thought Yi was the only person who surpassed him in skill and he killed Yi. Mencius said, “As for this event, Yi had his own fault.” Gongming Yi said, “He seemed to have no fault.” Mencius said, “His fault was not so serious. How could he have no fault? In old days, in Zheng State Zi Zhuo Ru Zi was dispatched to attack Wei State, and in Wei State Yu Gong Zhi Si was sent to run after him. Zi Zhuo Ru Zi said, 'Today I'm ill and can't take my bow so that I'm sure to die.' He asked his subordinates, 'Who is running after me?' His subordinates said, 'It is Yu Gong Zhi Si.' He said, 'I can survive.' His subordinates asked, 'Yu Gong Zhi Si is the famous shooter in Wei State but you say you can surivive. Why do you say so?' Zi Zhuo Ru Zi said, 'Yu Gong Zhi Si learned archery from Yin Gong Zhi Ta but the latter learned archery from me. Yin Gong Zhi Ta was an upright man and his student should also be upright.' Yu Gong Zhi Si caught Zi Zhuo Ru Zi and asked, 'Why didn't master take your bow?' Zi Zhuo Ru Zi answered, 'Today I'm ill and can't take my bow.' Yu Gong Zhi Si said, 'I learned archery from Yin Gong Zhi Ta who learned from you. I cannot use your craft to harm you, but this is state affair and I dare not refuse it.' Then he draw out arrows, knock them on wheels and rid of arrow-heads. After he shot four times he went back."

【注释】(1)逢蒙:亦作"逄蒙",páng ~,一读 péng ~,逢蒙既是羿的徒弟又是他的家将,后叛变,助寒浞杀羿。羿,神射手。篡夏自立。为夏代有穷国的君主。(2)愈己:胜过自己。(3)是:代词,此,这。(4)薄乎云尔:薄,少;轻。乎,词尾,没有相应的词对译,可以去掉。云尔,亦作"云耳",语气助词。用在语尾表示如此而已。(5)子濯孺子:郑国人夫。(6)庾公之斯:卫国大夫。(7)端人:正直的人。(8)扣轮:敲击车轮。扣同"叩"。敲击。(9)金:箭头。(10)乘矢:四支箭。乘 shèng,数词。古时以四为乘。

【原文】25 孟子曰:"西子蒙不洁,[1]则人皆掩鼻而过之;[2]虽有恶人,[3]齐戒沐浴,[4]则可以祀上帝。[5]"

【白话译文】

孟子说:"要是西施身上沾染了脏东西,那么别人走过她身旁时,都会捂住鼻子,怕闻恶臭;即使面目丑陋,要是他不饮酒不吃荤,又洗头又洗全身,心意诚实,身体干净,就可以祭祀上帝。"

【英语译文】

Mencius said, "If Xi Shi, the beauty was made dirty, the passersby would cover their noses for foul odor. If a person was ugly but he doesn't drink wine or eat meat, and has shower honestly, then he can sacrifice the God of Heaven."

【注释】(1)西子:西施,喻美妇人。蒙不洁:覆盖着脏东西。(2)掩鼻:捂住鼻子怕闻恶臭。(3)恶人:指丑人,丑妇。与"西子"对举。(4)齐:同"斋"。单说齐戒时,一般概念,包括沐浴在内;既言齐戒,又说沐浴,则"齐戒"的意义,只是不饮酒,不吃荤。(5)祀:祭祀。

【原文】26 孟子曰:"天下之言性也,[1]则故而已矣。[2]故者以利为本。[3]所恶于智者,为其凿也。[4]故智者若禹之行水也,则无恶于智矣。禹之行水也,行其所无事也。[5]如智者亦行其所无事则智亦大矣。天之高也星辰之远也,苟求其故,千岁之日至,可坐而致也。[6]"

【白话译文】

孟子说:"天下的人讨论人的本性或事物的性质时,以其本来的轨迹为准则就行了。本来的轨迹以顺势无阻自然而然为根本。厌恶聪明人的原因是,聪明人的穿凿附会。所以聪明人像大禹治水那样顺水向下之势,就没有厌恶聪明的事了。大禹治水不为违反自然的事。聪明人如果也不为违反自然的事,那么聪明也大了。天很高,星星很远,如果能够找到它们本来的轨迹,一千年后的冬至,都可以坐着推算出来。"

【英语译文】

Mencius said, "When people discuss human nature and things' characters, they shall regard the original track as criterion. The essence of the original track is going smooth and naturally. The reason for detesting smart men lies in that smart men make a far-fetched comparison. Therefore if smart men do things as Great Yu dredged water, then there is no one who detests them. Great Yu didn't do anything violating the nature when he dredged water. If smart men didn't do things violating the nature, they were really smart. The heaven is high and stars are far. If we can find out their tracks, one thousand years later we can figure out the exact time of winter solstice."

【注释】(1)言性:讨论人的本性或事物的性质。(2)则故而已矣:以其本来的轨迹为准则就行了。故,朱熹《四书集注》:"故者,其已然之迹,若所谓天下之故者也”。(3)利:顺势自燃。(4)凿:穿凿附会。(5)行其所无事:不为违反自然的事。(6)日至:指夏至或冬至。周曆以冬至为元旦。元旦意味着一年新的开始。

【原文】27 公行子有子之丧,[1]右师往吊。[2]入门,有进而与右师言者,有就右师之位而与右师言者。孟子不与右师言,右师不悦曰:“诸君子皆与驩言,孟子独不与驩言是简驩也。”孟子闻之,曰:“礼,朝廷不历位而相与言,[3]不逾阶而相揖也。我欲行礼,子敖以我为简,不亦异乎?”

【白话译文】

公行子死了儿子,右师前往吊唁。他一进门,有上前同他说话的,有走近他的座位同他说话的。只有孟子不同他说话,右师很不愉快,说:“各位大夫都同我说话,只有孟子不同我说话,这是简慢驩某了。”孟子听了,说:“依照礼节,在朝廷中不跨过位次来交谈,也不超过台阶来拱手作揖,我只想依礼而行,子敖却以为我简慢了谁,不是很奇怪吗?”

【英语译文】

Gong Xing Zi's son died and Wang Zi'ao went to offer condolences. Upon entering the door, some person talked to him, and others went to his seat and have a chat. Only Mencius didn't say a word to him and he wasn't glad, saying, “Every minister here has greeted me except Mencius. He has really contempt for me.” Hearing this Mencius said, “According to rites, in the court we shouldn't cross seats to have a talk, and we shouldn't cross steps to make a bow with hands folded in front. I just did a thing according to the rites, however Ziao thought that I had contempt for him. Isn't it quite strange?”

【注释】(1)公行子:齐国大夫。(2)右师:官名。其人即盖大夫王驩,字子敖(参见《公孙丑下》第六章)。(3)历位:越位。历,越过。(4)逾阶:超越台阶。揖:yī,拱手行礼。

【原文】28 孟子曰:“君子所以异于人者,以其存心也。君子以仁存心,以礼存心。[1]仁者爱人,有礼者敬人。爱人者,人恒爱之;敬人者,人恒敬之。[2]有人于此,其待我以横逆,[3]则君子必自反也;我必不仁也,必无礼也,此物奚宜至哉?[4]其自反而仁矣,自反而有礼矣,其横逆由是也,君子必自反也,我必不忠。自反而忠矣,其横逆由是也,君子曰:‘此亦妄人也已矣。[5]如此,则与禽兽奚择哉?[6]于禽兽又何难焉?[7]’是故君子有终身之忧,无一朝之患也。乃若所忧则有之:舜人也,我亦人也。舜为法于天下,可传于后世,我由未免为乡人也,[8]是则可忧也。忧之如何?如舜而已矣。[9]若夫君子所患则亡矣。[10]非仁无为也,非礼无行也。如有一朝之患则君子不患矣。”

【白话译文】

孟子说:“君子和一般人不同的地方,就在于居心不同。君子心里装着仁,装着礼。仁人爱别人,有礼的人尊敬别人。爱别人的人,别人总是爱他;尊敬别人的人,别人总是尊敬他。假如这里有个人,对我蛮横无理,那君子一定反躬自问,‘我一定不够仁,一定不够有礼,不然,这种态度,怎么可以冲着我来?’反躬自问后,觉得自己不是不仁不是无礼,这人的蛮横态度还是原样。君子一定又反躬自问,我一定不够忠心,反躬自问,自己是在忠心不二,他还是蛮横无理老一套。君子就会说:‘这也是个无知乱来的人罢了,这样不讲理,那和禽兽怎样区别呢?对于禽兽又何必责备呢?’所以君子有一辈子的忧虑,却没有突发的忧患。这样的忧虑是有的:舜是人,我也是人,舜为天下人树立了榜样,可以传于后世,我却仍然是个乡里无所作为的人,这个才是值得忧虑的事。这个忧虑怎么办呢?努力向舜学习罢了。至于君子别的忧患就没有了。不是仁爱的事不做,不是合于礼法的事不做,即使有意外飞来的横祸,君子也不以为痛苦了。”

【英语译文】

Mencius said, “The difference between a moral man and an ordinary person lies in that they have different intentions. A moral man cherishes humanity and rites. A humanistic man loves others and a man observing rites respects others. If a man loves others, others always love him; if a man respects others, then others always respect him. Suppose a person dealt with somebody unreasonably, a moral man would refleciou himself, ‘I must have been less humanistic and less being ritual, otherwise how could he be so impolite to me?’ After reflection the moral man found that he was very humanistic and ritual. But that man still dealt with him in the same way. The moral man reflected once again to find whether he is loyal or not. After reflection he found that he was very loyal. But that man still dealt with him in the same way. The moral man would say, ‘This man is a rough and unreasonable one who has no difference from beasts. How could we scold the beasts?’ Therefore, a moral man has a life-long worries but he doesn't have unexpected scourges. There were such kind of worries: Great Yu was a man and I am also a man. But Great Yu set a good example for people under the Heaven but I am just a countryman who achieves nothing. How can I deal with such kind of worry? I just have to learn from Great Yu. As for other scourges, a moral man don't have them. A moral man won't feel pain upon unexpected disasters if he doesn't do unkind and rites-violating things."

【注释】(1)存心:居心,心中怀着的意念。以仁(礼)存心,谓心中怀着仁(礼)。(2)恒:常常,经常。(3)横逆:谓强暴不顺理。(4)物:事情,事务。(5)妄人:无知妄为的人。(6)择:区别。(7)何难焉:为何责难。(8)乡人:普通人。(9)如:随顺,依照。(10)若夫:转折连词,表他转关系,可译作"至于""说到"。

【原文】29 禹、稷当平世,三过其门而不入,[1]孔子贤之。颜子当乱世,居于陋巷,一箪食一瓢饮,人不堪其忧,颜子不改其乐,孔子贤之。孟子曰:"禹、稷、颜回同道。[2]禹思天下有溺者,由己溺之也;[3]稷思天下有饥者,由己饥之也,是以如是其急也。禹、稷、颜子易地则皆然。[4]今有同室之人斗者,救之,虽被髮缨冠而救之,[5]可也;乡邻有斗者,被髪、缨冠而往救之,则惑也,[6]虽闭户可也。[7]"

【白话译文】

禹、稷处于政治清明的时代,三次经过自己的家门都不进去,孔子认为他们是贤人。颜子处于政治昏乱的时代,住在褊狭的小巷里,一小筐饭,一小瓢水,这样,别人都忧愁不忍,颜子却毫不改变自己的快乐。孔子认为他是贤人。孟子说:"禹、稷、颜子他们的思想原则相同。禹想到天下遭水淹的人,就好像是自己让天下人被淹一样,稷想到天下挨饿的人,就好像是自己让天下人挨饿一样,所以他们如此急迫不停地去拯救百姓。禹、稷、颜子他们,如果交换地位,也都会同样的干。如果有人在你所在的房间内打架斗殴,披着头发不戴帽子立即去排解,那是可以的。如果乡里的邻居打架斗殴,距离远,也披着头发不戴帽子立即去排解,那就糊涂了;即使把门关上,也是可以的。"

【英语译文】

Great Yu and Ji lived in political bright times, and they didn't go home while passed by their home. Confucius thought they were virtuous men. Yan Hui lived in political dark times, he stayed in a narrow lane eating a small basket of rice and drinking a small gourd of water. Other people worried about him but he himself felt happy and didn't change a little bit. Confucius thought that he was also a virtuous man. Mencius said, "Great Yu, Ji and Yan Hui had the same thinking principle. Great Yu thought that he himself made people drown while he perceived the situation of great flood. Ji thought that he himself made people suffer famine while he perceived the situation of hunger. If Great Yu, Ji and Yan Hui changed their positions they would do the same things. If some persons are fighting in your room, it is alright to deal with it without wearing hat and messed hair. If neighboring people in countryside are fighting in a distant place, it is muddled for you to do in the same way. Even closing the door is alright."

【注释】(1)平世:太平之世。与"乱世"对。三过:三次路过。(2)同道:同一思想,同一原则。(3)由:通"犹"。如同,好像。(4)皆然:都是一样。(5)斗:dòu,同"斗(dòu)。被髪缨冠:pī ~ ~ ~,谓忙得来不及束发结冠缨。(6)惑:糊涂,令人不解。(7)虽:连词,这里表示假设关系,相当于"纵然""即使"。

【原文】30 公都子曰:"匡章,通国皆称不孝焉,[1]夫子与之游,又从而礼貌之,[2]敢问何也?"孟子曰:"世俗所谓不孝者五:惰其四支,[3]不顾父母之养,一不孝也;博弈好饮酒[4],不顾父母之养,二不孝也;好货财私妻子,[5]不顾父母之养,三不孝也;从耳目之欲,[6]以为父母戮,[7]四不孝也;好勇斗狠,以危父母,五不孝也;章子有一于是乎?夫章子,子父责善而不相遇也。[8]责善,朋友之道也;父子责善,贼恩之大者。夫章子,岂不欲有夫妻子母之属哉?为得罪于父,不得近,出妻屏子,[9]终身不养焉。其设心以为不若是,[10]是则罪之大者,[11]是则章子已矣。[12]"

【白话译文】

公都子说:"匡章,全国都说他不孝,您却同他交往,而且还很敬重他,请问这是为什么呢?"孟子说:"一般人所说的不孝有五种:懒脚懒手不做事,不赡养父母,这是一不孝;喜欢下棋赌博和饮酒,不赡养父母,这是二不孝;贪爱钱财,偏爱妻室儿女,不赡养父母,这是三不孝;放纵耳目的欲望,而使父母受到羞辱,这是四不孝;耍狠斗勇,好打架,危及父母,这是五不孝。这五不孝,章子占一种吗?章子只是同他父亲相互要求从善,而不相合搞僵了。相互要求从善,是交朋友的做法,父子相互要求从善,总是损害亲爱之恩不小。章子难道不想有夫妻母子的团聚吗?就因为得罪了父亲,不能和他亲近,就把自己的妻室子女都赶走了,终身不要他们奉养,他心想不这样做,罪过会更大。这就是章子的为人了。"

【英语译文】

Gong Du Zi said, "People over the state have said that Kuang Zhang wasn't filial to his parents, but you are befriending him and respect him so much. Why?" Mencius said, "Ordinary people mention five kinds of non-filial-piety actions. The first one is that someone is lazy doing nothing and doesn't support his parents. The second one is that someone indulges in games and wine and doesn't support his parents. The third one is that someone is greedy on wealth and loves his wife and kids more but he doesn't support his parents. The fourth one is that someone indulges in desires of sight and hearing which makes his parents be shamed, but he doesn't support his parents. The fifth one is that someone loves fight which endangers his parents. Does Kuang Zhang have any kind of these five actions? Zhang Zi had made worse the relationship between him and his parents because he wanted his parents and he did kind things together mutually. Mutually doing kind things should be the method of making friends; father and son mutually doing kind things had harmed their relation a lot. Didn't Kuang Zhang want the reunion of the family members? Since he offended and could not get intimate with his father, he drove away his wife and kids and didn't require their support. He thought if he didn't do like this his guilt would be more serious. This is Kuang Zhang."

【注释】(1)匡章:齐人。传说,章子的母亲得罪了章子的父亲,章父杀了章母埋于马栈之下,大约章子曾谴责其父而不听,因此父子失和。通国:全国。(2)从而:连词,因而。礼貌:以庄肃和顺的仪容表示敬意;尊敬。(3)四支:即"四肢"。支,肢的古字。人体两上肢,两下肢合称四肢。(4)博弈:局戏和围棋,亦指赌博。(5)好货财:贪爱钱财。私妻子:偏爱妻室儿女。(6)从:zòng,"纵"的古字。放纵;纵情。(7)以为:犹而为,而成。以,而,连词。戮:羞辱。(8)相遇:相合。(9)出妻:休弃妻子。屏子:bǐng ~,排斥子女;抛弃子女。(10)设心:用心,居心。以为:认为。是则:这就,这就是。(11)已矣:语气词,用于句末与"矣"同义,根据语境可译作:啊、呀、啦、了、罢了、而已等。

【原文】31 曾子居武城,[1]有越寇。[2]或曰:"寇至,盍去诸?[3]"曰:"无寓人于我室,毁伤其薪木。"[4]寇退,则曰:"修我墙屋,我将反。"寇退,曾子反。左右曰:"待先生如此其忠且敬也,寇至,则先去以为民望;[5]寇退,则反,殆于不可。[6]"沈犹行曰[7]:

“是非汝所知也。昔沈犹有负刍之祸，[8]从先生者七十人，未有与焉。”子思居于卫，[9]有齐寇。[10]或曰：“寇至，盍去诸？”子思曰：“如伋去，君谁与守？”孟子曰：“曾子、子思同道。曾子，师也，父兄也；子思，臣也，微也。曾子、子思易地则皆然。”

【白话译文】

曾子住在武城，越国军队来侵犯。有人说：“强盗来了，何不离开呢？”曾子说：“好，不要让人住进我屋里，免得毁坏我的草和树。”强盗退走了，曾子说：“把我的墙和屋修理修理我要回来了。”强盗退了，曾子回来了。他旁边的人说：“武城人这样忠实恭敬对待您，强盗打来，您率先离开作为民众仿效的对象；强盗退了，就马上回来，这怕不可以吧？”沈犹行说：“这不是你们所能知道的。从前先生住在我那里，有打柴人闹事生祸，跟随先生的有七十人，先生带着他们全部离开了，没有参与。”子思住在卫国，齐国军队来侵犯，有人说：“强盗来了，何不离开呢？”子思说：“如果我离开了，国君与谁来守城呢？”孟子说：“曾子和子思处事的原则是一样的。曾子是国君的老师，是长辈；子思是国君的臣子，是小官。曾子和子思如果交换地位，他们的行为会是一样的。”

【英语译文】

Zeng Zi lived in Wucheng and troops of Yue State attacked it. Somebody asked, “Thieves have come. Why don’t you leave away?” Zeng Zi said, “Ok. But do not let anyone live in my room and damage my grasses and trees.” After the thieves retreated Zeng Zi said, “Please repair my walls and rooms, and I will come back.” His men beside him said, “People in Wucheng have respected you so much, however, when the enemy attacked you left first and set an example for them to flee and when the enemy retreated you came back right away. Is it right for you to do that?” Shen Youxing said, “You don’t know what is the real thing. In other days the Master lived in our place, and some woodcutters made troubles. The master led his seventy disciples leave away and didn’t take part in the event.” Zi Si lived in Wei State and troops of Qi State attacked. Somebody asked, “Thieves have come. Why didn’t you leave away?” Zi Si said, “With whom will the monarch defend the city if I leave away from here?” Mencius said, “Zeng Zi and Zi Si did things according to the same principle. Zeng Zi was the teacher of the monarch and superior. Zi Si was the minister of the monarch and subordinate. If they changed their posts, they would act in the same way.”

【注释】(1)武城:鲁邑名。在今山东费县西南九十里。(2)越寇:越灭吴后,与鲁交界。寇,名词,盗匪,侵略者;动词,侵略,侵犯。(3)盍:hé,副词,表示反诘。犹何不。去诸:去,动词,离开。诸,语气助词。在句末可以表感叹或疑问,在句中可以表停顿或舒缓语气。(4)薪木:赵岐注:"薪草树木。"(5)民望:民众仿效的对象。(6)殆:近。(7)沈犹行:曾子弟子。(8)负刍之祸:打柴人闹事。负刍,背柴草。谓从事樵采之事。朱熹《四书集注》:"言曾子曾舍于沈犹氏,时有负刍者作乱,来攻沈犹氏。"负刍者,即打柴人。一说"负刍"是人名。见赵岐注。(9)子思:(公元前483年——公元402年)战国初思想家。姓孔,名伋,孔子之孙,伯鱼之子。子思受业于曾子,作中庸,中庸是孔门传授心法,孟子受业于子思的门人,子思上承曾子,下启孟子,被尊为述圣。(10)齐寇:齐国的侵略军。齐军侵犯。

【原文】32 储子曰:[1]"王使人瞷夫子,[2]果有以异于人乎?[3]"孟子曰:"何以异于人哉?尧舜与人同耳。"

【白话译文】

储子说:"王派人来暗中察看您,看看当真有不同于人的地方吗?"孟子说:"有什么跟别人不同呢?尧舜也和一般人相同。"

【英语译文】

Chu Zi said, "The king sent someone privately inspect you, and he wanted to see whether you have anything different from other people." Mencius said, "Do I have anything different from other people? Yao and Shun were the same with ordinary men."

【注释】(1)储子:齐人。参见《告子下》第五章。(2)瞷:jiàn,窥视,侦伺。(3)果:副词,果真,当真,确实。谓与所预相符。

【原文】33 齐人有一妻一妾而处室者,其良人出,则必餍酒肉而后反。其妻问所与饮食者,则尽富贵也。其妻告其妾曰:"良人出,[1]则必餍酒肉而后反;问其与饮食者,尽富贵也,而未尝有显者来。吾将瞷良人之所之也。[2]"蚤起,[3]施从良人之所之,[4]遍国中无与立谈者。卒之东郭墦间,[5]之祭者乞其馀;不足,又顾而之他。此其为餍足之道也。其妻归,告其妾,曰:"良人者,所仰望而终身也,今若此。"与其妾讪其良人,[6]而相泣于中庭,[7]而良人未之知也,施施从外来,[8]骄其妻妾。由君子观之,则人之所以求富贵利达者,其妻妾不羞也,而不相泣者,几希矣。[9]

【白话译文】

齐国有一个同一妻一妾共处的人，作为丈夫，他每次外出，总是吃饱喝足了酒肉后才回家。他妻子问他和一些什么人同吃同喝，他回答的全是有钱有势的人。他妻告诉他妾说：“丈夫外出总是吃饱喝足了酒肉后才回家，问他和一些什么人同吃同喝，回答的全是有钱有势的人，但是从没有有头有脸的人到家里来，我想暗暗看看他到底去哪些地头。”第二天一早，她弯弯拐拐地尾随着丈夫，走遍城中，没看见一个人站着与丈夫说话；最后，她丈夫一直走到东城外墓地里，到祭墓人那里讨些剩余酒肉来吃喝。还没饱足，就东望西望，到另一个祭墓人那里去讨。这便是他吃饱喝足的妙招。他妻回去告诉了他妾，并且说：“丈夫是我们终身依靠的人，现在他竟然如此窝囊！”妻妾二人，又恨又骂无耻懦夫，没办法，一起在庭中痛苦。然而这个丈夫还不知情，自娱自乐地回家，照旧向妻妾夸耀。以君子的眼光来看，那就是一些人求荣华富贵的手段，不使妻妾感到羞辱而相对痛苦的，太少了。

【英语译文】

A man in Qi State lived together with his wife and concubine, and he always went home after eating and drinking enough. His wife asked with whom he ate together and his answer was that those were wealthy men in power. His wife told his concubine, “Our man always went home after eating and drinking enough and he always ate together with those wealthy men in power. But I never saw a wealthy man in power come to our home. I want to stealthily find out where he has gone.” The next morning she tracked this man in zigzagging path through the town but she found no one ever talked to him. Finally this man reached a tomb yard in east part out of the town and begged food and drink from those who did sacrificial ceremony. When he was filled up, he watched here and there, and then begged in another yard. This was his smart way to eat and drink enough. His wife went home and told his concubine the truth, “Husband should be the man on whom we depend in our lifetime, but he behaved so good-for-nothing.” The two women hated and scolded their man but they were sad since they had no way out. However, this man didn't know that his women had already known the truth. And he still boasted as usual to his wife and concubine. From the point of a moral man there are few means which are used to seek for wealth and glory and in the mean time not make one's wife ashamed.

【注释】(1)良人:古时女子对丈夫的称呼。(2)之所之:去去过的地方。(3)蚤起:同“早起”。(4)施:yí,曲折行进,逶迤行进。(5)东郭:东边的外城。亦指东城外,东郊。墦间:fán ~,坟墓间,墓地里。(6)讪:shàn,怨恨咒骂。(7)相泣:共同哭泣,一起哭泣。于中庭:于庭中。(8)施施:喜悦自得的样子。(9)则人之所以求富贵利达者,其妻妾不羞也,而不相泣者,几希矣:则,是承接连词。把上文和下文所说的两个相关情况连接起来。“人之所以求富贵利达者,其妻妾不羞也,而不相泣者”这是一个者字结构,是句子的主语部分;由两个“者字结构”合成。第二个“者字结构”中的“也”是语气助词表停顿。几希矣,是谓语部分。矣,语气助词。用在陈述句末,表已然、将然或必然。译为“了”“啦”。

孟子集注卷九　万章章句上　凡九章

【原文】1 万章问曰:“舜往于田,[1]号泣于旻天,[2]何为其号泣也?”孟子曰:“怨慕也。”[3]万章曰“‘父母爱之,喜而不忘;父母恶之,劳而不怨。’然则舜怨乎?”曰:“长息问于公明高曰:[4]‘舜往于田,则吾既得闻命矣;号泣于旻天,于父母,则吾不知也。’公明高曰:‘是非尔所知也。’夫公明高以孝子之心,为不若是恝,[5]我竭力耕田共为子职而已矣,[6]父母之不我爱,于我何哉?[7]帝使其子九男二女,百官牛羊廪备,[8]以事舜于畎亩之中。[9]天下之士多就之者,帝将胥天下而迁之焉。为不顺于父母,如穷人无所归。天下之士悦之,人之所欲也,而不足以解忧;好色,人之所欲,妻帝之二女,而不足以解忧;富,人之所欲也,富有天下,而不足以解忧;贵,人之所欲,贵为天子,而不足以解忧。人悦之、好色、富贵,无足以解忧,惟顺于父母,可以解忧。人少,则慕父母;知好色,则慕少艾;[10]有妻子,则慕妻子;仕则慕君,不得于君则热中。[11]大孝终身慕父母。五十而慕者,[12]予于大舜而见之矣。”

【白话译文】

万章问道:“舜到田地里去干活,却又仰天大哭,这是为什么呢?”孟子说:“他哀怨自己总是得不到父母的爱。”万章说:“父母爱,不要得意忘形;父母不喜欢,努力做事不抱怨。那么,舜抱怨吗?”孟子说:“从前,长息向公明高请教,说道:‘舜在历山到田地里去干活,您已经讲过了,可是他仰天大哭,这样对于父母如何?我不知道。’公明高说:‘这不是你们能懂得的。’公明高认为孝子之心不是这样淡漠的:我努力耕田,恭恭敬敬做儿子该做的事罢了;父母不爱,有什么关系?舜却不然,尽管帝尧使他的九男二女和各级官吏带着足够的牛、羊、粮食等到田野中来服侍他，天下的士人也有许多去支持他，帝尧还把整个天下都让给他，就因为没有得到父母的欢心，他老是像穷困人没有归宿一样。天下的士人都喜欢，是人们追求的，可他不足以解忧；美人，是人们追求的，已有帝尧的二女为妻，可他不足以解忧；富有，是人们追求的，他已富有天下，可他不足以解忧；显贵，是人们追求的，他已贵为天子，可他不足以解忧。众人喜欢、美人陪伴、富贵双全，都不足够解忧，只有能顺父母的心这一步，可以解忧。一般人，小时候，都爱念父母；长大了知道爱美，就爱念美女；有了妻室儿女，就爱念妻室儿女；做了官，就爱念君主；不得君主欢心，就急切追逐名利权势。大孝的人，一辈子都爱念父母。五十岁了还在爱念父母的，我在大舜那里看到了。”

【英语译文】

Wan Zhang asked, “Why did Great Shun labored in fields and cried aloud?” Mencius answered, “He lamented that he hadn't been loved by his parents.” Wan Zhang said, “If parents love you, you mustn't get lost in too much excitement; if parents don't love you, you must work hard and never complain. Did Great Shun complain?” Mencius said, “In the old days, Zhang Xi asked Gongming Gao for advice, ‘You have said Great Shun went to labor in fields when he lived in Lishan. But he cried aloud. How do you think he responded to his parents in this way? I don't know.’ Gongming Gao said, ‘You don't know such kind of things.’ Gongming Gao thought a filial kid shouldn't be so indifferent: I do farming jobs conscientiously and modestly what a son shall do. It dosen't matter if my parents don't love me. Great Shun was different. Although Sage Yao made his nine sons and two daughters and all officials go to serve Great Shun in the fields with enough ox, sheep and foodstuff, many scholars supported him, and Sage Yao Passed all the land to him, Great Shun still felt that he had no achievement just because his parents didn't love him. It is what we're pursuing that scholars in the world all love him, but this cannot rid of his worries. Beauties are what we're pursuing and Sage Yao's two daughters had been his wives, but this cannot rid of his worries. Being wealthy is what we're pursuing and he had owned the world, but this cannot rid of his worries. Being noble is what we're pursuing and he had become king, but this cannot rid of his worries. People all loving him, beauties accompanying him, being wealthy and noble can get rid of his worries. Only making parents happy can get rid of his worries. An ordinary man is in love with his parents when he is a kid; he is in love with beauties while growing up; he is in love with his wife and children after his marriage; he is in love with his monarch after becoming an official; he is in a hurry to chase fame, fortune and power if he fails to make the monarch happy. A man who has big filialness will be in love with his parents life long. I have seen a man of fifty years old who is still in love with his parents. That's Great Shun."

【注释】(1)舜往于田:舜在历山耕过田。往于田,即前往田地干活。(2)号泣:háoqì,放声大哭。旻天:mín ~,泛指天,特指秋天。(3)怨慕:朱熹《四书集注》:"怨己不得其亲而思慕也。"后泛指因不得相见而思慕。慕,因喜爱而研习模仿;思念。(4)长息:公明高弟子。公明高:曾子弟子。(5)恝:jiá,忽略;淡然。(6)共:gōng,通"恭",恭敬。(7)于我何哉:意近"于我何有哉"。对于我又怎么样?(8)百官:各级官吏。仓廪:贮藏米谷的仓库。备:齐备,全有。(9)畎亩:quǎnmǔ,田地;田野。(10)少艾:shàoài,指年轻美丽的女子。(11)热中:~zhōng,原指内心躁急,后多指急切追逐名利权势。(12)五十而慕者:舜摄政时年已五十。朱熹《四书集注》:"五十而慕,则其终身慕可知矣。"

【原文】2 万章问曰:"诗云:'娶妻如之何?必告父母'。[1]信斯言也,宜莫如舜。[2]舜之不告而娶,何也?"孟子曰:"告则不得娶。男女居室,[3]人之大伦也,如告,则废人之大伦,以怼父母,[4]是以不告也"。万章曰:"舜之不告而娶,则吾既得闻命矣。帝之妻舜而不告,何也?"曰:"帝亦知告焉则。不得妻也。"万章曰:"父母使舜完廪,捐阶,[5]瞽瞍焚廪。使浚井,[6]出,从而揜之[7]。象曰:[8]'谟盖都君咸我绩。[9]牛羊父母,仓廪父母,干戈朕,琴朕,弤朕,二嫂使治朕栖。[10]'象往入舜宫,舜在床琴。[11]象曰:'郁陶思君尔。[12]'忸怩。[13]舜曰:'惟兹臣庶。[14]汝其于予治'[15]不识舜不知象之将杀己与?"曰:"奚而不知也?[16]象忧亦忧,象喜亦喜。"曰:"然则舜伪喜者与?"曰:"否。昔者有馈生鱼于子产,子产使校人畜之池。[17]校人烹之,反命曰'始舍之圉圉焉,[18]少则洋洋焉[19],攸然而逝[20]'子产曰:'得其所哉!得其所哉!'校人出,曰:'孰谓子产智?予既烹而食之,曰:得其所哉?得其所哉。'故君子可欺以其方,[21]难罔以非其道。[22]彼以爱兄之道来,故诚信而喜之,奚伪焉?[23]"

【白话译文】

万章问道:"《诗经》上说:'迎娶妻子该怎么办?一定先报告父母。'当时,应该没有人比舜更信这样的话;舜不报告父母,娶了妻子,怎么解释?"孟子说:"报告了就娶不成。男女结婚同居,是人间最大的正常关系。舜父顽劣,舜母嚣张,如果报告了,就会毁掉这个正大关系,而结怨父母,所以不报告。"万章说:"舜不报告父母而娶妻,我懂您的教诲了。尧把女儿嫁给舜,也没给舜的父母说一声,又是什么道理呢?”孟子说:“尧也知道,如果说了,就不能把女儿嫁给舜了。”万章说:“舜的父母叫他整修谷仓,等舜上了屋顶,就抽去了梯子,他父亲瞽瞍立即放火焚烧谷仓。舜逃险后,父母叫他去把井眼挖深,等他下井后就用泥土填井把他埋葬,可他从井旁的洞穴逃走了。舜的异母弟象说:‘谋害舜都是我的功劳,牛羊分给父母,谷仓分给父母,干戈归我,琴归我,雕弓归我,两位嫂嫂给我铺床迭被。’象走进舜的住房,舜却在床上弹琴。象说:‘真的,真的我好想念你呀。’状态不大自在。舜说:‘我想念着这里的臣下和百姓,你替我管理管理罢!’我不明白,舜是否知道象要杀他。”孟子说:“怎么不知道呢? 象忧愁,他也忧愁,象高兴,他也高兴。”万章说:“这样,那么舜的高兴是假装的吗?”孟子说:“不是;从前,有个人送条活鱼给郑国子产,子产叫管水池的人把它养在池塘里,管水池的人把鱼煮起吃了,然后交差说:‘刚放进水塘时,它要死不活地,动又不动,一会儿摇头摆尾,转了个圈儿,忽然猛地一下飘走,不见了。’子产说:‘它得到了好地方呀! 它得到了好地方呀!’那人出来说道:‘谁说子产聪明,我把那条鱼煮起吃了,他还说它得到了好地方呀! 它得到了好地方呀!’所以对于君子,可以用合于情理的方法诳骗他,难用不合于情理的方法蒙蔽他。象用爱兄的方法来诳,所以舜信以为真而喜,为什么是假装的呢?”

【英语译文】

Wan Zhang asked. “*The Book of Songs* said ‘How does a young man marry a lady?He should inform his parents in advance. ’ There wasn’t anyone who believed it more than Great Shun did. But Great Shun didn’t inform his parents in advance when he married. How do you explain it?” Mencius answered, “If he reported he couldn’t get married. It is the most normal relation for man and woman to get married and live together. Shun’s father was crappy and his mother was unbridled. If Shun reported his marriage to his parents then they would destroy the great relation. Then he would be at deep enmity with his parents. Therefore he didn’t report. ” Wan zhang said, “I have known your explanation about why Great Shun didn’t inform his parents of his marriage. Why did Sage Yao make his daughter marry Great Shun but not tell Shun’s parents?” Mencius said, “Sage Yao knew that if he told Shun’s parents, then his daughter couldn’t marry Great Shun. ” Wan Zhang said, “Shun’s parents ordered him to repair the barn but after he climbed up the roof of the barn they removed the ladder. His father Gu Sou set a fire to burn the barn right away. Shun survived the disaster and his parents ordered him to deepen the well but after he went down to the well they filled the well in order to bury him alive. But he fled away through the side hole. Shun's half brother Xiang said, 'It's my contribution to murder Shun. Ox, sheep and barn are distributed to parents. And swords, zither, and bow belonged to me. The two sisters-in-law made bed for me.' As Xiang went into Shun's bedroom Shun was playing zither in the bed. Xiang said, 'I really miss you.' But he behaved awkwardly. Shun said, 'I am missing the ministers and people, so you manage these things for me.' I don't understand whether Shun knew that Xiang would murder him." Mencius said, "How couldn't he know it? If Xiang was worried he was also worried; if Xiang was glad he was also glad." Wan Zhang asked, "Then did Shun pretended to be glad?" Mencius said, "No, he didn't. In the old days a man gave a living fish to Zi Chan of Zheng State. Zi Chan asked the man the pond-keeper to raise the fish in the pond, but the man cooked it and ate it. After that he reported to Zi Chan, 'Upon being put in the pond, the fish was to die. But after a while it became energetic waving its tail, then it floated away suddenly. I couldn't see it anymore.' Zi Chan responded, 'It got a good place. It got a good place.' The man went out and said, 'Who thought Zi Chan was smart? I cooked and ate the fish but he said that it got a good place.' Therefore, it's easy to cheat a moral man by means of reasonable method, but it's difficult to blind him by means of unreasonable method. Xiang cheated Shun by means of loving his brother and Shun believed it and he was glad. Why do you think that he pretended to be glad?"

【注释】(1)诗云句:见《齐风·南山》。舜时,自然无此诗句;万章所说,不过是认为舜时已有此礼而已。(2)宜莫:应当没有人。(3)男女居室:指夫妇同居。(4)怼:duì,怨恨。(5)完廪:修缮谷仓,捐阶:除去阶梯。(6)浚井:jùn~,把井挖深。浚,除去淤塞物;深挖。(7)揜:yǎn,掩盖。(8)象:舜的异母弟。(9)谟盖:mó hài,谟害,同"谋害"。谟,计谋;谋略。盖,通"害"。都君:指舜。《史记·五帝本纪》:"〔舜〕一年而所举乘聚。二年成邑,三年成都。"故有都君之称。(10)朕、弤、二嫂、栖:朕 zhèn,我。弤 dǐ,舜弓名。二嫂,象称舜的两个妻子。栖 qī,床,古代坐卧之具。(11)琴:鼓琴。(12)郁陶:yù yáo,忧思集聚的样子。(13)忸怩:niǔní,惭愧的样子。(14)惟:思念。(15)于:为(wèi),替。(16)奚:为何,为什么。(17)校人:jiào,管理池沼的小吏。(18)圉圉:yǔyǔ,困而未舒的样子。少:shǎo,少顷;短暂。洋洋:舒缓的样子,迟缓的样子。(20)攸然:迅疾的样子。逝:消失不见。

(21)欺以其方:“方”与“道”同义。其方,指合乎事理的方法。(22)罔以:“罔”与“欺”同义。犹言诳骗、蒙蔽。非其道,指不合乎事理的方法。(23)奚伪:为何假装。

【原文】3 万章问曰:“象日以杀舜为事,立为天子,则放之,[1]何也?”孟子曰:“封之也,或曰放焉。”万章曰:“舜流共工于幽州,[2]放驩兜于崇山,[3]杀三苗于三危,[4]殛鲧于羽山,[5]四罪而天下咸服,[6]诛不仁也。象至不仁,封之有庳。有庳之人奚罪焉?[7]仁人固如是乎?在他人则诛之,在弟则封之。[8]”曰:“仁人之于弟也,不藏怒焉,不宿怨焉,[9]亲爱之而已矣。亲之欲其贵也,爱之欲其富也。封之有庳,富贵之也。身为天子,弟为匹夫可谓亲爱之乎?”“敢问或曰放者,何谓也?”曰:“象不得有为于其国,[10]天子使吏治其国,而纳其贡税焉,[11]故谓之放。岂得暴彼民哉?[12]虽然,欲常常而见之,故源源而来。[13]‘不及贡,以政接于有庳’,[14]此之谓也。”

【白话译文】

万章问道:“象每天都把谋杀舜作为大事来抓,舜做了天子,只把他搁置到外地,这是什么道理呀?”孟子说:“实际是封他为诸侯,有些人以为是搁置。”万章说:“舜把共工迁到幽州,把驩兜搁置于崇山,把三苗国君杀死于三危,把鲧诛杀于羽山。定了这四个人的罪,天下都归服。就因为是讨伐了不仁的人。象是最不仁的人,却封到有庳,有庳国的百姓有什么罪呢?仁人本来就是这样做事吗?对他人就惩罚,对弟弟就封赏。”孟子说:“仁人对于弟弟不隐藏愤怒,也不怀恨在心,只是亲他爱他罢了。亲他,便想让他贵,爱他,便想让他富。把有庳国土封给象,便是让他又富又贵。本人做了天子,弟弟却是一个老百姓,可以说是亲爱吗?”万章说:“请问,有人说是搁置,是什么意思呢?”孟子说:“象不能在封给他的国土上自由为政;天子派遣了官吏来给他治理国家,缴纳赋税,所以有人说是搁置。象能暴虐那里的百姓吗?即使如此,舜还想常常见到象,象也不断来见舜。‘不等诸侯朝贡,以政务接见有庳人’这话说的就是这个意思。”

【英语译文】

Wan Zhang asked, “Xiang regarded murdering Great Shun as a big task every day. But after Shun became king he was just laid aside. What's the reason for this?” Mencius answered, “Actually he was granted as vassal, but somebody thought that he had been laid aside.” Wan Zhang said, “Great Shun removed Gonggong to Youzhou, laid Huandou aside in Chongshan, killed the king of Sanmiao State in Sanwei, and killed Gun in Yushan. After these four men had been punished people under the heaven all submitted to his authority because he had attacked those men without humanity. Xiang was the least humanistic one but was granted as vassal in Youbi State. Did people in Youbi State commit crime? Did a humanistic man do things like this? He punished others but granted titles and territories to his brother." Mencius said, "A man with humanity doesn't hide his agony but he doesn't harbor resentment in his bosom, either. He just got intimate with his brother and he just loved his brother. Being intimate he wanted his brother noble; loving him he wanted his brother wealthy. He granted territory of Youbi State to Xiang in order to make him noble and wealthy. He himself became a king but his brother was just a common people. Could this be called intimacy and love?" Wan Zhang asked, "Somebody said that he just laid aside his brother. What does this mean?" Mencius said, "Xiang couldn't carry out administrative affairs freely in the territory granted to him. The king dispatched officials to govern his state, and to collect tax. Therefore somebody said that he was laid aside. Could Xiang maltreat people there? Even so, Great Shun always thought of Xiang and Xiang always came to visit Shun. 'Not awaiting the vassal to pay tribute, but receiving Youbi people officially' told the exact meaning."

【注释】(1)放之:朱熹《四书集注》:"放,犹置也;置之于此,使不得去也。"(2)流共工于幽州:把罪人迁徙到远方叫"流"。共工,人名。尧的臣下。与官名有别。幽州在今北京市密云区东北。(3)驩兜(huāndōu):尧舜时大臣。崇山:据清王夫之王鸣盛说:当在唐驩州境内,泗城之南(今广西凌云县和西林县一带。)(4)三苗:国名。三苗国君顽固不服。杀三苗,谓杀三苗国君。三危:古代西部边疆山名。其位置说法不一:一说今甘肃敦煌三危山即古三危。一说在甘肃 岷山之西南。一说在云南。(5)殛:jí,前人有两解。一作流放解;一作诛杀解。鲧:大禹之父。羽山:在今江苏赣县界。一说在今山东蓬莱市东南三十里。(6)四罪:四项治罪,四项判处。(7)有庳:~bì,古国名。在今湖南道县北。(8)在:介词,对,对于。(9)藏怒:藏匿其怒。宿怨:怀恨在心。(10)不得有为:谓不能自主政事。(11)纳:缴纳。贡税:犹赋税。田赋与捐税的合称。(12)暴彼民:暴虐那里的人民。(13)源源:如水之相继连续不断。(14)不及贡:不待到诸侯朝贡之期。

【原文】4 咸丘蒙问曰:[1]"语云:[2]'盛德之士,君不得而臣,父不得而子。'舜南面而立,[3]尧帅诸侯北面而朝之,[4]瞽瞍亦北面而朝之。舜见瞽瞍,其容有蹙。[5]孔子曰:'于斯时也,天下殆哉,岌岌乎![6]'不识此语诚然乎哉?"孟子曰:"否。此非君子之言,齐东野人之语也。[7]尧老而舜摄也,[8]尧典曰:'二十有八载,放勋乃徂落,[9]百姓如丧考妣,[10]三年四海遏密八音。[11]'孔子曰:'天无二日,民无二王。'舜既为天子矣又帅天下诸侯以为尧三年丧,是二天子矣。"咸丘蒙曰:"舜之不臣尧,则吾既得闻命矣。诗云:[12]'普天之下,莫非王土;率土之滨,莫非王臣。'而舜既为天子矣,敢问瞽瞍之非臣,如何?"曰:"是诗也非是之谓也;劳于王事,而不得养父母也。曰'此莫非王事,我独贤劳也。[13]'故说诗者,不以文害辞,[14]不以辞害志。以意逆志,[15]是为得之。如以辞而已矣,云汉之诗曰:'周余黎民,靡有孑遗。[16]'信斯言也,是周无遗民也。孝子之至,莫大乎尊亲;尊亲之至,莫大乎以天下养。为天子父,尊之至也;以天下养,养之至也。诗曰:'永言孝思,孝思维则。[17]'此之谓也。书曰:'祇载见瞽瞍,夔夔齐栗,瞽瞍亦允。[18]'是为父不得而子也?[19]"

【白话译文】

咸丘蒙问道:"俗话说:'品德高尚的人,君主不可把他当臣子,父亲不可把他当儿。'舜坐在向南的尊位上,尧带领诸侯向北朝见他。瞽瞍也向北朝见他;舜看见瞽瞍,神色不安。孔子说:'在这个时候,天下真是危险得很啦!'不知道这话是不是真实可信?"孟子说:"不,这不是君子的言语,这是齐国东部边远地带的人说的。尧衰老后,只是让舜代理政务。《尚书·尧典》上说:'过了二十八年,放勋才逝世。群臣好像死了父母一样,服丧三年,四海之内,都停止了音乐。'孔子说:'天上没有两个太阳,人间没有两个天子同场。'舜既然已为天子又带领天下诸侯来为尧服丧三年,那就是同时有两个天子了。"咸丘蒙说:"舜不以尧为臣,我已领受您的教诲了。《诗经》上说:'整个天下,没有哪里不是天子的土地,整个土地上,没有哪个不是天子的臣民。'舜既做了天子,请问,瞽瞍又不是臣,如何解释?"孟子说:"北山这首诗,不是你说的那意思,而是表明勤劳于王事的人,不能够奉养父母。诗人说,'这些事没有一件不是天子的事呀,都是臣民,为什么独我一人这么劳累呢?'所以解说诗句的人,不要拘于文字误解词句,不要拘于词句误解原意,要用自己对整个诗句的领会去推测原意,这样就对了。假如拘于词句不联系上下文,那《云汉》诗说,'周朝剩余的百姓,没有一个遗留。'相信这话,那就是相信周朝没有一个人活下来。这怎么行呢?孝子孝的极点,没有超过尊敬双亲的;尊敬双亲的,没有超过拿天下来奉养双亲的。瞽瞍做了天子的父亲,可以说尊贵到极点了;舜以天下来奉养他,可以说奉养到极点了。《诗经》上说;'长长讲孝心,孝心是法则。'说的正是这个意思。《书经》上说:'舜恭敬地服侍进献瞽瞍,态度庄敬谨慎,瞽瞍也很和顺了。这难道是'父亲不可把他当儿子'吗?"

【英语译文】

Xian Qiumeng asked, "An old saying goes that 'A monarch cannot regard a man of virtue as his minister, and a father cannot regard him as his son'. Sage Yao sat in the respectable and south-facing seat, Great Shun led ministers and paid respects to him north-facingly. Gu Sou also north-facingly paid respects to him. Great Shun noticed that Gu Sou looked uneasy. Confucius said, 'At that time the world was really endangered.' I wonder whether what Confucius said was reliable." Mencius said, "No. It's not what a moral man said. It's the words of persons in the east remote area of Qi State. After Sage Yao was old, Great Shun just acted on behalf of him in administrative position. *The Book of History* said, 'After twenty-eight years Sage Yao died. Ministers wore funeral clothes for three years just as if their parents died. People in the world stopped singing and playing music instruments.' Confucius said, 'There aren't two suns in the heaven and there aren't two kings in the world.' There were two kings at the same time since Great Shun led his ministers to wear funeral clothes for three years." Xian Qiu Meng said, "Great Shun didn't regard Sage Yao as his minister. I have known your teaching about that. *The Book of Songs* said, 'All places belong to the kingdom. It's possession of the royal king. All persons live in every place. They are king's ordinary men.' How do you explain that Gu Sou wasn't a minister since Great Shun had become a king?" Mencius said, "This poem *North Mountain* doesn't suggest what you understand, but it means that a diligent king cannot support his parents. The poet said, 'All these are king's things. People are all ministers and subjects. Why am I so tired?' Therefore, when you explain a poem you shall not misunderstand the real meaning due to the limits of words. You should guess the original meaning according to your own understanding. That's alright. If you are limited by words and don't heed the context, then the poem *Milky Way* said, 'People survived in Kingdom Zhou. No one can escape from disasters.' If you believe it, you surely believe that none of Zhou Dynasty had survived. How could it be? The limit of a filial son dosen't surpass his parents; respecting one's parents cannot surpass doing so by means of using the world. Gu Sou was the father of the king and he reached the limit. Great Shun supported him by means of all the world and he reached the limit. *The Book of Songs* said, 'He filially abides by ancestor's doctrines. He solidifies Kingdom following ancestors.'" It had exactly the same meaning. *The Book of History* said, 'Great Shun modestly attended Gu

Sou in a cautious way, and Gu Sou became amiable. Didn't the father regard him as his son?"

【注释】(1)咸丘蒙:孟子弟子。(2)语:俗话,谚语,古书中的话。(3)南面而立:~~~wèi,古代坐北朝南为尊。因用南面指帝王、长辈的尊位。立,通"位"。南面而立,即居于向南的尊位上。(4)北面而朝:面向北行礼。古礼,臣拜君,卑幼拜尊长,皆面向北行礼。(5)有蹙:~cù,有,词头。只起构词作用无义。蹙,急促不安。(6)天下殆哉,岌岌乎:殆,读 dài,危亡;危险。岌岌,读 jíjí,危急的样子。古人多用来作状语。本句,为了强调状语把它析出置于重读位置上,还原后即,"天下殆岌岌乎殆哉!"(7)野人:上古谓居国城郊野的人。与"国人"对。(8)摄:代理。(9)放勋:亦作"放勋"。帝尧的名。徂落:cú~,亦作"殂落"。死亡。(10)百姓:百官。考妣:~bǐ,父母的别称。按,考妣仅指死去的父母,惟曲礼有此异说。(11)遏密八音:指帝王等死后停止举乐。孔传:"遏,绝;密,静也。"八音,我国古代对乐器的总称。金、石、丝、竹、匏、土、革、木为制造乐器的八种质材,故称。亦泛指音乐。(12)诗云;普天之下……莫非王臣:见《诗·小雅·北山》。《毛序》:"北山,大夫刺幽王也。役使不均,已劳于从事,而不得养其父母也。"率土之滨,谓沿着国土直至海边,训"四海之内"。率,循,沿着。(13)贤劳:劳苦;辛劳。(14)不以文害辞:文,指"字"。辞,指"句子,话语"。意,指字句表现的意义。(15)以意逆志:意,指字句表现的意义。逆,揣测。志,指作者的本意。(16)云汉之诗:见《诗·大雅·云汉》。黎民:老百姓。孑遗:jié~,残存;遗民。(17)诗曰两句:见《诗·大雅·下武》。'永言,长讲。孝思,孝亲之思。与孝心同义。则,法则。(18)书曰三句:见《书·大禹谟》。祇,读 zhí,恭敬。载,侍奉。见,读 xiàn,进献。夔夔,读 kuíkuí,戒惧谨慎的样子。齐,同"斋"。庄敬。栗,谨敬。允若,和顺。(19)也:语气助词,用在是非问句或反问句的末尾,表疑问语气。译为"吗""么"。

【原文】5 万章曰:"尧以天下与舜,有诸?"孟子曰:"否;天子不能以天下与人。""然则舜有天下也,孰与之?"曰:"天与之。""天与之者,谆谆然命之乎?[1]"曰:"否;天不言以行与事示之而已矣。"曰:"以行与事示之者,如之何?"曰:"天子能荐人于天,不能使天与之天下;诸侯能荐人于天子,不能使天子与之诸侯;大夫能荐人于诸侯,不能使诸侯与之大夫。昔者,尧荐舜于天,而天受之;暴之于民而民受之;故曰,天不言,以行与事示之而已矣。"曰:"敢问荐之于天,而天受之;暴之于民[2],而民受之,如何?"曰:"使之主祭,而百神享之,是天受之;使之主事,而事治,百姓安之,是民受之也。天与之人与之故曰,天子不能以天下与人。舜相尧二十有八载,非人之所能为也,天也。尧崩,[3]三年之丧毕,舜避尧之子于南河之南[4],天下诸侯朝觐者,[5]不之尧之子而之舜;讼狱者,[6]不之尧之子而之舜;讴歌者,不讴歌尧之子而讴歌舜,故曰,天也。夫然后之中国,践天子位焉,[7]而居尧之宫,[8]逼尧之子,是篡也,[9]非天与也。《泰誓》曰:[10]'天视自我民视,天听自我民听'此之谓也。"

【白话译文】

万章问道:"尧把天下给舜,有这回事吗?"孟子说:"不,天子不能把天下给人。"万章又问:"那么,舜得到的天下,是谁给的?"答道:"天给的。"又问:"天给他时,反复告诫过吗?"答道:"不,天不说话,拿行动和事情来表示罢了。"又问:"拿行动和事情来表示,是怎么表示的呢?"答道:"天子能把人推荐给天,却不能促动天把天下给人;诸侯能把人推荐给天子,却不能促动天子把诸侯之位给人;大夫能把人推荐给诸侯,却不能促动诸侯把大夫之位给人。从前,尧把舜推荐给天,天接受了,把他显露在百姓面前,百姓也接受了;所以说,天不说话,拿行动和事情来表示而已。"万章说:"请问,把他推荐给天,天接受了,把他显露在百姓面前,百姓也接受了,是怎么知道的?"孟子说:"叫他主持祭祀,神明们都来享用,这便是天接受了。叫他主持政务,事情都能办好,百姓满意,这便是百姓接受了。天给他,人给他,不是天子给他。所以说,天子不能把天下给人。舜辅佐尧二十八年,这不是哪一个人的意志能够做到的,而是天意了。尧去世后,三年服丧完了,舜为了避开尧的儿子丹朱,自己逃到南河的南边去。可是,天下诸侯朝见天子的,不到尧的儿子那里,却到舜那里;打官司的,不到尧的儿子那里,却到舜那里;唱赞歌的人,不歌颂尧的儿子,却歌颂舜。所以说,这是天意。这样,舜才回到首都,登上天子位。如果他住在尧的宫室里而不避开,便有逼迫尧的儿子让位的嫌疑;逼迫让位是"篡夺"不是"天授"。《尚书·泰誓》说:'百姓的眼睛就是天的眼睛,百姓的耳朵就是天的耳朵'正是我现在讲的意思。"

【英语译文】

Wan Zhang asked, "Sage Yao gave the world to Great Shun, didn't he do so?" Mencius answered, "No, he didn't. The Son of the Heaven can't give the world to others." Wan Zhang asked again, "Then who gave the world to Shun?" Mencius answered, "The Heaven gave it to him." Wan Zhang asked again, "Did the Heaven admonish him repeatedly while it gave the world to him?" Mencius answered, "No. The Heaven couldn't speak a word but it expressed by actions." Wan Zhang asked again, "In what way did the Heaven express its will?" Mencius answered, "The Son of the

Heaven can recommend someone to the Heaven but he can't urge it to give the world to a man. A vassal can recommend someone to the Son of the Heaven but he can't urge him to grant the post of vassal to a man. A minister can recommend someone to a vassal but he can't urge him to grant the post of minister to a man. In the old days, Sage Yao recommended Great Shun to the Heaven and the Heaven accepted. Common people accepted Great Shun when he was exposed to them. Therefore, the Heaven can't speak a word but express its will by actions." Wan Zhang asked, "In what way did we know that Sage Yao recommended Great Shun to the Heaven and the Heaven accepted him and common people accepted Great Shun when he was exposed to them?" Mencius answered, "He was asked to host sacrificial ceremony, and the gods came to share, which showed that the Heaven accepted him. When he was asked to be in charge of governance he completed well and people were very gratified, which showed that common people accepted him. The heaven and common people gave him the world but the Son of the Heaven couldn't do so. Great Shun assisted Sage Yao for twenty eight years, which wasn't a person's will but the Heaven's will. Yao died and three years' funeral duration finished. Great Shun fled to the south of Nan He in order to dodge Yao's son Dan Zhu. However, vassals didn't go to Dan Zhu's place but Shun's place to pay respects to the Son of the Heaven. People didn't go to Dan Zhu's place but Shun's place to file in a lawsuit. People didn't sing praise to Dan Zhu but Shun. Therefore, this was the Heaven's will. As a result, Great Shun went back to the capital and ascended the throne. If he had lived in Yao's palace and hadn't dodged Yao's son, then he was suspecious to force Yao's son to resign sovereignty which was usurping the throne but not being granted by the Heaven. *The Book of History* said, 'People's eyes are the Heaven's eyes and people's ears are the Heaven's ears.' It had exactly the same meaning."

【注释】(1)谆谆:zhūnzhūn 反复告诫、再三叮咛的样子。(2)荐:jiàn,推荐。暴:pù,今读 bào,显露;暴露。(3)崩:bēng,古代帝王、皇后之死称"崩"。(4)南河:古代河名。指黄河自今潼关以下由西向东流的一段。张守节《正义》:"河在尧都之南故曰南河。"(5)朝觐:~jìn,谓臣子朝见君主。(6)讼狱:诉讼。(7)践:担当,升任。特指登基,即帝王位。(8)而:连词。表假设,犹"如果"。(9)篡:cuàn,用强力夺取。特指臣子夺取君位。(10)泰誓:《尚书》篇名。

【原文】6 万章问曰:"人有言,'至于禹而德衰,不传于贤而传于子。'有诸?"孟子说:"否,不然也。天与贤,则与贤;天与子,则与子。昔者舜荐禹于天,十有七年,舜崩。三年之丧毕,禹避舜之子于阳城。[1]天下之民从之,若尧崩之后不从尧之子而从舜也。禹荐益于天,七年,禹崩,三年之丧毕,益避禹之子于箕山之阴,[2]朝觐讼狱者不之益而之启,[3]曰,'吾君之子也。'讴歌者,不讴歌益而讴歌启,曰,'吾君之子也。'丹朱之不肖,[4]舜之子亦不肖。舜之相尧、禹之相舜也,历年多,施泽于民久。启贤,能敬承继禹之道。益之相禹也,历年少,施泽于民未久。舜禹益相去久远,[5]其子之贤不肖,皆天也,非人之所能为也。莫之为而为者,天也;莫之致而至者,命也。匹夫而有天下者,德必若舜禹,而又有天子荐之者,故仲尼不有天下。继世以有天下,天之所废,必若桀纣者也,故益伊尹周公不有天下。伊尹相汤以王于天下,汤崩太丁未立,外丙二年,仲壬四年。[6]太甲颠覆汤之典刑,伊尹放之于桐。[7]三年,太甲悔过,自怨自艾,[8]于桐处仁迁义,[9]三年,以听伊尹之训己也,复归于亳。[10]周公之不有天下,犹益之于夏、伊尹之于殷也。孔子曰,唐虞禅,[11]夏后殷周继,[12]其义一也。'"

【白话译文】

万章问道:"人们说,'从尧发展到禹,道德开始衰微,帝位不传给贤良,却传给儿子。'是这样的吗?"孟子说:不,不是这样的。天让传给贤良,便传给贤良;天让传给儿子,便传给儿子。从前,舜把禹推荐给天,十七年过后,舜去世了。服丧三年完毕,禹为了避开舜的儿子让他继位,住在阳城。可是,天下的百姓跟随着禹,就像尧去世后百姓不跟随尧的儿子而跟随舜一样。禹把益推荐给天,七年过后,禹去世了。服丧三年完毕,益为了避开禹的儿子让他继位,住在箕山的北边,当时朝见天子的人、打官司的人都不到益那里去而到启那里去,并且还说,'他是我们君主的儿子呀!'唱赞歌的人,不歌颂益,却歌颂启,并且还说,'他是我们君主的儿子呀!'尧的儿子丹朱赶不上父亲,舜的儿子也赶不上父亲。舜辅佐尧,禹辅佐舜,经过的年数多,为老百姓普施恩泽的时间长,启贤明,能够认真继承禹的传统。益辅佐禹呢,经过的年数少,为老百姓普施恩泽的时间短。舜、禹、益之间相距时间的长短,他们儿子的贤或不贤,都是天意,不是人力所能做到的。没有人做过却做了的,这是天意;没有人招来过却招来了,这是命运。一个普通人却得到了天下的,他的德行必然像舜和禹一样,而且还有天子推荐。所以孔子由于没有天子推荐,不能得到天下。继承前人来拥有天下又被天废弃的,必然是像夏桀和殷纣一样的恶人了,所以益 、伊尹 、周公不能得到天下。伊尹辅佐汤行王道于天下,汤去世后,太丁是太子,未继位就死了,外丙在位二年,仲壬在位四年;太丁的儿子太甲继位，破坏汤的法度，伊尹把他搁置于桐。三年后，太甲悔过，悔恨自己的过错而予以改正，在桐地那里，心里有仁，行为向义转变。三年后，凭接受伊尹的训导，回到了亳都。周公不能得到天下，就像益在夏朝、伊尹在殷朝一样。孔子说，'唐尧虞舜以天下让贤，夏、商、周三朝，天下以子孙继承，都是天命，意义相同。

【英语译文】

Wan Zhang asked, "From Sage Yao to Great Shun, morality began to decline and the throne was given to the king's son not to a man with virtue. Was it true?" Mencius answered, "No, it wasn't true. In the old days, Great Shun recommended Yu to the Heaven and seventeen years later Great Shun died. After wearing funeral clothes for three years, Yu dodged Great Shun's son and lived in Yangcheng. People in the world followed Yu just as those who had followed Great Shun but not Sage Yao's son after Sage Yao's death. Yu recommended Yi to the Heaven and three years, later Yu died. After wearing funeral clothes for three years, Yi dodged Yu's son and lived in the north of Jishan. At that time people went to the place of Qi not that of Yi to pay their respects and file in lawsuit and they said, 'He is the son of our king. ' People praised Qi but not Yi and they said, 'He is the son of our king. 'sage Yao's son couldn't match his father, and Shun's son couldn't match his father, either. Great Shun assisted Sage Yao and Yu assisted Great Shun for a long time and they showed more mercy on common people. And Qi was wise and virtuous and he could inherit Yu's tradition. However, Yi assisted Yu for a short time and he showed less mercy on common people. The time duration among Great Shun, Yu, and Yi was decided by the Heaven's will. Whether or not their sons are wise and virtuous was also decided by the Heaven's will. These couldn't be accomplished by manpower. It's the Heaven's will that one has done a thing which no one else did before. It's fate that one has summoned a thing which no one else did before. If an ordinary man has got the world, he is surely wise and virtuous and he was surely recommended by the Son of the Heaven. Therefore, Confucius didn't get the world because he hadn't been recommended by the Son of the Heaven. Those who got the world by inheriting their predecessors but was finally ousted must be evildoers as King Jie of Xia Dynasty and King Zhou of Shang Dynasty, therefore, Yi, Yi Yin and Duke Zhou couldn't get the world. Yi Yin assisted Tang to carry out Kingly Way. After Tang died the crowned prince was Tai Ding who died without ascending the throne. Wai Bing was in power for two years and Zhong Ren was in power for four years. Tai Ding's son, Tai

Jia succeeded to the throne and he violated Tang's regulations and laws. So Yi Yin laid him aside in the place of Tong. Three years later, Tai Jia repented his error and corrected the faults. In the place of Tong, he cherished humanity and turned to righteousness. Another three years passed and he returned to Bo, the capital under Yi Yin's guidance. Duke Zhou couldn't get the world, which was the same that Yi of Xia Dynasty and Yi Yin of Yin Dynasty. Confucius said, 'Sage Yao and Great Shun gave the world to the person of virtue; in Xia, Shang and Zhou dynasties offspring of kings succeeded the throne. All these were the mandate of the Heaven, which had the same meaning.'"

【注释】(1)阳城:山名。在今河南登封市北三十八里,禹曾避居于此。又邑名。在今河南登封市东南三十五里,今为告成镇。或以为禹曾避居于此。(2)箕山之阴:箕山,在今河南登封市东南。阴,水的南面或山的北面。亦泛指北面。(3)启:禹之子。是否贤良,古籍中有异说。(4)丹朱之不肖:丹朱本名朱,后封于丹,故称丹朱。不肖,读~xiào,谓子不似父。(5)舜、禹、益相去久远:意谓舜相尧二十八年、禹相舜十七年、益相禹七年,舜、禹为相时间长,拥有优势;益为相时间短,没有优势。(6)外丙二年,仲壬四年:外丙、仲壬,皆太丁弟。《卜辞》作卜丙、中壬。二年、四年,一说古人谓岁为年,汤崩时,外丙方二岁,仲壬方四岁,惟太甲少长,故立之。太甲,太丁子。(7)桐:地名。在今山西万荣西。(8)自怨自艾:谓悔恨自己的过错而予以改正。(9)处仁:犹"居仁"。谓内心存仁。迁义:犹"徙义"。谓见义即改变意念而从之。(10)亳:商汤时都城。共有三处:1)在今河南商丘市东南,相传汤曾居于此,又名南亳。2)在今河南 商丘市北,相传诸侯拥戴汤为盟主于此,又名北亳。3)在今河南偃师市西,相传汤攻克夏时居此又名景亳、西亳。(11)禅:shàn,以帝位让人。(12)继:帝位由子孙继承。

【原文】7 万章问曰:"人有言'伊尹以割烹要汤,[1]有诸?"孟子曰:"否,不然,伊尹耕于有莘之野,[2]而乐尧、舜之道焉。非其义也,非其道也,禄之以天下,弗顾也,繫马千驷,[3]弗视也。非其义也,非其道也,一介不以与人,[4]一介不以取诸人。汤使人以币聘之,[5]嚣嚣然曰:[6]'我何以汤之聘币为哉?[7]我岂若处畎亩之中,由是以乐尧、舜之道哉?'汤三使往聘之,既而幡然改曰:[8]'与我处畎亩之中,[9]由是以乐尧、舜之道,吾岂若使是君为尧、舜之君哉?[10]吾岂若使是民为尧、舜之民哉?吾岂若于吾身亲见之哉?天之生此民也,使先知觉后知,使先觉觉后觉也。予,天民之先觉者也;予将以斯道觉斯民也。非予觉之,而谁也?思天下之民匹夫匹妇有不被舜之泽者，[11]若己推而内之沟中，[12]其自任以天下之重如此，故就汤而说之以伐夏救民[13]。吾未闻枉己而正人者也，况辱己以正天下者乎？圣人之行不同也，或远，或近；或去，或不去；归洁其身而已矣。吾闻其以尧、舜之道要汤，未闻以割烹也。伊训[14]曰：'天诛造攻自牧宫，朕载自亳。'"

【白话译文】

万章问道："人们说，'伊尹以当厨师做菜肴来向汤讨好求用，'有这事吗？"孟子曰："不，不是这样的；伊尹在有莘国郊野耕田，以行尧、舜之道为乐。不是正义的，不是正道的，纵使拿天下作为俸禄，他也不屑顾。良马四千匹，他也不屑看。不是正义的，不是正道的，一丝儿也不给别人，一丝儿也不要别人的。汤派人用贵重礼物去延请，他淡淡地说道：'我要汤的聘礼干什么呢？哪有我在田野中，就这样遵行尧、舜之道快乐呢？'汤多次派人用礼物去延请，不久，他完全改口说：'与其就这样处在田野中以尧、舜之道为乐，哪里赶得上使这个君主做尧、舜一样的君主呢？哪里赶得上使百姓做尧、舜的百姓呢？哪里赶得上在我活着的时候亲眼看到这些呢？上天生育人民，叫先知道的启发后知道的，叫先觉悟的启发后觉悟的。我，群众中先觉悟的人；我将用尧、舜之道启发人民了。不是我启发他们，会是谁启发他们呢？'他想到天下的百姓中，如果有一个普通男女还没沾受尧、舜之道的恩泽，就好像自己把他推到山沟中一样。他就是这样以天下的重担作为自己的责任；所以他去劝说汤讨伐夏桀拯救人民。我没听说过自己不正却能纠正别人的，何况以侮辱自己来纠正天下的呢？圣人的行为各有不同，或远离君王，或靠近君王；或离开官场，或不离开官场，归根到底，是要自身干干净净罢了。我听说他以尧、舜之道要求汤，未听说他当厨师做菜肴的事。《伊训》上说：'上天的诛罚是从桀的牧宫开始进行的，我是从亳都开始进行的。'"

【英语译文】

Wan Zhang asked, "People said 'Yi Yin acted as a cook and begged Tang's employment by preparing soup.' Was that true?" Mencius answered, "No, it wasn't true. Yi Yin plowed in the fields in You Shen State, and he was happy to conduct the Way of Sage Yao and Great Shun. He disdained to take things which were not righteous or not in right way even he was given the world as his salary. He disdained to look at four thousand good horses. As for things which were not righteous or not in right way, he didn't give or accept a little bit. Tang dispatched somebody to invite him by giving precious gifts but he said slightly, 'Why do I accept Tang's gift? Could it make me happy as I conduct the Way of Sage Yao and Great Shun in the fields?' Tang dispatched somebody to invite him by giving precious gifts for several times. Soon he modified his previous remark and said, 'I'd rather make this king become a king like Yao and Shun than conducting the Way of Sage Yao and Great Shun in the fields. I'd rather make people become the same as those of the times of Yao and Shun. I'd rather see all these come into being while I am still alive. The Heaven produces people and makes those who are firstly enlightened to enlighten others and makes those who are firstly aware to make others aware. I am the first who become aware in the masses and I will enlighten people by means of the Way of Yao and Shun. If I don't enlighten them, who will do that?' He thought that if a man or a woman hadn't been benefited from the Way of Yao and Shun they are just thrown into valley by him. He regarded the burden of the world as his own task and persuaded Tang to attack Jie of Xia Dynasty to save common people from distress. I haven't heard that one can correct others if he himself isn't upright. Let alone insulting oneself to save people in the world. The actions of sages were different. Some stayed far away from kings and some stayed intimately with kings. Some left official circle and some didn't do so. In a word they just stayed whitehanded themselves. I have heard that he required Tang by means of the Way of Yao and Shun, but I haven't heard that he prepared soup. *The Book of History* said, 'The death penalty of the Heaven started from the Mugong Palace of Jie of Xia Dynasty, and I started to spread the Way of Yao and Shun in the Capital Bo.'"

【注释】(1)割烹:亦作"割亨"。割切烹调,泛指烹饪。要汤:求汤。按,《史记·殷本纪》云:"伊尹名阿衡。阿衡欲干汤而无由,乃为有莘媵臣,负鼎俎,以滋味说汤,致于王道,或曰,伊尹处士,汤使人聘迎之,五反然后肯往从汤,言素王及九主之事。汤举任以国政。"(2)有莘:~shēn,古国名。1)亦称有辛、有侁。在今山东曹县西北。汤娶有辛氏之女即其国。2)姒姓,在今陕西合阳东南。周文王妃太姒,即此国之女。繫马:xì~,廐内繫养的良马;良马。(4)一介:介,通"芥"。一介,指微小的事物。(5)以币聘之:币,泛指车马皮帛玉器等礼物。聘,以礼延请。(6)嚣嚣然:xiāoxiāo ~,自得无欲的样子。(7)聘币:古时聘人所备的礼物。(8)既而:时间副词,犹不久。幡然:fān~,剧变的样子。幡,通"翻",变动,反复。(9)与:选择连词,相当于"与其"。(10)岂若:何若,不如。(11)不被:没有蒙受。(12)内:"纳"的古字。入;使入。(13)说:shuì,劝说别人听从自己的意见。(14)伊训曰两句:伊训,《尚书》遗篇名。伊尹训太甲之文。天诛,上天(或帝王)的诛罚。造,开始,起始。牧宫,夏桀的王宫。朕,伊尹自称。载,开始。

【原文】8 万章问曰:"或谓孔子于卫主痈疽,[1]于齐主侍人瘠环,[2]有诸乎?"孟子曰:"否,不然也;好事者为之也。[3]于卫主颜雠由。[4]弥子之妻与子路之妻,[5]兄弟也。[6]弥子谓子路曰:'孔子主我,卫卿可得也。'子路以告。孔子曰:'有命'。[7]孔子进以礼,退以义,得之不得曰'有命'。[8]而主痈疽与侍人瘠环,是无义无命也。孔子不悦于鲁卫,[9]遭宋桓司马将要而杀之,[10]'微服而过宋。[11]是时孔子当阨,主司城贞子,为陈侯周臣。[12]吾闻观近臣,以其所为;[13]观远臣以其所主。[14]若孔子主痈疽与侍人瘠环,何以为孔子?"

【白话译文】

万章问道:"有人说孔子在卫国住在卫灵公宠幸的宦官痈疽家里,在齐国住在侍人瘠环家里,有这两回事吗?"孟子曰:"不,不是这样的;这是爱兴事端的人在说谎。孔子在卫国,住在颜雠由家中。弥子妻子和子路之妻子姊妹。弥子瑕对子路说:'孔子如果住我家,卫国卿相的位置就可以得到了。'子路把这话转告了孔子。孔子说:'一切顺从命运。'孔子依礼法进,依道义退,当不当官都顺从命运。如果他住在痈疽和宦官瘠环家中,这便是不讲礼义和命运了。孔子在鲁国和卫国都不乐意居住,又碰上宋国司马桓魋打算把他拦截着杀死,只得改换装束悄悄过宋。这时孔子正在困境中,寓居司城贞子家,做了陈侯周的臣子。我听说过,观察在朝的臣子,看他所招待的客人;观察外来的臣子,看他所寓居的主人。如果孔子真的曾经以痈疽和宦官瘠环为寓居的主人,还怎么能算孔子呢?"

【英语译文】

Wan Zhang asked, "People said 'When Confucius stayed in Wei State, he lived in Yong Ju's home , who was the favorite minister of Duke Ling of Wei State. And when he stayed in Qi State, he lived in servant Ji Huan's home. ' Was that true?" Mencius answered, " No, it wasn't true. This is the lying. of those trouble-makers When Confucius stayed in Wei State, he lived in Yan Luoyou's home. Mi Zixia's wife and Zi Lu's wife were sisters. Mi Zixia said to Zi Lu, 'If Confucius lived in my home, he had got the post of prime minister of Wei State. ' Zi Lu told Confucius what Mi Zixia said and Confucius said, ' All depends on the mandate of the Heaven. ' Confucius head forward according to rites and laws, and he retreats according to the way and righteousness. Whether or not being an official depends on fate. It was not based on rites and fate if he lived in Yong Ju's home and Ji Huan's home. While in Lu State and Wei State, Confucius was reluctant to stay. And when military general Huan Tui decided to hold him up and murder him, he had to make up and fled privately to Song State. At that time, Confucius was in difficult position, and lived in SiCheng ZhenZi's home, and became a minister of Duke Chen. I have heard that if you observe a minister in court you should observe the guests he received. If you observe a minister outside you should observe the host who received him. If Confucius really lived in Yong Ju and Ji Huan and regarded them as his hosts, could he be himself? "

【注释】(1)主:寓居。痈疽:yōngjū,《说苑》作雍雎。卫灵公宠幸的宦官。(2)侍人:宫中的近侍小臣。多由阉人充任。瘠环:姓瘠,名环。(3)好事者:hào～～,爱兴事端的人;喜欢多事的人。(4)颜雠由:《史记·孔子世家》作颜浊邹。(5)弥子:卫灵公的宠臣弥子瑕。(6)兄弟:古代"姊妹",亦称"兄弟"。(7)有命:由命运主宰。(8)得之不得曰:之,连词。相当于"与""和""而"。曰,为;是。(9)不悦:不乐意。于:居。按:"不悦于鲁",指"齐人馈女乐,季桓子受之"事;"不悦于卫",指"招摇过市"之事。(10)宋桓司马:宋司马桓魋。(魋,读 tuí。)将:欲;打算。要:拦截。(11)微服:为隐藏身份而改变常服。指由高改低。按:《史记·孔子世家》:"孔子去曹适宋,与弟子习礼于大树下,宋桓司马桓魋欲杀孔子,拔其大树。孔子去。"(12)司城贞子:陈国人。陈侯周:赵岐注:"陈怀公子也。为楚所灭,故无谥,但曰陈侯周。"(13)近臣:在朝之臣。以其:介词短语。根据他(它),按照他(它)。(14)远臣:远方来仕者。

【原文】9 万章问曰:"或曰:'百里奚自鬻于秦养牲者,五羊之皮,[1]食牛以要秦穆公。[2]'信乎?'"孟子曰 :"否,不然;好事者为之也。百里奚,虞人也。晋人以垂棘之璧与屈产之乘假道于虞以伐虢,[3]宫之奇谏,百里奚不谏。[4]知虞公之不可谏而去,之秦,年已七十矣;曾不知以食牛干秦穆公为污也,[5]可谓智乎?不可谏而不谏,可谓不智乎?知虞公之将亡而先去之,不可谓不智也。时举于秦,知穆公之可与有行也而相之,[6]可谓不智乎?相秦而显其君于天下,可传于后世,不贤而能之乎?自鬻以成其君,乡党自好者不为,而谓贤者为之乎?"

【白话译文】

万章问道:"有人说:'百里奚把自己卖给秦国一个养牲畜的人;得价五张羊皮,帮他养牛,借此寻找机会巴结秦穆公。'真是这样吗?"孟子说 :"不,不是这样的;这是喜欢多事的人编造的。百里奚,是虞国人。晋人用垂棘的美玉和屈地所产的良马做交易,向虞国借路攻打虢国。虞国大臣宫之奇谏阻虞公,劝他不要允许;百里奚却不谏阻,知道虞公不会听从劝说,便离开虞国,进了秦国,当时已经七十岁了;他竟不知用养牛的办法来巴结秦穆公是一种恶浊行为,算得上聪明吗?预见到不可劝阻而不劝阻,可以说是不聪明吗?预见到虞公将要被灭亡就先离开,不能说不聪明。当他在秦国被推举的时候便知道,秦穆公是一位可以帮助而有作为的君主就决定辅佐他,能说不聪明吗?为秦国的卿相,使穆公显赫于天下,而且足以流传于后代,不是贤人做得到吗?卖掉自己来成全君主,乡村中洁身自好的人都不肯干,能说贤人肯干吗?"

【英语译文】

Wan Zhang asked, "People said 'Bai Li Xi sold himself to a man who reared livestock and he got five sheets of sheepskin. Then he helped the man to raise ox so that he could fawn on Duke Mu of Qin State.' Was that true?" Mencius answered, "No, it wasn't true. Those were lying of trouble-makers. Bai Li Xi was a native of Yu State. People of Jin State traded with Yu State by fine jade in Chuji and good horses in Qu so that they could march through Yu State to attack Guo State. A minister Gong Zhi Qi admonished Duke Yu not permit them to walk through; but Bai Li Xi didn't do so since he knew that Duke Yu wouldn't listen to his admonishment. He left Yu State and entered Qin State at the age of seventy. He didn't know it's a dirty action to fawn on Duke Mu of Qin State by means of raising ox. Could we say that he was smart? He foresought it's no use to admonish and he didn't admonish Duke Yu. Couldn't we say that he wasn't smart? He was so smart that he left Yu State when he foresought that Yu State would be defeated. When he was recommended in Qin State he knew that Duke Mu of Qin State was an ambitious king and he decided to assist him. Couldn't we say that he wasn't smart? Being a minister of Qin State he made Duke Mu of Qin State eminent in the world, and the cause of Qin State was succeeded by offspring. Could a man without virtue manage to do so? A self-disciplined person in village refused to sell himself and help a king to achieve his aim. Could we say that a virtuous man was willing to do that?"

【注释】(1)百里奚:奚,亦作"傒"。春秋时秦国大夫。百里氏,一说百氏,字里,名奚。原为虞大夫,虞亡时为晋所俘,作为晋献公女陪嫁之臣入秦。后出走,为楚人所执,又被秦穆公以五张牡黑羊皮赎回,用为大夫,世称五羖大夫。与蹇叔、由余等共同辅佐秦穆公创立霸业。鬻:yù,卖。(2)食牛:sì,喂牛,养牛。(3)垂棘:晋国地名。屈产之乘:~ ~ ~ shèng,屈地所生的马。乘,指“马”。假道:jiǎ dào,借路。虞:古国名。舜之先封于虞,故城在今山西平陆县东北。夏禹封舜子商均于虞,为今河南省虞城县。虢:guó,古国名西周文王弟虢仲之封地。在今陕西省宝鸡市东,是为西虢。虢叔之封地。在今河南成荥阳市虢亭,是为东虢。(4)宫之奇谏,百里奚不谏:虞国大臣宫之奇谏阻虞公,劝他不要允许;百里奚却不谏阻。(5)曾:zēng,副词。乃,竟。干:求。污:污的异体字。(6)有行:有所作为。

孟子集注卷十　万章章句下　凡九章

【原文】1 孟子曰:“伯夷,目不视恶色,耳不听恶声。非其君不事,非其民不使。[1]治则进,乱则退。[2]横政之所出,[3]横民之所止,[4]不忍居也。思与乡人处,如以朝衣朝冠坐于涂炭也。[5]当纣之时,居北海之滨,[6]以待天下之清也。[7]故闻伯夷之风者,[8]顽夫廉,[9]懦夫有立志。[10]伊尹曰:‘何事非君? 何使非民?[11]治亦进,乱亦进。’曰:‘天之生斯民也,使先知觉后知,使先觉觉后觉。予,天民;之先觉者也;予将以此道觉此民也。’思天下之民匹夫匹妇有不与被尧舜之泽者,若己内之沟中,其自任以天下之重也。柳下惠,不羞污君,不辞小官。进不隐贤,[12]必以其道。遗佚而不怨,[13]阨穷而不悯。[14]与乡人处,由由然不忍去也。[15]‘尔为尔,我为我,虽袒裼裸裎于我侧,[16]尔焉能浼我哉。’[17]故闻柳下惠之风者,鄙夫宽,薄夫敦。[18]孔子之去齐,接淅而行;[19]去鲁,曰:‘迟迟吾行也。’去父母国之道也。可以速而速,[20]可以久而久,可以处而处,可以仕而仕,孔子也。”孟子曰:“伯夷,圣之清者也;伊尹,圣之任者也;柳下惠,圣之和者也;孔子,圣之时者也。孔子之谓集大成。集大成也者,金声而玉振之也。金声也者,始条理也;玉振之也者,终条理也。始条理者,智之事也;终条理者,圣之事也。智,譬则巧也;圣,譬则力也。由射于百步之外也,其至,尔力也;其中,非尔力也。[21]”

【白话译文】

孟子说:“伯夷,眼睛不看不好的颜色,耳朵不听不好的声音。不是如意的君主不服事,不是如意的百姓不使唤。政治清明就做官,政治黑暗就退隐。施行暴政的国家,不法之徒居住的地方,他都不忍心居留。他认为同乡下那些没开化的人相处,就好像穿戴着上朝的礼帽礼服坐在污泥炭灰上。当商纣在位的时候,他住在北海边上,等待天下的清平。所以听到伯夷音讯的人,贪婪的廉洁起来了,懦弱的能自立起来了。伊尹说:'服侍哪一个都是君,使唤哪一个都是民,政治清明也做官,政治混乱也做官。'还说:'上天生育这些下民呀,叫先知道的启发后知道的,叫先觉悟的启发后觉的。我,天生下民的先觉悟的人呢;我要用尧舜之道启发天下人民。'他认为天下的人民,只要有一个男的或女的没有沾受到尧舜仁义的恩泽,就如自己亲手把他推进了沟中一样。他把天下的重担扛在自己肩上。柳下惠不以服侍坏君主为羞辱,也不推辞做小官。推荐人才,不埋没贤能的人,一定走正路,不走后门。被遗弃不怨恨,遭困穷不忧愁。同乡下那些没开化的人相处,十分愉快,舍不得离开。认为'你是你,我是我,即使不穿衣裳,对我无礼,这样怎么能玷污我呢?'所以听到柳下惠音讯的人,狭隘的宽大起来了,刻薄的厚道起来了。孔子离开齐国时,捧着已经淘湿的米不煮就走。离开鲁国时,他说:'我们缓缓地走吧!'这是他离开祖国时的道德情韵。能够加快就加快,能够持久就持久,能够相处就相处,能够出来做官就出来做官,这就是孔子了。"孟子说:"伯夷,是圣人中的清高者;伊尹,是圣人中的自责者;柳下惠,是圣人中的随和者;孔子,是圣人中的应时者。孔子被称为集大成的人。集大成的意思是以钟发声以磬收韵,奏乐从始至终;乐音的脉络层次从钟声开始一贯不乱直到磬声结束。引起脉络层次,是智的作用;结束脉络层次是圣的作用。智,比如技巧;圣,比如功力。犹如在百步以外射箭,射到,是你的功力;射中却不是你的功力。"

【英语译文】

Mencius said, "Bo Yi refused to look at bad color, and he refused to listen to bad sound. He didn't serve unsatisfactory king and he didn't order unsatisfactory people. When political brightness appeared he would become an official; when political darkness appeared he would retreat. He couldn't bear to live in a tyrant state or a place in which lawless persons lived. He regarded staying with uncivilized village men as wearing ritual hats and clothes of court and sitting on dirty mud and coal-ash. When King Zhou of Shang Dynasty was in power he lived in the coast of the North Sea waiting for pure politics. Therefore after hearing the message of Bo Yi those greedy men became whitehanded and those coward men became self-helped. Yi Yin said, 'I can serve any king and I can order any person. I can be an official when politics is pure or dark.' He also said, 'The Heaven produces people and makes those who are firstly enlightened to enlighten others and makes those who are firstly aware to make others aware. I am the first who become aware in the masses and I will enlighten people by means of the Way of Yao and Shun.' He thought that if a man or a woman hadn't been benefited from the Way of Yao and Shun they are just thrown into valley by him. He regarded the burden of the world as his own task and shouldered it. Liu Xiahui didn't feel ashamed to serve a bad king, and he didn't refuse to be a small official, either. While he recommended talents he took the right way not neglecting virtuous ones. He wasn't agonized while being rejected and he wasn't worried while being trapped and poor. He was very happy to stay with those uncivilized village men and didn't want to leave them. He thought 'You are you and I am myself. Even you are baked, how could you make me dirty?' Therefore after hearing the message of Liu Xiahui those narrow-minded men became broad-minded, and those harsh men became honest. When Confucius left Qi State, he set off handing rice which was washed but not cooked. When leaving Lu State Confucius said, 'Let's walk slowly.' This was what he felt passionately when he left his motherland. He would hurry up if possible, he would persist if possible, he would become an official if possible. This was Confucius." Mencius said, "Bo Yi was aloof among sages, Yi Yin was self-abuse among sages, Liu Xiahui was easygoing among sages, Confucius was time-needed among sages. Confucius was regarded as a synthesizer. Synthesization meant that he used bell to produce voice and *qin* to draw up from the beginning to the end. Hierarchy of the music from bell voice to draw-up of *qin* was kept the same. It's the function of wisdom to initiate the hierarchy of music, and it's the function of sage to draw it up. Wisdom is like skill and sage is like ability. It's just like shooting in a place one hundred paces away. If the arrow touched the target, it's your ability; but if the arrow hit the bull's eyes, it isn't your ability."

【注释】(1)非其:非,不是。其,指意之所属。犹言"那,那个(如意的、合适的)"。(2)治则进,乱则退:治、乱,政治局面,清明叫治,黑暗叫乱。进,谓出仕。退,谓退隐。(3)横政:hèng~,暴政;没有法度的政事。横政之所出,谓暴政施行的国家。(4)横民:hèng~,不法之徒;不讲道理的人。横民之所止,谓不法之徒居住的地方。(5)涂炭:污泥炭灰。比喻肮脏或肮脏处。(6)北海之滨:北海,古代泛指北方边远的地方。滨,边境。(7)清:太平。(8)闻……风:听到……的音讯或传闻。(9)顽夫廉:贪婪的人变得廉洁。(10)懦夫有立志:懦弱的人能够自己站立。(11)何事非君?何使非民:何,疑问代词,作"事"与"使"的宾语。意谓服侍哪一个不是君?使唤哪一个不是民?为了直白,译文将反问句译作陈述句。(12)进不隐贤:进,举荐,推荐;引进。隐贤,同"蔽贤"。埋没贤能的人。说文:"隐,蔽也。"

(13)遗佚:yíyì,亦作“遗逸”。遗弃而不用。(14)阨穷:è~,亦作“厄穷”。艰难困苦。悯:mǐn,忧愁;忧伤。(15)由由然:愉悦的样子。(16)袒裼裸裎:tǎnxī luǒchéng,赤身露体。谓粗野无礼。(17)尔焉能:这怎么能。浼:měi,沾污;玷污。(18)鄙夫、薄夫:狭隘的人、刻薄的人。(19)接淅:捧着已经淘湿的米。朱熹《四书集注》:“接,犹承也;淅,渍米也。渍米将炊,而欲去之速,故以手承米而行,不及炊也。”后以“接淅”指行色匆忙。(20)可以速而速:连下文四个“而”,承接连词,和“则”相同。前此说明原因、理由或情况,后此说明相应的措施或结果。译为“于是”“就”“便”。(21)金声而玉振之:谓以钟发声以磬收韵,奏乐从始至终。振,收;约束。按:钟以金制,磬以玉制。朱熹《四书集注》:“并奏八音,则于其未作,而先击镈钟以宣其声,俟其既阕,而后击特磬以收其韵。(22)由:同“犹”。

【原文】2 北宫锜问曰:[1]“周室班爵禄也,[2]如之何?”孟子曰:“其详不可得闻也。诸侯恶其害己也,而皆去其籍;然而轲也尝闻其略也。[3]天子一位,公一位,侯一位,伯一位,子、男同一位,凡五等也。君一位,卿一位,大夫一位,上士一位,中士一位,下士一位,凡六等。天子之制地,方千里。[4]公侯皆方百里,伯七十里,子、男五十里,凡四等。不能五十里,不达于天子,附于诸侯,曰附庸。天子之卿受地视侯,大夫受地视伯,元士受地视子、男。[5]大国地方百里,君十卿禄,卿禄四大夫,大夫倍上士,上上倍中士,中士倍下士,下士与庶人在官者同禄,禄足以代其耕也。次国地方七十里,君十卿禄,卿禄三大夫,大夫倍上士,上士倍中士,中士倍下士,下士与庶人在官者同禄,[6]禄足以代其耕也。小国地方五十里,君十卿禄,卿禄二大夫,大夫倍上士,上士倍中士,中士倍下士,下士与庶人在官者同禄。禄足以代其耕也。耕者之所获,一夫百亩;百亩之粪,农夫食九人,上次食八人,中食七人,中次食六人,下食五人,庶人在官者,其禄以是为差。”

【白话译文】

北宫锜问道:“周王朝制定的官爵和俸禄的等级是怎样的?”孟子说:“详细情况已不能知道了。诸侯厌恶这制度妨害自己,把关于这方面的文书都销毁了。但是我听说过它的大概。天子一等,公一等,侯一等,伯一等,子、男同一等,共五等。君一等,卿一等,大夫一等,上士一等,中士一等,下士一等,共六等。以上是爵位,天子直管的土地,一千平方里,公、侯皆一百平方里,伯,七十平方里,子、男,各五十平方里,共四等。不足五十平方里的,不能朝见天子,附属于诸侯,叫作附庸。天子的卿,所受的封地比照侯,大夫所受的封地比照伯,元士所受的封地比照子、男。大国土地一百平方里,君主的俸禄为卿的十倍,卿为大夫的四倍,大夫为上士的两倍,上士为中士的两倍,中士为下士的两倍,下士与平民任职于官署的俸禄相同。这等俸禄足够代替耕田的收入。耕田的收入,一夫一妇分田百亩;百亩田地努力耕作施肥,上等农夫可以养九个人,其次的可以养八个人,中等的可以养七个人,中次的可以养六个人,下等的可以养五个人,平民任职于官署,他们的俸禄,比照这个分等级。

【英语译文】

Beigong Qi asked, "What were the ranks of official and standards of salaries in Zhou Dynasty?" Mencius answered, "We cannot know the exact details. Princes detested and got rid of them because they thought these systems would do harm to themselves. However, I have heard a rough framework about them. The Son of the Heaven (*tianzi*) ranked first; duke (*gong*) ranked the second; marquis (*hou*) ranked the third; earl (*bo*) ranked the third; viscount (*zi*) and baron (*nan*) ranked the fourth. King (*jun*) ranked the first; minister (*qing*) ranked the second; sub-minister (*dafu*) ranked the third; upper scholar (*shangshi*) ranked the fourth; middle scholar (*zhongshi*) ranked the fifth, and lower scholar (*xiashi*) ranked the sixth. The above are the titles of nobility. The Son of the Heaven owned land of one thousand square *li*. Duke and marquis owned land of one hundred square *li* respectively. Earl owned land of seventy square *li*. Viscount and baron owned land of fifty square *li*. These were four grades. Those who owned land of less than fifty square *li* could not pay their respects to the Son of the Heaven and they could only attached to princes and they were called dependencies. The manor owned by minister who's under the Son of the Heaven was granted according to that of marquis. The manor owned by sub-minister was granted according to that of earl. The manor owned by scholar was granted according to that of viscount and baron. The land of a big state extends to one hundred square *li* and its king's salary was ten times of that of minister. Minister's salary was four times of that of sub-minister. Sub-minister's salary was twice of that of upper scholar. Upper scholar's salary was twice of that of middle scholar. Middle scholar's salary was twice of that of lower scholar. Lower scholar's salary was the same as common people who have official posts. The obtained salary could completely replace the income of farming. As for income of farming, a couple could get field of one hundred *mu*. If people tried hard to do farming jobs in field of one hundred *mu*, the best farmer could keep nine persons alive; the better farmer could keep eight persons alive; the good farmer could keep seven persons alive; the bad farmer could keep six persons alive; the worse farmer could keep five persons alive. If a common person had an official post, his salary was granted according to this standard."

【注释】(1)北宫锜:~~qí,姓北宫,名锜。卫人。(2)班:分等列序;排列。爵禄:官爵和俸禄。(3)轲:孟子名。(4)天子之制地,方千里:已往的版本标点误作:天子之制,地方千里。于文不通。原意不是"制,地方"两个词,"也不是"制、地、方"三个词,而是"制地,方" 两个词。制地,意谓控制土地,语出《国语·齐语》。方,古代计量面积用语。后加表示长度的数字或数量值,表示纵横若干长度的意思。多用于计量土地方千里即言纵横各千里。纵横各千里即言一千平方里。下文"公侯皆方百里"句,省略了"制地"二字,"伯七十里,""子、男五十里"。视:比照,比拟。(5)元士:周代天子之士的称谓。(6)庶人在官:在职为官;任职于官署。

【原文】3 万章问曰:"敢问友。"孟子曰:"不挟长,不挟贵,不挟兄弟而友[1]。友也者,友其德也,不可以有挟也。孟献子,百乘之家也,有友五人焉;[2]乐正裘,牧仲,其三人,则予忘之矣。献子之与此五人者友也,无献子之家者也。此五人者,亦有献子之家,[3]则不与之友矣。非惟百乘之家为然也,虽小国之君亦有之。费惠公曰,[4]'吾于子思,则师之矣;吾于颜般,则友之矣;王顺、长息则事我者也。'非惟小国之君为然也,虽大国之君亦有之。晋平公之于亥唐也,[5]入云则入,坐云则坐,食云则食,[6]虽蔬食菜羹,[7]贵贵尊贤,其义一也。未尝不饱,盖不敢不饱也。然终于此而已矣。弗与共天位也,弗与治天职也,弗与食天禄也,士之尊贤者也,非王公之尊贤。舜尚见帝[8],帝馆甥于贰室,[9]亦飨舜,迭为宾主,[10]是天子而友匹夫也。用下敬上,谓之贵贵;用上敬下,谓之尊贤。"

【白话译文】

万章问道:"请问结交的原则。"孟子说:"不要仗恃自己年长,不要仗恃自己有地位,不要仗恃自己兄弟的势力与人结交。与人结交,是结交他的品德,不可以有什么仗恃。孟献子,兵车一百辆的大夫之家,有朋友五个;乐正裘,牧仲,其余三个我忘记了。献子与这五位相交,没有自己是大夫的想法。这五个人,假如有献子是大夫的想法,那就不会同他结交了。不仅仅是有兵车一百辆的大夫这样,就是小国的君主也这样。费惠公说:'我对子思,敬为老师;我对颜般,结为朋友;王顺和长息便是为我做事的人。'不仅仅是小国的君主也这样,就是大国的君主也这样,晋平公对亥唐,亥唐叫他进,便进,叫他坐,便坐,叫他吃饭,便吃饭,即使是糙米饭蔬菜汤,从未不吃饱,因为朋友的饭菜,不敢不饱。然而晋平公也只是做到这一步罢了,没有同他一起共有官位,没有同他一起治理政事,没同他一起享受俸禄,这只是一般士人尊敬贤者的态度,不是王公尊敬贤者所应有的态度。舜谒见尧,尧请他这位女婿住在另一宫殿中,还请他吃饭,舜也请尧吃饭,他们交替做宾主。这是天子同老百姓交友的范例。不揣地位低的人去尊敬地位高的人,叫尊重贵人;不仗恃地位高的人去尊敬地位低的人,叫尊重贤人。尊重贵人和尊重贤人,道理是一致的。”

【英语译文】

Wan Zhang asked, “Could you please tell me the principle of making friends?” Mencius answered, “Don’t make friends according to age, post and your brother’s power. To make friends with others is to focus on his virtue but not to consider anything else. Meng Xian Zi owned one hundred carts but had only five friends among whom were Le Zhengqiu and Mu Zhong and I could not remember the other three. Meng Xian Zi made friends with them without thinking that he was a minister. If the five persons thought Meng Xianzi was a minister, they didn’t make friends with him, either. A minister owning one hundred carts as well as a king of a small state did like this. Duke Hui of Bi State said, ‘I regarded Zi Si as my teacher; I made friends with Yan Ban; Wang Shun and Zhang Xi served me.’ A king of a small state as well as a king of a big state did like this. When Duke Ping of Jin State told Hai Tang to go in, he went in; when the Duke told him to sit down, he sat down; when the Duke told him to have meal, he did so even if it was rough meal with vegetable soup and ate up. He dared not to do so since it was friend’s meal. However, Duke Ping of Jin State just did things like that. He didn’t share official posts with Hai Tang; he didn’t deal with governance together with Hai Tang; he didn’t enjoy salaries together with Hai Tang. It was just the way a scholar respected a virtuous man but not the way a duke respected a man of virtue. Great Shun paid respect to Sage Yao, Yao made Shun, his son-in- law live in another palace and dined him. Shun also dined Yao and they changed their roles of host and guests. This was a model for the Son of the Heaven making friends with common people. It was respecting the noble man not using lower-rank man to respect higher-rank man; it was respecting the virtuous man not relying on higher-rank man to respect lower-rank man; and it was the same to respect the noble man and the virtuous man.”

【注释】(1)挟:xié,依恃;倚仗。(2)孟献子:鲁国的贤大夫仲孙蔑。(3)亦:连词。假如;如果。(4)费:bì,古国名。(5)之:结构助词。用在复句的前一分句的主语、谓语间,使句子在形式上转化为偏正词组,从而取消分句的独立性,使读者的感觉是话没说完,还有下话要说,现代汉语没有这种用法,可以去掉不译。“晋平公之于亥唐也”是偏正词组作状语。(6)入云则入,坐云则坐,食云则食:这是三个紧缩句。“入云”“坐云”“食云”是“云入”“云坐”“云食”的倒装。(7)蔬食菜羹:糙米饭蔬菜汤。(8)见:即“上见”。进见地位或辈分较高的人。尚,同“上”。(9)帝馆甥于贰室:帝,指尧。馆,使居住;安置。甥,女婿。贰室,贰,“二”的大写。在这里当为序数。贰室,即二室,即第二室或别室。(10)迭:dié,交替,更迭,轮流。

【原文】4 万章问曰:“敢问交际何心也?[1]”孟子曰:“恭也。”曰:“‘却之却之为不恭’何哉?[2]”曰:“尊者赐之,[3]曰,‘其所取之者义乎,不义乎?’而后受之,以是为不恭,[4]故弗却也。”曰:“请无以辞却之,[5]以心却之,曰,‘其取诸民之不义也’,而以他辞无受,不可乎?”曰:“其交也以道,其接也以礼,斯孔子受之矣。”万章曰:“今有御人于国门之外者,[6]其交也以道,其馈也以礼,斯可受御与?[7]”曰:“不可;康诰曰:‘杀越人于货,闵不畏死,凡民罔不譈。[8]’是不待教而诛者也。殷受夏,周受殷,所不辞也;[9]于今为烈,[10]如之何其受之?”曰:“今之诸侯取之于民也,犹御也。苟善其礼际矣,斯君子受之,敢问何说也?”曰:“子以为有王者作,将比今之诸侯而诛之乎[11]?其教之不改而后诛之乎?夫谓非其有而取之者盗也,充类至义之尽也。[12]孔子之仕于鲁也,鲁人猎较,孔子亦猎较。[13]猎较犹可,而况受其赐乎?”曰:“然则孔子之仕也,非事道与?[14]”曰:“事道也。”“事道奚猎较也?”曰:“孔子先簿正祭器,[15]不以四方之食供簿正。”曰:“奚不去也?”曰:“为之兆也。[16]兆足以行矣,而不行,[17]而后去,[18]是以未尝有所终三年淹也。[19]孔子有见行可之仕,[20]有际可之仕[21],有公养之仕。[22]于季桓子,见行可之仕也;于卫灵公,际可之仕也;于卫孝公,公养之仕也。[23]”

【白话译文】

万章问道:“请问同人家往来接触,当存什么心肠?”孟子说:“恭敬心肠。”万章说:“常说‘一再拒绝或推辞,是不恭敬。’为什么呢?”孟子说:“辈分或地位高的人有所赐予,暗自说道,‘他所取得的东西是正义的呢?还是不正义的呢?’然后才接受。因此便是不恭,所以不拒绝。”万章说:“让我不用口头拒绝用心底拒绝,内心深处说‘这是他从百姓那里取来的不义之财呀’,然后用别的话岔开来推辞,这也不可以吗?”孟子说:“别人从正路来,依礼相接触,这样,孔子都会接受的。”万章说:“假如有个在国门外杀人抢财的人,他也从正路来,依礼相接触,可以接受他的行为和赃物吗?”孟子说:“不可以;《尚书·康诰》上说:‘杀害别人,抢夺财物,强悍不怕死,这号人,没有哪个不痛恨。’这是不必先给予教育就可诛杀的了。这条法律,殷朝从夏朝接受下来,周朝又从殷朝接受下来,一直没有不接受的;现在杀人抢劫的情况更厉害了,怎么能接纳这种人呢?”万章说:“今天这些诸侯从民间收取财物,和拦路抢劫一样。一旦依礼往来接触,这样君子就接受,请问如何解说呢?”孟子说:“你以为若有王者兴起,将连今日的诸侯在内不必先给予教育就诛杀呢?还是先教育,如果不改,然后诛杀呢?所谓不是自己所有却去取得它便是抢劫,这只是类推到义的最高处的话,和拦路杀人夺财不同,孔子在鲁国做官的时候,鲁国人争夺禽兽作祭品,孔子也参与。争夺禽兽作祭品还可以,何况接受赐予呢?”万章说:“那么,孔子做官,不是为了推行他的政治主张吗?”孟子说:“是为了推行他的政治主张。”万章说:“既然是为了推行他的政治主张,为什么要参与争夺禽兽作祭品?”孟子说:“孔子先用文书规定祭器,不用外地寻来的食物作文书规定祭品。这样,争夺禽兽作祭品的风习就将自然废弃。”万章说:“孔子为什么不辞官离去呢?”孟子说:“孔子为行道做官,得先打基础作验证,验证显现能够行道,为什么要离去?如果朝廷不肯行道,然后离去不迟。所以孔子不曾在一个朝廷驻留过整整三年。孔子有因为可以行道而做官的情况,也有因为君主对他礼遇而做官的情况,还有因为国君养贤而做官的情况。对于鲁国的季桓子,是因为可以行道而做官;对于卫灵公,是因为礼遇而做官;对于卫孝公,是因为国君养贤而做官。”

【英语译文】

Wan Zhang asked, “When we are in contact with others, what intention should we have?” Mencius answered, “Modest and humble intention. ” Wan Zhang asked, “People often say that it isn’t modest and humble to refuse or decline. Why?” Mencius said, “When a superior gives you something, you talk to your self privately ‘Is it righteous or not if I accept it?’ and then you take it. Therefore, this isn’t modest. So you needn’t refuse it. ” Wan Zhang asked, “I don’t refuse it explicitly but express implicitly in heart ‘This is ill-gotten gains that he has obtained from common people ’, and then I will refuse it by digressing the topic. Isn’t it all right?” Mencius said, “If he has obtained it in a right way and contacted you according to rites, even Confucius would accept it. ” Wan Zhang asked, “Suppose a man murdered others and robbed things of others outside of the state gate and he came in the right road, contacted us according to rites can we accept his action and things?" Mencius answered, "No, we can't. *The Book of History* said, 'if someone murdered others and robbed things of others being rough and not fearing death, everyone would hate him.' He could be killed without beforehand education. As for this law, Shang Dynasty inherited from Xia Dynasty, and Zhou Dynasty inherited from Shang Dynasty. Nobody didn't accepted it. Nowadays murdering and robbery have taken place increasingly, how could we accept such kind of man?" Wan Zhang said, "Nowadays the dukes and princes collected wealth from people just as the murderers and robbers had done. Once contacting according to rites a moral man will accept things given by them. How would you explain it?" Mencius said, "If a kingly monarch appears, do you think it's proper without education evil men as well as princes are put to death, or we should educate them first and then put them into death? If we say it's robbery to obtain something which doesn't belong to us, then this is analogy of the highest point of being righteous, which is different from murdering and robbery. When Confucius was an official in Lu State, people strived for beasts as sacrifice and he himself also participated in it. It's all right to strive for beast as sacrifice, let alone acception of things granted by others." Wan Zhang asked, "Then didn't Confucius carry out his political stand when he was an official?" Mencius answered, "Yes, he acted as an official in order to carry out his political stand." Wan Zhang asked, "Why did he participate in striving for beasts as sacrifice since he wanted to carry out his political stand?" Mencius said, "Confucius stipulated the sacrificial utensils in written form, and food found in other places couldn't be stipulated as sacrifice. Thus the custom of striving for beasts as sacrifice would be naturally abandoned." Wan Zhang asked, "Why didn't Confucius resigned and left away?" Mencius answered, "Confucius acted as an official in order to carry out the Way and he had to lay foundation and tested it. After test, the Way could be carried out. Why did he leave away? It wasn't late to leave if the court refused to carry out the Way. Therefore Confucius stayed in one court for not more than three years. Confucius acted as an official because the court could carry out the Way. Sometimes he did so because the king dealt with him according to rites, and sometimes he did so because the king kept virtuous men. He acted as an official in Lu State when Ji Huan Zi carried out the Way. He did so in Wei State when Duke Ling of Wei State dealt with him according to rites. he also did so in Wei State when Duke Xiao of Wei State kept virtuous men."

【注释】(1)交际:人与人之间往来接触。何心:什么心肠。(2)却之:拒绝,推辞。(3)尊者:辈分或地位高的人。(4)以是:因此,用这,拿这。(5)请:请求,要求。引申为"让我"。(6)御人于国门之外:朱熹《四书集注》:"御,止也。止人而杀之,且夺其货也。国门之外,无人之处也。"(7)受御:此御为"御人于国门之外者"之省文。(8)《康诰》曰:'杀越人于货,闵不畏死,凡民罔不譈。'今本《尚书·康诰》作"杀越人于货,暋不畏死,罔弗憝。越,劫夺,抢劫。于,取。《诗·豳风·七月》:"昼尔于茅,宵尔索绹。""于货"与"于茅"语法相同,谓取其货。闵同暋(mǐn)强悍。譈,读 duì,同"憝"。怨恨。(9)殷受夏,周受殷,所不辞也:"受"与"辞"是一对反义词。谓"不必先给予教育就可诛杀"这条法律,殷朝从夏朝接受下来,周朝又从殷朝接受下来,一直没有不接受的。(10)烈:甚,厉害。(11)比:介词,连,同。(12)充类:推类,类推。至义之尽:谓(类推)到义的极高处或极精微处。(13)猎较:争夺猎物。谓田猎时夺取禽兽作祭品,春秋时有这风俗。(14)事道:实践道;推行自己的政治主张。(15)簿正:谓立文书以正其不正。朱熹《四书集注》引徐氏曰:"先以簿书正其祭器,使有定数,不以四方难继之物实之。夫器有常数,实有常品,则其本正矣,彼猎较者,将久而自废矣。"(16)兆:起始,发端。为之兆,犹言为行道打基础做验证。(17)而:假设连词,如果。(18)而后:承接连词,然后。(19)终三年淹:停留整整三年。(20)见行可:见其道可行。(21)际可:接遇以礼,礼遇。(22)公养:国君养贤。(23)季桓子:鲁卿季孙斯。卫灵公:卫侯元。卫孝公:春秋、史记皆无卫孝公。疑为出公辄。一人而二谥有先例。

【原文】5 孟子曰:"仕非为贫也,而有时乎为贫;娶妻非为养也,而有时乎为养。[1]为贫者,辞尊居卑,辞富居贫。[2]辞尊居卑,辞富居贫,恶乎宜乎?[3]抱关击柝。[4]孔子尝为委吏矣,[5]曰,'会计当而已矣。[6]'尝为乘田矣,[7]曰,'牛羊茁壮长而已矣。[8]'位卑而言高,罪也;立乎人之本朝,[9]而道不行,耻也。"

【白话译文】

孟子说:"做官不是因为贫困,但有时也因为贫困;娶妻不是因为孝养父母,但有时也因为孝养父母。因为贫困做官的,不做高官,担任低下职位,不求厚禄,只取工资。不做高官,担任低下职位,不求厚禄,只取工资,那担任什么职位才合宜呢?守门打更都可以。孔子曾经做过管理仓库的小吏,他说:'我对财物的管理出纳没出过错误。'他也做过主管畜牧的小吏。他说:'只要牛羊生长旺盛就好了。'职位低下,却妄议朝廷大事,便是罪行;在君主的朝廷上做官,而自己的正义主张不能实现,这是耻辱。"

【英语译文】

Mencius said, "Being poor isn't the reason why a man becomes an official but sometimes he does so because he is poor. Being filial to one's parents isn't the reason why a man gets married but sometimes he does so because he is filial to his parents. Due to being poor someone becomes an official but he just takes a low rank post and he doesn't seek large amount of money but get salary. Not being a higher rank official, taking low-rank post, not seeking a large amount of money but getting salary, what kind of post can a man take? To be a doorkeeper and time-teller is all right. Confucius was ever a small official as a barn-keeper and he said, 'I hadn't made any mistake when managing the barn.' He was also a small official in charge of livestock and he said, 'It's all right only if sheep and ox grow lively.' It's committing crime for a low-rank official to talk boldly about big affairs in court. It's a shame for a high-rank minister in court whose opinion cannot be implemented."

【注释】(1)养:yàng,今读 yǎng,孝养父母。(2)富、贫:谓俸禄的厚薄。(3)恶:疑问代词,何,什么。(4)抱关击柝:~ ~ ~tuò,守门打更,守门打更的人。借指小吏。关,门。柝,古代巡夜人敲着报更的木梆。(5)委吏:管仓库的小吏。(6)会计当:kuàijì dàng,会计,管理财物及其出纳等事。(后指监督和管理财务的工作。)会计当,谓对财物的管理出纳正确无误。(7)乘田:shèng ~,春秋时鲁国主管畜牧的小吏。(8)茁壮:zhuó ~,生长旺盛。(9)本朝:朝廷。古代以朝廷为国之本,故称。

【原文】6 万章曰:"士之不托诸侯,[1]何也?"孟子曰:"不敢也。诸侯失国,[2]而后托于诸侯,礼也;士之托于诸侯,非礼也。"万章曰:"君馈之粟,则受之乎?"曰:"受之。""受之何义也?"曰:"君之于氓也,[3]固周之。[4]"曰:"周之则受,赐之则不受,何也?"曰:"不敢也。"曰:"敢问其不敢何也?"曰:"抱关击柝者皆有常职以食于上。无常职而赐于上者,[5]以为不恭也。"曰:"君馈之,则受之,不识可常继乎?"曰:"缪公之于子思也,亟问,[6]亟馈鼎肉。[7]子思不悦。于卒也,摽使者出诸大门之外,[8]北面稽首再拜而不受,[9]曰:'今而后知君之犬马畜伋。'盖自是台无馈也,[10]悦贤不能举,又不能养也,可谓悦贤乎?"曰:"敢问国君欲养君子,如何斯可谓养矣?"曰:"以君命将之,[11]再拜稽首而受。其后廪人继粟,庖人继肉,[12]不以君命将之。子思以为鼎肉使己仆仆尔亟拜也,[13]非养君子之道也。尧之于舜也,使其子九男事之二女女焉,百官牛羊仓廪备,以养舜于畎亩之中,后举而加诸上位,[14]故曰,王公之尊贤者也。"

【白话译文】

万章说:"士人不依靠诸侯生活,这是为什么呢?"孟子说:"不敢这样。诸侯丧失了自己的国家,然后依靠其他诸侯,这是合于礼的;士人依靠诸侯,是不合于礼的。"万章说:"如果君主送给他谷米,就接受吗?"孟子说:"接受。"万章说:"接受,又是什么道理呢?"孟子说:"君主对于外来的百姓本来都是要救济的。"万章说:"救济便接受,赐予便不接受,为什么呢?"孟子说:"不敢呀。"万章说:"请问为什么不敢呢?"孟子说:"守门打更的人都有一定的职务才接受上面给的工资。没有一定的职务而接受上面赐予的行为,被认为是不恭敬的。"万章说:"君主馈赠,就接受,不知道可以经常这样不?"孟子说:"鲁缪公对于子思,就是屡次问候他,屡次馈赠他熟肉,子思因此不高兴。最后一次,他让使者退出大门外,自己面向北方磕头作揖,拒绝了礼物。说道:'从今以后我知道君主是在把我当犬马喂养。'大概从此才没给子思送熟肉了。喜悦贤人不能起用,又不能正常奉养,可以说喜悦贤人吗?"万章说:"请问国君要奉养君子,怎么样才算奉养呢?"孟子说:"第一次称述君主的旨意供养贤人,贤人作揖磕头接受。以后掌管粮仓的人继续恭送米谷,掌管膳食的人继续恭送肉食,都不称述君主的旨意了,贤人也不作揖磕头了;这叫正常奉养。子思觉得为了一块熟肉使自己一次又一次地烦恼跪拜,这不是养君子的做法了。尧对于舜,使他的九个儿服侍舜、两个女嫁给舜,各种官吏和牛、羊、仓廪齐全,用来养舜于田野中,后来起用,提拔到高位上。所以说这才是王公尊敬贤人。"

【英语译文】

Wan Zhang asked, "Scholars don't live on princes. Why?" Mencius answered, "They dare not to do so. It's ritual for a prince who lost his state and had to live on other princes. It isn't ritual for a scholar to live on prince." Wan Zhang asked, "If a king gives him grain, does he accept it?" Mencius said, "Yes, he does." Wan Zhang asked, "Why does he accept it?" Mencius said, "A king should relieve people coming from other places." Wan Zhang asked, "Why do we accept relief but refuse grant?" Mencius said, "We dare not accept grant." Wan Zhang asked, "Why did you say that we dare not accept grant?" Mencius said, "To be a doorkeeper and time-teller one has a certain official post and dares to accept salary. It is regarded as immodest to accept grant without any official post." Wan Zhang asked, "If a king grants something one may accept it. I wonder whether we can do this always?" Mencius said, "Duke Mu of Lu State visited Zi Si for many times and granted him cooked meat for many times, which made Zi Si very unhappy. For the last time, he let the messenger out of door, and he himself made a bow with hands folded in front while facing the north, and then he refused the gift and said, 'From now on, I know that the king raises me as dogs and horses.' Duke Mu of Lu State didn't give cooked meat anymore. Can loving a virtuous man but not employing him be called loving him?" Wan Zhang asked, "How can a king do to support a moral man?" Mencius said, "For the first time a king expressed his intention to support a virtuous man; the virtuous man made a bow with hands folded in front, and then accepted it. Later on, people in charge of grain gave him rice; people in charge of food gave him meat and they never expressed king's intention. The virtuous man didn't bow. Such kind of doings are normal support. Zi Si thought he was made bow repeatedly just for a piece of meat and it wasn't the way to support a moral man. Sage Yao made his nine sons serve Great Shun, and he married his daughter to Shun. Various ranks of officials, sheep and ox were all prepared for keeping Shun in fields. Later Shun was employed and promoted to the highest post. Therefore, this was the way duke respected a virtuous man."

【注释】(1)托:寄托,依靠。(2)失国:丧失国家的统治权;亡国。(3)氓:从外地迁来之民。(4)固:本来,原来。周:救济,周济。(5)赐于上:来自上面的赐予。于,介词。自,从。(6)亟问:qì ~,屡次问候;屡次或问讯。(7)亟馈:屡次馈赠。鼎肉:已经解割的牲肉。亦指熟肉。(8)摽:biāo,挥之使去;驱逐。(9)稽首再拜:qǐ ~ ~ ~,古代的一种隆重礼节。先叩首至地后,又先后拜两次。下文的"再拜稽首"是连拜两次后,叩首至地。(10)盖:副词,大概,大约。台:通"始"。(11)将:供养,奉养。(12)廪人、庖人:掌管粮仓的官吏、掌管膳食的官吏。(13)仆仆尔:犹"仆仆然",烦琐的样子。(14)加诸:加,义同加官晋爵的"加",即晋升、提拔的意思。诸,介词,相当于"于"。

【原文】7 万章曰:"敢问不见诸侯,何义也?"孟子曰:"在国曰市井之臣,[1]在野曰草莽之臣[2],皆谓庶人。庶人不传质为臣,不敢见于诸侯,礼也。[3]"万章曰:"庶人,召之役则往役;君欲见之,召之,则不往见之,何也?"曰:"往役,义也;往见,不义也。且君之欲见之也,何为也哉?"曰:"为其多闻也,为其贤也。"曰:"为其多闻也,则天子不召师,而况诸侯乎?为其贤也,则吾未闻欲见贤而召之也。缪公亟见于子思[4],曰:'古千乘之国以友士,何如?'子思不悦,曰:'古之人有言曰,事之云乎,[5]岂曰友之云乎?'子思之不悦也,岂不曰[6]'以位,则子,君也;我,臣也;何敢与君友也?以德,则子事我者也,奚可以与我友?'千乘之君求与之友而不可得也,而况可召与?齐景公田,招虞人以旌,不至,将杀之。志士不忘在沟壑,[7]勇士不忘丧其元。[8]孔子奚取焉?取非其招不往也。"曰:"敢问招虞人何以?"曰:"以皮冠,[9]庶人以旃,士以旂,大夫以旌。[10]以大夫之招招虞人,虞人死不敢往;以士之招招庶人,庶人岂敢往哉?况乎以不贤人之招招贤人乎?欲见贤人不以其道,犹欲其入而闭之门也。夫义,路也;礼,门也。唯君子能由是路。出入是门也。诗云:[11]'周道如底,[12]其直如矢;君子所履,小人所视'"万章曰:"孔子,君命召,不俟驾而行。然则[13]孔子非与?"曰:"孔子当仕有官职,而以其官召之也。"

【白话译文】

万章说:"请问您不去见诸侯,是什么道理呢?"孟子说:"没有职位的人住在城市里叫市民,住在郊野外叫草民,这都叫老百姓。老百姓不需要提着见面礼物去请求为民,不敢求诸侯接见,这是合于礼的。"万章说:"老百姓,被召服役就去服役;君主想见老百姓,来人召唤,却不去见君主,这是什么道理呢?"孟子说:"去服役,是应该的;去谒见君主是不应该的。而且君主想老百姓去会晤他,为的是什么呢?"万章说:"为的是他见闻广博,为的是他品德高尚。"孟子说:"为的是他见闻广博的话,那么天子应以他为师而不可召唤,何况诸侯呢?为的是他品德高尚的话,那么我也未听说过,想要同品德高尚的人相见而随便召唤的。鲁缪公屡次访晤子思,说道:'古代具有千辆兵车的国君同士人交友,怎么样啊?'子思不高兴,说:'古时的人是说,拜他为师罢,哪里是说跟他交友呢?'子思的不高兴,难道不是说'论地位,你是君主,我是臣下,哪敢同君主交友呢?论道德,你是向我学习的人,怎么可以与我交友?'有千辆兵车的国君请求与他交友还不行,何况可以召唤吗?齐景公田猎,用旌召唤掌管山泽园囿的官员,他不来,齐景公要杀他。有志气的人不怕抛尸山沟,勇敢的人不怕丢脑袋。孔子对这位官员取他哪一点呢?取他对不合于礼的召唤死也不应招。"万章说:"请问该用什么召唤掌管山泽园囿的官员?"孟子说:"用皮帽子。召唤平民用赤色无装饰的曲柄旗,召唤士人用画有两龙并在竿头悬铃的旗。召唤大夫,用竿头有牦牛尾或兼五彩羽毛做装饰的旗。用召唤大夫的旗帜去召唤掌管山泽园囿的官员,那个官员死不敢往;用召唤士人的旗帜去召唤平民,平民难道敢去吗?何况用召唤不贤之人的礼节去召唤贤人呢?想同贤人会晤,却不依规矩礼节,就像要请人进屋,却又把门关着。义,是路;礼,是门。只有君子能走这条路,出入这道门。《诗经》上说:‘大路平如磨刀石,直处好像箭竿子;君子常在上面走,小人偷偷地窥视。’”万章说:“孔子,听说国君召唤他,不等驾好车马就起步前行。照前面的说法,那么孔子错了吧?”孟子说:“孔子正在做官,有职务在身,国君因其职务召唤他。”

【英语译文】

Wan Zhang asked, “Master, why didn’t you go to see the prince?” Mencius answered, “A man who without an official post lives in a town is called townspeople, and a man without an officialpost lives in suburb is called vulgar people. They are all common people. It’s ritual for a common person not to require for being civilian person with gifts and not dare to visit a prince.” Wan Zhang said, “Common people went to take service when they were summoned. The king wanted to see a common person and sent someone to summon him, but he refused to see the king. Why?” Mencius answered, “He should go taking service but he shouldn’t go to visit the king. What’s more, for what purpose did the king want the common person to see him?” Wan Zhang said, “It’s because he was knowledgeable and he was a virtuous man.” Mencius said, “If the king thought he was knowledgeable, then the king should regard him as teacher and shouldn’t summon him, let alone prince. If the king thought he was a virtuous man, then I haven’t heard one could casually summon anyone else to see him. Duke Mu of Lu State visited Zi Si for many times and asked, ‘In the old days, a king with one thousand carts made friends with scholars. What do you think about it?’ Zi Si felt unhappy and said, ‘The ancient men meant that the king made him his teacher. How could the king make friends with him?’ Zi Si’s unhappiness really meant that ‘As for social status, you are a king and I am a minister. How can you make friends with me? As for morality, you are the man who learns from me, how can you make friends with me?’ A king with one thousand carts couldn’t make friends with him, let alone summoning him. When Duke Jing of Qi State hunted, he summoned the woods-keeper by banners. But the woods-keeper refused to approach him and he wanted to kill the keeper. A man with ambition wasn’t afraid to be thrown dead into valley and a man with courage wasn’t afraid to be killed. Which point of this small official did Confucius praise? Confucius praised that he refused the indecorous summon even he would face death.” Wan Zhang asked, “Please tell me, what should be used to summon the woods-keeper?” Mencius answered, “Fir-hat should be used. When summoning common people, a red flag without decore was used; when summoning scholars, a flag with two-dragons design and hanging-bell was used; when summoning a minister, a banner with yak tail and colorful feather was used. When the woods-keeper was summoned by a banner which was used for summoning a minister, the keeper never went even if he would face death. If a common person was summoned by the flag which was used for summoning scholar, would the common person go? Now the virtuous man was summoned in the same way a man without virtue was summoned. Someone wanted to meet a virtuous man but he didn't act according to rites. It was the same when you invite someone to your home but you close the door. Righteousness is the path and rites is the door. Only a moral man can take this path and go in and out of this door. *The Book of Songs* said, ' Roads extend smooth as grindstone. As arrow flies they reach straight. Those rich and empowered walk on. Average people have to dodge along. ' " Wan Zhang asked, "When Confucius was summoned by the king, he set off right away with carriage unprepared. According to the above, had Confucius surely made mistake?" Mencius answered, "Confucius was an official and had a post. The king summoned him due to his official post. "

【注释】(1)在国曰市井之臣:国,国都,亦泛指城邑。市井:古代城邑中集中交易之处;街市;市场;交易之处;街市;市场。臣:民众。(2)庶人不传质:在野外叫草莽之臣,和市井之臣,都叫庶人。传质(~ zhì),初次见人时所执的礼物叫"质"(质通"贽")。庶人的质用鹜(wù,家鸭)。提着礼物求见时,必须先由看门人传达,叫作"传质"。庶人不传质,是说庶人没有见诸侯的格。(3)欲见贤而召之:真诚见贤应当延请不是征召。(4)见于子思:意谓去见子思,访晤子思。(5)事之:事,谓从师求学。事之,即跟他学习,拜他为师的意思。(6)岂不曰:难道不是。曰,为;是。(7)不忘在沟壑:没有忘记抛在沟壑中的尸体。(8)不忘丧其元:没有忘记失去头颅的人。以上两句的意思是明知所为的正义而不怕弃尸、斩首。(9)皮冠:古代打猎时戴的皮帽子。加于礼冠之上,用以御尘,亦以御雨雪。(10)旃,旂,旌:旃,读 zhān,赤色无饰曲柄的旗。旂,读 qí,古代画有两龙并在竿头悬铃的旗。旌,读 jīng,古代用牦牛尾或兼五彩羽毛饰竿头的旗。(11)诗云以下四句:见《诗经·小雅·大东》。(12)周道如底:周道,大路。底,通"砥",磨刀石。(13)然则:连词,用在句子开头,表示既然这样,那么。

【原文】8 孟子谓万章曰:"一乡之善士斯友一乡之善士,一国之善士斯友一国之善士,善士斯友天下之善士。以友天下之善士为未足,又尚论古之人。[1]颂其诗,[2]

读其书,不知其人,[3]可乎?是以论其世也。[4]是尚友也。[5]”

【白话译文】

孟子对万章说:“一乡知名的优秀人物便结交一乡知名的优秀人物,一国知名的优秀人物便结交一国知名的优秀人物,天下知名的优秀人物便结交天下知名的优秀人物。认为停止于结交天下知名的优秀人物为不够广阔深入,又上溯历史议论古代人物,吟咏他们的诗歌,研读他们的著作,不了解他们的为人,可以吗?所以要讨论他们所处的时代状况,这便是回顾历史同古人交友。

【英语译文】

Mencius told Wan Zhang, “A famous and prominent man in a township makes friends with other famous and prominent ones in the same township. A famous and prominent man in a state makes friends with other famous and prominent ones in the same state. A famous man and prominent in the world makes friends with other famous and prominent ones in the world. If you regard making friends with famous and prominent persons as superficiality, you date back history and comment ancient persons, and you chant their poems and read their books. How could it be if you don't understand their way of being human? Therefore we should discuss the epoch when they lived, which was to date back history and make friends with ancient people.”

【注释】(1)尚:同“上”。(2)颂:同“诵”。(3)知人:了解某人的真实状况。(4)论世:研讨所在的时世。(5)尚友:与古人交友。

【原文】9 齐宣王问卿。孟子曰 :“王何卿之问也?”王曰:“卿不同乎?”曰:“不同;有贵戚之卿,[1]有异姓之卿。”王曰:“请问贵戚之卿。”曰:“君有大过则谏;反复之而不听,则易位。[2]”王勃然变乎色。[3]曰:“王勿异也。王问臣,臣不敢不以正对。[4]”王色定,然后请问异姓之卿。曰:“君有过则谏,反复之而不听,则去。”

【白话译文】

齐宣王提卿爵事宜。孟子说 :“王要问哪一类卿呢?”王说:“卿不是一样吗?”孟子说曰:“不一样;有和王室同宗族的卿,有不和王室同宗族的卿。”王说:“我请问和王室同宗族的卿。”孟子说 :“君王若有重大错误,他便加劝阻;反复劝阻了还不听从,就废掉昏君另立新君。”齐宣王突然愤怒变了脸色。孟子说:“王不要奇怪,王问我,不敢不拿老实话回答。"齐宣王的脸色平静了,又请问不和王室同宗族的卿。孟子说:"君王若有错误,便加劝阻;反复劝阻了还不听从,自己就离职。"

【英语译文】

King Xuan of Qi State asked Mencius things concerning ministers. Mencius asked, "Which kind of minister do you want to know?" The king asked, "Aren't ministers the same?" Mencius said, "No. They are not the same. There are ministers who are in the same clan with royal family. But there are ministers who are in different clan with royal family." The king said, "I want to know ministers who are in the same clan with royal family." Mencius said, "If the king made mistakes they would admonish him. After repeated admonishment if the king refused to correct his mistakes, they would abolish the fatuous and self-indulgent king." Suddenly King Xuan became agonized. Mencius said, "You needn't feel surprised. Since you asked me I dare not reply you with dishonest answer." King Xuan calmed down and asked about ministers who have different clan with royal family. Mencius said, "If the king made mistakes, they would admonish him. After repeated admonishment if the king refused to correct his mistakes, they would leave their posts."

【注释】(1)贵戚之卿:贵戚,帝王的亲族。贵戚之卿,即帝王的亲族之卿。与下文"异姓之卿"相对,解作"同姓之卿"也可以文从字顺。(2)易位:变更君位。(3)勃然:因生气或惊慌等变脸色的样子。犹突然泛起。变乎色:变了脸色。(4)正:真诚。

孟子集注卷十一　告子章句上　凡二十章

【原文】1 告子曰:"性犹杞柳也,[1]义犹桮棬也[2];以人性为仁义,犹以杞柳为桮棬。"孟子曰:"子能顺杞柳之性而以为桮棬乎?将戕贼杞柳而后以为桮棬也?[3]如将戕贼杞柳而以为桮棬,则亦将戕贼人以为仁义与?率天下之人而祸仁义者,[4]必子之言夫![5]"

【白话译文】

告子说："人的本性好像榉柳树，义礼好像杯盘；把人的本性导入仁义，正好像用榉柳树来制成杯盘。"孟子说："你是顺着榉柳树的本性来制成杯盘呢？还是毁伤榉柳树的本性来制成杯盘呢？如果要毁伤榉柳树的本性后才制成杯盘，那不也要毁伤人的本性后才导之入仁义吗？率领天下的人来祸害仁义的一定是您的这种说法吧！"

【英语译文】

Gao Zi said, "Human nature is just like willow tree, whereas righteousness and rites are like willow-made cup. Leading human nature toward humanity and righteousness is just like weaving willow twigs into a cup." Mencius said, "Did you make cup from willow twigs according to its nature, or did you do it after destroying its nature? If you could only make cup from willow twigs after destroying its nature, didn't you lead human nature toward humanity and righteousness after you destroyed it? You are surely the man who has led men in the world to destroy humanity and righteousness!"

【注释】(1)告子：战国时人，名不详，一说名不害。提出性无善恶论，同孟子的性善论对立。杞柳：落叶乔木(或说落叶灌木)，枝条细长柔韧，可编织箱筐等器物，也称红皮柳。旧说都以为就是榉树。(2)桮棬：桮，同"杯"；棬，读 quān，用曲木制作的盂类饮器。(3)戕贼：qiāng ~，摧残，破坏。(4)率：shuài，带领，率领。(5)必：副词。一定，必定。

【原文】2 告子曰："性犹湍水也，[1]决诸东方则东流，决诸西方则西流。人性之无分善不善也，犹水之无分东西也。"孟子曰："水信无分于东西，[2]无分于上下乎？人性之善也，犹水之就下也。人无有不善，水无有不下。今夫水，搏而跃之，可使过颡；[3]激而行之，可使在山。[4]是岂水之性哉？其势则然也。人之可使为不善，其性亦犹是也。"

【白话译文】

告子说："人性好像快速旋流的水，东边开口向东流，西边开口向西流。人性的不分善与不善，好像水的不分向东流向西流。"孟子说："水的确是没有东流西流的分别，难道也没有向上或向下的区别吗？人性的善良，正好像水性向下流。人没有不善良的，水没有不下流的。假若水被拍打跳跃起来，可以使他翻过我们的额头;被阻挡流行,可以使他留在山上。这难道是水的本性吗?是情势所迫使。人可以使为不善,其性也是像这样。"

【英语译文】

Gao Zi said, "Human nature is like whirling water which flows eastward when rivermoath is in the east and flows westward when rivermoath is in the west. That human nature isn't good or evil is the same as that water flows either eastward or westward." Mencius responded, "Water really flows either eastward or westward and there's no difference. But isn't there the difference of flowing upward or downward? Human nature being good is the same as water flows downward. No man is not good and no water does not flow downward. If water is beaten to jump up, it can cross our foreheads; if water is blocked to flow, it can stay in a mountain. Is it the original nature of water? It is forced by outer factor. Man can be made evil and his nature is the same."

【注释】(1)湍水:tuān ~,急而萦回的水。湍,水势急而旋。(2)信:诚,真的。(3)今:连词,假若。夫:fú,句中语气助词。搏:拍打。而:他,它。跃之:使它跳跃(飞溅)。颡:sǎng,额。(4)激而行之:阻挡它流行。

【原文】3 告子曰:"生之谓性。[1]"孟子曰:"生之谓性也,犹白之谓白?[2]"曰:"然。""白羽之白也,犹白雪之白;白雪之白犹白玉之白与?"曰:"然。""然则犬之性犹牛之性,牛之性犹人之性与?[3]"

【白话译文】

告子说:"天生的资质叫作性。"孟子说:"天生的资质叫作性,好比一切东西的白色叫做白吗?"答道:"是的。""白羽毛的白如同白雪的白,白雪的白如同白玉的白吗?"答道:"是的。""那么狗性如同牛性,牛性如同人性吗?"

【英语译文】

Gao Zi said, "The inborn disposition is called nature." Mencius asked, "If the inborn disposition is called nature, can whiteness of all things be called white?" Gao Zi answered, "Yes." Mencius asked, "Is the whiteness of white feather the same as that of white snow, and is the whiteness of white snow the same as that of white jade? Gao Zi answered, "Yes." Mencius asked, "Then is the nature of dog the same as that of ox, and is the nature of ox the same as that of human being?"

【注释】(1)生之谓性:朱熹《集注》:"生,指人物之所以知觉运动者而言。告子论性前后四章,语虽不同,然其大指不外乎此,与近世佛氏所谓作用是性者略相似。"(2)与:yú,语气词,表疑问,下同。(3)牛之性犹人之性与:牛之性和人之性相同吗?于是告子自知其说之非,不能对答。

【原文】4 告子曰:"食色,性也。[1]仁,内也,非外也;义,外也,非内也。[2]"孟子曰:"何以谓仁内义外也?"曰:"彼长而我长之,非有长于我也;犹彼白而我白之,从其白于外也,故谓之外也。[3]"曰:"异于白马之白也,无以异于白人之白也;不识长马之长也,无以异于长人之长与?且谓长者义乎?长之者义乎?[4]"曰:"吾弟则爱之,秦人之弟则不爱也,是以我为悦者也,故谓之内。长楚人之长,亦长吾之长,是以长为悦者也,故谓之外也。[5]"曰:"耆秦人之炙,无以异于耆吾之炙,夫物则亦有然者也。然则耆炙亦有外与?[6]"

【白话译文】

告子说:"饮食男女,是人的本性。仁,是内在的品质,不是外在的品质;义,是外在的品质,不是内在的品质"孟子说:"为何说仁是内在的质量,义是外在的品质呢?"告子说:"他人年老我尊敬他,这尊敬,是他年老引起的;正好比那东西是白色的,我才说它是白东西;而且我是从他外表认定是白的,所以义,是外在的质量。"孟子说:"不同于白马的白色没有什么不同于白人的白色;不知道对老马的怜悯和对老者的尊敬没有什么不同吗?而且你是说老者义还是说尊敬老者的人义?"告子答道:"对我的弟弟便爱,对秦国人的弟弟便不爱,这是我的喜爱,所以说仁是内在的质量。尊敬楚国的老者也尊敬我自己的老者,这是因为他们都是老者,所以说义是外在的质量。"孟子说:" 喜欢吃秦国人的烧肉,和喜欢吃自己的烧肉没有什么不同,各种事物也都有这样的情形。难道喜欢吃烧肉的心也是外在的质量?"

【英语译文】

Gao Zi said, "It's Human Nature for man to eat and to get married. Humanity is inner quality but not external quality. Righteousness is external quality but not inner quality. " Mencius asked, "Why do you say that humanity is inner quality and righteousness is external quality?" Gao Zi replied, "Others are old and I respect them. This respect is caused by the fact that they are old. It's the same as that thing is white so I say it's a white thing. What's more, I consider it white from its appearance. Therefore, righteousness is external quality." Mencius said, "There is no difference between the whiteness of white horse and that of white people. Don't you know there's no difference between the pity for old horse and that for old man? Do you say it's righteous of being old or it's righteous to respect old man?" Gao Zi replied, "I love my younger brother, but I don't love any younger brother of people in Qin State. This is my specific love. Therefore humanity is inner quality. I respect old man in Chu State and I also respect my own old man because they are all old man. Therefore righteousness is external quality." Mencius said, "There is no difference between liking roast pork of Qin State and liking one's own roast pork? Such situation in many cases does exist. Isn't liking roast pork the external quality?"

【注释】(1)食色,性也:《礼记·礼运》:"饮食男女,人之大欲存焉。"没有饮食,不能生活;没有男女相配,不能生育。所以说饮食男女是人人最大最基本的要求。但这不能区别于其他动物而且是本能不是本性。(2)义,外也,非内也:朱熹《集注》:"义不在彼之长,而在我长之之心,则义之非外明矣。"(3)从:承认,认可。(4)长之者:犹敬重长者的人。(5)外:外表,外在。(6)耆炙:shì zhì,爱好烤熟的肉。耆,今作"嗜"。

【原文】5 孟季子问公都子曰[1]:"何以谓义内也?"曰:"行吾敬,[2]故谓之内也。""乡人长于伯兄一岁,则谁敬?[3]"曰:"敬兄。""酌则谁先?[4]"曰:"先酌乡人。""所敬在此,所长在彼,果在外非由内也。[5]"公都子不能答,以告孟子。[6]孟子曰:"敬叔父乎?敬弟乎?彼将曰,'敬叔父。'曰,'弟为尸,[7]孟则谁敬?'彼将曰,'敬弟。'子曰,'恶在其敬叔父也?[8]'彼将曰,'在位故也。[9]'子亦曰'在位故也。庸敬在兄,斯须之敬在乡人。[10]'"季子闻之,曰:"敬叔父则敬,敬弟则敬,[11]果在外[12],非由内也。"公都子曰:"冬日则饮汤,夏日则饮水[13],然则饮食亦在外也?"

【白话译文】

孟季子问公都子,"为什么说义是内在的品质?"公都子答道:"表示我的敬意是我内心主使的,所说是内在品质。""本乡人比你长兄大一岁,你恭敬哪一个?"答道:"恭敬大哥。""那么先给谁斟酒?"答道:"先给本乡长者斟酒。""你心里恭敬的是大哥却向本乡长者行礼,果然义是外在的质量,不是内心的品质。"公都子不能对答。因此报告孟子。孟子说:"你可以说'恭敬叔父?还是恭敬弟弟呢?'他会说

‘恭敬叔父。’你又说，‘弟弟若代替死者或神受祭，那又恭敬谁呢？’他会说，‘恭敬弟弟。’你就说‘那你起先为什么说恭敬叔叔呢？’他会说‘由于弟弟在那尊位上。’你也可以说因为本乡长者在那尊位上。平常的恭敬，在于哥哥，短时的恭敬在于本乡长者。”季子得知这话说道：“恭敬叔父的恭敬，恭敬弟弟的恭敬，终究在外不是出于内心。”公都子说；“冬天就喝热汤，夏天就喝凉水。那么饮食是由外在的天气所决定的吗？”

【英语译文】

Meng Ji Zi asked Gong Du Zi why righteousness is inner quality. Gong Du Zi answered, “ Expressing my respect is stirred from my inner heart so that we say righteousness is inner quality. ” Meng Ji Zi asked, “If a village fellow is one year older than your eldest brother, whom do you respect?” Gong Du Zi answered, “I respect my eldest brother. ” Meng Ji Zi asked, “For whom will you pour a drink first?” Gong Du Zi answered, “I will pour a drink for the elder in our village first. ” Meng Ji Zi said, “In your heart you respect your eldest brother but you show respect first to the elder of your village. Righteousness is really an external quality. ” Gong Du Zi couldn’t reply to that and reported it to Mencius. Mencius said, “You may ask ‘ Do you respect your uncle or your younger brother. ’ He may say ‘ Respecting my uncle. ’ You may further ask ‘ If one’s younger brother receives sacrifice in place of the dead or the god, whom do you respect?’ He may say ‘ Respecting my younger brother. ’ You may ask ‘ Why did you say respecting your uncle at first?’ He may say ‘ Because my younger brother is now in the respectful post. ’ You may also say that the elder of your village is also in the respectful post. In ordinary time you respect your eldest brother and for a short while you respect the elder in your village. ” After hearing this Meng Ji Zi said, “Both respecting one’s uncle and respecting one’s younger brother come from outside not from inner heart. ” Gong Du Zi said, “In winter we drink hot soup and in summer we drink cool water. Then are food and drink decided by weather?”

【注释】(1)孟季子：其人不详，疑为孟仲子之弟；一说，即任国国君之弟季任。参看告子下(12.5)。公都子：孟子弟子。(2)行吾敬：表示我的敬意。(3)长于：zhǎng ~，相比之下年纪大于。伯兄：长兄。谁敬：犹口语“敬谁”，文言语法，疑问代词作宾语位置在动词前。(4)酌 zhuó：斟酒(把酒注入酒杯供饮)。则谁先：省略句，意思是“那么先给谁斟酒”。(5)所敬长：所敬爱的人和所尊敬的人。果：副词,果真;果然指事实与预料的相同。(6)以:连词。因而;因此。以告孟子,即言因而告诉孟子。(7)弟为尸:尸是古代祭祀时代死者受祭的人。弟为尸,犹言弟替死者或神居尊位受祭。(8)恶:wū,疑问代词。"何""安""怎么"。在:通"才"。其,语气助词。恶在其敬叔父也?(哪种情况才恭敬叔父呢?)(9)在位故:在尊位的原因。(10)庸:平常。斯须:须臾,片刻,短时间。(11)则敬:则,结构助词。相当于"之",可译为"的"。(12)果:副词。究竟;终究。(13)汤,水:相对而言,汤指开水,热水。水指生水;冷水。

【原文】6 公都子曰:"告子曰:'性无善无不善也。[1]'或曰;'性可以为善,可以为不善;是故文武兴,则民好善;幽厉兴,则民好暴。[2]'或曰;'有性善,有性不善;是故以尧为君而有象;以瞽瞍为父而有舜;以纣为兄之子,且以为君,而有微子启、王子比干。[3]'今曰'性善',然则彼皆非与?[4]"孟子曰:"乃若其情[5],则可以为善矣,乃所谓善也。若夫为不善,非才之罪也。[6]恻隐之心,人皆有之;羞恶之心,人皆有之;恭敬之心,人皆有之;是非之心,人皆有之。恻隐之心,仁也;羞恶之心,义也;恭敬之心,礼也;是非之心,智也。[7]仁义礼智,非由外铄我也,我固有之矣,弗思耳矣。[8]故曰,'求则得之,舍则失之。[9]或相倍蓰而无算者,不能尽其才者也。[10]诗曰:"天生蒸民,有物有则。民之秉彝,好是懿德。"[11]孔子曰:'为此诗者!其知道乎!故有物必有则;民之秉彝也,故好是懿德'。"[12]

【白话译文】

公都子说:"告子说:'本性没有善和不善。'有人说:'本性可以行善,也可以行不善;所以周文王和周武王在位,民众喜爱善良;周幽王和周厉王在位,民众喜爱暴虐。'有人说:'有的本性善,有的本性不善'因此以尧为君主而有为恶的象;以残忍的瞽瞍为父而有仁孝的舜;以暴虐的纣是哥哥的儿做君主,而有贤叔忠臣微子、启、王子比干。'现在讲'本性善',那么,他们说的都不对吗?"孟子说:"至于人们的情——显露的本性,就可以算是善了,也就是我讲的本性善。如果行为不善,不是本性的罪过。同情怜悯之心,人人都有;羞耻厌恶之心,人人都有;谦恭讲礼之心,人人都有;明对错,辨正误之心,人人都有。同情怜悯之心属于仁,羞耻厌恶之心属于义,谦恭讲礼之心属于礼,明对错,辨正误之心属于智。仁义礼智,不是由外界渗入的,是我本来就有的,未曾思考罢了。所以说一经思考,便会明白,不思考 ,就不明白。'有些人相差几倍,甚至无数倍,而不能发挥其本性之善。《诗经》说:"天然生成的众民,拥有万物也拥有法则。众民的执持常道,是喜爱固有美德。"孔子说:'这首诗的作者,真懂人间之道啊!本来存在事物,必定存在法则;众民掌握了法则,喜爱本来的美德。'"

【英语译文】

Gong Du Zi said, "Gao Zi said 'The original nature is neither good nor evil.' Someone said 'The original nature can lead to good, and it can lead to evil. When King Wen and King Wu of Zhou Dynasty were in power, people tended to be good. But when King You and King Li of Zhou Dynasty were in power, people tended to be evil.' Someone said 'Some original nature is good and other is evil'. Therefore when Yao was the king, Xiang was evil. Cruel father Gu Shou had a filial son Shun. Tyrant King Zhou of Shang Dynasty had a royal uncle Wei Zi, Qi and prince Bi Gan. Now we talk about that original nature is good. Then was what they said not right?" Mencius said, "As for feeling, that is, explicit nature can be good. This is what I mean orginal nature is good. If one's action is evil then it's not due to original nature. Everybody has the feeling of compassion; everybody has the feeling of shame; everybody has the feeling of modesty, and everybody has the feeling of the distinction between the right and the wrong. The feeling of compassion is the beginning of humanity; the feeling of shame is the beginning of righteousness; the feeling of modesty is the beginning of rites, and the feeling of the distinction between the right and the wrong is the beginning of wisdom. Humanity, righteousness, rites and wisdom don't penetrate from outside but I originally own them. I just don't think about them. Therefore, upon thinking about them one can understand. If he doesn't think about them, he won't understand. These people have large differences so that they cannot develop their original nature's good. *The Book of Songs* said, 'Common people are born fraternally. And they have similar morality. People naturally observe natural way. They worship virtue without violating.' Confucius said, 'The author of this poem really understood the way of human world. While there exist things, all things observe certain rules. When people observe the rules, they worship the original virtue.'"

【注释】(1)告子:战国时人,名不详,一说名不害。提出无善恶论。性无善无不善:人性没有善与不善的分别。(2)是故:因此,所以。文武:周文王和周武王。幽厉:周幽王和周厉王。好暴:任性暴虐。(3)有性善有性不善:有的人性善,有的人性不善。关于微子的身世,也即微子与纣的关系,典籍所载有如下三种说法:1)纣之同母庶兄。2)纣之异母庶兄。3)纣之叔父。现取第三种。(4)然则:连词,连接句子,表示连贯关系。犹言“如此,那么”或“那么”。彼皆非与:他们都不是吗?(5)乃若:发语词,犹言至于(至于)。其情:其本性。俞樾《群经平议·孟子二》:“盖性、情二字,在后人言之,则区以别矣而在古人言之,则情即性也……”一说情者性之动也(情是性的动态表现)。(6)乃所谓:就是所说的。若夫:如果,假如。夫,语助词。非才之罪:不是本性的罪过。才,通“材”,本性,资质。(7)恻隐:同情,怜悯。羞恶:xiūwù,对自己或别人的坏处感到羞耻厌恶。(朱熹注:“羞,耻己之不善也;恶,憎人之不善也。”)恭敬:对人谦恭有礼貌。是非:明对错,辨正误。(8)仁义礼智:犹言仁爱正义,宽惠正直,规范有节,聪明智慧。铄:shuò,渗入。一说授予。弗思耳矣:没有思考罢了啊。(9)求:思索,思考,搜寻。得:知晓;明白。舍,失:意义与“求,得”对立相反。(10)倍蓰:bèixǐ,倍,与原数相等的数。蓰,原数的五倍。倍蓰,概言思舍之间的差距很大。而无算者:甚至有不计其数的。不能尽其才:不能发挥其本性之善。(11)天生蒸民:天然生成的众民。蒸,《诗》作“烝”。有物有则:有事物有法则。民之秉彝:民众的执持常道。好是懿德:喜爱这美德。选自《诗经·大雅·烝民》。(12)其知道乎:他知道人间之道啊。故有物必有则:本来存在事物,必定存在法则。故,副词。本,本来。

【原文】7 孟子曰:“富岁,子弟多赖;[1]凶岁,子弟多暴,非天之降才尔殊也,其所以陷溺其心者然也。[2]今夫麰麦,播种而耰之,[3]其地同,树之时又同,浡然而生,至于日至之时,皆熟矣。[4]虽有不同,则地有肥硗,雨露之养、人事之不齐也。[5]故凡同类者,举相似也,何独至于人而疑之?[6]圣人,与我同类者。故龙子曰:‘不知足为屦,我知其不为蒉也。’[7]屦之相似,天下之足同也。[8]口之于味,有同耆也;易牙先得我口之所耆者也。[9]如使口之于味也,其性与人殊,若犬马之与我不同类也,则天下何耆皆从易牙之于味也?[10]至于味,天下期于易牙,是天下之口相似也。[11]惟耳亦然,至于声,天下期于师旷,是天下之耳相似也。[12]惟目亦然,至于子都,天下莫不知其姣也。不知子都之姣者,无目者也。[13]故曰,口之于味也,有同耆焉;耳之于声也,有同听焉;目之于色也,有同美焉。至于心,独无所同然乎?[14]心之所同然者何也?谓理也,义也。[15]圣人先得我心之所同然耳。故理义之悦我心,犹刍豢之悦我口。[16]”

【白话译文】

孟子说:“丰年,年轻后辈懒惰的较多;荒年,年轻后辈凶恶的较多。不是天生的资质这样不同;是其心受了侵害的,认为自己所为正确适宜。大麦这种粮食作物,播了种子,也系碎土块覆盖了种子,其土地同,而且这些种植活动都是同时的,麦苗顺势生长发育,到了夏至,都成熟了。即使有所不同,那便是由于土地的肥瘦,雨露的多少,人工的粗细,不可能绝对相同。所以凡是同类都相似,为何唯独讲到人就怀疑相似了?圣人与我们是同类的人。所以龙子说:‘不知道足的码子而做鞋,我知道不是做草筐或草鞋。’单底鞋(或鞋)的相似,由于天下人的足形体相同。口对于味道有相同的爱好,易牙早先就拥有我们这种爱好。假如使口对于味道,人与人的本性不同像狗马的与我们不同类一样,那么天下人为何都认同易牙的味道爱好?讲到味道,天下人都期望像易牙那样能调味,这是天下人的口都相似的原因。耳也是这样。讲到声音,天下人都期望像师旷那样能调音,这是天下人的耳都相似的原因。眼睛也是这样,讲到子都,天下人莫不知道他是美男子。不知子都的帅美的人,是没有眼光的瞎子。所以说口对于味道,有同样的爱好;耳对于声音,有同样的听觉美;眼睛对于形色,有同样的视觉美。讲到心,就唯独没有相同的了吗?心相同的是什么呢?是公理是正义。道德极高尚智慧又极高超的人早先就拥有了我们心所同的了。所以公理正义适合我们的心,就像肉类食品适合我们的口。”

【英语译文】

Mencius said, “In harvest years youth are lazy and in famine years they are cruel. It’s not because they have different disposition. It’s because they think their actions are appropriate after their hearts have been badly influenced. Barley can grow from hard earth after sowing. The earth is the same and barley grow in the same way. Till summer solstice they ripe. Even if there is difference, the difference lies in different earth quality, different quantity of rain, and different human labor. Therefore things of the same kind have similar quality. Why do we doubt when talking about human beings? The sages are the same kind with us. Therefore Long Zi said, ‘When I make shoes without knowing feets’ sizes, I know I am not making grass baskets or grass shoes. ’ The form of shoes are similar because man’s feet have the same forms. Our mouths have similar liking for taste and Yi Ya had the same liking as ours. Suppose our taste, different people have different nature just as dogs and horses do, and then why people in the world all tend to Yi Ya’s liking? As for taste, people all want to do seasoning like Yi Ya did. It is because people’s mouths are similar. Our ears are also like this. As for sound, people all want to tune as Shi Kuang did. It’s because human being’s ears are similar. Our eyes are also like this. As for Zi Du people all know he was a handsome man. Those who didn’t know Zi Du was handsome were blind men. Therefore our mouths have the same liking to taste; our ears have the same liking to sound; our eyes have the same liking to form. As for feelings, isn't there any similarity? What is the similarity of feelings? It is generally acknowledged truth. It is righteousness. Those who were highly moral and wise had already the same feelings as ours. Therefore, truth and righteousness being appropriate to our feelings is the same as meat and food being proper to our mouths."

【注释】(1)富岁:丰年。子弟:泛指年轻后辈。(2)凶岁:凶年,荒年。暴:凶恶,残酷。非天之降才尔殊也:不是天生才质如此不同。其所以陷溺其心者然也:其,近指代词,这。所以,原因,情由。陷溺,浸润,影响,使变坏。者,指代"子弟(年轻后辈)"。然,认为正确;相适宜。(3)今夫:发语词。麰麦:móumài,大麦。耰:yōu,击碎土块覆种。(4)树:种植,栽种。浡然:bó~顺势兴起,事物自始生而发展起来,由小而大或由少而多。日至之时:此指夏至之时。(5)虽有不同:谓成熟的大麦不会完全一个样。则:连词,这里表逆承,原来。肥硗:~qiāo,谓土质有肥沃和贫瘠之别。雨露之养:谓雨露滋养有别。人事之不齐:谓人工管理有别。(6)同类:同一种类。举相似:全相似,皆相似。何独至于人而疑之:为何唯独讲到人类就怀疑了。(7)圣人:品德最高尚、智慧最高超的人。与我同类:圣人和我们同是人类。龙子:古时贤人。不知足为屦:不知道足的码子做单底鞋。屦:jù,麻、葛等制成的单底鞋,亦泛指鞋。(8)足同:谓天下人类的足形体基本相同(只是大小有别)。不为蒉也:不是做草鞋。蒉:kuì,草鞋,草筐。(9)口之于味:人口之对于味。有同耆也:有相同的爱好。耆,shì,爱好,后作嗜。易牙:人名,又称狄牙、雍巫,春秋时齐桓公宠臣。长于调味,喜逢迎,传说曾烹其子为羹以献桓公。先得我口之所耆者也:先前具有我们口的所爱好的知名者。(10)如:假如尝味时。其性与人殊:人性各不相同。若犬马之与我不同类也:像狗和马与我们不同类一样。则天下何耆皆从易牙之于味也:那么天下人为何对味的爱好都跟随易牙。(11)至于味:讲到味道。天下期于易牙:天下的人期望如易牙一样善于调和味道。相似:相像,相类似。(12)师旷:春秋晋国乐师,善于辨音。(13)惟目亦然:眼睛也是这样。惟,语首助词,无实义。子都:古美男子名。姣:jiāo,谓容貌美丽,体态健美。(14)同耆:相同的爱好,同听:相同的听觉。色:颜色,悦目的仪容身段。同美:相同的感觉。独无所同然乎:唯一没有相同的吗。(15)理:公理。义:正义。(16)所同然:相同的东西。悦我心:适合我心。刍豢:chúhuàn,牛羊犬豕之类的家畜,泛指肉类食品。悦我口:适合我口。

【原文】8 孟子曰:"牛山之木尝美矣,[1]以其郊于大国也,斧斤伐之,[2]可以为美乎？是其日夜之所息，雨露之所润，非无萌蘖之生焉[3]，牛羊又从而牧之，是以若彼濯濯也，[4]人见其濯濯也，以为未尝有材焉，[5]此岂山之性也哉？虽存乎人者，岂无仁义之心哉？[6]其所以放其良心者，亦犹斧斤之于木也。[7]旦旦而伐之，可以为美乎？[8]其日夜之所息，平旦之气，其好恶与人相近也者几希，则其旦昼之所为，有梏亡之矣。[9]梏之反复，则其夜气不足以存；[10]夜气不足以存，则其违禽兽不远矣。[11]人见其禽兽也，而以为未尝有才焉者，是岂人之情也哉！[12]故苟得其养，无物不长；苟失其养，无物不消。[13]孔子曰：'操则存，舍则亡；出入无时，莫知其乡。'惟心之谓与[14]"

【白话译文】

孟子说："牛山的树木曾经是盛美的，由于那里在国都城外，老是有各种斧头去砍伐，盛美能够继续吗？因为白天夜晚不停生长和雨露滋润，不是没有长出嫩芽新条啊，可是又放牧牛羊来践踏啃啮，所以那么光秃秃的了。人们看见那光秃秃的样儿，认为这山从未有过可作木材的大树，这难道是山的本性吗？本来存于人身的素质，难道没有仁义的心吗？那些违背仁义这种良心的人的缘由也和斧头对于树木一样，天天不断摧毁，能够美盛吗？他们白天夜晚的生长，清晨的新爽，与人好恶相近的成分极少。然而通过白天的行为后，这极少的相近成分，又因为受约束而丧失了。约束限制一次又一次地连续重复，所以晚上静思所产生的良知善念（夜间的清凉之气），就不能够保存。夜间的清凉之气不能够保存，那么他们就与禽兽距离不远了。人们看见他们不知礼义如禽兽而认为他们不曾具有人的本性，这哪是人的真实情况？所以只要得到适当的滋养，没不成长之物；只要失去适当的滋养，没不消亡之物。孔子说：'执持就存在，舍弃就不存在，作息不定时，不知道他向往什么。'说的是人心吧？"

【英语译文】

Mencius said, "Trees on Ox Mountain ever grew prosperously. People cut trees by ax because it is located out of the capital. Could prosperity continue? New buds grow due to the nourishing of rain and dew but many bulls and goats feed on them, consequently Ox Mountain became bald. Upon seeing the baldness, people thought there weren't big trees on the mountain. But is it the nature of the mountain? Since original quality lives in man, isn't there feeling of humanity and righteousness? The reason why people violate the virtue of humanity and righteousness is the same as the ax did to the trees. Since damage continued day after day, how could prosperity continue? Trees grow day after night and become fresh in the morning, which has little similarity with human being's preference. The little similarity disappears after daytime's activities due to constraints. Constraints repeat again and again, therefore kind and good thinking at night cannot be kept. Consequently these persons are almost the same as beasts. People notice that these persons don't have humanity and righteousness but are almost the same as beasts. How can it be the real situation? Therefore upon proper nourishing, everything will grow up; once losing proper nourishing everything will disappear. Confucius said, 'On insistence it will exist; once giving up, it will lose. Disorder of work and rest will lead him nowhere. This is surely about human feelings.'"

【注释】(1)牛山之木尝美:牛山,山名,在今山东省淄博市。春秋时齐景公泣牛山,即此地,当时位于齐国国都临淄之南。尝美:曾经是茂盛美丽的。尝(cháng),副词,曾经。(2)以:因果连词,因为,由于。郊:《尔雅》:"邑外谓之郊。"于:在。大国:指齐国都城临淄。斧斤:亦作"斧斫"。泛指各种斧头。(3)可以:表示可能或能够。是:因果连词,相当于"因为","因此"。日夜之所息:日夜生长。雨露之所润:雨露滋润。萌蘖:méngniè,指草木砍伐后长出的新芽。(4)牛羊又从而牧之:又因而至此放牧牛羊。从而,然后;因而。之,至;往。是以若彼濯濯也:所以那样光秃秃的。濯濯,zhuó~,光秃的样子。(5)未尝:未曾,不曾。材:木材;可作木材的树。(6)虽:通"须",副词。本,本来。(7)其所以放其良心者:~~~fāng~~~~,那些人违背良心的原因。放,fāng。违逆,违背。于:对于。(8)旦旦:天天。而:语助词,用于句中舒缓语气。(9)所息:滋息;生长。平旦:清晨。好恶:hàowù,爱好与嫌恶。相近:接近;靠近。几希:jī xī,相差甚微;极少。旦昼:清晨。有:yòu,通"又"。梏亡:gùwáng,谓因受束缚而致丧失;亦泛指丧失。(10)梏之反复:约束限制一次又一次地连续重复。夜气:儒家谓晚上静思所产生的良知善念。夜间的清凉之气。不足以存:不能够保存。(11)违:相距;距离。(12)见其禽兽:看见不知礼义的人。未尝有才焉者:从来没有人的本质的人。是岂人之情也哉:这哪是人的实际情况。(13)苟:假如;如果;只要。养:滋养。长:长进。消:消减。(14)操:执持;拿着。舍:放弃。出入无时:作息不定时。莫知其乡:不知道他向往什么。乡,通"向"。惟心之谓与:说的是人心吧。惟,犹是;为。

【原文】9 孟子曰:"无或乎王之不智也。[1]虽有天下易生之物也,一日曝之,十日寒之,未有能生者也。[2]吾见亦罕矣,吾退而寒之者至矣,吾如有萌焉何哉?[3]今夫弈之为数,小数也;[4]不专心致志,则不得也。[5]弈秋,通国之善弈者也。[6]使弈秋诲二人弈,其一人专心致志,惟弈秋之为听。[7]一人虽听之,一心以为有鸿鹄将至,思援弓缴而射之,虽与之俱学,弗若之矣。[8]为是其智弗若与?曰:非然也。[9]"

【白话译文】

孟子说:"不要疑惑王的不明智。纵使天下容易生长的植物,晒它一天,冷它十天,没有能够生长的。我和王相见实在稀少了,我退回住处,谄谀的人们,天天见王,胜过十日寒冷,我对他的善良的萌生能怎么样呢?下棋是技艺,是小技艺。不用心专一,聚精会神,就学不到这个技艺。弈秋,是全国下棋的顶尖人物。假使弈秋教道甲乙两个人下棋,甲用心专一,聚精会神。只要弈秋吩咐就听从。乙虽也听吩咐,却满心认为将有天鹅飞来,思考拿弓箭去射它,乙虽与甲同学,他比不上甲。原因是智慧比不上吗?肯定不是这样的。"

【英语译文】

Mencius said, "Don't doubt king's lack of wisdom. Plants which can grow easily cannot grow anymore when they are exposed to the sun one day and are frozen for ten days. I seldom met king but when I retreated to my residence flattering men met king each day. It's just like being frozen for ten days and how could I arouse his kindness? Playing chess is a small craft. If one cannot concentrate on it he cannot master it. Yi Qiu was the top chess player all over the country. Suppose Yi Qiu taught A and B to play chess. A concentrated on it and he would do anything ordered by Yi Qiu. On the contrary, although B obeyed Yi Qiu's order he always thought swan would fly nearby and he wanted to shoot it by his bow and arrow. Therefore his craft of chess couldn't match that of A. Was B's wisdom match that of A? It was certainly not so."

【注释】(1)无或乎:不要疑惑于。或,通"惑"。乎,介词。同"于"。王:疑指齐王(见朱熹《四书集注》)。(2)易生之物:容易生长之物。一日曝之,十日寒之:晒它一天,冷它十天。曝(pù),晒。(3)吾见亦罕矣:见,此谓谒见;拜见。亦,实在;毕竟。罕(hǎn),少;稀。退而寒之者至矣:退,指从王前退回住处。寒之者,指谄谀的人(他们天天见王,犹如十日之寒)。吾如有萌焉何哉:我对王的新萌善念能如何呢。(4)今夫:发语词。弈:yì,围棋。亦指"下棋"。为数:是技艺。小数也:小技艺呢。(5)专心致志:用心专一,聚精会神。则不得也:就不能获得(这技艺)呢。(6)通国:全国。(7)惟弈秋之为听:只要弈秋吩咐就听从。(8)鸿鹄:hónghú,俗称天鹅。援弓缴:手里拿着弓箭。援,执,持。缴,系着生丝绳的箭。若:及得上,比得上。(9)为是:wèi ~,因为是,原因是。曰:肯定。非然也:不是这样的。然,代词。如此,这样。

【原文】10 孟子曰:“鱼,我所欲也,熊掌亦我所欲也;[1]二者不可得兼,舍鱼而取熊掌者也。[2]生亦我所欲也,义亦我所欲也;二者不可得兼,舍生而取义者也。生亦我所欲,所欲有甚于生者,故不为苟得也;[3]死亦我所恶,所恶有甚于死者,故患有所不辟也。[4]如使人之所欲莫甚于生,则凡可以得生者,何不用也?使人之所恶莫甚于死者,则凡可以辟患者,何不为也?由是则生而有不用也,由是则可以辟患而有不为也,[5]是故所欲有甚于生者,所恶有甚于死者。非独贤者有是心也,人皆有之,贤者能勿丧耳。[6]一箪食,一豆羹,得之则生,弗得则死,嘑尔而与之,行道之人弗受;蹴尔而与之,乞人不屑也;[7]万钟则不辨礼义而受之。万钟于我何加焉?为宫室之美、妻妾之奉、所识穷乏者得我与?[8]乡为身死而不受,今为宫室之美为之;乡为身死而不受,今为妻妾之奉为之;乡为身死而不受,今为所识穷乏者得我而为之,[9]是亦不可以已乎?此之谓失其本心。[10]”

【白话译文】

孟子说:“鱼,我喜爱的美味,熊掌也是我喜爱的美味;这两种美味,不可能同时得到时,放弃鱼而选取熊掌。生命也是我喜爱的,正义也是我喜爱的;这两样至宝不可能同时保有时,放弃生命而选取正义。生存也是我喜爱的,但喜爱的有超过生存的,所以不做不正当的事来取得生存;死亡亦是我厌恶的,但厌恶的有超过死亡的,所以祸患有不逃避的。假如一个人的喜爱没有超过生存的,那么凡是可以取得生存的手段有什么不采用的?假使一个人的厌没有超过死亡的,那么凡是可以逃避祸患的事,有什么不干的?奉行此道就可以得生却有人不干,奉行此道就可以逃避祸患却有人不为。所以喜爱的有超过生存的,厌恶的有超过死亡的。不只是贤人有这种心,人人都有这种心,贤人能够不消耗这种心而已。一碗饭,一盆汤,得到了就生存,得不到就死亡。如果呵斥地给予,路中饥渴的人,不会接受。践踏地给予,乞丐看不起,认为不值得。优厚的俸禄却不考问是否合乎礼法道义就接受,万钟优厚的俸禄对自己增加什么呢?增加住房的美好、妻妾的侍奉、认识的穷困人的亲悦吗?从前是身死而不接受,现在为了住房的美好而接受;从前是身死而不接受,现在为了妻妾的侍奉而接受;从前是身死而不接受,现在为了认识的穷困人的亲悦而接受,这些也是不可以不干的吗?这叫作消耗本来的羞恶之心。”

【英语译文】

Mencius said, "Fish is my delicious food and bear's paws are also my delicious food. When I cannot have these two simultaneously, I will give up fish and have bear's paws. Both life and righteousness are what I love. When I cannot have these two simultaneously I will give up life and keep righteousness. Being alive is what I love. But when what I love surpasses being alive, I won't do bad things to be alive. Being dead is what I hate. But when what I hate surpasses being dead, I won't dodge any disaster. If what one loves doesn't surpass being alive, he will adopt any methods to be alive. If what one hates doesn't surpass being dead, he will use any method to dodge disaster. Only if adopting this method can one be alive, and only if adopting this method can one dodge disaster. But there are still people who refuse to do so. Therefore what one loves may surpass being alive and what one hates may surpass being dead. Both virtuous men and ordinary men cherish such feelings but virtuous men don't deplete such kind of feeling. A person will be alive if he obtains a bowl of rice and a basin of soup. He will die if he doesn't obtain them. A hungry and thirsty person on the road won't accept if they are given food and water with disdain. A beggar won't accept either if they are given food and water with disdain. If one accepts dear salary without considering if it is appropriate for righteousness, what could it add to him? Is beautiful housing, wife and concubine's service, or poor men's admiration? In old days one wouldn't accept it even he would die, but nowadays for beautiful housing he will accept it. In old days one wouldn't accept it even he would die, but nowadays for wife and concubine's service he will accept it. In old days one wouldn't accept it even he would die, but nowadays for poor men's admiration he will accept it. Must these things be done? It is depleting original feelings of shame."

【注释】(1)鱼,熊掌:鱼,泛指鱼类。熊掌,熊脚掌。鱼和熊掌都是美味;而熊掌比鱼,其味更美。所欲:喜爱的。(2)得兼:同时都得到。取:采取,选择。者也:语气助词。(3)生,义:生命;正义。甚:超过,胜过。不为:不干,不做。苟得:不当得而得。(4)故患有所不辟:所以有不可躲避的祸患。(5)由是则生而有不用也:奉行此道就可以得生却有人不干。而,转折连词,然而,却。有,同"或"有人,有的人。用,行,为。下文仿此。(6)能勿丧耳:能够不消耗(此心)而已。勿,副词,不。丧 sàng,消耗,耗费。(7)一箪食,一豆羹:一箪饭食,一豆羹汤。同"箪食豆羹",谓少量饮食。箪 dān ,用来盛饭食的盛器,用竹或苇编成,圆形有盖。豆 dòu,古代食器,形似高足盘,多为陶质,也有用青铜木竹制成的。嘑尔:hù ~,呵斥的样子。行道之人:指路中饥渴的人。蹴尔:cù ~,践踏的样子。乞人:讨饭的人,乞丐。不屑:认为不值得;看不起。(8)万钟:谓优厚的俸禄。钟,古容量单位。不辨礼义:不考问是否合乎礼法道义。万钟于我何加焉:万钟对自己增加什么。为宫室之美、妻妾之奉、所识穷乏者得我与陈设:增加住房的美好、妻妾的侍奉、认识的穷困人的亲悦自己。为 wéi 陈设,设置。训为“增加”。(9)乡为:xiàngwéi,从前是。今为:~wèi,现在为了。为之:wéi ~,干;接受。(10)是亦不可以已乎:这也是不可以停止的吗。本心:指羞恶之心。

【原文】12 孟子曰:“今有无名之指屈而不信,[1]非疾痛害事也,[2]如有能信之者,则不远秦楚之路,[3]为指之不若人也。指不若人,[4]则知恶之;心不若人,则不知恶,此之谓不知类也。”[5]

【白话译文】

孟子说:“假若有个人,手的第四指弯曲而不能伸直,他怨恨疼痛又碍事。如果有能够使手指伸直的人,他一定去拜访,即使到秦楚,路也不为远,因为手指比不上别人。手指比不上别人,就知道厌恶,心比不上别人,就不知道厌恶,这叫作不懂类比的轻重等差。”

【英语译文】

Mencius said, “If a person’s ring finger bends seriously and cannot stretch, he hates pain and thinks it’s a hindrance. If there is a man who can make his ring finger stretch he will surely pay a visit to that man. Even if it is a long journey to Qin or Chu State, he will think it isn’t a long way because his finger cannot match other persons’ fingers. Once his finger cannot match other persons’ fingers he begins to hate it. But when his feeling cannot match others’ he doesn’t hate. This is not knowing the signifilene of analog.”

【注释】(1)今:假设连词。犹“若”。无名之指:手的第四指称无名指。屈而不信:~ ~ ~shēn,弯曲而,不能伸直。(2)非疾痛害事:怨恨疼痛碍事。非,怨恨;仇恨。疾痛,疼痛。害事,妨事,碍事。非,解作“不是”,于此不安。(3)不远秦楚之路:不以去秦楚之路为远。(4)为指之不若人:因为手指比不上别人。(5)恶:wù,厌恶。不知类:谓不懂类比的轻重等差。

【原文】13 孟子曰:“拱把之桐梓,[1]人苟欲生之,皆知所以养之者。[2]至于身,而不知所以养之者,[3]岂爱身不若桐梓哉?弗思甚也。[4]”

【白话译文】

孟子说:“还未成材的小桐树和小梓树,人们只要想使他们生长,便都是知道小桐树和小梓树是可以培养的。讲到身体,却不知道身体是可以培养的。难道爱身体还不及爱桐树、梓树?太没思考了。”

【英语译文】

Mencius said, “Young tung trees and *zi* trees can be nurtured if people want them to grow into useful timber. As for human body, people do not know it can also be nurtured. Isn’t loving human body not as loving trees? It is thoug htless.”

【注释】(1)拱:两手所围的圆周。把:一手所围的圆周。桐梓:两种树名,桐树与梓树,两者皆良材,拱把之桐梓,泛指还未成材的小桐树和小梓树。(2)人苟欲生之:人们只要想使它们生长。所以养之:可以培养。(3)至于身:讲到身体。(4)弗思甚也:太没思考了。

【原文】14 孟子曰:“人之于身也,兼所爱。[1]兼所爱,则兼所养也。无尺寸之肤不爱焉,则无尺寸之肤不养也。[2]所以考其善不善者,岂有他哉?于己取之而已矣。[3]体有贵贱,有小大。无以小害大,无以贱害贵。养其小者为小人,养其大者为大人。[4]今有场师,舍其梧槚,养其樲棘,则为贱场师焉。[5]养其一指而失其肩背,而不知也,则为狼疾人也。[6]饮食之人,则人贱之矣,为其养小以失大也。[7]饮食之人无有失也,则口腹岂适为尺寸之肤哉?[8]”

【白话译文】

孟子说:“人对于身体,各部分都爱。都爱,就都保养。没有一点一片皮肤不爱,也没有一点一片皮肤不保养。所以考察保养得好不好,难道有别的方法吗?在于自己的趋向罢了。身体有重要部分和次要部分,有小的部分和大的部分。不要因为小的部分损害大的部分,不要因为次要的部分损害重要的部分。保养小的部分是小人,保养大的部分是君子。若有园艺工匠舍弃良木梧桐和山楸,培养酸枣和荆棘,那么他是最差的园艺工匠。保养一根指头而损害肩膀和背脊,自己还不知道,那么他是糊涂的人。专门吃喝的人,人们就轻视他,因为他保养小的部分损害大的部分。专门吃喝的人没有损失哪样,那么口腹难道仅仅是一点一片皮肤样的小部分吗?"

【英语译文】

Mencius said, "People love each part of human body. Since they love each part, they maintain each part. There isn't one piece of skin that they don't love, and there isn't one piece of skin that they don't maintain. Isn't there any other way to check whether the skin is mainta ned well or not? It is just one's tendency. There are major parts and minor parts, small parts and big parts of human body. One shouldn't harm big parts due to small parts, and he shouldn't harm major parts due to minor parts. Those who maintain small parts are mean men and those who maintain big parts are moral men. If a gardener nurtures sour jujube and brambles but gives up Phoenix Tree and Rowan Oak, then he is the least qualified one. If one maintains one finger and harms his shoulder and back but he doesn't know the reason, then he is the most muddled man. People contempt those who just eat and drink because they maintain the small one and harm the big one. Are mouth and stomach just small pieces of skin if those who just eat and drink don't lose anything?"

【注释】(1)人之于身:人对于身体。兼所爱:全部都爱。(2)兼所养:全部都保养。尺寸之肤:一小点儿皮肤。尺寸,形容事物些许、细小或低微。(3)考其善不善者:谓考察保养好不好。于己取之而已矣:在于自己的趋向罢了。取,qū,通"趋",趋向。(4)体有贵贱,有小大:身体有重要部分和次要部分,有小的部分和大的部分。无以:不要因为。害:损害。朱熹《四书集注》:"贱而小者口腹也;贵而大者,心志也。"(5)场师:古代园艺匠师(匠师:主管众工匠的官员;泛指工匠)。梧檟:~jiǎ,亦作"梧榎",梧桐和山楸。两者都是良木,因而并称比喻良材。樲棘:èrjí,果木名,即酸枣,不是良材。一说,"樲"是酸枣"棘"是荆棘。大人:君子。贱场师:低下的,小的园艺工匠。(6)养其一指而失其肩背:治养一根指头而丢失肩和背。狼疾人:昏乱人;糊涂人。(7)饮食之人,则人贱之:讲吃喝的人,人们轻视他。贱,轻视,鄙视。(8)饮食之人无有失:讲吃喝的人没有失去什么。适:通"啻chì"。但,仅仅。

【原文】15 公都子问曰:"钧是人也,[1]或为大人,或为小人,何也?"孟子曰;"从其大体为大人,从其小体为小人。[2]"曰:"钧是人也,或从其大体 ,或从其小体,何也?"曰:"耳目之官不思,而蔽于物。[3]物交物,则引之而已矣。[4]心之官则思,思则得之,不思则不得也。此天之所与我者。[5]先立乎其大者,则其小者不能夺也。[6]此为大人而已矣。[7]"

【白话译文】

公都子问道:"同样是人,有些是君子,有些是小人,是什么缘故?"孟子回答说:"随从大的体是君子,随从小的体是小人。"又问:"同样是人,有些随从大的体,有些随从小的体,是什么缘故?"孟子回答说:"耳目的功能不能思考,易被外物蒙蔽,物与物相接触,耳目易被外物牵引而去呀。心的功能就是思考,思考就明白得当;行为适宜。不思考就不明白不得当,行为不适宜。这是大自然对人类的优厚。先确立大体心,耳目等小体就不能篡夺。这样便是君子了。"

【英语译文】

Gong Du Zi asked, "Why are there mean men and moral men since they are both human beings? Mencius answered, "Moral men follow big part but mean men follow small part. " Gong Du Zi asked again, "Why do some follow big part but some follow small part?" Mencius answered, "Ears and eyes don't have the function of thinking and they are easily blinded. When contacting things ears and eyes are easily digressed by them. The function of mind is to think. As long as one thinks it over he will get enlightened and act appropriately. If someone doesn't think it over, he won't be enlightened and he won't act appropriately. This is bestowed by the Nature. When the big part, mind is established first, the small parts ears and eyes cannot usurp its function. Thus one can become a moral man. "

【注释】(1)钧:通"均"。相同;相等。(2)或:代词。这里代人,即"有人""有些人"。何也:为什么,什么缘故。从:随。大体?:指"心"。耳目之类叫"小体"。(3)耳目之官:耳目的功能。不思:不能思。蔽于物:易被外物蒙蔽。(4)物交物:物与物相接触;特指耳目与外物接触。则引之而已矣:谓易被外物牵引而去。(5)得之:明白得当;行为适宜。天之所与我者:我,泛指自己的一方。在大自然中,我意谓人类。(6)立、夺:确立、夺取。

【原文】16 孟子曰:"有天爵者,有人爵者。[1]仁义忠信,乐善不倦,此天爵也;[2]公卿大夫,此人爵也。[3]古之人修其天爵,而人爵从之。[4]今之人修其天爵,以要人爵;[5]既得人爵,而弃其天爵,则惑之甚者也[6],终亦必亡而已矣。[7]"

【白话译文】

孟子说:"有天下公认的爵位,有朝廷授予的爵位。仁义忠信,乐于坚持做好事,这是天下公认的爵位;三公九卿和各级大夫,这是朝廷授予的爵位。古时的人修养天下公认的爵位,而后朝廷授予的爵位跟上。现今的人修养天下公认的爵位,用来要求朝廷授予的爵位;得到了朝廷授予的爵位后,就抛弃天下公认的爵位,因此昏乱极了,最后朝廷授予的爵位也必然抛弃下场。"

【英语译文】

Mencius said, "There are commonly-recognized titles of nobility and there are titles of nobility granted by the court. Humanity, righteousness, royalty, credibility, and insistence on doing good things are commonly-recognized titles of nobility. Dukes, ministers and high-rank officials are titles of nobility granted by the court. Ancient people nurtured the commonly-recognized titles of nobility, and then the court-granted titles of nobility followed up. Nowadays people nurture commonly-recognized titles of nobility and use them to demand titles of nobility granted by the court. After they obtain the titles granted by the court they reject the commonly-recognized titles of nobility. Therefore confusion reaches extremity and the titles of nobility granted by the court are certainly rejected."

【注释】(1)有天爵者:有天下公认的爵位。有人爵者:有朝廷授予的爵位。者,用在名词后表语气停顿并引出下文。(2)乐善不倦:乐于坚持做好事。乐 lè,乐于。(3)公卿大夫:三公九卿和各级大夫。(4)修其天爵:修养天下公认的爵位。而人爵从之:于是朝廷授予的爵位随之而至。(5)以要人爵:用来要求朝廷授予。(6)则惑之甚者:因此昏乱到了极点。则,因果连词。犹因此,所以。(7)终亦必亡而已矣:最后朝廷授予的爵位也必然抛弃下场。

【原文】17 孟子曰:"欲贵者,人之同心也。[1]人人有贵于己者,弗思耳矣。[2]人之所贵者,非良贵也。[3]赵孟之所贵,赵孟能贱之。[4]诗云:'既醉以酒,既饱以德。[5]'言饱乎仁义也,所以不愿人之膏粱之味也;[6]令闻广誉施于身,所以不愿人之文绣也。[7]"

【白话译文】

孟子说:"希望地位显要,是人的共同心愿。人人都有显要于贵于己的存在,没有思考罢了。人以爵位加身而后显要。这不是本来的善良显要。赵孟是晋国的卿,他的显要能取消别人的显要而使他低贱。如果是善良的显要,怎么能使他低贱?《诗·大雅·既醉》说:'宴会上醉酒了,德行充实不乱。'即是说仁义充足,因此不羡慕人家的肥美之味。美好广传的声誉表白于身,因此不羡慕人家华丽的衣服。"

【英语译文】

Mencius said, "It's common people's desire for being in eminent status. Everyone wants to be more eminent and nobler, and just doesn't think about it purposely. Man becomes eminent after he is granted title of nobility. This isn't original philanthropic eminence. Zhao Meng was a minister of Jin State. His eminence could overshine other's eminence and make other humble. If it was philanthropic eminence, how could it make other humble? *The Book of Songs* said, 'Your fine wine made me drunk. I am very glad you are honest.' This means that he wouldn't admire other's delicious food and drink if someone was humanistic and righteous. Widely spread one's good reputation he wouldn't admire other's gorgeous clothes."

【注释】(1)欲贵者:希望地位显要。者,语气助词。人之同心也:人的共同心愿。(2)人人有贵于己者:人人都有显要于己的存在。(显要于己的:指天下公认的爵位。)弗思耳矣:没有思考罢了。(3)人之所贵者:谓人以爵位加身而后显要。非良贵也:不是本来的善良显要。(4)赵孟之所贵:赵孟的显要。赵孟,晋国的卿。赵孟能贱之:赵孟能取消别人的显要而使他低贱。如果是善良的显要,怎么能使他低贱?(5)既醉以酒,既饱以德:见《诗·大雅·既醉》。宴会醉酒,德行充实不乱。饱,满足;充足。(6)言饱乎仁义也:是说仁义充足。所以不愿人之膏粱之味也:因此不羡慕人家的肥美之味。膏粱,肥美的食物。(7)令闻广誉施于身:美好广传的声誉表白于身。施,显扬;表白。所以不愿人之文绣也:因此不羡慕人家华丽的衣服。文绣,刺绣华丽的丝织品或衣服。

【原文】18 孟子曰:"仁之胜不仁也,犹水胜火。今之为仁者,犹一杯水救一车薪之火也[1];不熄。则谓之水不胜火,此又与于不仁之甚者也[2]。亦终必亡而已矣。"

【白话译文】

孟子说:“仁胜过不仁,就像水能胜过火一样。如今行仁的人,好像用一杯水去扑灭一车木柴的大火一样,火焰不熄。便说水不能扑灭火,这些人又大大帮助不仁的人。到头来他们已行的一点点仁也会消亡的。”

【英语译文】

Mencius said, “That kumanity conquers inhumanity is the same as water conquers fire. Nowadays men who do good things are just like those who put off big fire of a cart of wood by means of a cup of water. The flame can't be extinguished. People will say water cannot put off fire and begin to help those inhumane men. Finally their good doings will disappear gradually. ”

【注释】(1)一车薪:一车木柴。(2)与:帮助,援助。

【原文】19 孟子曰:“五谷者,[1]种之美者也;[2]苟为不熟,不如荑稗。[3]夫仁,亦在乎熟而已矣。[4]”

【白话译文】

孟子说:“有五种谷物是种了植物中的优良品种;只要是不成熟,还不如稊米和稗子。仁,其本质也在于成熟罢了。”

【英语译文】

Mencius said, “There are five kinds of grain which are fine varieties. if they aren't ripe, they can not match barnyard grasses. The essence of humanity just lies in being ripe. ”

【注释】(1)五谷:五种谷物,所指不一。1)《周礼·天官·疾医》:“以五味、五谷、五药养其病。”郑玄注:“五谷,麻、黍、稷、麦、豆也。” 2)《孟子·滕文公上》:“树艺五谷,五谷熟而民人育。”赵岐注:“五谷谓稻、黍、稷、麦、菽也。”3)《楚辞·大招》:“五谷六仞”,王逸注:“五谷,稻、稷、麦、豆、麻也。”4)《素问·藏气法时论“五谷为养。”王冰注:“谓粳米、小豆、麦、大豆、黄黍也。”5)《苏悉地羯啰经》卷中:“五谷谓大麦、小麦、稻谷、大豆、胡麻。”后以五谷为谷物的通称,不一定限于五种。

(2)种:种子植物。(3)苟为不熟:只要是不成熟。熟,植物的果实完全长成,成熟;有收成。荑稗:tíbài,两种草名。似禾,其实(稊米和稗子)比谷小。也可食。(4)在乎:同"在于"。指出事物的目的、本质所在。

【原文】20 孟子曰:"羿之教人射,必志于彀;[1]学者亦必志于彀。大匠诲人必以规矩,学者亦必以规矩。[2]"

【白话译文】

孟子说:"羿教人射箭,一定力求拉满弓;学习的人也一定力求拉满弓。技艺高超的木工教导徒弟,一定依照规矩,学习的徒弟也一定依照规矩。"

【英语译文】

Mencius said, "When master of archery, Yi taught others to shoot, he surely required others to pull their bows fully and the learners also tried to pull the bows fully. When a skilled carpenter taught his disciples, he surely did things according to rules, and the disciples certainly did things according to rules."

【注释】(1)羿:yì,古代神话传说中善射的人。必志于彀:一定力求拉满弓。彀 gòu,张满弓。(2)大匠:技艺高超的木工。诲人:huì ~,教导徒弟。以规矩:依照规矩。规矩,校正圆形和方形的两种工具。

孟子集注卷十二　告子章句下　凡十六章

【原文】1 任人有问屋庐子曰:[1]"礼与食孰重?"曰:"礼重。""色与礼孰重?[2]"曰:"礼重。"曰:"以礼食,则饥而死;不以礼食,则得食,必以礼乎？亲迎,[3]则不得妻;不亲迎,则得妻,必亲迎乎?"屋庐子不能对,明日之邹以告孟子。[4]孟子曰:"于答是也,何有？不揣其本,而齐其末,[5]方寸之木可使高于岑楼。[6]一钩金？与一舆羽之谓哉?[7]取食之重者与礼之轻者而比之,奚翅食重?[8]取色之重者与礼之,轻者比之奚翅色重？往应之曰:'紾兄之臂而夺之食,[9]则得食;不紾,则不得食,则将紾之乎?逾东家墙而搂其处子[10],则得妻;不搂,则不得妻;则将搂之乎?"

【白话译文】

有个任国人问屋庐子:“礼和食哪样重要?”他答道:“礼重要。”“情欲和礼哪样重要?”他答道:“礼重要。”任国人又问:“依礼进食,就挨饿而死;不依礼进食就能得到食物,一定要依礼吗?按照婚礼到女家迎接新娘,就得不到妻子,不行亲迎礼,便会得到妻子,一定要按照婚礼到女家迎接新娘吗?”屋庐子不能对答。第二天他去邹国把问题告诉孟子。孟子说:“回答这个问题,有什么困难呢?不量度底端高低,就看顶端高低,树苗极矮小,如果移到高处,可以高于如高山的高楼。金属是重于羽毛的,难道是说一只带钩的金属重于一车羽毛吗?吃食物的重要方面比礼制的细节,何止说吃更重要?拿婚姻的重要方面比礼制的细节,何止说娶妻更重要?你去回答说:‘扭哥哥的胳膊抢夺他的食物,便得到吃的;不扭抢夺,便得不到吃的。那会去扭抢夺吗?翻过东邻的墙去搂抱处女,便得到妻室;不去搂抱,便得不到妻室,那会去搂抱吗?’”

【英语译文】

A man of Ren State asked Wu Lu Zi, “As for rite and food which is more important?” Wu Lu Zi answered, “Rite is more important.” The man asked, “Sexual desire and rite, which is more important?” Wu Lu Zi answered, “Rite is more important.” The man of Ren State asked once again, “If one eats food according to rite he will die of hunger; if he doesn’t eat food according to rite he will obtain food. Should he do it according to rite? If one welcomes his bride according to marriage rites, he won’t obtain his wife; if he doesn’t welcome his bride according to marriage rites he will obtain his wife. Should he do it according to rite?” Wu Lu Zi couldn’t answer this question. The next day he went to Zou State and asked Mencius the same question. Mencius replied, “It isn’t difficult to answer the question. A tree will be short if you just measure its bottom but not its top. It will surpass a high building if you measure its top. Metal is heavier than feather. Is a metallic hook heavier than a cart of feather? If you compare the importance of eating food with details of rites, why do you say eating is important than rite? If you compare the importance of marriage with details of rites, why do you say marrying is important than rite? You may answer, ‘If you twist your brother’s arms and rob him of his food, you can get food; if you don’t do so, you cannot get food. Then will you twist his arms and rob him? If you climb over east neighbor’s wall and hug the virgin, you can get a wife; if you don’t do so, you cannot get a wife. Then will you hug the virgin?’”

【注释】(1)任:rén,周代国名,风姓,在今山东济宁市。屋庐子:孟子弟子。(2)礼与食:礼,指社会生活的行为准则、道德规范和各种礼节。食,指粮食之類的养命物和吃喝。色:情欲,性欲。(3)亲迎:古代婚礼,“六礼(古代在确定婚姻过程中的六种礼仪,即纳采、问名、纳吉、纳征、请期、亲迎)”之一。夫婿至女家迎新娘入室,行交拜合卺之礼。(4)明日:第二天。之邹以告孟子:去邹把问题告诉孟子。以,并列连词。(5)于答是也:回答这个问题。于,语气助词,用于句首或句中,无义。何有:用于反问语气表示没有什么,意谓不难。不揣其本:不量度底端高低。揣 chuǎi,量度;衡量。而齐其末:就看顶端高低。齐,相同,一样。(6)方寸之木:犹方始之木。谓树苗,极矮小。岑楼:cénlóu,楼之高锐似山者。(7)一钩金:谓一只带钩之金,比喻轻少。一舆羽:一车羽毛。羽毛轻,积轻就重。一车羽毛重于一只带钩之金。(8)奚翅:xīchì,亦作“奚啻”,岂但;何止。(9)往应之:去回答。纱:zhěn,戾,捩,扭转。(10)逾东墙而搂其处子:翻过东邻的墙抱住他家的处女。

【原文】2 曹交问曰:[1]“人皆可以为尧舜,有诸?”孟子曰:“然。”“交闻文王十尺,汤九尺,今交九尺四寸以长,[2]食粟而已,如何则可?”曰:“奚有于是?亦为之而已矣。有人于此,力不能胜一匹雏,[3]则为无力人矣;今日举百钧,则为有力人矣。然则举乌获之任,是亦为乌获而已矣。[4]夫人岂以不胜为患哉?弗为耳。徐行后长者,岂人所不能哉?所不为也。尧舜之道,孝弟而已矣。子服尧之服,诵尧之言,行尧之行,是尧而已矣。子服桀之服,诵桀之言,行桀之行,是桀而已矣。”曰:“交得见于邹君,可以假馆,愿留而受业于门。”曰:“夫道若大路然,岂难知哉?人病不求耳。子归而求之,有余师。[5]”

【白话译文】

曹交问道:“人人都可以做尧舜,有这话吗?”孟子说:“有啊。”“我听说文王身高一丈,汤身高九尺;如今我身高九尺四寸多,只会吃饭罢了,我要怎样才行呢?”孟子说:“这有什么难呢?只要有作为就行了。当前无论谁力不能抓住家小鸭,算是没有能力的人了;当前能举三千斤,那就是有能力的人了。既然这样,那么举起乌获举的重量,也就是乌获罢了。一个人怎么能因不能担任而忧虑呀?只是不肯作为罢了。走慢点儿,走在长者的后面,叫作悌,快速地走在长者的前面,叫作不悌。走慢点儿,难道是人所不能的吗?不作为罢了。尧舜之道,也不过就是孝和悌嘛。你穿尧的衣服,说尧的话,做尧的举动,便是尧了。你穿桀的衣服,说桀的话,做桀的举动,便是桀了。”曹交说:“我必须谒见邹君,向他借个住处留在您门下学习。”孟子说:“道就像大路一样,能说难于了解吗?一般人的缺点是不寻求罢了。你回去自己寻求吧,老师多得很。”

【英语译文】

Cao Jiao asked, “Everybody can become Sage Yao and Great Shun. Is there such saying?” Mencius said, “Yes.” Cao Jiao said, “I heard that King Wen of Zhou Dynasty was one *zhang* tall and Tang was nine *chi* tall. And I am nine *chi* and four *cun* tall but I can just eat. How can I become Yao and Shun?” Mencius said, “It's not so difficult. It's all right if you do something. Nowadays whoever cannot pick up a small duck, he is an unable man. And whoever can lift something three-thousand-*jin* he is an able man. So, if someone lifts a heavy thing that Wu Huo, a strong man ever lifted, then he is Wu Huo. How can a man worries about that he cannot do anything? It is just because he refuses to do things. It's fraternity for one to walk slowly after an elder, and it isn't fraternity for one to walk fast ahead of an elder. Can't a man walk slowly? It is just because he refuses to do so. The Way of Sage Yao and Great Shun is filial piety and fraternity. You will become Sage Yao if you wear his clothes, say his words and do his actions. You will become Tyrant Jie if you wear his clothes, say his words and do his actions.” Cao Jiao said, “I will have an audience with King of Zou State, and request him of a residence to stay and become your disciple.” Mencius said, “The Way is like road. Could we say it's hard to understand? The drawback of average people is that they refuse to seek for it. You can go back and search for it. There are many men who can teach you.”

【注释】(1)曹交:赵岐注,“曹交,曹君之弟也。”(2)人皆可以为尧舜:疑为古语或孟子所尝言。以:yǐ,有。长:zhàng,多,多余。(3)食粟:吃公家饭。粟,俸禄意谓无能。奚有于是:这有什么难呢。奚有犹“何有”。亦:副词。仅仅;只是。有人于此:不论谁当前。匹雏:pǐchú 同“鸣雏”,家小鸭。(4)百钧:三千斤。钧,古代衡量单位之一,三十斤为一钧。然则:承接连词。既然这样,那么。举乌获之任:举起乌获举的重量。乌获,wūhuò,古之力士。(5)以不胜为患:因不能担任而忧虑。孝弟:xiàotì 孝顺父母,敬爱兄长。诵尧之言:述说尧的言论。得见:必须谒见。假馆:借个房舍(住处)。受业于门:在老师门下学习。人病不求耳:人的缺点是不寻求。病:缺点;错误。有余师:师不少;很多可受教之处;很多可效法之处。

【原文】3 公孙丑问曰："高子曰：[1]《小弁》，[2]小人之诗也。"孟子曰："何以言之？"曰："怨。"[3]曰："固哉，高叟之为诗也！[4]有人于此，越人关弓而射之，则己谈笑而道之；无他，疏之也。[5]其兄关弓而射之，则己垂涕泣而道之；无他，戚之也。[6]之怨，亲亲也。亲亲，仁也。固矣夫，高叟之为诗也！"曰："《凯风》何以不怨？[7]曰："《凯风》，亲之过小者也；《小弁》，亲之过大者也。亲之过大而不怨，是愈疏也；亲之过小而怨，是不可矶也。[8]愈疏，不孝也；不可矶，亦不孝也。孔子曰：'舜其至孝矣，五十而慕。[9]'"

【白话译文】

公孙丑问："高子说：'《小弁》是小人作的诗。是吗？'"孟子说："为什么这样说呢？"公孙丑说："因为它吐露了幽怨。"孟子说："高老论诗太拘泥了！现实生活中的人，越国人拉满弓去射他，于是他自己谈笑地喊话，这没有别的缘故，关系疏远啦。他哥哥拉满弓去射他，于是他自己淌着涕泪喊话。这没有别的缘故，关系亲密呀。《小弁》的怨恨，正是爱亲人的缘故。爱亲人，是仁的表现。高老论诗实在太拘泥了！"公孙丑说："《凯风》为什么不吐露幽怨呢？"孟子说："《凯风》这诗由于母亲的过失小；《小弁》这诗由于父亲的过失大。父母的过失大而不抱怨，是淡漠行为，是疏远父母的表现；父母的过失小而抱怨，是激怒行为，也是不孝顺父母的表现。孔子说："舜是极孝顺的人，五十岁了仍然和小儿一样思念父母。"

【英语译文】

Gongsun Chou asked, "Gao Zi said that 'Little Crow' was composed by mean man. Wasn't it?" Mencius asked, "Why did he say so?" Gongsun Chou said, "Because it expressed deep complaint." Mencius said, "Gao Zi was too confined in commenting poetry. In reality, people in Yue State pulled bow fully to shoot at him, and he just responded loudly. It was just due to alienated relation and without any other reason. His brother pulled bow fully to shoot at him, and he just responded with tears. It was just due to intimate relation and without any other reason. The complaint of 'Little Crow' just originated from intimacy. Loving one's relatives shows that one is humanistic. Gao Zi was really too confined in commenting poetry." Gongsun Chou asked, "Why didn't 'South Wind' express deep complaint?" Mencius said, "The poem 'South Wind' had little to do with mother's fault but the poem 'Little Crow' had much to do with father's fault. If a person's parents had much fault and he didn't complain to them, he was indifferent to and alienated from his parents. If a person's parents had little fault and he did complain, he was enraged and not filial to them. Confucius said, ' Great Shun was the most filial man who still missed his parents when he was fifty years old.' "

【注释】(1)高子:齐人。见《四书集注》。(2)《小弁》:《小雅》篇名。弁,音pán。(3)小人:指识见浅狭的人。怨:谓哀痛迫切。周幽王娶申后,生太子宜臼;又得褒姒,生伯服,而黜申后废宜臼。于是宜臼之傅为作此诗,以叙其哀痛迫切之情。(4)固哉:固执,拘泥。高叟:高老。为诗:讲诗,论诗。(5)越人:越国人。关弓:wāngōng,拉满弓。关,同"弯"。则己谈笑而道之:于是他自己谈笑地喊话。无他,疏之也:没有别的缘故,关系疏远啦。(6)则己垂涕泣而道之:于是他自己淌着涕泪喊话。戚之也:关系亲密呀。(7)亲亲:爱自己的亲属。《凯风》:见《国风·邶风》,凡四章通篇都是自责而慰母之辞。《诗序》说:"《凯风》美孝子也。卫之淫风流行,虽有七子之母,犹不能安其室,故美七子能尽其孝道,以慰母心,而成其志尔。"(8)矶:jī,水冲击岩石。引申为激怒,触犯。(9)至孝:谓极尽孝道。慕:指小儿思念父母的啼哭声。《礼记·檀弓上》:"其往也如慕,其反也如疑。"郑玄注:"谓小儿随父母啼呼。"孔颖达疏:"谓父母在前,婴儿在后,恐不及之,故在后啼呼而随之。"

【原文】4 宋牼将之楚,孟子遇于石丘,[1]曰:"先生将何之?"[2]曰:"吾闻秦楚将构兵,我将见楚王说而罢之。[3]楚王不悦,我将见秦王说而罢之。二王我将有所遇焉。[4]"曰:"轲也请无问其详,愿闻其指。说之将何如?[5]"曰:"我将言其不利也。"曰:"先生之志则大矣,先生之号则不可。[6]先生以利说秦楚之王,[7]秦楚之王悦于利,以罢三军之师,[8]是三军之士乐罢而悦于利也。为人臣者怀利以事其君,为人子者怀利以事其父,为人弟者怀利以事其兄,是君臣父子兄弟终去仁义,怀利以相接,[9]然而不亡者未之有也。[10]先生以仁义说秦楚之王,秦楚之王悦于仁义,而罢三军之师,是三军之士乐罢而悦于仁义也。为人臣者怀仁义以事其君,为人子者怀仁义以事其父,为人弟者怀仁义以事其兄,是君臣、父子、兄弟去利,怀仁义以相接也,然而不王者未之有也。何必曰利?"

【白话译文】

宋牼将去楚国,孟子在石丘那儿遇到他,问道:"宋先生您到哪里去?"他答道:"我听说秦楚两国交兵,打算去谒见楚王,劝告他停战。如果楚王不高兴我的话,打算去谒见秦王,劝告他停战。这两个国王,我会有所遇合。"孟子说:"请让我不问详情,想听大意。你将怎样劝告?”回答:“我打算说,交兵是不利的。”孟子说:“先生的志向很好,提法却不行。先生用利来劝告秦王、楚王,秦楚二王由于喜欢有利而停止全军征伐,于是全军官兵乐于停战而喜欢有利了。当人臣的心中装着利来服侍君主,当人儿子的心中装着利来服侍老子,当人弟娃的心中装着利来服侍他哥,于是君臣、父子、兄弟终于不要仁义来会合,这样而国家不灭亡的还没有过。先生用仁义劝告秦楚之王,秦楚之王喜欢仁义而停止全军征伐,于是全军官兵乐于停战而喜欢仁义了。当人臣的心中装着仁义来服侍君主,当人儿子的心中装着仁义来服侍老子,当人弟娃的心中装着仁义来服侍他哥,于是君臣、父子、兄弟心中都去掉利而装着仁义来会合,这样而国家不以德政统一天下的还没有过。为什么必要讲‘利’呢?”

【英语译文】

Song Keng would go to Chu State. Mencius met him in Shi Qiu of Song State and asked, “Mr. Song, where are you going?” Song Keng answered, “I heard that Qin State and Chu State are at war. I want to pay a visit to King of Chu State and persuade him to bring out a truce. If King of Chu State doesn’t accept my suggestion, I am going to pay a visit to King of Qin State and persuade him to bring out a truce. I have predestined affinity with these two states.” Mencius said, “I just want to know roughly how you will persuade them?” Song Keng said, “I will say that it’s not beneficial for them to be at war.” Mencius said, “Your intention is very good but your wording isn’t workable. If you admonish kings of Qin and Chu states by means of benefit, they will bring out truce because they like benefit. Their generals and soldiers will be glad at truce and begin to like benefit. If ministers serve their king with intention for benefit; sons serve their fathers with intention for benefit, and younger brothers serve their elder brothers with intention for benefit, king and ministers, father and sons, elder and younger brothers meet together not for humanity and righteousness. and Such a state is destined to perish. If you admonish kings of Qin and Chu states by means of humanity and righteousness, they will bring out truce because they like humanity and righteousness. Their generals and soldiers will be glad at truce and begin to like humanity and righteousness. If ministers serve their king with intention for humanity and righteousness, sons serve their fathers with intention for humanity and righteousness, and younger brothers serve their elder brothers with intention for humanity and righteousness, and then king and ministers, father and sons, elder and younger brothers meet together not for benefit but for humanity and righteousness. Such a state is destined to unify the world by means of government of virtue. Why do we necessarily mention ‘benefit’?”

【注释】(1)宋牼:sòngkēng,亦名宋钘(～jiān)、宋荣。战国时宋国人。石丘:宋国地名。(2)何之:去何处。(3)构兵:gòubīng,交战。说罢之:劝告他罢兵。说:shuì:劝说别人听从自己的意见。而:代词,他。(4)有所遇焉:有遇合的。(5)轲也请无问其详:我请允许不问详情,愿意听听意旨。请,敬辞。表示请对方允许自己做愿意做的事。说之将何如:将如何进言(劝说)。(6)志则大:志向好。大:善。号则不可:提法不行。号:名义,提法。(7)以利说秦楚之王:用利劝告秦楚之王。(8)罢三军之师:停止全军征伐。师:出兵征伐,进军。(9)怀利以相接:心中装着利来会合。(10)然而:“然”是近指代词,相当于“此”“如此”。“而”是顺承连词。现代汉语还用,可以不译或去掉。

【原文】5 孟子居邹,季任为任处守,[1]以币交,受之而不报。[2]处于平陆,储子为相,[3]以币交,受之而不报。他日,由邹之任见季子;[4]由平陆之齐,不见储子。[5]屋庐子喜曰:“连得间矣。[6]”问曰:“夫子之任见季子;之齐,不见储子,为其为相与?[7]”曰:“非也。书曰:‘享多仪,仪不及物曰不享,惟不役志于享。[8]’为其不成享也。”屋庐子悦。或问之。屋庐子曰:“季子不得之邹,储子得之平陆。[9]”

【白话译文】

孟子住在邹国时,季任为任国留守,代理国政。他送礼物来和孟子交友,孟子接受了礼物没有回赠。孟子住在平陆时,储子是齐国的卿相,他也送礼物来和孟子交友,孟子接受了礼物没有回赠。过了一些日子,孟子从邹国到任国,拜访了季子;从平陆到齐都,没有拜访储子。屋庐子高兴地说:“难得提问老师的机会呀!”他问道:“老师到任国拜访了季子;到齐都不拜访储子,是因为储子只是卿相吗?”孟子说:“不是。《尚书》里说:‘进献重视仪节,仪节比不上礼品叫作没有进献,因为没有把心用在进献上。’”屋庐子听了很高兴。有人问他这件事,屋庐子说:“季子在代理国政,不能亲自到邹国去,而储子作为卿相是能亲自到平陆去的。”

【英语译文】

When Mencius lived in Zou State, Ji Ren acted on behalf of his elder brother and was in a responsible position of the king. After he presented gift to Mencius and intended to make friends, Mencius accepted the gift but didn’t send a present in return.

When Mencius lived in Pinglu, Chu Zi acted as a minister of Qi State. After he presented gift to Mencius and intended to make friends, Mencius accepted the gift but didn't send a present in return. After several days Mencius went to Ren State from Zou State and paid a visit to Ji Ren; but when he went to the capital of Qi State from Pinglu he didn't visit Chu Zi. Wuluzi said happily, "We seldom have a chance to ask our master a question. " He asked Mencius, "Master visited Ji Ren when you arrived at Ren State, but you didn't visit Chu Zi when you arrived at the capital of Qi State. Is it because Chu Zi is just a minister?" Mencius said, "No. *The Book of History* said, 'When people are dedicating something, they must pay attention to rituals. If rituals don't match gift, it cannot be called dedication since one doesn't attach importance to dedicating. '" After hearing this Wulu zi was very happy. And somebody asked him about it, Wulu zi said, "Ji Ren couldn't go to Zou State personally because he acted on behalf of his elder brother and was in a responsible position of the king. However, as a minister of Qi State, Chu Zi could go to Zou State personally. "

【注释】(1)季任:任国国君之弟。赵岐说:"季任,任君之弟。任君朝会于邻国,季任为之居守其国也。" 处守:犹留守。古时国君离开京城命大臣留守其地。(2)以币交:~bì~,用礼物交友。币:缯帛。古代常用作祭祀或馈赠的礼品。不报:没有回赠。(3)平陆:战国时齐邑,故城在今山东省汶上县北。储子为相:储子任齐国的卿相(执政大臣)。(4)他日:过了一段时间。由邹之任见季子:从邹国到任国,拜访了季子。(5)由平陆之齐不见储子:从平陆邑到齐都,没有拜访储子。(6)连得间矣:难得提问的机会呀。连:难。间:可乘的机会。(7)为其为相与:因为他只是卿相。(8)书曰:'享多仪,仪不及物:见《尚书·周书·洛诰》曰:"享多仪,仪不及物曰不享,惟不役志于享。" 说:"享献(进献长者或上级)重视仪节(礼节),仪不及物(礼品)曰不享,没有礼节只有礼物或者礼节不到位。叫作没有进献。惟不役志(用心)于享:因为没有把心用在进献上。"(9)得:能够。

【原文】6 淳于髡曰:[1]"先名实者,为人也;后名实者,自为人也。[2]夫子在三卿之中[3],名实未加于上下而去之,仁者固如此乎?[4]"孟子曰:"居下位不以贤事不肖者,伯夷也;五就汤,五就桀者伊尹也;不恶污君,不辞小官者,柳下惠也。三子者不同道,其趋一也。[5]一者何也? 曰:仁也。君子亦仁而已矣,何必同?"曰:"鲁缪公之时,公仪子为政,子柳、子思为臣,鲁之削也滋甚。[6]若是乎贤者之无益于国也!"曰:"虞不用百里奚而亡,秦穆公用之而霸。不用贤则亡,削何可得与?"曰:"昔者王豹处于淇,而河西善讴;[7]绵驹处于高唐,而齐右善歌;[8]华周杞梁之妻善哭其夫而变国俗。[9]有诸内必形诸外。为其事而无其功者,髡未尝睹之。[10]是故无贤者也,有则髡必识之。”曰:“孔子为鲁司寇,不用,从而祭,燔肉不至,[11]不税冕而行。[12]不知者以为为肉也。其知者以为为无理也。乃孔子则欲以微罪行,不欲为苟去。[13]君子之所为,众人固不识也。”

【白话译文】

淳于髡说:“看重名誉功业是为了济世救民,轻视名誉功业是要独善其身。您作为齐国的三卿之一没有建立上辅君王下济臣民的名誉功业,就要离开,仁德的人原来是这样的吗?”孟子说:“处在低下的职位不以自己的贤德服侍不贤的人,这是伯夷;五次到汤那里,五次到桀那里,这是伊尹;不厌恶坏君主,不拒绝小官职,这是柳下惠。三位贤人的行为不相同,他们前进的方向却是相同的。相同什么呢?就是仁德。君子只要仁德就行了,为什么要一模一样呢?淳于髡说:“鲁缪公在位的时候,公仪子主持国政,泄柳和子思都在朝中为臣,鲁国却越来越削弱了。像这样嘛,贤人对国家没有益处啊!”孟子说:“虞国不用百里奚而灭亡,秦穆公重用百里奚而称霸。不用贤人的国家就会亡国,割地苟安都办不到,还能得到什么?”淳于髡说:“从前王豹住在淇水旁,河西的人都会唱歌;绵驹住在高唐,齐国西部地方的人都会唱歌;华周、杞梁的妻子痛哭她们的丈夫,因而改变了国家的风俗。里面有什么一定会表现在外面。干一件事而没有使其好坏有所改变的人,髡未曾见过。所以现在没有贤人;如果有,我一定会知道他。”孟子说:“孔子当鲁国的司寇,不被重用,然后祭祀,不分祭肉给他,这是君相俱无礼呀。他连礼帽都没取下就急忙离开了鲁国。不知道实情的人以为他是为争祭肉而离去,知道实情的以为他是为鲁国不守礼法而离去。至于孔子,却是想要自己背一点小罪名而走,不想随便离去。君子的做法,一般人本来就是不知道的。”

【英语译文】

Chunyu Kun said, “If one pays attention to reputation and achievements, he wants to serve the people; if he looks down on these, he wants to be righteous alone. You haven't established your reputation and achievement to assist the king and serve the people but you want to leave. Is a humanistic man with virtue like this?” Mencius answered, “It was Bo Yi who was in low position and didn't assist the king without virtue by means of his own virtue. It was Yi Yin who went to King Tang for five times and went to King Jie for five times. It was Liu Xiahui who didn't loathe bad king and didn't despise low-rank official. The three virtuous men's actions were different but their direction of moving was the same. That was humanity and virtue. Moral men should be virtuous and humanistic. Why did they behave all the same?" Chunyu Kun said, "When Duke Mu of Lu State was in power, Gongyi Zi was in charge of administrative affairs. Xie Liu and Zi Si were ministers in the court but Lu State became increasingly weak. If so, virtuous men weren't beneficial to a state." Mencius said, "Yu State perished when Bai Li Xi wasn't employed in it, on the contrary Qin State succeeded in seeking hegemony when Baili Xi was employed in it. A state which doesn't use virtuous man would perish. Since it cannot seek momentary ease by ceding territory, what else can it obtain?" Chunyu Kun said, "In other days Wang Bao lived nearby Qi River, people in the west part of the river could sing songs; when Mian Ju lived in Gaotang, people in the west part of Qi State could sing songs; wives of Hua Zhou and Qi Liang cried bitterly about them because custom of state had been changed. Words are the voice of the mind. I haven't seen a man who did a thing but didn't change anything. Therefore, nowadays there isn't any virtuous man. If there is, I have surely known him." Mencius said, "Confucius acted as secretary of justice (*si kou*) in Lu State but he wasn't paid attention to. Then when he sacrificed he wasn't given sacrificial meat. This showed that the king and ministers weren't acting according to the rites. Without taking off his ritual hat he hurried in leaving Lu State. Those who didn't know the reality thought that he left because he didn't obtain sacrificial meat. But those who knew the reality thought that he left because people in Lu State didn't observe the rites. Confucius left being blamed by a small accusation but he didn't do it casually. An ordinary man doesn't understand what a moral man does."

【注释】(1)淳于髡:chúnyú kūn,人名。战国齐辩士。淳于,复姓。(2)先名实者:把声誉事功放在前头的人,即重视声誉事功的人。为人:是为济世救民。后名实者:与先名实者对立,是轻视声誉事功的人。自为人:是为独善其身。(3)夫子在三卿之中:三卿,指古代上中下三卿。(4)仁者固如此:有德行的人本来就是像这样吗。(5)不肖:不正派。伯夷:商末孤竹君长子。伊尹:商汤大臣,名伊,一名挚,尹,是官名。相传生于伊水,故名。是汤妻陪嫁的奴隶,后助汤伐桀,被尊为阿衡(商代官名)。柳下惠:春秋鲁大夫展获,字季,又字禽,曾为士师官,食邑柳下,谥惠,故称其为展禽、柳下季、柳士师、柳下惠等。以柳下惠之名最为著称。相传他与一女子共坐一夜,不曾淫乱。后用以借指有操行的男子。不同道:方法不同。

其趋一也:大方向相同。(6)亦仁而已矣:只要行人道就对了。亦,副词。仅仅;只是。何必同:不需要(不必)一个样子。鲁缪公:《史记》作鲁穆公。鲁哀公孙,名显。公仪子:当是公仪休。《史记·循吏列传》:"公仪休者,鲁博士也,以高第为鲁相。奉法循礼,无所变更。"为政:执掌国政。子柳:泄柳。子思:孔伋,孔子之孙。为臣:这里指做相位下的臣子官员。削:削弱。滋甚:更加快速,更加厉害。《史记·六国年表》,"齐宣公四十四年,伐鲁莒及安阳;四十五年,伐鲁,取都;四十八年,取鲁郕;齐康公十一年,伐鲁,取最;十五年,鲁败我(齐)平陆;二十年,伐鲁,破之。"这些事都在鲁缪公之世。(7)若是乎:像这样嘛。削何可得与:削地求和怎么得到呢。百里奚:"奚"一作"傒"。春秋时秦国大夫。百里氏,一说百氏,字里,名奚。原为虞大夫,虞亡时为晋所俘,作为晋献公女陪嫁之臣入秦。后出走楚,为楚人所执,又被秦穆公用五张牡黑羊皮赎回,用为大夫,世称"五羖大夫"。王豹:春秋时卫人,善讴。居于淇,而河西之人化之亦善讴。淇:卫国水名,是古黄河支流,在黄河西岸。(8)绵驹处于高唐,而齐右善歌:绵驹,齐国人,善于唱歌。高唐:齐国地名,在今山东禹城市西南。齐右:高唐在齐国西部,以朝南论,西在右,所以叫齐右。(9)华周、杞梁之妻善哭其夫:赵岐《注》:"华周,华旋也;杞梁,杞殖也。二人俱为齐将伐莒而战败。事见《左传·襄二十三年》。《说苑善说篇》:"昔华舟、杞梁战而死,其妻悲之,向城而哭隅为之崩,城为之阤(zhì 崩塌也)。"国俗:一国的风俗。(10)有诸内必形诸外:里面有什么一定会表现在外面。为其事而无其功者:谓干一件事而没有使其好坏有所改变的人,髡以此讥孟子仕齐无功。(11)从而:连词。然后;因而。燔肉不至:燔,fán,亦作"膰",祭肉。古礼,宗庙、社稷诸祭,必分祭肉与同姓之国以及有关的人,表示"同福禄"。至,通"致"。给予;加给。燔肉不至,谓祭肉不分给大夫,是君相俱无礼。(12)不税免而行:税通"脱",没脱下礼貌就走了。极言匆忙,不辞而别。(13)乃孔子则欲以微罪行,不欲为苟去:乃,转折连词。译作"至于"。

【原文】7 孟子曰:"五霸者,[1]三王之罪人也;[2]今之诸侯,五霸之罪人也;今之大夫,今之诸侯之罪人也。[3]天子适诸侯曰巡狩,诸侯朝于天子曰述职。[4]春省耕而补不足,秋省敛而助不及。[5]入其疆,土地辟,田野治,养老尊贤,俊杰在位,则有庆;庆以地。[6]入其疆,土地荒芜,遗老失贤,掊克在位,则有让。[7]一不朝,则贬其爵;再不朝则削其地;三不朝则六师移之。[8]是故天子讨而不伐,诸侯伐而不讨。[9]五霸者,搂诸侯以伐诸侯者也,故曰,五霸者,三王之罪人也。[10]五霸,桓公为盛。葵丘之会,诸侯束牲载书而不歃血。[11]初命曰,诛不孝,无易树子,无以妾为妻。[12]再命曰,尊贤育才,以彰有德。[13]三命曰,敬老慈幼,无忘宾旅。[14]四命曰,士无世官,官事无摄,取士必得，无专杀大夫。[15]五命曰，无曲防，无遏籴，无有封而不告。[16]曰，凡我同盟之人，既盟之后，言归于好。[17]今之诸侯皆犯此五禁，故曰，今之诸侯，五霸之罪人也；长君之恶其罪小，逢君之恶其罪大。[18]今之大夫皆逢君之恶，故曰今之大夫，今之诸侯之罪人也。

【白话译文】

孟子说："五霸是三王的罪人，现在的诸侯又是五霸的罪人；现在的大夫，又是现在诸侯的罪人。天子到诸侯的国家去，叫作巡狩。诸侯朝见天子叫作述职。天子春天视察耕种情况，补助耕种投入不足的人；秋天视察收获情况，周济歉收的人。一进入某个国家的境界，如果土地已开辟，庄稼长得很好，老人得赡养，贤者受尊重，出色人才在朝廷，那么就有赏赐；赏赐用土地。如果一进入某个国家的境界，土地荒废，老人被遗弃，贤者不被任用，搜刮钱财的人立于朝廷，那么就有责罚。诸侯一次不朝，就降低他的爵位；两次不朝，就削减他的土地；三次不朝，就用天子的直属部队去惩罚其人而废弃他。所以天子发出命令惩治有罪，而使方伯连帅带领诸侯去征伐，这是讨而不伐。诸侯奉天子之命，声明其罪而征伐这是伐而不讨。五霸呢，是拉拢部分诸侯而攻另外的诸侯的人，所以我说五霸是三王的罪人。五霸，齐桓公最强。葵丘盟会上，捆绑了牺牲没杀，把盟约放在牺牲体上，没有饮血。盟约的第一告诫是：惩罚不孝的人，不变换世子，不要立妾为妻。第二告诫是：尊重贤人，养育人才和表彰有德行的人。第三告诫是：敬老爱幼，不要怠慢在本国做官的外国人和客居异乡的人。第四告诫是：士人的官职不要世代相传。官府的事，不要兼职。选取士人，一定要正当。不要任意杀死职官。第五告诫是：不要到处筑堤，为害邻邦，不要阻止邻国购粮，不要有所封赏而不告诉盟主。最后说，所有参与盟会的人从订立盟约后，完全恢复旧好。今日的诸侯都违犯了这五条告诫。所以说，今天的诸侯是五霸的罪人。臣下助长君上的恶行，这罪行，还算小；臣下以谄媚逢迎而导君为非，这罪行可就大了。今天的大夫，都逢迎君主的恶行，所以说，今天的大夫又是诸侯的罪人。"

【英语译文】

Mencius said, "The Five Overlords were criminals of the Three Great Kings, and nowadays princes are criminals of the Five Overlords, and ministers are criminals of princes. It was called imperial inspection tour when the Son of the Heaven went to princes' states. It was called report on one's work when princes were presented at the court. In spring the Son of the Heaven inspected farming work and he added up farming men without sufficient supplies. In autumn the Son of the Heaven inspected harvesting work and he gave alms to those who had crop failure. When he entered a state, he would grant a reward by means of land if in the state its land had been tilled and crops grew prosperously, and the elders were raised well, and the virtuous were respected, and talents were in the court. When he entered a state, he would give punishment if in the state its land had been deserted, and the elders were abandoned, and the virtuous weren't employed, and men who plundered, money were in the court. If a prince didn't pay respect to the court once, his title of nobility would be degraded. If he didn't pay respect to the court twice, his land would be reduced. If he didn't pay respect to the court thrice, the army of the Son of the Heaven would attack him and abolish him. Therefore the Son of the Heaven issued order of punishment, and the leader of princes led troops to attack him. This was denouncement before attack. The princes were ordered by the mandate of the Son of the heaven to claim his crimes and then to attack him. This was attack before denouncement. The Five overlords drew some princes to their sides and then attacked other princes. Therefore I said that the Five Overlords were criminals of the Three Great Kings. Among the Five Overlords, Duke Huan of Qi State was the strongest. At the Kuiqiu Alliance Meeting, sacrifices were bound but were not killed, and the alliance members didn't smear the blood of sacrifice on their mouths. The first admonishment of the covenant was to punish unfilial son, not to change lord's heir, not to change a concubine into a wife. The second admonishment of the covenant was to respect the virtuous, to nurture talents and to commend men of morality. The third admonishment of the covenant was to respect the elder and care about the younger, not neglect foreigners who were officials and lived in the state. The fourth admonishment of the covenant was the official post of scholar shouldn't inherited; one could not hold two or more official posts concurrently, and it should be normal to select scholars, and officials could not be killed casually. The fifth admonishment of the covenant was not to dam everywhere and harm neighbors, not to hinder neighbor states from purchasing grain, not to keep silent to the alliance leader while being rewarded. The covenant said finally that all members became friendly as usual after they signed the covenant. Nowadays princes all violated these five admonishments. Therefore, princes nowadays are criminals of the Five Overlords. If ministers assisted their king's crime, they committed small crime. If ministers led their king to commit crime by means of flattery, they committed great crime. Nowadays ministers all flatter king's evil doings, therefore nowadays ministers are criminals of princes."

【注释】(1)五霸:两种说法:一说指齐桓公、晋文公、秦穆公、宋襄公、楚庄王。一说指齐桓公、晋文公、秦穆公、楚庄王、吴王阖闾。(2)三王:这里指夏禹、商汤、周文王、武王。(3)今之大人:指在高位者,如王公贵族。(4)天子适诸侯曰巡狩,诸侯朝于天子曰述职:适 shì,去,往。巡狩,亦作"巡守"。谓天子出行视察邦国州郡。朝于,于是语气助词,古代凡见人皆称朝,这里指诸侯定期朝见天子报告封国情况。述职,诸侯向天子陈述职守,后指外任官员向朝廷陈述职守,今泛指向主管部门陈述汇报工作情况。(5)春省耕而补不足,秋省敛而助不及:省 xǐng,视察。(6)入其疆:谓进入其国境。土地辟,田野治:开垦了土地,庄稼长得好。养老尊贤,俊杰在位:赡养老人尊重贤人,出色人才在朝廷。则有庆;庆以地:就有赏赐,用土地赏赐。(7)土地荒芜,遗老失贤:土地被荒废,老人被遗弃,贤人不得用。掊克:póukè,聚敛;搜刮民财之人。让:责备,责问。(8)六师移之:谓用天子的直属部队去惩罚其人而废弃他。六师,指天子的军队。(9)讨而不伐:天子发出命令惩治有罪,而使方伯连帅(诸侯之长)带领诸侯去征伐。伐而不讨:伐,伐是奉天子之命,声明其罪而征伐。(10)搂诸侯以伐诸侯者:(五霸是)拉拢诸侯而伐诸侯的称霸者。搂 lōu,挟持,拉拢。(11)葵丘之会:齐桓公建立霸权后,于桓公三十五年(公元前651年)在葵丘(今河南民权东北)邀集周公及鲁、宋、卫、郑、许、曹等国相会结盟,规定不可壅塞水源,不可阻碍各地粮食流通,不可改换嫡子,不可随便杀死大夫,并尊贤育才、选拔贤士,不让士世袭官职,同盟者皆言归于好。束牲载书而不歃血(捆绑用作牺牲的牲畜不杀,把盟约文书放在牲畜身体上,不微吸牲血)。歃血:shà ~,古代盟会中的一种仪式。盟约宣读后,参加者用口微吸所杀生的血,以示诚意。一说,以指蘸血,涂于口旁。(12)初命:第一告诫。(再命:第二告诫。)(初,再,表序次相当于第一、第二;首先,其次)。命,告诫。无易树子:古代诸侯立为世子的嫡子。(13)以:等立平列连词。译作"与""和"。(14)无忘宾旅:忘,玩忽,怠忽。宾旅,客卿(秦国请其他诸侯国的人来秦做官其位为卿。而以客礼待之,故称。后亦泛称在本国做官的外国人);羁旅之人,指客居异乡的人。(15)世官:父子相继为官。官事无摄:官府的事,不要兼职。取士必得:选取士人,一定要正当。无专杀大夫:不要任意杀死职官,擅自杀人叫专杀。次于卿的职官是大夫,后因以大夫为任官职者之称。(16)曲防:遍设堤防。朱熹注:"无曲防,不得曲为堤防,壅泉激水,以专小利,病邻国也。"遏籴:èdí 阻止买进谷物。无有封而不告:不要以私恩擅自封赏而不告盟主。(17)言归于好:~ ~ ~hǎo,谓相好如初。言,助词。(18)长君之恶:君上为恶臣下助力。逢君之恶:君上之恶心未发,臣下以谄媚逢迎而导君为非。

【原文】8 鲁欲使慎子为将军。[1]孟子曰:"不教民而用之,[2]谓之殃民。[3]殃民者不容于尧舜之世。[4]一战胜齐,遂有南阳,然且不可。[5]"慎子勃然不悦曰:"此则滑厘所不识也。[6]"曰:"吾明告子。天子之地方千里;不千里,不足以待诸侯[7]。诸侯之地方百里;不百里不足以守宗庙之典籍。[8]周公之封于鲁,为方百里也;地非不足,而俭于百里。[9]太公之封于齐也,亦为方百里也;地非不足,而俭于百里。今鲁方百里者五,子以为有王者作,则鲁在所损乎,在所益乎?[10]徒取诸彼以与此,然且仁者不为,况于杀人以求之乎?[11]君子之事君也,务引其君以当道,志于仁而已。[12]"

【白话译文】

鲁国想要叫慎子当将军。孟子说:"不先教导百姓懂礼义,便用他们打仗,这叫为害百姓。为害百姓的人,在尧舜时代是容不下的。打一次仗便胜了齐国而取得南阳,这样也是不可以的。"慎子突然变了神色,愤愤地说:"这个就是我不知道的了。"孟子说:"我明白地告诉你吧。天子的土地纵横一千里;如果不到一千里,便不够待遇诸侯。诸侯的土地,纵横一百里;如果不到一百里,便不够守护传统的礼法制度和正统政权。周公受封于鲁,是应该纵横一百里的;土地不是不够,但实际上少于一百里。太公受封于齐,也应该纵横一百里的;土地不是不够,但实际上少于一百里。如今鲁国有五个纵横一百里,你认为如有圣主明王兴起,鲁国的土地在被减少之列呢?还是在被增加之列呢?不动武,将土地从一个国家取来给另一个国家,仁德的人尚且不干,何况杀人来求得土地呢?君子服侍君王,一定用合于正道的路子引其君有志于仁罢了。"

【英语译文】

The authority of Lu State wanted Shen Zi to be a general. Mencius said, "It is doing harm to common people to use them fight before teaching them rites and rituals. People who did harm to common people could not be tolerated in the times of Sage Yao and Great Shun. It was still not alright if one got Nanyang and won over Qi State after one fight." Shen Zi became enraged and said angrily, "I don't know that at all." Mencius said, "I tell you clearly. The land of the Son of the Heaven extends one thousand square *li*. If it is less than that, then the Son of the Heaven has no way to treat vassals. The land of vassal extends one hundred square *li*. If it is less than that, then a vassal has no way to observe traditional systems of rites and governance. Duke Zhou was given title and land in Lu State and his land should extend one hundred square *li*. But his land extended less than that even there was enough land. Tai Gong was given title and land in Qi State and his land should extend one hundred square *li*. But his land extended less than that even there was enough land. For present time, in Lu State there are five areas which extends one hundred square *li*. Do you think it should be added or reduced in land area? A virtuous and humanistic man refuses to obtain land from one state and give it to another without war. Let alone getting land by means of killing men. A moral man should serve his monarch in a right way and lead him to virtue and humanity."

【注释】(1)使慎子为将军:慎子,鲁臣,名滑厘(gǔlí)。将军:春秋、战国为军中统帅泛称,亦作为高级武官尊称。(2)不教民而用之:《论语·子路篇》:"以不教民战,是谓弃之"与此同意。朱熹注:"教民者,教之礼义,使知入事父兄出事长上也。不教民而用之:不以义礼教民而使知入事父兄出事长上而使用民。(3)谓之殃民:叫为害百姓。(4)殃民不容于尧舜之世:殃民在尧舜时代不容纳。(5)一战胜齐,遂有南阳,然且不可:当时由于鲁国想要使慎子伐齐取南阳(即汶阳,在泰山的西南,汶水的北边,本属鲁,后逐渐被齐所侵夺。)所以孟子说即使慎子善战有功如此,然而不可以。(6)勃然不悦曰:神色突变愤愤地说。此则滑厘所不识也:这就是我所不知道的了。(7)待诸侯:待遇诸侯。(8)宗庙:祖宗的庙宇;朝廷国家的代称。典籍:指法典图集等重要文献。(9)俭于百里:不到一百里。俭:薄,少。(10)今鲁方百里者五:现在鲁国土地有五个纵横一百里。子以为有王者作:你认为有王者兴起时。则鲁在所损乎,在所益乎:那么鲁国在削减土地之列吗还是在增加土地之列呢?(11)徒取:谓不动武而取。(12)务引其君以当道:务,必须,一定。当道,dáng~合于正道。志于仁而已:有志于仁罢了。志,向慕;有志于。

【原文】9 孟子曰:"今之事君者皆曰,'我能为君辟土地,充府库。'[1]今之所谓良臣,古之所谓民贼也[2]。君不乡道,不志于仁,而求富之,是富桀也。[3]'我能为君约与国,战必克。'[4]今之所谓良臣,古之所谓民贼也。君不乡道,不志于仁,而求为之强战,是辅桀也。[5]由今之道,无变今之俗,虽与之天下[6],不能一朝居也。[7]"

【白话译文】

孟子说:"今天服侍君主的人都说,'我能够帮君主扩展土地,增加国家的财物和兵甲。'今天所谓的好臣子正是古代所谓的残害人民的人。君主不向往道德,无意行仁,却想使他钱财富实,这等于使夏桀钱财富实。他们还说,'我能够帮君主邀结同盟国,打仗必胜。'今天所谓的好臣子正是古代所谓的残害人民的人。君主不向往道德,无意行仁,却想帮他勉力作战。这等于帮助夏桀。顺着现在的路走,不改变现在的风俗习气,纵使把天下全都交给他,一个早晨他也坐不安稳。"

【英语译文】

Mencius said, "Nowadays people who serve their monarch say, 'I can assist the monarch to expand territory and strengthen the state's finance and armaments.' Nowadays the so-called good ministers are the same as those who did harm to people in ancient times. When the monarch doesn't yearn for morality and refuses to conduct virtue and humanity, they still want him to be wealthy. This is the same as that someone made Tyrant Jie of Xia Dynasty become wealthy. They also say, 'I can assist the monarch to invite alliance and win a war.' Nowadays the so-called good ministers are the same as those who did harm to people in ancient times. When the monarch doesn't yearn for morality and refuses to conduct virtue and humanity, they still help him to fight. This is just helping Tyrant Jie of Xia Dynasty to do evils. If the monarch goes on like this and refuses to change customs he cannot stay stably for one morning even all the world is passed over to him."

【注释】(1)辟土地:开拓土地。充府库:增加国家的财物和兵甲,让国家的库房严实无虚。(2)民贼:残害人民的人。(3)乡道:向往道德,追求道德。乡:通"向"。(4)约与国:约,邀结,邀请。与,同盟者,党与。(5)强战:qiǎng ~ 勉力作战。(6)由今之道:顺着现在的路走。虽与之天下:纵使把天下交给他。(7)不能一朝居也:不能安居一个早晨。

【原文】10 白圭曰:[1]"吾欲二十而取一,何如?[2]"孟子曰:"子之道,貉道也。[3]万室之国,一人陶,则可乎?[4]"曰:"不可,器不足用也。"曰:"夫貉,五谷不生,惟黍生之;[5]无城郭、宫室、宗庙、祭祀之礼,无诸侯币帛饔飧"[6],无百官有司,故二十取一而足也。今居中国,去人伦,无君子,[7]如之何其可也?陶以寡,且不可以为国,况无君子乎?欲轻之于尧舜之道者,大貉小貉也;欲重之于尧舜之道者,大桀小桀也。[8]"

【白话译文】

白圭说:"我想把税率定为二十抽一,怎么样?"孟子说:"你的主张是貉国的主张。一万户的国家,只有一个人做瓦器,就可以了吗?"回答道:"不可以,瓦器不够用。"孟子说:"貉国,各种谷类作物大都不宜生长,只有黍这种谷物能够生长;又没有城墙、房屋、祖庙和祭祀的礼节;也没有诸侯分治交往、没有币帛之用、没有馈食及宴饮之礼、没有各种衙署和官吏,所以二十抽一就够了。如今在中国,不要社会上一切伦常,不要各种官吏那怎么行呢?想要比尧舜的十分抽一的税率还轻的是大貉、小貉;想要比尧舜的十分抽一的税率还重的是大桀、小桀。"

【英语译文】

Bai Gui said, "I want to set tax rate as one twentieth. How about it?" Mencius said, "Your proposal is that of Mo State. In a state of ten thousand households, only one person makes earthernwares. Is that alright?" Bai Gui said, "It isn't alright because earthernwares are not enough." Mencius said, "In Mo State many grains and crops cannot grow except millet. In the state there aren't city walls, houses, temples and sacrificial rites and rituals. There aren't contact and communication between princes; there aren't use of silk; there aren't rites of cooked food as sacrificial ceremony and those of having dinner, and there aren't various government offices and different ranks of officials. Therefore tax rate of one twentieth is completely enough. Nowadays in the Mid-state how could there be not any ethical relations and any officials? Those who want lighter tax rate than one tenth of Sage Yao and Great Shun are people of Mo State. Those who want heavier tax rate than one tenth of Sage Yao and Great Shun are people of Tyrant Jie's time."

【注释】(1)白圭:战国史周人,名丹。曾任魏惠王大臣。善于修筑堤防,兴修水利。主张减轻田税,征收生产物二十分之一。年代与孟子相值而略少于孟子。(2)二十而取一:谓税率订为二十分之一。(3)貉道:mò~,貉国主张。貉同"貊",北方的一个国名。(4)万室之国:万室,犹万家,万户。一人陶:一个人烧制陶器。(5)五谷不生,惟黍生之:不是各类谷物都能生长只有黍类能够生长。(6)无诸侯币帛饔飧:没有诸侯分治、没有币帛之用、没有馈食及宴饮之礼。(7)有司:官吏。人伦:人间的正常关系。无君子:特指正面官吏。(8)尧舜之道:即"仁道"。

【原文】11 白圭曰:"丹之治水也愈于禹。[1]"孟子曰:"子过矣。[2]禹之治水,水之道也,[3]是故禹以四海为壑。[4]今吾子以邻国。水逆行谓之洚水。洚水者洪水也。[5]仁人之所恶也。吾子过矣。"

【白话译文】

白圭说:"我治水患胜过大禹。"孟子说:"您错了。禹治水患是按水性就低归海疏导的。所以大禹使水流注到四海去。而今您先生却使水流注到邻近的国家去。水上涨甚至泛滥叫作洚水。洚水就是洪水。是有仁爱之心的人所最厌恶的。先生您错了。"

【英语译文】

Bai Gui said, "I am better than Great Yu in regulating rivers and watercourses." Mencius said, "You are wrong. Great Yu regulated rivers by dredging them and led them to flow into seas according to the nature of water. Therefore Great Yu made river water flow into seas. Nowadays you are making river water flow into neighboring states. When water swells it becomes flooding, which is loathed by any person who cherishes humanity. Therefore, Mister, you are wrong."

【注释】(1)愈:胜过。(2)过矣:错了。(3)水之道:就低归海。(4)壑:沟壑,陆上受水处。(5)水逆行:受阻上涨甚至泛滥。(6)吾子:男子间的爱称。可译作:先生您,您先生,我的先生,等等。视场合而定。

【原文】12 孟子曰:"君子不亮[1],恶乎执?[2]"

【白话译文】

孟子说:"君子没有诚信,操守什么?"

【英语译文】

Mencius said, "If a moral man isn't honest, what will he stick to?"

【注释】(1)亮:信,与"谅"同。(2)恶乎:wū ~,亦作"恶虖"。疑问代词。作状语译作"怎么""哪(里)";作宾语、定语,译作"什么"" 哪里"。执:执持,操守。

【原文】13 鲁欲使乐正子为政。[1]孟子曰:"吾闻之,喜而不寐。"公孙丑曰:"乐正子强乎?”曰:“否。”“有知虑乎?[2]”曰:“否。”“多闻识乎?[3]”曰:“否。”“然则奚为喜而不寐?[4]”曰:“其为人也好善。”“好善足乎?”曰:“好善优于天下,而况鲁国乎?[5]夫苟好善,则四海之内皆将轻千里而来告之以善,[6]夫苟不好善,则人将曰,予既已知之矣。[7]” 訑訑之声音颜色距人于千里之外。士止于千里之外,则谗谄面谀之人至矣。[8]与谗谄面谀之人居,国欲治,可得乎?”

【白话译文】

鲁国想叫乐正子执掌国政。孟子说:“我听到这个消息高兴得睡不着。”公孙丑说:“乐正子很坚强吗?”答道:“不。”“有智慧和谋略吗?”答道:“不。”“知识广,学问多吗?”答道:“不。”“那么你为什么高兴得睡不着呢?”答道:“他的为人喜欢听取善言。”“喜欢听取善言就够了吗?”答道:“喜欢听取善言处于整个天下都有余力,何况处于鲁国呢?如果喜欢听取善言,那么四面八方的人就会不远千里赶来把善言告诉他。如果不喜欢听取善言,那么别人会说,‘他洋洋自得的样儿我早已知道。’洋洋自得的声音和脸色拒人于千里之外。士人在千里之外不来,那进谗言、说坏话、毁谤、讨好、当面恭维的人来了。同他们在一起,要把国家治理好,做得到吗?”

【英语译文】

The authority of Lu State wanted Yue Zheng Zi to be in charge of state administrative affairs. Mencius said, “On hearing this news, I cannot fall asleep.” Gongsun Chou asked, “Is Yue Zheng Zi strong?” Mencius replied, “No, he isn’t.” Gongsun Chou asked, “Is he wise and strategic?” Mencius replied, “No, he isn’t.” Gongsun Chou asked, “Is he far-sighted and knowledgeable?” Mencius replied, “No, he isn’t.” Gongsun Chou asked, “Then why can’t you fall asleep?” Mencius replied, “Because he likes listening to good-intended words.” Gongsun Chou asked, “Is it enough to listen to good-intended words?” Mencius said, “Of course, one can govern the whole world if he likes listening to good-intended words, let alone Lu State. If someone likes good-intended words, then people from all places ten thousand *li* away will come to him and tell him their good-intended words without hesitation. If someone doesn’t like good-intended words, then other people will say, ‘I have already known his being pleased with himself.’ Voice and appearance of being pleased with oneself will hinder persons approaching him. Scholars are in the place thousand *li* away and refuse to come near him, then people who love slanderous talk, bad-mouthing others, slandering, currying favors with others, and face to face compliments will spring out. Can you succeed in managing a state together with these men?"

【注释】(1)乐正子:yuè ~ ~,即乐正克。(2)知虑:zhìlǜ,同"智虑",智慧和谋略。(3)闻识:知识,学问。(4)奚为:为何,为什么。奚:xī,疑问词。何,什么。(5)优于天下:谓处于整个天下有余力。优,宽绰,有余力。而况:何况。(6)轻千里:不以千里为远难行。(7)訑訑:yī ~,洋洋自得的样子,沾沾自喜的样子。(8)距:通"拒",拒绝,排斥。谗谄面谀:chánchǎn miànyú,背后说坏话毁谤,当面讨好恭维。

【原文】14 陈子曰:[1]"古之君子何如则仕?"孟子曰:"所就三,所去三。[2]迎之致敬以有礼,[3]则就之;礼貌未衰言弗行也则去之。其次,虽未行其言也,迎之致敬以有礼,则就之;礼貌衰,则去之。其下,朝不食,夕不食,饥饿不能出门户。[4]君闻之曰:'吾大者不能行其道,又不能从其言也,使饥饿于我土地,吾耻之。'周之,亦可受也,[5]免死而已矣。"

【白话译文】

陈子说:"古代的君子要怎样才出来做官?"孟子说:"就官职的情况有三种,离官职的情况也有三种。迎接极其恭敬而有礼物,并说自己能实践的话,便就职。礼貌虽未衰减,说的话未实践,便离职。其次,虽未实践他自己说的话,迎接极其恭敬而有礼貌,便就职。礼貌一天不如一,便离职。第三,早上没饭吃,太阳落山了也没饭吃,饿得不能出门。君主知道了,说:'大节上我没实行他的学说,细节上我没听从他的话,使他在我国土上饿肚皮,我很耻辱。'于是救济他。这也可以接受,免于死亡罢了。"

【英语译文】

Chen Zi asked, "In ancient times, how could a moral man be willing to become an official?" Mencius answered, "There were three types of being an official, and there were also three types of resigning from a post. Firstly, someone was welcomed politely and presented gift; furthermore, he could practice his words. In that case he could accept his post. He could resign when his words couldn't be realized although politeness didn't reduce. Secondly, he would accept his post when his words couldn't be practiced but he was welcomed very politely and presented gift. Politeness reduced day after day and he would resign. Thirdly, he had nothing to eat in the morning , even at sunset he didn't eat anything. And he was too weak to walk out of door due to hunger. After knowing this the monarch said, 'For general aspect I didn't carry out his teachings and for specific details I didn't accept his advice so that he suffered hunger and I am ashamed.' Consequently, the monarch offered relief to him. That could be accepted because he wouldn't die of starvation."

【注释】(1)陈子:陈臻。(2)所就三,所去三:就官职三种情况,离官职三种情况。(3)以有礼:而有礼物。《礼记·表记》:"无礼,不相见也。"郑玄注:"礼,谓挚(贽)也。"孔颖达疏:"礼,谓贽币也。贽币所以示己情,若无贽币之礼不得相见。所以然者,欲民之无相亵渎也。"言将行其言:说能履行其言。将:能。(4)其下:下,谓次序或时间在后。此"其下"当是"第三"。(5)周之:周济他。

【原文】15 孟子曰:"舜发于畎亩之中,[1]傅说举于版筑之间,[2]胶鬲举于鱼盐之中,[3]管夷吾举于士,[4]孙叔敖举于海,[5]百里奚举于市。[6]故天将降大任于斯人也,必先苦其心志,劳其筋骨,饿其体肤,空乏其身,行拂乱其所为,所以动心忍性,[7]曾益其所不能。[8]人恒过,然后能改;困于心,衡于虑,[9]而后作;征于色,发于声,而后喻。[10]入则无法家拂士,出则无敌国外患者,[11]国恒亡。然后知生于忧患而死于安乐也。[12]"

【白话译文】

孟子说:"舜在田野耕作中被提拔起来,傅说在筑墙劳役中被提拔起来,胶鬲从鱼盐商中被提拔起来,管夷吾从狱官手里被提拔起来,孙叔敖从海边被提拔起来,百里奚从市场里被提拔起来。所以上天打算把重大任务落到这个人身上,一定先要使他心志苦闷,使他筋骨劳动,使他躯体挨饿,使他两袖清风、身无半文。让他的行为差错多到位少。这样来振奋他的信心,磨炼他的韧性,把所不能增加为能。一个人常有过失,然后能够改正过失;把在心中的困惑,平息在思考中,而后振作起来;表现于形色上,发散于声音中,而后通晓明白。入朝竟然没有守法度的世臣和足为辅弼的士子,出国竟然没有抗衡的国家和外患,这样,国家总是容易灭亡。如此可知忧愁患害足以使人生存,安逸快乐足以使人死亡。"

【英语译文】

Mencius said, "Great Shun was promoted when he was plowing fields. Fu Yue was promoted when he was building walls. Jiao Ge was promoted when he was selling fish. Guan Zhong (Yiwu) was promoted by a prison officer. Sun Shu'ao was promoted when he lived nearby sea coast. BaiLi Xi was promoted when he labored in a fair. Therefore when the Heaven decides to bestow great mission on someone, the Heaven will make the man depressed, completely exhausted, and suffered starvation. The Heaven will make him possess nothing but his personal belongings. The Heaven will make him do less correct things and make more mistakes. By doing so, the Heaven stirs his confidence and tempers his tenacity, and consequently incapability will change into capability. A man often makes mistakes but can correct them. He clears his confusion and then pulls himself together. He expresses it in his appearance and voice, and then he becomes enlightened. When one is in court there aren't ministers abiding laws and scholars as assistants. When one goes to other state there aren't rivalry state and foreign aggression. In that case a state is easy to perish. From this we know that worries and disasters can make men exist, whereas ease and happiness can make men perish."

【注释】(1)发于畎亩之中:舜曾耕于历山(古山名,其今地所在,说法不一,较著者有七。)畎亩:quǎn mǔ,田地;田野。(2)举于版筑之间:《史记·殷本纪》:"武丁夜梦得圣人,名曰说。以梦所见视群臣百吏,皆非也。于是乃使百工营求之野,得说于傅险中。是时说为胥靡(服劳役的奴隶)筑于傅险。见于武丁,武丁曰:"是也。"得而与之语,果圣人。举以为相,殷国大治。故遂以傅险姓之,号曰傅说。"版筑,古人筑墙,用两版相夹,实土于其中以杵筑之。(3)胶鬲举于鱼盐之中:商周时人,纣时因遭世乱,曾隐遁为商。(4)管夷吾举于士:管夷吾即管仲。"士"为狱官之长。(5)孙叔敖举于海:春秋时楚国期思(今河南淮滨东南)人。蔿氏,名敖字孙叔,一字艾猎。楚庄王时官令尹(宰相)。为政注重法治任用贤能,曾在邲之战中率军大败晋军。又在期思、雩娄(今河南商城东)兴修水利。开凿芍陂(今安徽寿县安丰塘),蓄水灌田。(6)百里奚举于市:见前9.9中【注释】(1)。(7)是人:这人。拂乱:违反其意愿以乱之。动心忍性:振奋信心磨炼韧性。(8)曾:同增。(9)恒过:常有过失。衡于虑:谓通过思考,困惑平息了。衡:平,平息。(10)作:振作,兴起。(11)法家:守法度的世臣。拂士:足为辅弼的士子。拂,同"弼"。(12)国恒亡:国家固定灭亡。恒,固定。

【原文】16 孟子曰:"教亦多术矣,[1]予之教诲也者[2],是亦教诲之而已矣。[3]"

【白话译文】

孟子说："教育方法实在是多呢，我认为不值得的训导嘛，是又一种训导罢了。"

【英语译文】

Mencius said, "There are so many methods to instruct. That I think someone is not deserved instruction is another method to instruct."

【注释】(1)亦：毕竟。术：方法。不屑：认为不值得。(2)教诲：教导，训导。也者：语气助词，用于此表提示。

孟子集注卷十三　尽心章句上　凡四十六章

【原文】1 孟子曰："尽其心者，知其性也。知其性，则知天矣。[1]存其心，养其性，所以事天也。[2]夭寿不贰，修身以俟之，所以立命也。[3]"

【白话译文】

孟子说："尽量发挥善良的本心，这就懂得了人的本性。懂得了人的本性，就懂天意了。保持人的本心，培养人的本性，就是侍奉天命的方法。短命长寿都一样，不三心二意，只是陶冶身心涵养德性，等待天命，这便是修身养性以奉天命了。"

【英语译文】

Mencius said, "If one tries his best to develop rininate conscience, one has known human nature. Once he knows human nature he understands the will of the Heaven. To stick to innale conscience and nurture human nature is to serve the will of the Heaven. Whether living short or living long, one shouldn't be of two minds but cultivate his morality and wait for the mandate of the Heaven. This is cultivating one's moral character to obey the mandate of the Heaven."

【注释】(1)尽心：竭尽心力。(2)所以事天：用来侍奉上天，侍奉上天的方法。(3)立命：谓修身养性以奉天命。

【原文】2 孟子曰:“莫非命也,顺受其正;[1]是故知命者不立乎岩墙之下。[2]尽其道而死者,正命也。[3]桎梏死者,非正命也。[4]”

【白话译文】

孟子说:“人人都有命啦。但是顺理而行,接受正命;所以懂命的人,不站在有倾倒危险的墙壁下。尽力行正路而死的人接受的是正命,犯罪而死的人接受的不是正命。”

【英语译文】

Mencius said, “Everyone has his destiny. But he should behaves according to rites and accepts right destiny. Therefore a man who understands destiny doesn't stand under the dangerous wall. A man who behaves in the right way and dies accepts right destiny but a man who commits crime and dies doesn't accept right destiny.”

【注释】(1)莫非命也:没有谁没有命啦(人人都有)。非:无,没有。顺受其正:顺,指行为顺理。其正,谓命之正,即下文“正命”之义。(2)岩墙:将要倒的墙。(3)正命:行正路而死者的命。

【原文】3 孟子曰:“求则得之,舍则失之,[1]是求有益于得也,[2]求在我者也。[3]求之有道,得之有命,[4]是求无益于得也,求在外者也。[5]

【白话译文】

孟子说:“探求,便会得到,放弃,便会失掉,这是探求有益于获得,是探求存在于自身内的。探求有正路,得到由命运主宰,这是探求无益于获得,是探求存在于自身外的。”

【英语译文】

Mencius said, “You will obtain something if you explore; and you will lose something if you give up. This means that exploration is helpful to attainment and exploration exists inside oneself. Exploration requires the right way and attainment is destined by fate. This means that exploration doesn't benefit attainment and exploration exists outside of oneself.”

【注释】(1)舍:放弃。(2)得:获得。(3)在我者:存在于自身的。(4)有命:由命运主宰。

【原文】4 孟子曰:“万物皆备于我矣。[1]反身而诚,[2]乐莫大焉。[3]强恕而行,[4]求仁莫近焉。”[5]

【白话译文】

孟子说:“天地间的一切都为我们人相对蓄备着,反过来要求自己,自己又是诚实的,便没有更大的快乐了。勉力不懈地按推己及人的恕道做去,达到仁德的道路没有比这更近的了。”

【英语译文】

Mencius said, “All things are bestowed on us. If we demand ourselves and we are honest, there isn't anything more pleasant. If we do things in the way considering others in our own places, there isn't shortcut to reach humanity and virtue.”

【注释】(1)万物皆备于我:万物,统指宇宙间的一切事物。备于我,为我们人相对蓄备着。(2)反身而诚:反过来要求自己(反身自问),又是诚实的。(3)乐莫大焉:没有更大的快乐了。(4)强恕而行:勉力不懈地按推己及人的恕道而行。(5)求仁莫近焉:追求仁德此路最近。

【原文】5 孟子曰:“行之而不着焉,[1]习矣而不察焉,[2]终身由之而不知其道者,[3]众也。[4]”

【白话译文】

孟子说:“干一件事,起初不明白却这样干,习惯了却不清楚如此干的原因或道理。一辈子干这事却不知道到底是什么事的人,多啊。”

【英语译文】

Mencius said, “There are many people who don't understand something but just do it, and don't know the reason after they get accustomed, and keep doing all the lifetime without realize the reasons.”

【注释】(1)著者,知之明。(2)察者,识之精,言方行之而不能明其所当然。(3)终身由之而不知其道者:既习矣而犹不识其所以然,所以终身由之而不知其道者。(4)众也:多啊。

【原文】6 孟子曰:“人不可以无耻[1],无耻之耻,无耻矣。”

【白话译文】

孟子说:“人不可以没有羞耻,没有羞耻的羞耻,不知耻辱啊!”

【英语译文】

Mencius said, “One shouldn’t have no feelings of shame, and one doesn’t feel ashamed if he doesn’t have feelings of shame.”

【注释】(1)耻:羞耻。

【原文】7 孟子曰:“耻之于人大矣,为机变之巧者,[1]无所用耻焉。不耻不若人,[2]何若人有?”

【白话译文】

孟子说:“羞耻对于人关系重大,耍机智权变的人,没有哪里用得上羞耻。不以比不上别人为羞耻,有什么比得上别人?

【英语译文】

Mencius said, “Feelings of shame affect a man greatly. Those who play petty tricks needn’t have feelings of shame. If a man doesn’t feel shameful when he cannot match others, how can he match other people?”

【注释】(1)机变:机智权变。(2)若:及得上,比得上。

【原文】8 孟子曰:“古之贤王好善而忘势;[1]古之贤士何独不然?乐其道而忘人之势,故王公不致敬尽礼,[2]则不得亟见之。[3]见且由不得亟,[4]而况得而臣之乎?[5]”

【白话译文】

孟子说:"古代的贤明君王乐于善言善行,因而淡忘了自己的威权势力;古代的贤士,哪个不是这样? 乐于走他自己的道路,因而淡忘了别人的威权势力;所以王公不对他表示恭敬竭尽礼仪,这就不能够多次和他相见。相见都不够多,何况要他做臣下?"

【英语译文】

Mencius said, "Ancient wise and virtuous monarchs were glad to do kind things and speak kindly so that they forgot their power and post. Ancient virtuous scholars all did like this and they were glad to walk on their own road so that they forgot their power and post. Consequently, dukes and princes didn't show respect to them according to rites and rituals so that they couldn't meet them for many times. They didn't meet them for many times, let alone made them their ministers."

【注释】(1)好善而忘势:乐于善言善行不顾念威势。(2)何独不然:谁不是这样。致敬尽礼:表示恭敬竭尽礼仪。(3)亟见:qì ~ 屡次相见,一再相见。(4)且由:亦作"且犹",尚且。(5)得而臣之:得他作臣。

【原文】9 孟子谓宋勾践曰:[1]"子好游乎?[2]吾语子游。[3]人知之,亦嚣嚣,[4]人不知,亦嚣嚣。"曰:"何如斯可以嚣嚣矣?"曰:"尊德乐义,则可以嚣嚣。故士穷不失义,达不离道。穷不失义,故士得己焉;[5]达不离道,故民不失望焉。古之人得志,泽加于民;不得志,修身见于世。[6]穷则独善其身,达则兼善天下。[7]"

【白话译文】

孟子对宋勾践说:"你喜欢游说吗? 我告诉你如何游说。别人理解也自得其乐,别人不理解也自得其乐。"宋勾践说:"要怎样才能自得其乐呢?"答道:"崇尚德喜爱义,就可以自得其乐了。所以士人穷困时,不丢掉义,显达时,不离开正道。穷困时,不丢掉义,所以自得其乐;显达时,不离开正道,所以百姓不致失望。古代的人,志愿实现,恩泽普施于百姓;志愿未张,修养个人品德表现于世。穷困就独自行善,显达还同天下行善。"

【英语译文】

Mencius said to Song Goujian, "Do you like lobbying? I tell you how to lobby.

You become happy no matter others understand you or not." Song Goujian asked, "How can I become happy myself?" Mencius said, "You can be happy yourself if you worship virtue and like righteousness. Therefore scholars don't give up righteousness when they are in difficult position, and they don't digress from right way when they are illustrious and influential. Do not giving up righteousness when they are in difficult position then they become happy themselves. Do not digressing from right way when they are illustrious and influential, then they don't make common people disappointed. Ancient people showed mercy on common persons when their ambitions were realized. They cultivated their integrity and showed to others when their ambitions weren't realized. When they were in difficult position, they did kind things alone; when they were illustrious and influential, they did kind things together with others."

【注释】(1)谓:对……说;说。宋勾践:姓宋,名勾践。(2)游:游说。指战国时代策士们周游列国,劝说君主采纳其政治主张的一种活动。后泛指劝说别人意见、主张。(3)语子游:告诉你游说。(4)嚣嚣:xiāo ~,自得无欲的样子。(5)得己焉:谓不失己志。俗语谓"不丢志(气)。"(6)修身见于世:见,同"现"。(7)达则兼善天下:达,谓"显达"。兼善天下,言为天下做善事。

【原文】10 孟子曰:"待文王而后者,[1]凡民也。[2]若夫豪杰之士,[3]虽无文王犹兴。"

【白话译文】

孟子说:"要等到文王出来后才奋发的,是一般百姓,至于才能出众的人,纵使没有文王也能奋发起来。"

【英语译文】

Mencius said, "Those who roused themselves after King Wen appeared were ordinary people. If someone was outstanding, he would rouse himself even if there wasn't King Wen."

【注释】(1)兴:感动兴发之意。(2)凡民:一般百姓。(3)若夫:放在句首无上文,和单用一个"夫"字差不多,是语助词,表议论的开始可以去掉不译。有上文,表他转关系,是转折连词,可以译为"至于"。豪杰之士:才能出众的人。

【原文】11 孟子曰:“附之以韩魏之家,[1]如其自视欿然,[2]则过人远矣。”[3]

【白话译文】

孟子说:“用韩、魏两家的财富来增加给他,如果他看得很淡,接受与不接受都一样;这样的人就远远超过一般人了。”

【英语译文】

Mencius said, “When someone was presented wealth of two families of Han and Wei, he neglected it. And he behaved all the same whether he accepted it or not. Such kind of person surely excels ordinary men greatly.”

【注释】(1)附:增益,增加。韩魏之家:韩、魏,春秋时晋六卿中之两家大臣,家财富有。(2)如其:假如,如果。自视:自己看,自己认为。欿然:kǎn ~,不自满之意。(3)过人远矣:远远超过一般人了。

【原文】12 孟子曰:“以佚道使民,[1]虽劳不怨。以生道杀民,[2]虽死不怨杀者。[3]”

【白话译文】

孟子说:“用使百姓安乐之道来使用百姓,百姓虽然劳苦,也不怨恨。用使百姓之生存之道来杀人,那人虽被杀,也不怨恨杀他的人。”

【英语译文】

Mencius said, “If people are employed by way that makes them happy, they won't complain even if they work hard. If a man is killed by way that makes him live, he won't hate the man who had killed him.”

【注释】(1)佚道:yì ~,使百姓安乐之道。(2)生道:使百姓生存之道。

【原文】13 孟子曰:“霸者之民驩虞如也,[1]王者之民皞皞如也。[2]杀之而不怨,利之而不庸,[3]民日迁善而不知为之者。[4]夫君子所过者化,所存者神,上下与天地同流,岂曰小补之哉?[5]”

【白话译文】

孟子说:“霸主的百姓欢喜快乐,圣王的百姓,心情舒畅。杀了他,也不怨恨,给了他好处,也不酬谢。民间天天改过向善,也不知道是谁在作为。圣人经过的地方,人们深受感化,驻步停留的地方,感化更是神秘,上与天下与地之化同运并行。难道是小小的补益吗?”

【英语译文】

Mencius said, “Subjects of a hegemony love pleasure and those of sage king enjoy ease of mind. They won't complain even if they are killed. They won't acknowledge even if they are rewarded. Ordinary men correct errors and tend to kindness each day but they don't know whom is contributed to. Where sages pass people are deeply influenced and where sages stop the influence is more mysterious. The influenced of Heaven and Earth carries on at the same time. Is it a small benefit?”

【注释】(1)驩虞:与欢娱同。如:副词、形容词词尾。和“然”的作用差不多,常常和表声貌情态的词语后面有“……的样子”的意思;现代汉语中没有相应的词,可以去掉不译。(2)皞皞:广大自得的样子。(3)杀之而不怨,利之而不庸:杀他不怨,利他不谢。(4)民日迁善而不知为之者:民众一天天好转不知谁在推动。(5)君子:指君王和圣人。所过者:谓经过的地方。化:感化。所存者:驻足处,停留处。神:谓更神秘。同流:相类似。

【原文】14 孟子曰:“仁言,不如仁声之入人深也。[1]善政,不如善教之得民也。[2]善政,民畏之,善教,民爱之。善政得民财,善教得民心。”

【白话译文】

孟子说:“仁德的言语不及仁德的声誉打动人心那么深。良好的政治不及良好的教化得到民心。良好的政治,百姓畏惧,良好的教化,百姓爱护。良好的政治,得民财,良好的教化,得民心。”

【英语译文】

Mencius said, “Humanistic and virtuous words impress men less than humanistic and virtuous reputation. Good politics is less popular than good education. People fear good politics and they protect good education. Good politics obtains wealth from common people and good education obtain their support."

【注释】(1)仁言:朱熹集注,"程子曰,'仁言,谓以仁厚之言加于民。仁声,谓仁闻,谓有仁之实而为众所称颂者也。此尤见仁德之昭著,故其感人尤深也。'"人人:打动人,为人所感受、理解。(2)善政:政,谓法度禁令,所以制其外也。教,谓道德齐礼,所以格其心也。

【原文】

孟子曰:"人之所不学而能者,其良能也;[1]所不虑而知者,其良知也。[2]孩提之童,无不知爱其亲者,[3]及其长也,无不知敬其兄也。亲亲,仁也;敬长,义也;无他,达之天下也。[4]"

【白话译文】

孟子说:"人所不等学习便会的能力是天赋的良能;不等思考便知道,是良知,是人类先天具有的道德意识。两三岁的小孩儿,没有不爱他父母的,等到他长大,没有不恭敬兄长的。亲爱父母是仁,恭敬兄长是义。没有别的原因,因为仁、义两种品德可以通行天下。"

【英语译文】

Mencius said, "The ability without learning is bestowed by the heaven, and the knowledge without thinking is conscience and inborn moral awareness. Kids of two or three years old all love their parents and when they grow up, they all respect their elder brothers. Loving one's parents is humanity and respecting one's elder brothers is righteousness. There isn't any reason for that. It is just because these two can pass through the land under the heaven."

【注释】(1)其良能也:其,副词,表论断。良能,天赋之能。(2)良知:人类先天具有的道德意识。(3)孩提之童:两三岁之间的幼童。孩提,谓小儿笑父母提抱中的样子。(4)亲亲:爱父母。达之天下:通行天下。

【原文】16 孟子曰:"舜之居深山之中,与木石居,与鹿豕游,其所以异于深山之野人者几希;[1]及其闻一善言[2],见一善行,若决江河,沛然莫之能御也。[3]"

【白话译文】

孟子说:"舜住在深山中时,与石头树木为邻居,和鹿子野猪同游。跟山野一般人不同之处很少。到他在大位上时,听到一句好言语,看到一个好行为,就如江河决口了一样急速,谁也不能延缓他采纳。"

【英语译文】

Mencius said, "When Great Shun lived in big mountains his neighbors are rocks and trees and he walked together with deers and wild pigs. At that time he wasn't different from ordinary men. As he was empowered nobody could hinder him from adopting constructive suggestions after he noticed good-doings or heard good words. He did this rapidly just like rivers burst."

【注释】(1)野人:上古指居国城郊野之人。与"国人"相对。(2)及其闻一善言:到他在大位上时,听到一句好言语。(3)沛然莫之能御:疾速采纳谁也阻挡不了。

【原文】17 孟子曰:"无为其所不为,无欲其所不欲,如此而已矣。"[1]

【白话译文】

孟子说:"不做自己所不愿做的事,不要自己所不想要的东西,这就行了。"

【英语译文】

Mencius said, "One shouldn't do things that he isn't willing to do, and shouldn't obtain things that he doesn't want. It is all right."

【注释】(1)朱熹集注:"李氏曰:'有所不为不欲,人皆有是心也。至于私意一萌,而不能以礼义制之,则为所不为、欲所不欲者多矣。能反是心,则所谓扩充其羞恶之心者而义不可胜用矣,故曰如此而已矣。'"

【原文】18 孟子曰:"人之有德慧术知者,[1]恒存乎疢疾,[2]独孤臣孽子,[3]其操心也危,[4]其虑患也深,故达。[5]"

【白话译文】

孟子说:"人之有德行、智慧、道术、知识的,经常存在忧患感。只有孤立之臣和庶子他们时常担心危险，思考忧患很深，所以通达。”

【英语译文】

Mencius said, “Men with morality, wisdom, way and wit usually have sense of urgency. Only the isolated ministers and concubine children worry about dangers and think deeply, therefore they are reasonable.”

【注释】(1)德慧术知：赵岐注：“德行、知慧、道术、才智”。(2)疢疾：chèn～，忧患。(3)孤臣：孤立无助或不受重用的远臣。孽子：niè～，亦作“孼子”，庶子，非正妻所生之子，地位卑贱。(5)达：通达事理。

【原文】19 孟子曰：“有事君人者，[1]事是君则为容悦者也；[2]有安社稷臣者，[3]以安社稷为悦者也；有天民者，[4]达可行于天下而后行之者也；[5]有大人者，正己而后物正者也。[6]”

【白话译文】

孟子说：“有侍奉君主的人，那是侍奉一个君主就曲意顺从，迎合讨喜欢的人；有安定国家为臣的人，那是以安定国家为乐的人；有全尽天理的天民，那是道可行于天下然后行之的人；有圣人，那是端正了自己，便随着端正外物的人。”

【英语译文】

Mencius said, “If there is a person who serves monarch, he must be a man who flatters and pleases the monarch against his will; if there is a minister who tranquilizes the state, he must be a man who is satisfied with tranquility of state; if there are heavenly subjects who know heavenly principles, they must be men who carry out the Way in the world when the Way can be carried out; if there is sage, he must be a man who correct himself and then correct others.”

【注释】(1)君人：义同人君，君主。(2)容悦：谓曲意奉迎，以取悦于上。(3)安社稷臣者：为臣而安定国家的人。(4)天民：全尽天理，作天之民。(5)达：畅通。(6)正己而后物正：先正己而后正物。

【原文】20 孟子曰：“君子有三乐，而王天下不与存焉。[1]父母俱存，兄弟无故，[2]

一乐也;仰不愧于天,俯不怍于人,[3]二乐也;得天下英才而教育之,[4]三乐也。君子有三乐,而王天下不与存焉。”

【白话译文】

孟子说:“君子有三种乐趣,但天下之乐不在其中。父母都健在,兄弟没有灾患,是第一种乐趣;抬头对天没有惭愧,低头对人没有惭愧,是第二种乐趣;得到天下优秀人才而对他们进行教育,是第三种乐趣。君子有三种乐趣,但天下之乐不在其中。”

【英语译文】

Mencius said, “A moral man has three kinds of happiness but he isn’t happy at the world. His parents are alive and his brothers don’t have disasters. This is his first happiness. He isn’t ashamed towards the Heaven and he isn’t ashamed towards other people, either. This is his second happiness. He gets talents from everywhere and educates them. This is his third happiness. A moral man has three kinds of happiness but he isn’t happy at the world. ”

【注释】(1)而王天下不与存焉:赵岐注,“天下之乐。不得与此三乐之中。”与存(yùcún),参与其间。(2)无故:没有事故,没有灾患。(3)怍:zuò,羞惭。(4)英才:杰出的才智。

【原文】21 孟子曰:“广土众民,君子欲之,所乐不存焉;[1]中天下而立,定四海之民,君子乐之,所性不存焉。[2]君子所性,虽大行不加焉,虽穷居不损焉,分定故也。[3]君子所性,仁义礼智根于心,[4]其生色也睟然。见于面,盎于背,施于四体,四体不言而喻。[5]”

【白话译文】

孟子说:“广大的土地,众多的人民,君子想要,但乐趣不在此。居于天下中心,安定四海人民,君子乐于这样,但本性不在此。君子的本性,纵使他的理想广为推行也不因此而增,纵使穷困隐居也不因此而减。这是本分已固定的缘故。君子的本性,仁义礼智植根于心,那显现的外表嘛,清和润泽现于脸,洋溢于背,散布于四肢。四肢不用说就明白。”

【英语译文】

Mencius said, "A moral man desires for spacious land and masses but his happiness doesn't lie in these. A moral man is happy to live in the center of the world and to calm people down but his original nature doesn't lie in these. A moral man's original nature doesn't increase even if his ideal has been spread or his original nature doesn't decrease even if he lives as a hermit due to difficult position. This is because his role has been fossilized. A moral man's original nature is humanity, righteousness, rites and wisdom which have been rooted in his mind. Clearness, harmony, and smoothness appear in his face, dwell in his back and spread his four limbs. Four limbs feel these without words."

【注释】(1)所乐不存焉:乐趣不在此。存,在。焉,此。(2)中天下而立:居于天下中心。所性不存焉:本性不在此。(3)大行:广为推行,普遍流行。穷居:谓隐居不仕。分定故也:fèn ~ ~ ~,本分所定的缘故。(4)根于心:植根于心。(5)其生色也:那显现的外表嘛。睟然:cuì ~,清和润泽的样子。见于面:现于脸。盎于背:洋溢于背。施于四体:散布于四肢。施,散布,铺开。不言而喻:不用说就明白。

【原文】22 孟子曰:"伯益辟纣,居北海之滨。[1]闻文王作兴,曰:[2]'盍归乎来!,吾闻西伯善养老者。[3]'太公辟纣,居东海之滨。闻文王作兴,曰:'盍归乎来!吾闻西伯善养老者。'天下有善养老,则仁人以为己归矣。[4]五亩之宅,树墙下以桑,匹妇蚕之,[5]则老者足以衣帛矣。五母鸡,二母彘,无失其时,老者足以无失肉矣。[6]百亩之田,匹夫耕之,八口之家足以无饥矣。所谓西伯善养老者,制其田里,教之树畜,导其妻子,使养其老。五十非帛不暖,七十非肉不饱,不暖不饱,谓之冻馁。[7]文王之民无冻馁之老者,此之谓也。[8]"

【白话译文】

孟子说:"伯益避开纣王,住在北海的边上,听说文王兴起来了,兴奋地说'何不回去吧!我听说西伯善养年老的人。'姜太公避开纣王,住在东海的边上,"听说文王兴起来了,兴奋地说'何不回去吧!我听说西伯善养年老的人.'天下有人善养年老的人,那么行仁德的人便认为他是自己可靠的人了。五亩大小的里(乡村聚居地),在围墙下栽种桑树,一个妇女养蚕,那么老人能够穿较厚的丝织物了。五只母鸡,二只母猪,顺时饲养,使它们繁殖,老人能够不缺肉食了。百亩之田,男人去耕种,八口之家,能够告别饥饿了。所谓西伯善养年老的人,就是规定了土地制度,教育人民栽种畜牧,引导他们的妻子儿女奉养老人。五十岁的人不穿厚丝织物不暖和,七十岁的人不吃肉不饱。穿不暖,吃不饱,叫作受冻挨饿。文王的百姓没有受冻挨饿的老人,就是这个意思。”

【英语译文】

Mencius said, “Bo Yi dodged King Zhou of Shang Dynasty and lived nearby the North Sea. When he heard King Wen of Zhou Dynasty had risen, he said happily, ‘Why not go back? I hear that King Wen kindly supports the elders.’ Jiang Shang dodged King Zhou of Shang Dynasty and lived nearby the East Sea. When he heard King Wen of Zhou Dynasty had risen he said happily, ‘Why not go back? I hear that King Wen kindly supports the elders.’ If there is man who kindly supports the elders, then people who carry out humanity and virtue think that he is the most reliable man. In settlement of five *mu* area, mulberry trees are planted, and one woman raises silkworms, and then the elders can wear thick silk clothes. Five hens and two swines are raised according to the season and they reproduce so that the elders can eat chicken and meat. Men plow field of one hundred *mu* and a family of eight persons will say goodbye to famine. That King Wen kindly supports the elders means that he stipulates that mulberry trees are planted and livestock are raised, and instruct men's wives and kids support the elders. People of fifty years old don't feel warm if they haven't worn thick silk clothes, and people of seventy years old aren't full if they haven't eaten meat. If one doesn't feel full and warm, he is suffering hunger and famine. The elder people of King Wen didn't suffer hunger and famine. That is the case.”

【注释】(1)辟:同“避”。(2)作兴:zuò xīng,兴起。(3)盍归乎来:何不回归呀,盍,何不。归,返回。乎、来,都是助词。西伯:即周文王,因为他曾受纣王命为西方诸侯之长故称。(4)以为己归矣:认定为自己的意向所归。(5)五亩之宅:五亩大小的里(乡村聚居地)。

【原文】23 孟子曰:“易其田畴[1],薄其税敛,[2]民可使富也。食之以时,用之以礼,[3]财不可胜用也。民非水火不生活,昏暮叩人之门户求水火,无弗与者,至足矣。[4]圣人治天下,使有菽粟如水火。[5]菽粟如水火。而民焉有不仁者乎?”

【白话译文】

孟子说："整治农田，减轻税收，可使百姓富足。耕种按时，费用按礼，财物是用不尽的。百姓没有水、火便活不下去，黄昏敲别人的门讨水火，没有不给与的，由于水火极多啦。圣人治理天下，要使粮食像水火那么多。粮食像水火那么多了，哪有百姓不仁爱的呢？"

【英语译文】

Mencius said, "It can make people wealthy to renovate farmland and reduce tax. Wealth cannot run off if farming is seasonable and fee is ritual. Without water and fire people cannot live. At dusk someone knocks at neighbors' doors for water and fire, he can get them because other people have already owned water and fire. Sages administrate the world to make grains as plenty as water and fire are. If grains are as plenty as water and fire are, why don't people love humanity?"

【注释】(1)易其田畴：易，整治。田，泛言耕种用的土地。畴，已耕作的田地，也指良田。(2)薄其税敛：减轻税收。敛，征收，索取。(3)食之以时：耕种按时。食，耕种。《周礼·地官·遂师》："经牧其田野，辨其可食者。"郑玄注："可食，谓今年所当耕者也。"《礼记·檀弓上》："我死则择不食之地而葬我焉。"郑玄注："不食，谓不垦耕也。"用之以礼：费用按礼。(4)昏暮：黄昏，傍晚。至足矣：最多了。矣，语气助词。用在陈述句末表行为的已然，将然或必然，和"也"差不多，可译作"了""啦"。(5)菽粟：shūsù，豆和小米 。泛指粮食 。

【原文】24 孟子曰："孔子登东山而小鲁，登泰山而小天下，[1]故观于海者难为水，[2]游于圣人之门者难为言。[3]观水有术，必观其澜。日月有明，容光必照焉。流水之为物也，不盈科不行；[4]君子之志于道也，不成章不达。[5]"

【白话译文】

孟子说："孔子上了东山，便觉得鲁国实在是小；上了泰山，便觉得天下也小；所以看过海洋的人，就轻视不如海洋的水面；曾在圣人之门学习过的人，就轻视别的言论。看水有方法，一定要看大波浪。太阳月亮都有光亮，一点儿细微的缝隙都一定照到。流水这东西不充满地面凹陷处不再往前流；君子的立志于道，没有发展的形象表现，也就不能达到目的。"

【英语译文】

Mencius said, "Confucius ascended the East Mountain and thought Lu State was really small. He also thought the world was small, too, after he ascended Taishan Mountain. Therefore a man who has seen a sea surface is in contempt of narrower surface. A man who ever learned under guidance of sages is in contempt of other's words. There is certain method to observe water and we should observe big waves. The sun and the moon shine bright and they can shine each crack. Flowing water doesn't move on until it fills pits on the ground. A moral man who sticks to the Way cannot reach his goal if there isn't developing sign."

【注释】(1)孔子登东山而小鲁:东山,当即蒙山,在今山东蒙阴县南。是山东第二高山。小,认为小;轻视。(2)难为水:轻视小于海的水面。难为,谓使人困窘,使人为难;轻视,糟蹋。(3) 游于圣人之门者难为言:在圣人们中学习过的人轻视一般言论。(4)有术:有方法。澜:lán,大波浪。明:指日月的光亮。容光:细微的缝隙。盈科:充满地面凹陷处。科,同"坎""坑"。(5)志于道:立志于道。不成章:没有发展的形象表现。章,事物发展的步骤所显露的形象、规模。达:达到目的。

【原文】25 孟子曰:"鸡鸣而起,孳孳为善者,[1]舜之徒也。鸡鸣而起,孳孳为利者,跖之徒也。[2]欲知舜与跖之分,无他,利与善之间也。[3]"

【白话译文】

孟子说:"鸡叫就起床,努力行善的人,是舜一类人物;鸡叫就起床,努力求利的人,是跖一类人物。要晓得舜和跖的分别,没有别的,求利和行善不同道。"

【英语译文】

Mencius said, "Men who got up upon roosters crowing and tried hard to show mercy belong to Sage Shun. Men who got up upon roosters crowing and tried hard to search for benefit belong to thief Zhi. If you want to differentiate Shun from Zhi, you just pay attention that searching for benefit and showing mercy aren't on the same Way."

【注释】(1)孳孳:zī~,同"孜孜"。勤勉;努力不懈。(2)跖:zhí,亦作"蹠",相传为柳下惠的弟弟,春秋时的大盗。(3)间:jiàn,差别,距离。

【原文】26 孟子曰:“杨子取为我[1],拔一毛以利天下,不为也。墨子兼爱,[2]摩顶放踵利天下,为之。[3]子莫执中。[4]执中为近之,执中无权,犹执一也。[5]所恶执一者,为其贼道也,举一而废百也。[6]”

【白话译文】

孟子说:“杨子趋向为己,拔一根汗毛来使天下人得利,都不肯干。墨子主张兼爱,从头顶到脚跟都磨伤,不辞辛苦,舍己为人。子莫在这两人之间走中间道路,叫作执中。其实是近路。如果不能掌握灵活性,就是拘泥于一点。为什么厌恶拘泥于一点呢?因为它为害仁义之道,拿一端废百端。”

【英语译文】

Mencius said, “Yang Zhu benefited himself and he refused to benefit other people even if a hair was picked out of him. Mo Zi advocated universal love and he didn't fear hardship but sacrificed himself for others and was hurt in whole body from head to heel. Zi Mo chose middle way between these two, which was called impartiality. In fact, impartiality is shortcut. If one doesn't master flexibility, he will stick to one point. Why do we hate sticking to one point? Because it does harm to the Way of humanity and righteousness and it destroys one hundred aspects by means of one aspect.”

【注释】(1)杨子:指杨朱,战国初哲学家,先秦古书中又称他为阳子居或阳生。魏国人相传他反对墨子的兼爱和儒家的伦理思想,主张“贵生”“重己”,“全性葆真,不以物累形。”重视个人生命的保存,反对别人对自己的侵夺,也反对侵夺别人。为我:为己。取:qū,通“趋”。趋向。一解“主张”,也通。(2)墨子:名翟(约公元前468年——公元前376年)。春秋战国之际思想家、政治家、墨家的创始人。相传原为宋国人,后长期住在鲁国,曾学习儒术,因不满烦琐的“礼”,另立新说,聚徒讲学,成为儒家的主要反对派。兼爱:墨子主张爱无差别等级,不分厚薄亲疏。(3)摩顶放踵:módǐngfǎng zhǒng,从头顶到脚跟都磨伤。形容不辞辛苦,舍己为人。(4)子莫:鲁之贤人。他知道杨墨之失中,故度于二者之间而执其中。(5)近:近路。权:秤锤。(6)所恶执一者:厌恶执一的原因。贼:害,伤害。

【原文】27 孟子曰:“饥者甘食,渴者甘饮,是未得饮食之正也,饥渴害之也。[1]岂惟口腹有饥渴之害?人心亦皆有害。人能无以饥渴之害为心害,则不及人不为忧矣。”

【白话译文】

孟子说:"饥饿的人总觉得食物甜美好吃,干渴的人总觉得饮水甘甜好喝。这是由于他没尝到所吃所喝的正常味道,因为他的口腹遭受了饥饿干渴的打击而疲惫了。难道只是口腹才有饥渴的损害?人心也都有受害的情况。如果人能做到预防自己的心遭受饥渴那样的打击,就不会以赶不上别人而忧虑了。"

【英语译文】

Mencius said, "A hungry man always feels his food delicious and a thirsty man always feels his drink sweet. This is because he doesn't taste his food and drink normally and his mouth and stomach are tired for hunger and thirst. Are mouth and stomach only harmed by hunger and thirst? Men's mind can also be harmed. If one manages to prevent harm which is the same as that of hunger and thirst, he won't be worried about that he can't catch up with others."

【注释】(1)饥渴害之也:饥渴损伤了口腹的正常运作功能。

【原文】28 孟子曰:"柳下惠[1]不以三公易其介[2]。"

【白话译文】

孟子说:"柳下惠不因多次被贬降而改变对祖国的情谊。"

【英语译文】

Mencius said, "Liu Xiahui didn't change his passion for his motherland due to demoted thrice."

【注释】(1)柳下惠:春秋鲁大夫展获,字季,又字禽,曾为士师官,食邑柳下,谥惠,故称其为展禽、柳下季、柳士师、柳下惠等。以柳下惠之最为著名。《论语·微子》:"柳下惠为士师,三黜(三次被贬降)人曰:'直道而事人焉往而不三黜?枉道而事人,何必去父母之邦?'"(2)介:朱熹注,"介,有分辨之意。柳下惠,进不隐贤,必以其道遗佚不怨,厄穷不悯,直道事人,至于三黜,是其介也,此章言柳下惠和而不流,与孔子论夷齐不念旧恶正相类,皆圣贤微显阐幽之意也。"

【原文】29 孟子曰:"有为者辟若掘井[1],掘井九轫而不及泉[2],犹为弃井也。[3]"

【白话译文】

孟子说:"做一件事譬若挖井,挖到七八丈深却不见泉水,还是一眼废井。"

【英语译文】

Mencius said, "Doing one thing is like digging a well. It is an abandoned one if it's dug to seven or eight *zhang* deep but no springwater comes out."

【注释】(1)有为者:犹"作为"。指学习、工作、搞事业等。辟若:同譬若。(2)轫:通"仞"。八尺为仞。(3)弃:废,废除。

【原文】30 孟子曰:"尧舜,性之也;[1] 汤武,身之也;[2] 五霸,假之也。[3] 久假而不归,恶知其非有也[4]。"

【白话译文】

孟子说:"尧舜实行仁义政治是出于本性,彻底自然没有做作。商汤和周武王行仁义是修身自励推行;五霸行政是假借仁义而谋权夺利。长久假借不还,民众怎么知道他们没有仁义?"

【英语译文】

Mencius said, "Sage Yao and Great Shun carried out government of humanity out of their nature without any affectation. King Tang of Shang Dynasty and King Wu of Zhou Dynasty carried out humanity and righteousness due to their moral cultivation. The Five Hegemonys carried out government to search for right and benefit with the excuse of humanity and righteousness. They didn't return the excuse for a long time. How could masses know whether they were humanistic and righteous or not?"

【注释】(1)性之也:本性的作用。(2)身之也:修身的作用。(3)假之也:假借的作用。(4)归:还原。恶:wū,怎么。非有:没有(仁义),不存在(仁义)。

【原文】31 公孙丑曰:"伊尹曰:'予不狎于不顺,[1] 放太甲于桐,[2] 民大悦。太甲贤,又反之,[3] 民大悦。'贤者之为人臣也,其君不贤,则固可放与?[4]"孟子曰:"有伊尹之志,则可;无伊尹之志,篡也。[5]"

【白话译文】

公孙丑说:"伊尹曾经说过'我不亲近不顺义理的人,于是把太甲放逐到桐邑,百姓大为高兴。太甲变好了,又让他返回大位,百姓又大为高兴。'贤人作为臣下,君王不好有过失,原来可以把他放逐吗?"孟子说:"有伊尹公天下的态度,就可以;没有伊尹公天下的态度,就是臣子夺取君位。"

【英语译文】

Gongsun Chou said, "Yi Yin ever said 'I didn't get intimate with men who weren't righteous so that I had exiled Tai Jia to Tongyi. Common people got excited. After Tai Jia changed for good he was reinstated so that common people also got excited.' When virtuous men are ministers but their monarch wasn't virtuous and made mistakes, could they exile him?" Mencius said, "They could do so if they take the attitude of Yi Yin's regarding the land under heaven as the public's. They usurped the throne if they don't take the attitude of Yi Yin's regarding the land under heaven as the public's."

【注释】(1)不狎于不顺:狎,xiá,接近;亲近。不顺,这里是说太甲不顺义理。(2)放太甲于桐:事见《万章上》第六章。放,放逐。(3)又反之:又返回他的大位。(4)与:yú,同"欤"。用在是非问句或反问句末表疑问语气。译为"吗""么"。(5)伊尹之志:朱熹注,"伊尹之志,公天下以为心而无一毫之私者也。"篡:cuàn,用强力夺取,特指臣子夺取君位。

【原文】32 公孙丑曰:"《诗》曰:'不素餐兮'[1],君子之不耕而食,何也?"孟子曰:"君子居是国也,其君用之,则安富尊荣;[2]其子弟从之,则孝悌忠信。'不素餐兮',孰大于是?"

【白话译文】

公孙丑说:"《诗经》说:'不是不劳而食啊!'可是君子不种庄稼也来吃饭,这是为什么呢?"孟子说:"居住在一个国家,君王用他,就会平安、富有、光荣;少年子弟信从他,进而孝顺父母、重兄长、忠实、守信。'不白吃饭'同这些效应相比哪个更好?"

【英语译文】

Gongsun Chou said, "*The Book of Songs* said 'Aren't you eaters without toiling!'

But why did moral men come to eat a meal when they didn't grow crops?" Mencius answered, "He would be peaceful, wealthy and glorious when he lived in a state where the monarch employed him? The youth and kids followed him and became filial to their parents, respected their elder brothers, and were honest and faithful. 'Being eaters without toiling' and these effects, which is more important?"

【注释】(1)素餐:不劳而食,无功而食,无功受禄。语出《诗经·魏风·伐檀》。

【原文】33 王子垫问曰:[1]"士何事?"孟子曰:"尚志"[2]。曰:"何谓尚志?"曰:"仁义而已矣,杀一无罪非仁也。非其有而取之,非义也。居恶在?仁是也。路恶在?义是也。居仁由义,大人之事备矣。"

【白话译文】

王子垫问道:"士做什么事?"孟子答道:"要使自己的志气行为高尚。"又问道:"怎样才算自己的志气行为高尚?"答道:"实行仁义罢了。杀一个无罪的人,是不仁;不是自己所有,却把它揽取了,是不义。他住在哪里呢?仁那里;他走在哪里呢?义那里。住在仁的屋子里,走在义的大路上,就够格做一个大写的人了。"

【英语译文】

Wang Zidian asked, "What should a scholar do?" Mencius said, "He should make his ambition and action become respectable." Wang Zidian asked again, "How can one make his ambition and action become respectable?" Mencius answered, "Just carry out humanity and righteousness. It isn't humanistic to kill a man without crime. It isn't righteous for a man to obtain what doesn't belong to him. Where does he live? It's humanity. Where does he walk? It's righteousness. Living in the house of humanity and walking on the road of righteousness can make a real Man."

【注释】(1)王子垫:赵岐注,"齐王子,名垫也。"(2)尚志:高尚其志;崇尚志节。

【原文】34 孟子曰:"仲子,不义与之齐国而弗受,[1]人皆信之,是舍箪食豆羹之义也。[2]人莫大焉亡亲戚君臣上下。以其小者信其大者,[3]奚可哉?[4]"

【白话译文】

孟子说:“陈仲子,假定不合理地把齐国交给他,那么他不会接受,别人都相信他。他那种义是放弃一筐饭一碗汤的义。人的不义没有比不要父兄君臣尊卑还大的,而因为他有小节操,就相信他的大节操,如何可以呢?”

【英语译文】

Mencius said, “If Qi State was passed unreasonably to Chen Zhongzi he wouldn’t take it over. Others would believe him. His righteousness was one of giving up one basket of rice and a bowl of soup. There isn’t anything more unrighteous than neglecting the grade of his father, his elder brothers, his monarch and ministers. How can we believe his great moral integrity since he has little integrity?”

【注释】(1)仲子:即陈仲子。详《滕文公下》第十章。而弗受:而,承接连词。和“则”相同,在承认前面所说事实或所假定的情况下接过来申说其相应的结果。译为“那么”。(2)箪食豆羹:一筐饭一碗汤。(3)人莫大焉亡亲戚君臣上下:焉,介词,犹“于”。亡,同无。仲子避兄离母,耻其兄为齐卿,故孟子大不以为然,说他无亲戚君臣上下。(4)奚:疑问词,犹何。

【原文】35 桃应问曰:[1]“舜为天子,皋陶为士,瞽瞍杀人,则如之何?”孟子曰:“执之而已矣。”“然则舜不禁与?”曰:“夫舜恶得而禁之?夫有所受之也。[2]”“然则舜如之何?”曰:“舜视弃天下犹弃敝蹝也。[3]窃负而逃,遵海滨而处,终身欣然,乐而忘天下。[4]”

【白话译文】

桃应问道:“舜当天子,皋陶当法官,假如瞽瞍杀了人,那怎么办?”孟子说:“把他逮捕起来罢了。”“那么,舜不阻止吗?”孟子答道:“舜怎么能阻止呢?皋陶之法,有所传授,天子也不例外。”“那么,舜该怎么办呢?”答道:“舜把抛弃天子之位看成抛弃破草鞋一样。偷偷背着父亲逃走,沿着海边住下,一辈子快乐,不想天下。”

【英语译文】

Tao Ying asked, “Great Shun was the Son of the Heaven. Gao Yao was a judge. Suppose Gu Shou killed a man, what should they do?” Mencius answered, “Just arrest him.” Tao Ying asked, “Then, couldn’t Great Shun hinder them?” Mencius answered, "How could he hinder them? The Gao Yao's Law had been inherited. Even the Son of the Heaven should not be an exception." Tao Ying asked, "Then what should Great Shun do?" Mencius answered, "Great Shun regarded giving up the post of the Son of the Heaven as giving up torn grass-shoes. He would stealthily flee away with his father, and he would live nearby the sea. Then he would be happy for lifetime without thinking about the land under the heaven."

【注释】(1)桃应:孟子弟子。(2)夫有所受之也:夫,代词,他(指皋陶)。有所受之:朱熹注,"言皋陶之法,有所传受,非所敢私,虽天子之命亦不得而废之也。"(3)敝蹝:bìxǐ,亦作"敝躧",破烂的草鞋。(4)窃负:偷偷地背起。欣:同"欣"。

【原文】36 孟子自范之齐,[1]望见齐王之子,喟然叹曰:"居移气,养移体,大哉居乎!夫非尽人之子与?[2]"孟子曰:"王子宫室、车马、衣服多与人同,而王子若彼者,其居使之然也,况居天下之广居者乎?[3]鲁君之宋,呼于垤泽之门。[4]守者曰:'此非吾君也,何其声之似我君也?此无他,居相似也。"

【白话译文】

孟子从范邑到齐都,在较远处望见了齐王的儿子,感叹地说:"居处的地位改变人的气质,奉养改变人的形貌。居处的地位真正重要啊!他难道不也是人的儿子吗?"又说:"王子的住所、车马、衣服多半和别人相同,为什么他现在是那样呢?是他居处的地位促成的;何况以仁为居处地位的人呢?鲁国君主到宋国去,在宋国的东南城门下呼喊,守门的说:'这不是我们的君主呀,为什么他的声音像我们的君主呢?'这没有别的缘故,居处的地位相似罢了。"

【英语译文】

Mencius set off his journey at the place of Fan and reached the capital of Qi State. On seeing the son of King of Qi State he sighed, "Dwelling place can change one's disposition, and wealth can change one's appearance. Dwelling place is really important. Isn't he an ordinary man's son?" He said once more, "The prince's dwelling place, carriages, horses and clothes are the same as others'. Why does he look like that? It is his dwelling place that has contributed to it. Let alone a man who regards humanity as his dwelling place? The Monarch of Lu State went to Song State and shouted under the southeast city gate. The doorkeepers said, "This isn't our monarch. But why does his voice sound like that of ours?' There isn't other reason for it but the dwelling place is the same."

【注释】(1)自范之齐:范,齐邑。故城在今山东范县东南二十里为从梁(魏)到齐的要道。(2)喟然:kuì ~,感叹、叹息的样子。居移气:居处的地位改变人的气质。居,谓所养处之位。养移体:奉养改变人的形貌(容貌,风度)。夫非尽人之子与:夫,他。非,不合,不同。尽人,人人,所有的人。(3)广居:指仁。见《滕文公下》第二章。(4)泽之门:宋东城南门。垤,dié。

【原文】37 孟子曰:"食而弗爱,豕交之也;爱而不敬,兽畜之也。[1]恭敬者,币之未将者也。[2]恭敬而无实,君子不可虚拘。[3]"

【白话译文】

孟子说:"养活他却不爱怜他,等于养猪;爱怜他,却不恭敬他,等于养狗马。恭敬的心情是在致送礼物前早就具有的。只有恭敬的外表没有恭敬的真实心情,君子不可被这种虚假的礼仪所笼络。"

【英语译文】

Mencius said, "Supporting him but not loving him equalizes raising pigs. Loving him but not respecting him equalizes raising dogs and horses. Before one presents gift to somebody else he should have feeling of respect. If a man only has respecting appearance but no really respecting mind, a moral man shall not be seduced by the fault rites and rituals."

【注释】(1)食:sì,拿东西给人吃。交:接。兽:指犬马之类。畜:养。(2)将:奉,送。(3)无实:不真实。虚拘:以虚假的礼仪笼络人。

【原文】38 孟子曰:"形色天性也;惟圣人然后可以践形。[1]"

【白话译文】

孟子说:"人的身体容貌是天然生成的;只有圣人才能体现天赋的质量。"

【英语译文】

Mencius said, "Man's body and appearance are inborn. Only sages can embody quality endowed by Heaven."

【注释】(1)践形:体现人所天赋的品质。

【原文】39 齐宣王欲短丧。公孙丑曰:"为期之丧,犹愈于已乎?[1]"孟子曰:"是犹或紾其兄之臂,子谓之姑徐徐云尔,亦教之孝悌而已矣。[2]王子有其母死者,其傅为之请数月之丧。公孙丑曰:"若此者何如也?[3]"曰:"是欲终止而不可得也。虽加一日愈于已,谓夫莫之禁而弗为者也。[4]"

【白话译文】

齐宣王想要缩短守丧的时间。公孙丑说:"三年丧改为守孝一年,不是也比完全不守孝好些吗?"孟子说:"这就像有一个人在扭他哥哥的胳膊,你却对他说,暂且慢慢地扭吧。不要紧,只是教导他孝父母敬兄长便行了。"王子中有个最近死了生母的,他的师傅为他请求守孝几个月。公孙丑问道:"像这样的怎么样?"孟子答道:"这个是由于王子想要把三年丧期守满而办不到的后续,那么,我说纵使多守孝一天也比不守孝好,是对那些没有人阻止守孝而是自己不去守孝的人说的。"

【英语译文】

King Xuan of Qi State wanted to shorten the duration of mourning for one's parect. Gongsun Chou said, "Three years' observing for one's parent is shortened for one year. Isn't it alright?" Mencius said, "It is the same as that one is twisting his elder brother's arm, and you say 'You may twist it slowly.' It doesn't matter. You need only educate them to be filial to his parents and to respect his elder brothers." One prince's birth mother recently died and his master requested for several months' mourning. Gongsun Chou asked, "What do you think about this?" Mencius replied, "It is the consequence of the prince failing to observe mourning for three years. Then I said that it's better to observe one day more than not to do so, which issuitable to those who themselves are unwilling to observe mourning without anyone hindering them."

【注释】(1)期:jī。这里指"期服"。服丧一年。已:犹止。(2)紾:zhěn,扭转,拗折。谓:对……说。亦:但是,只是,仅仅。(3)王子有其母死者:王子中有个最近死了生母的。(4)夫:那些人。莫之禁:没有人阻止他(们)。

【原文】40 孟子曰:“君子之所以教者五;[1]有如时雨化之者,[2]有成德者,[3]有达财者,[4]有答问者,[5]有私淑艾者。[6]此五者,君子之所以教也。[7]”

【白话译文】

孟子说:“君子教人的方式有五种:有像及时雨那样沾溉万物的,有成全品德的,有培养才能的,有解答疑问的,还有让不可能及门的人间接学习的,不加任何条件。这五种,就是君子教育人的方式。”

【英语译文】

Mencius said, “A moral man educates people in five ways. The first one is that he educates people like timely rain. The second one is that he cultivates people's morality. The third one is that he nurtures people's capability. The fourth one is that he gets rid of people's doubts. The fifth one is that he makes those who can't become his disciples learn from him indirectly. These are the five approaches for a moral man to educate people.”

【注释】(1)所以教者五:用来教人的方式方法有五种。者,代词。代事物。(2)如时雨化之者:像及时雨那样沾溉万物的。(3)成德者:成全品德的。(4)达财者:培养才能的。(5)答问者:解答疑问的。(6)私淑艾者:~ ~yì~,焦循《正义》,“私淑艾者,即私拾取也……未得为孔子之徒,而拾取于相传之人,故为私。”本文译作“让不能及门者间接学习,不加任何条件”。

【原文】41 公孙丑曰:“道则高矣,美矣,宜若登天然,[1]似不可及也。何不使彼为可几及而日孳孳也?[2]”孟子曰:“大匠不为拙工改废绳墨,羿不为拙射变其彀率[3]。君子引而不发,跃如也。中道而立能者从之。[4]”

【白话译文】

公孙丑说:“这道是很高很好了,好像登天一样,似乎不可触及。为何不使它成为可以达到的胜境而让人天天努力去登攀呢?”孟子说:“高明的工匠不因为拙劣的工人改变或者废弃规矩,羿也不因为拙劣的射手变更拉开弓的标准。君子教人正如善于教射箭的人,拉满弓只做跃跃欲射的姿态,以正确的示范引导有能力的跟着来。”

【英语译文】

Gongsun Chou said, “The Way is very good and high but it cannot be reached like climbing up to the Heaven. Why not change it into a wonderland which attracts people to climb each day?" Mencius said, "A brilliant craftsman won't change or reject the rule due to unskilled worker. Hou Yi never changed the standard to pull the bow due to bad shooter. A moral man educates people in the same way that a master teaches other to shoot. He pulls the bow not shooting and just poses to shoot. He leads the way correctly and the capable people follow up."

【注释】(1)宜若:似乎,好像。(2)几及:jī ~,达到;几乎达到。孳孳:zī ~,努力不懈。(3)彀率:标准。(4)引而不发,跃如也:拉满弓弦而不发箭,只作跃跃欲射的姿态,以便学的人观摩领会。原指善于教射;后比喻善于引导而不代庖或比喻做好准备待机行事。

【原文】42 孟子曰:"天下有道,以道殉身;[1]天下无道,以身殉道。[2]未闻以道殉乎人者也。[3]"

【白话译文】

孟子说:"天下清明,君子便施行他的'道';天下黑暗,君子就不惜为'道'而死;未听说过牺牲'道'来迁就别人的。"

【英语译文】

Mencius said, "When the rule is clear and bright, moral men carry their Way. When the rule is dark, moral men won't hesitate to die for the Way. I have never heard that one sacrificed the Way to give in to others."

【注释】(1)以道殉身:意思是"道"为己所运用。殉,如殉葬之殉。(2)以身殉道:朱熹注,"道屈则身在必退,以死相从而不离也。"(3)殉:随,跟从。

【原文】43 公都子曰:"滕更之在门也,[1]若在所礼。而不答,何也?"孟子曰:"挟贵而问,挟贤而问,挟长而问,挟有勋劳而问,挟故而问,皆所不答也。[2]滕更有二焉。[3]"

【白话译文】

公都子说:"滕更在您门下的时候,似乎该在以礼相待之列,可是您却不回答他,为什么呢?"孟子说:"倚仗着自己的权势而来发问,倚仗着自己的贤能而来发问,倚仗着自己的年纪大而来发问,倚仗着自己的功劳而来发问,倚仗着自己是老交情而来发问,都是我所不回答的。滕更占了两条。"

【英语译文】

Gongdu Zi asked, "When Teng Geng was your disciple, it seemed that you should treat him according to rites but you refused to respond to him. Why did you do that?" Mencius said, "If one asks me relying on power and influence, or if one asks me relying on his competence, or if one asks me relying on his old age, or if one asks me relying on contribution, or if one asks me relying on old acquaintance, I will refuse to respond to him. Teng Geng relied on power and competence."

【注释】(1)滕更:赵岐注,"滕君之弟,来学于孟子者也。"(2)挟:xié,依恃,倚仗。(3)有二:赵岐注,"二,谓挟贵、挟贤"。

【原文】44 孟子曰:"于不可已而已者,[1]无所不已。于所厚者薄,无所不薄也。其进锐者,[2]其退速。"

【白话译文】

孟子说:"对于不可停止的事停止了,那就没有什么不可停止的了;对于所当厚的薄了,那就没有什么不可薄的了。前进过快,后退也快。"

【英语译文】

Mencius said, "If one stops things which cannot be stopped, then everything can be stopped. If one is stingy to things to which one should be liberal, then to everything one can be stingy. If one heads forward too fast, he will be back ward fast, too."

【注释】(1)已:止。不可止,谓不可不为的。所厚,谓所当厚的。(2)进锐:前进快速。前进快速,用心太过,其气易衰故退速。

【原文】45 孟子曰:"君子之于物也,[1]爱之而弗仁;[2]于民也,仁之而弗亲。亲亲而仁民,仁民而爱物。"

【白话译文】

孟子说:“君子对于禽兽草木,爱惜它,却不拿仁德对待它;对于百姓,拿仁德对待他,却不亲爱他。君子亲亲爱人,因而仁爱百姓,仁爱百姓,因而爱惜禽兽草木等万物。”

【英语译文】

Mencius said, “A moral man cherishes livestock and plants but doesn't treat them with virtue and humanity. He treats common people with virtue and humanity but doesn't love them. A real moral man loves his parents and common people. He loves common people and then cherishes livestock and plants.”

【注释】(1)物:谓禽兽草木。(2)弗仁:不拿仁德对待它。

【原文】46 孟子曰:“知者无不知也,当务之为急;[1]仁者无不爱也,急亲贤之为务。尧舜之知而不遍物,急先务也;尧舜之仁不遍爱人,急亲贤也。不能三年之丧,而缌、小功之察,放饭流歠,而问无齿决,是之谓不知务。[2]”

【白话译文】

孟子说:“有知识的人没有不该知道的,只是急于当前办首先必办的事;仁者没有不爱的,只是必须先关爱亲人和贤者。尧舜的智慧不能完全知道一切事物,因为急需知道首要事务。尧舜的仁德不能普遍爱一切人,因为急需亲爱亲人和贤者。如果不能够施行守孝三年的丧礼,却对缌麻三月、小功五月的丧礼过细讲求;在尊长面前用餐,大口吃饭,大口喝汤,却讲求不要用牙齿啃断干肉,这些都叫不识大体。”

【英语译文】

Mencius said, “A wise man knows everything and he is busy with urgent thing. A humanistic man loves everyone but he firstly loves his parents and virtuous men. With wisdom, Sage Yao and Great Shun couldn't know all things because they should know utmost thing. With virtue, Sage Yao and Great Shun couldn't love all people because they should firstly love their parents and virtuous men. One cannot observe mourning for one's parent for three years but scrutinizes the trivial things of wearing linen clothes for three or five months. One swallows food, drinks fast, and demands not to gnaw bones when eating before the elder. Such actions can be called failing to see the larger issue."

【注释】(1)当务:当前(眼前)应办的事。(2)不知务:不识大体。

孟子集注卷十四 尽心章句下 凡三十八章

【原文】1 孟子曰:"不仁哉梁惠王也!仁者以其所爱及其所不爱,不仁者以其所不爱及其所爱。[1]"公孙丑问曰:"何谓也?""梁惠王以其土地之故,糜烂其民而战之,大败,将复之,恐不能胜,故驱其所爱子弟以殉之,是之谓以其所不爱及其所爱也。"

【白话译文】

孟子说:"太没有仁德了,梁惠王这个人呀!仁人把他对待所喜爱者的恩德也给予所不爱的人,不仁者把他加给所不爱者的祸害也加给所爱的。"公孙丑问道:"这是什么意思呢?"孟子说:"梁惠王为了争夺土地,驱使百姓抛尸战场,骨肉糜烂。大败后企图再战,怕不能得胜,又驱使他喜爱的子弟去死战,这就叫把他加给所不爱者的祸害也加给所爱的人。"

【英语译文】

Mencius said, "King Hui of Liang State was really not virtuous and humanistic! A humanistic man transfers his mercy for his loved one to those he doesn't love. An in-humanistic man forces his harm for those he doesn't love to those he loves." Gongsun Chou asked, "What does it mean?" Mencius said, "In order to seize land, King Hui of Liang State made people die, and the dead bodies rot in the air. After being defeated he wanted to fight again and feared failure, therefore he pushed his loved men to fight deadly in battlefields. It was called forcing his harm for those he doesn't love to those he loves."

【注释】(1)及:给,给予。

【原文】2 孟子曰:"春秋无义战,[1]彼善于此,则有之矣。征者上伐下也,敌国不相征也。"

【白话译文】

孟子说:“春秋时代没有正义战争。那国的君主比这国的君主好一点儿是有的。但是征讨的意思是上级讨伐下级,同等级的国家是不能互相征讨的。”

【英语译文】

Mencius said, “In Spring and Autumn Period, there wasn’t righteous war. It was normal that the monarch of one state was better than that of another one. However, crusade refers to that the higher rank crusades the lower rank and states of the same rank can not attack each other.”

【注释】(1)义战:正义战争。

【原文】3 孟子曰:“尽信《书》,则不如无《书》。吾于《武成》,[1]取二三策而已矣。[2]仁人无敌于天下,以至仁伐至不仁,而何其血之流杵也?”

【白话译文】

孟子说:“完全相信《尚书》,那不如没有《尚书》。我对于《武成》篇只采取两三策罢了。仁人在天下没有敌手,以周武王极为仁道的人讨伐商纣极为不仁的人,怎么会厮杀到流的血多得飘走杵这种武器呢?”

【英语译文】

Mencius said, “If we totally believe in *The Book of History*, it’s better for us not to have it. As for chapter *Wu Cheng*, I just absorb two to three sections. A man of humanity has no rival in the world. King Wu of Zhou Dynasty, the most humanistic man crusaded King Zhou of Shang Dynasty, the most inhumane man. How could blood so much that pestles were floating on blood river?”

【注释】(1)尽信《书》,则不如无《书》。吾于《武成》:《书》,即《尚书》。《武成》,《尚书》篇名。叙述周武王伐纣时的事。现存的《尚书·武成》,据说是伪古文,有“血流漂杵”一句。杵(chǔ),古代一种棒状的武器。(2)策:cè,古代用以记事的竹、木片。一片叫简,编在一起的叫“策”。

【原文】4 孟子曰:“有人曰:‘‘我善为陈,[1]我善为战。’大罪也。国君好仁,天下无敌焉。南面而征,北狄怨;[2]东面而征,西夷怨;曰:‘奚为后我?’武王之伐殷也,革车三百两,虎贲三千人。王曰:‘无畏!宁尔也,非敌百姓也。’若崩厥角稽首。[3]征之为言正也,各欲正己也,焉用战?[4]”

【白话译文】

孟子说:“有人说:‘我善于布阵,我善于作战。’这是大罪呀。一国的君主如果爱好仁德,天下没有敌手。征讨南方,北方狄族抱怨。征讨东方,西方夷族抱怨,说:‘为什么后到我们这里来?’周武王讨伐殷商,兵车三百辆,勇士三千人。武王说:‘不要害怕!我是来安定你们的,不是同你们为敌的。’百姓都一下子把额角触地叩起头来。征的意思是正,各个人都希望端正自己了,又何必要战争呢?”

【英语译文】

Mencius said, “Somebody boasted ‘I’ m good at embattling and I’ m good at fighting. ’ This is really a big crime! If a monarch of a state loves virtue and humanity, then he has no rivals in the world. When he crusaded the south, Di Minority in the north complained. When he crusaded the east, Yi Minority in the west complained. They asked, ‘Why did you come here so late?’ King Wu of Zhou Dynasty crusaded Shang Dynasty with three thousand warriors and three hundred fighting carts. He said, ‘Don’t be frightened. I come to tranquilize you and I won’t be hostile to you. ’ Then common people kowtowed to him. Zheng (crusade) means correctness. If everyone wished to correct himself, why should there be any war?”

【注释】(1)陈:同“阵”。军伍行列,战斗队形。(2)南面而征,北狄怨:征讨南方,北方狄族抱怨。(3)若崩厥角稽首:若,他们(指百姓)。崩厥角,像崩溃一样一下子把额角垂到地面。稽首(qǐ ~),叩头至地。

【原文】5 孟子曰:“梓匠轮舆,[1]能与人规矩,不能使人巧。”

【白话译文】

孟子说:“各种木工师傅能传授工艺的法则,却不能使学徒更巧些。”

【英语译文】

Mencius said, "All craftsmen can impart laws of crafts but they cannot make their disciples nimble."

【注释】(1)梓匠轮舆:古代对梓人(造工具)、朱熹注:匠人(搞建筑)轮人(造车轮)舆人(造车)的并称。亦泛指木工。(2)规矩:"……规矩,法度可告者也。巧则在其人,虽大匠亦未如之何也已。盖下学(谓学习人情事理)可以言传,上达(谓进而认识自然法则)必由心悟,……"

【原文】6 孟子曰:"舜之饭糗茹草也[1],若将终身焉;[2]及其为天子也,被袗衣,鼓琴,二女果,[3]若固有之。"

【白话译文】

孟子说:"舜吃干粮咽野菜的时候,好像打算一辈子就那样似的。到他做了天子后,穿着单衣,弹着琴,尧的两个女儿侍候着,又好像这些是本来就有的。"

【英语译文】

Mencius said, "It seems that Great Shun wished to eat dry grain and swallow wild vegetables all his life. After he became the Son of the Heaven, he wore thin clothes, played harp, and was served by Sage Yao's two daughters. It seemed that he had owned these at first."

【注释】(1)饭糗:饭(fàn),动词。吃饭,亦泛指吃。糗(qǐu),炒熟的米麦。亦泛指干粮。茹草:rú~,吃野菜。茹,吃,吞咽。(2)若将终身焉?:若,好像,似乎。将,副词。打算,欲。焉,助词。用在句末,与若,如配合,表示比拟,相当于"然"。犹言"那样""似的"。(3)被:pī,穿着。袗衣:zhěn~,单衣。鼓琴:弹琴。二女:指尧的两个女儿。果:wǒ,通"婐",侍女,引申为侍候。

【原文】7 孟子曰:"吾今而后知杀人亲之重也:[1]杀人之父,人亦杀其父;杀人之兄,人亦杀其兄。然则非自杀之也,一间耳。[2]"

【白话译文】

孟子说:"我从今以后,知道杀人父的重罪了;杀了别人之父,别人又杀自己之父;杀了别人之兄,别人又杀自己之兄。这样,虽然父亲和哥哥不是自己杀的,也和自己杀的差不多。”

【英语译文】

Mencius said, “From now on I know the grave crime of killing other's father. If one kills other man's father, his father will be killed by other man. If one kills other man's elder brother, his elder brother will be killed by other man. As a result, though one's father and elder brother aren't killed by himself, the situation is almost the same.”

【注释】(1)今而后:从今以后。杀人亲之重:重,谓“重罪”。(2)一间:~jiàn,谓相距极近。间,间隙 。

【原文】8 孟子曰:“古之为关也[1],将以御暴;今之为关也,将以为暴。”

【白话译文】

孟子说:“古代设立关卡,是要用抵御残暴;今天设立关卡,是要用来实行残暴。”

【英语译文】

Mencius said, “In ancient times, passes were set up in order to defend tyrann. However, nowadays passes are set up to conduct tyranny.”

【注释】(1)为关:设立关卡。

【原文】9 孟子曰:“身不行道,不行于妻子;使人不以道,[1]不能行于妻子。”

【白话译文】

孟子说:“自身不行道,道在妻子儿女身上也行不通;使唤别人不依道,妻子儿女也使唤不了。”

【英语译文】

Mencius said, “If one doesn't conduct the Way, it cannot go smoothly in respect of his wife and kids. If one doesn't order other people according to the Way, he cannot order his wife and kids."

【注释】(1)不以道:不依道。

【原文】10 孟子曰:"周于利者凶年不能杀[1],周于德者邪世不能乱。"

【白话译文】

孟子说:"财利富足的人荒年不能伤害他,道德完美的人乱世不能迷惑他。"

【英语译文】

Mencius said, "A wealthy man cannot be harmed in a famine year, and a virtuous man cannot be baffled in chaotic time."

【注释】(1)周:朱熹注,"足也,言积之厚则用有余。"杀:伤害。

【原文】11 孟子曰:"好名之人能让千乘之国,苟非其人,[1] 箪食豆羹见于色。"

【白话译文】

孟子说:"好名之人可以把有一千辆兵车的国家君位让给别人,若不是他心目中的人,即使要他让一筐饭一碗汤,脸上也会显出不高兴的神色。"

【英语译文】

Mencius said, "A man who cherishes reputation can hand over the throne of a state which has one thousand fighting carts to other person. However, if the person isn't his preference, he will appear unhappy even if he is requested for a basket of rice or a bowl of soup."

【注释】(1)其人:他心目中的人。

【原文】12 孟子曰:"不信仁贤,则国空虚;无礼义,则上下乱;无政事,则财用不足。[1]"

【白话译文】

孟子说:“不信任仁德贤能的人,那国家就会空虚;没有礼义,那上下的关系就会混乱;没有良好的政事,那国家需要运用的财富就会不够。”

【英语译文】

Mencius said, “If virtuous and humanistic men weren’t trusted, then a state would weaken. If there weren’t rites and righteousness, then the relation among the ruler and the masses would be in disorder. If there wasn’t good administration, then there wasn’t enough wealth for running the state.”

【注释】(1)财用:财富。

【原文】13 孟子曰:“不仁而得国者,有之矣;不仁而得天下者,未之有也。[1]”

【白话译文】

孟子说:“不仁道却得到了国家的,有这样的事呀;不仁道却得了天下的,就不曾有过。”

【英语译文】

Mencius said, “There ever existed that man without humanity obtained a state. However, There never existed that a man without humanity obtained the whole land under the heaven.”

【注释】(1)未之有:未有之。

【原文】14 孟子曰:“民为贵,社稷次之,君为轻。[1]是故得乎丘民而为天子,得乎天子为诸侯,得乎诸侯为大夫。[2]诸侯危社稷,则变置。[3]牺牲既成,粢盛既絜,祭祀以时,然而旱干水溢,则变置社稷。[4]”

【白话译文】

孟子说:“百姓是最贵重的,土神和谷神在其次,君主轻微在第三。所以得到百姓的欢心能做天子,得到天子的欢心做诸侯,得到诸侯的欢心做大夫。诸侯危害国家,那就改立。牺牲既已肥壮,祭品又已洁净,便按时祭祀,但是还遭受旱灾水灾,那就改立土神和谷神。"

【英语译文】

Mencius said, "Common people are the most precious, and the gods of land and grain come to the next, and the monarch ranks the third. Therefore, one can become the Son of the Heaven if he is loved by common people, and one can become a vassal if he is loved by the Son of the Heaven, and one can become a minister if he is loved by a vassal. If a vassal does harm to state, he should be rejected. If sacrifices are fat, and sacrificial objects are cleansed, then sacrificial ceremony should be held timely. After the ceremony flood and drought still fall on, the gods of land and grain should be changed."

【注释】(1)社稷:土神和谷神。(2)丘民:田野之民。

【原文】15 孟子曰:"圣人,百世之师也,伯夷、柳下惠是也。故闻伯夷之风者,顽夫廉,懦夫有立志。闻柳下惠之风者,薄夫敦,鄙夫宽。[1]奋乎百世之上,百世之下,闻之莫不兴起也。[2]非圣人而能若是乎?而况于亲炙之者乎?[3]"

【白话译文】

孟子说:"圣人是百代的老师,伯益和柳下惠就是这样的人。所以听到伯益的风操故事,贪得无厌的人,清廉起来了,懦弱的人,也能挺立不屈了;听到柳下惠的风操故事,刻薄的人,也厚道起来了,心胸狭隘的人,也宽宏大量起来了。他们在百代以前发奋作为,在百代以后,听了他们的故事,没有不感动奋发的人。不是圣人能够像这样吗?何况亲自接受熏陶的人呢?"

【英语译文】

Mencius said, "Sages are teachers for hundred generations. Bo Yi and Liu Xiahui were such men. On hearing Bo Yi's story greedy men became white-handed and cowards became strong. On hearing Liu Xiahui's story harsh men became honest and narrow-minded men became generous. One hundred generations ago, they roused themselves. One hundred generations later no one won't be moved by their stories. Who could be like this if he wasn't a sage? Let alone they were personally nurtured by sages."

【注释】(1)顽夫:贪婪的人。懦夫:nuò ~,软弱无能的人。薄夫:刻薄的人。鄙夫:心胸狭隘的人。(2)兴起:感动奋发。(3)亲炙:亲近而熏炙之。

【原文】16 孟子曰:“仁也者,人也。合而言之,道也。[1]”

【白话译文】

孟子说:“仁是为人之理,仁和人合起来说,便是道。”

【英语译文】

Mencius said, “Humanity is the reason for being a man. The Way is the combination of man and humanity.”

【注释】(1)仁:谓人之所以为人之理。然而仁是理,人是物。以仁之理合于人之身而言之,乃所谓道者也。

【原文】17 孟子曰:“孔子之去鲁,曰:‘迟迟吾行也。’去父母国之道也。[1]去齐,接淅而行,去他国之道也。[2]”

【白话译文】

孟子说:“孔子离开鲁国,说:‘我们慢慢走吧。’这是离开祖国的态度。离开齐国时,捧着已经淘湿的米匆忙而走。这是离开外国的态度。”

【英语译文】

Mencius said, “When Confucius left Lu State he said, ‘Let's walk slowly.’ This was his attitude toward leaving his motherland. When he left Qi State he hurried walking while holding wet rice. This was his attitude toward leaving a foreign state.”

【注释】(1)孔子之去鲁:另见《万章下》第一节。这里重出。(2)接淅而行:捧着已经淘湿的米匆忙而走。

【原文】18 孟子曰:“君子之戹于陈蔡之间,[1]无上下之交也。[2]”

【白话译文】

孟子说:“孔子被困在陈、蔡两国之间,是由于对两国的君臣没有交往的缘故。”

【英语译文】

Mencius said, “Confucius was confined between Chen State and Cai State because he didn't get well along with monarchs and ministers of the two states.”

【注释】(1)君子之戹于陈蔡之间:君子,指孔子。《论语·卫灵公》:“在陈绝粮,从者病,莫能兴。”即是此事。戹,通“厄”。(2)无上下之交也:指君臣。

【原文】19 貉稽曰[1]:“稽大不理于口。[2]”孟子曰:“无伤也。士憎兹多口。[3]《诗》云:‘忧心悄悄,愠于群小。[4]’孔子也。‘肆不殄厥愠,亦不陨厥问。’文王也。[5]”

【白话译文】

貉稽说:“我被人家说得很糟。”孟子说:“不要紧,士人憎恨这些不该说的话。《诗经》说,‘不让烦恼上眉梢,小人合围不目逃。’这是孔子啊。又‘虽未消除戎狄怒,王的声誉并未污。’这是说的文王啊。”

【英语译文】

Mo Ji said, “I was commented badly by other people.” Mencius said, “It doesn't matter and scholars hate these commentaries. *The Book of Songs* said ‘Ice, coal, water, fire cannot get together. Mean man traps me while I move a bit,’ which described Confucius. *The Book of Songs* also said ‘Agony of ethnic minority hadn't been rid off. Reputation of King Wen was still in purity.’, which described King Wen of Zhou Dynasty.”

【注释】(1)貉稽:mòjī,赵岐注,“貉,姓,稽,名;仕者也。”(2)大不理于口:犹言很不理于人口。理,顺。(3)憎兹多口:朱熹注,“赵氏曰:‘为士者,益多为众口所讪。’按此憎当从土,今本皆从心,盖传写之误。”多口,多言,不该说而说。(4)忧心两句:见《诗·邶风·柏舟》。(5)肆不殄两句:见《诗·大雅·绵》。肆,故。殄,绝。

【原文】20 孟子曰:“贤者以其昭昭使人昭昭,[1]今以其昏昏使人昭昭。[2]”

【白话译文】

孟子说:“贤人用自己的聪明智慧促使别人聪明智慧,现在是用自己的昏庸愚昧促使别人聪明智慧。”

【英语译文】

Mencius said, “A virtuous man makes other people wise by means of his wisdom. However, people nowadays make others wise by means of his foolishness.”

【注释】(1)昭昭:谓聪明智慧。(2)今:现在。昏昏:谓昏庸愚昧。

【原文】21 孟子谓高子曰:“山径之蹊,[1]间介然用之而成路;[2]为间不用,则茅塞之矣。[3]今茅塞子心矣。[4]”

【白话译文】

孟子对高子说:“山中道路之间的近便路线,经常有人行走,也就成了一条路。只要隔一段时间无人行走,它就会被茅草所堵塞。现在茅草把你的心堵塞了。”

【英语译文】

Mencius told Gao Zi, “The shortcut among mountains can change into a path if people often walk on it. It will be blocked by thatch on condition that no people walk on it for sometime. Now your mind has already been blocked.”

【注释】(1)山径之蹊间:山中道路之间的近便之路。走的人次少甚至没了,就会被野草所堵塞。(2)介然用之:频繁不断有人行走。(3)为间不用:隔一段时间无人行走。(4)茅塞:被茅草所堵塞。

【原文】22 高子曰:“禹之声尚文王之声。[1]”孟子曰:“何以言之?”曰:“以追蠡。[2]”曰:“是奚足哉?城门之轨,两马之力与?[3]”

【白话译文】

高子说:“禹的音乐比文王的音乐好。”孟子说:“你根据什么这样说呢?”答道:“因为禹传下来的钟,那纽都快断了。”孟子说:“这个怎么能证明呢?城门下车轮印迹那么深，难道只是几匹马的力量吗？"

【英语译文】

Gao Zi said, "Great Yu's music was better than that of King Wen of Zhou Dynasty." Mencius asked, "why do you say so?" Gao Zi answered, "The bell which was passed down by Great Yu was almost broken in the bellpull." Mencius said, "How could this prove your words? The track under city gate is so deep. Can you say it was made just by several horses?"

【注释】(1)声：谓音乐。尚：超过，胜过。(2)追蠡：duīlí，钟纽欲断的样子。钟纽(钮)，古钟悬挂处。(3)两马：几匹马。(习惯用法。概数，万马言其多，两匹马、几匹马言其少。)

【原文】23 齐饥。陈臻曰："国人皆以夫子将复为发棠，殆不可复。[1]"孟子曰："是为冯妇也。晋人有冯妇者，善搏虎。卒为善，[2]士则之，[3]野有众逐虎，虎负嵎，莫之敢撄。[4]望见冯妇趋而迎之，冯妇攘臂下车，[5]众皆悦之，其为士者笑之。"

【白话译文】

齐国遭了饥荒，陈臻对孟子说："国内的人都以为老师会再次劝请齐王打开棠地的仓库来赈济灾民，大概不可以再这样做罢。"孟子说："再这样做就是冯妇了。晋国有个叫冯妇的人，善于和老虎搏斗，后来年龄大了改行打虎之外的善事。士人都拿他做榜样。有一次，野地里许多人正追逐老虎，老虎背靠着山角没有人敢迫近它。人们望见了冯妇，便快步向前去迎接。冯妇也就捋起袖子伸出胳膊，走下车来。大家都喜欢他，可是作为士的那些人却在讥笑他。"

【英语译文】

Qi State was suffering famine. Chen Zhen said to Mencius, "Master, people of Qi State think that you will persuade the King to use grain in the barn of Tangyi to relieve people. Maybe you cannot do this again." Mencius said, "If I do this again I am Feng Fu. In Jin State a man called Feng Fu was good at fighting with tiger but later on he was old and changed to do good deeds except fighting with tiger. Scholars set him as an example. Once upon a time, there was a tiger that was run after by many persons. The tiger stood against a corner in the mountain and nobody dared to approach it. People noticed Feng Fu and hurried to welcome him. Feng Fu rolled his sleeve, stretched his arms, and got off his carriage. People all liked him but scholars jeered at him."

【注释】(1)复为发棠:先时齐国发生饥荒,孟子劝齐王发棠邑之仓以振贫穷。至此又饥,陈臻因齐人望孟子再劝齐王发棠而问孟子。(2)搏虎:打虎,和老虎搏斗。卒为善:后改行打虎之外的善事。(3)士则之:士人效法他。(4)负嵎:背靠山的弯曲处。莫之敢撄:没有人敢触犯。撄 yīng,迫近,触,触犯。(5)攘臂:捋起衣袖,伸出胳膊。常形容奋激的样子。

【原文】24 孟子曰:"口之于味也,目之于色也,耳之于声也,鼻之于臭也,[1]四肢,之安佚也,性也,有命焉,君子不谓性也。[2]仁之于父子也,义之于臣也,礼之于宾主也,知之于贤者也,圣人之于天道也,有性焉,君子不谓命也。[3]"

【白话译文】

孟子说:"口的对于美味,眼的对于美色,耳的对于好听的声音,鼻的对于芬芳的气味,手足四肢的对于舒服,这些都是人的天性,但是得到与否,要看天命,君子不助长生来的天性。仁对于父子之间,义对于君臣之间,礼对于宾主之间,智慧对于贤者,圣人对于天道,能够实现与否,也有天性的作用,君子不助命运。"

【英语译文】

Mencius said, "Mouth is to good taste; eyes are to beautiful things; ears are to fine sound; nose is to fragrant smell. All these are men's original nature. However, thet whether or not men can obtain them depends on heaven's mandate and moral men don't promote inborn nature. Humanity is to relationship among a father and his kids; righteousness is to relationship among a monarch and his ministers; rites is to relationship among a host and his guests; wisdom is to virtuous men, and sages are to the Way. Whether or not these are realized depends on heaven's nature and moral men don't promote fate."

【注释】(1)臭:xiù,气味。(2)不谓性:不助性。谓,犹勤,帮助。君子直道而行不任个性而偏离正道。(3)不谓命:不助命。君子直道而行,不因天命如何而忘乎其形。

【原文】25 浩生不害问曰：[1]“乐正子何人也？”孟子曰：“善人也，信人也。[2]”“何谓善？何谓信？”曰：“可欲之谓善，[3]有诸己之谓信，[4]充实之谓美，[5]充实而有光泽之谓大，[6]大而化之之谓圣，[7]圣而不可知之之谓神。[8]乐正子，二之中、四之下也。[9]”

【白话译文】

浩生不害问道：“乐正子是怎样的人？”孟子说：“好人，诚实的人。”“怎么叫好？怎么叫诚实？”答道：“那人值得喜欢便叫‘好’；好处确实存在于他自身便叫‘诚实’；好处充满了自身便叫‘美’；不但充满，还光辉地表现出来了便叫‘大’；既大了又能融化贯通，便叫‘圣’；圣德达到神妙不可测度的境界，便叫‘神’。乐正子是介于‘好’和‘诚实’两者之中，‘美’‘大’‘圣’‘神’四者之下的人物。”

【英语译文】

Haosheng Buhai asked, “What kind of man was Le Zhengzi?” Mencius answered, “He was a good man and an honest man.” Haosheng Buhai asked, “What kind of man was a good man, and what kind of man was an honest man?” Mencius said, “A man who deserves loving is a good man. And if being good is expressed in themselves, it was called ‘honest’. If being good fill oneself, then it is called ‘perfection’. If being good not only fill oneself but also is expressed, then it is called ‘greatness’. If being good express out and go through all things, then it is called ‘sage’. If sage's virtue reaches unfathomable level, then it is called ‘deity’. Le Zhengzi is a man who is between ‘good’ level and ‘honest’ level but below the levels of ‘perfection’, ‘greatness’, ‘sage’, and ‘deity’.”

【注释】(1)浩生不害：浩生，姓；不害，名；齐人。(2)善人也，信人也：好人，诚实的人。(3)可欲之谓善：值得喜欢的叫“好”。(4)有诸己之谓信：所说的好确实存在于它自身叫诚实。(5)充实之谓美：好处充满了他自身便叫‘美’。(6)充实而有光泽之谓大：好处充实显现光辉叫大。(7)大而化之之谓圣：又大又能融化贯通叫圣。(8)圣而不可知之之谓神：又大又能融化贯通而至于不可知其边际叫神。(9)二之中、四之下也：在好人诚实人之中，神、圣、美、大人之下。

【原文】26 孟子曰：“逃墨必归于杨，逃杨必归于儒。[1]归，斯受之而已矣。[2]今之与杨墨辩者，[3]如追放豚，既入其苙，又从而招之。[4]”

【白话译文】

孟子说:“逃离墨子一派的,一定归入杨朱这一派;逃杨朱一派的一定归附于儒家。来归附,就接受算了。今天同杨墨两家相辩论的人,好像追逐走散失了的猪一样,已经关进猪圈了,还要把它的脚绊住。”

【英语译文】

Mencius said, “Those who fled from the School of Mo Zi must come to the School of Yang Zhu. Those who fled from the School of Yang Zhu must come to Confucianism. If they come to Confucianism, we just accept them. Nowadays those who debate with the School of Yang Zhu and the School of Mo Zi are just pigs that have been dispersed. They have left their sty and their feet have been stopped.”

【注释】(1)归于儒:归附儒家。朱熹注:“墨氏务外而不情,杨氏太简而近实,故其反正之之渐,大略如此。”(2)归,斯受之:归附,就接受。(3)与杨墨辩者:指当时的儒家一部分人。(4)放豚:散失的猪。放,散失,散落。豚 tún,小猪;泛指猪。既入其苙:关进猪圈后。入,使进入。苙 lì,畜圈,猪栏。又从而招之:从而,然后;因而。招:朱熹注,“招,罥也,羁其足也。”

【原文】27 孟子曰:“有布缕之征,[1]粟米之征,力役之征。君子用其一,缓其二。用其二而民有殍,用其三而父子离。”

【白话译文】

孟子说:“有征收布与线的赋税,有征收谷米的赋税,还有征发劳役的赋税。君子于三者之中采用一种,那两种便暂时不用。如果同时用两种,百姓便会有饿死的;如果同时用三种,那父子之间只能离散互不相顾了。”

【英语译文】

Mencius said, “There is tax for cloth and thread, or tax for grains, or tax for corvee. Moral men choose one from three and suspend the other two. If the two are simultaneously taxed, common people will be starved to death. If the three are simultaneously taxed, a father and his sons will be separated and cannot ta be care of each other.”

【注释】(1)布缕之征:朱熹注:“征赋之法,岁有常数,然布缕取之于夏,粟米取之于秋,力役取之于冬,当各以其时;若并取之,则民力有所不堪矣。”布缕 ~ lǚ,布与线。亦泛指织物。

【原文】28 孟子曰:“诸侯之宝三:[1]土地、人民、政事。宝珠玉者,殃必及身。[2]”

【白话译文】

孟子说:“诸侯的贵重东西有三件:土地、人民和政事。珍爱珠玉的,祸害一定临头。”

【英语译文】

Mencius said, “There are three precious things for vassals, which are land, citizen and administrative affairs. Those who cherish jewelry and jade will surely suffer disasters.”

【注释】(1)诸侯之宝:诸侯的贵重东西。(2)宝珠玉者:珍爱珠玉的人。

【原文】29 盆成括仕于齐,[1]孟子曰:“死矣盆成括!”盆成括见杀,门人问曰:“夫子何以知其将见杀?”曰:“其为人也小有才,未闻君子之大道也,[2]则足以杀其躯而已矣。”

【白话译文】

盆成括在齐国做官,孟子说:“要死了盆成括!”盆成括被杀,学生问道:“老师怎么知道他会被杀?”答道:“他为人有些小聪明,但是不曾知道君子之大道,这就足以惹来杀身之祸罢了。”

【英语译文】

When Pencheng Kuo was an official in Qi State, Mencius said, “Pencheng Kuo will die!” After Pencheng Kuo was killed his disciples asked, “Master, how do you know that he will be killed?” Mencius replied, “He is a man having some clever tricks, but he doesn't know the Way of being a moral man. That will surely invite disaster of being killed.”

【注释】(1)盆成括:盆成,姓;括,名。(2)为人:做人,处世,接物。小有才:在小事小道方面有才智。未闻:未领会。

【原文】30 孟子之滕,馆于上宫。[1]有业屦于牖上,馆人求之弗得。[2]或问之曰:“若是乎从者之廋也?[3]”曰:“子以是为窃屦来与?”曰:“殆非也。夫子之设科也,[4]往者不追,来者不拒。苟以是心至,斯受之而已矣。”

【白话译文】

孟子到了滕国,住在旅馆楼上。据说窗台上有还未编织完工的单底鞋,旅馆中的人去取,却不见了。有人问孟子,说:“这个样儿,随从的人把它藏起来了吧?”孟子说:“你以为他们是为了偷单底鞋而来的吗?”答道:“大概不是。你老人家开设的课程,去的学生不追问,来学的人不拒绝。只要怀着学习的心来,就接受罢了。”

【英语译文】

Mencius reached Teng State and stayed in second floor of the hostel. It was reported that on the windowsill there was an uncompleted shoes but it was gone when people in the hostel went to get it. Someone asked, “One of your attendants must have hidden it.” Mencius asked, “Do you think that he had come here for stealing the shoes?” The man answered, “No, it seemed that he hadn't. For the courses you lectured, you didn't inquire those who left and you didn't refuse those who attended. If only they intended to study under your guidance, you just accepted them.”

【注释】(1)馆于上宫:馆,寓居;留宿。上宫:赵岐注:“上宫,楼也。孟子舍止宾客所馆之楼上也。”(2)业屦:还未编织完工的单底鞋。(3)若是乎从者之廋也:从者,指孟子的随行者。廋:sōu,藏匿,隐藏。(4)设科:开设课程,教授。

【原文】31 孟子曰:“人皆有所不忍,达之于其所忍,仁也;人皆有所不为,达之于其所为,义也。人能充无欲害人之心,而仁不可胜用也;人能充无穿逾之心,而义不可胜用也;人能充无受尔汝之实,[1]无所往而不为义也。士未可以言而言,是以言餂之也;[2]可以言而不言,是以不言餂之也,是皆穿逾之类也。”

【白话译文】

孟子说:“人人都有所不忍的心情,把它推移到自己所忍的心情上,这便是仁;人人都有所不愿干的事,把它推移到自己愿干的事上,这便是义。人能充满不想害人的心，于是仁便用不尽了；人能充满不挖洞翻墙的心，于是义便用不尽了；人能充满不受鄙视的言行举止所辱的实质，没有亏缺，那随便到哪里都合于义了。同一个不可以同他谈论的士人谈论，这是用言语去挑逗他，以便自己取利；不同一个可以同他谈论的士人谈论，这是用沉默去挑逗他，以便自己取利，这些都是属于挖洞翻墙这一类型的。”

【英语译文】

Mencius said, “Everyone has feeling of unbearing. If it is spread to the things one cannot bear, it is called humanity. Everyone has things that he is unwilling to do. If it is spread to the things that he is willing to do, it is called righteousness. If a man cherishes feeling of not harming others, his humanity won't run off. If a man cherishes feeling of digging holes in wall and fleeing, his righteousness won't run off. If a man cherishes feeling of not being affected by disdainful words and actions, he will be righteous wherever he goes. If one talks with a scholar to whom he shouldn't talk, he is teasing the scholar so that he can obtain benefit. If one doesn't talk with a scholar to whom he may talk, he is teasing the scholar by means of silence so that he can obtain benefit. These all belong to the things of digging holes in wall and fleeing.”

【注释】(1)无受尔汝之实：“尔、汝”为古代尊长对卑幼的对称代词，如果平辈用了，便表示轻视、贱视对方。孟子之意，若要不受别人的轻贱，自己便先应该有不受轻贱的言语行为。(2)餂：tiǎn，取，诱取。

【原文】32 孟子曰：“言近而指远者，善言也；守约而施博者，[1]善道也。君子之言也，不下带而道存焉；[2]君子之守，修其身而天下平。人病舍其田而芸人之田，[3]所求于人者重，而所以自任者轻。”

【白话译文】

孟子说：“言语浅近而意指深远的，是“善言”；操守简易而施与广大的，是“善道”；君子的言语，讲的虽是常见的事情，但是“道”就在其中；君子的操守，从修养自身开始从而使天下太平。有些人的毛病就在于丢荒自己的田，却去除别人田里的草。要求别人的很重，自己负担的很轻。”

【英语译文】

Mencius said, "They are kind words which is simple but with compliceted implications. And it is kind Way which has simple moral integrity but spreads widely. A moral man is about cemnuon things but contains 'Way'. A moral man's integrity starts to cultivate himself to pacify the land under the Heaven. Somebody has the fault to deject his own fields but to do weeding in others' fields. He demands others more but demands himself less."

【注释】(1)守约而施博:所操守简易而所施与广大。(2)不下带:带,束腰之带。朱熹注:"古人视不下于带,则带之上,乃目前常见至近之处也。举目前之近事,而至理存焉。"(3)芸人之田:除别人田里的草。芸,通"耘"。除草。

【原文】33 孟子曰:"尧舜,性者也;汤武,反之也。[1]动容周旋中礼者,盛德之至也[2]。哭死而哀,非为生者也。[3]经德不回,非以干禄也。[4]言语必信,非以正行也。[5]君子行法,以俟命而已矣。[6]"

【白话译文】

孟子说:"尧舜的美德,出于本性。汤武,便是通过修身恢复本性而至于善美的。举止仪容、应对进退,没有不合于礼的,是美德中极高的品位了。哭死者而悲哀,不是做给在生者看的。始终不变的品德,不是为了做官谋俸禄。说话一定诚实,是本性的自然,不是为了证明自己的行为。君子按天理之当然行事,听天由命罢了。"

【英语译文】

Mencius said, "The virtue of Sage Yao and Great Shun came from their original nature. King Tang of Shang Dynasty and King Wu of Zhou Dynasty reached the summum bonum through cultivating themselves and recovering original nature. Their manners and actions were all ritual and the highest level concerning virtue. To cry for the dead and to be sad wasn't a show for the people alive. Unchanging morality wasn't for obtaining an official post or getting salary. While speaking they were honest but not to prove their actions. Moral men do things according to the Heavenly principle and just obey the mandate of the Heaven."

【注释】(1)反之也:返回本性。(2)动容周旋中礼者:举止仪容、应对进退,没有不合于礼的。(3)非为生者也:不是做给在生者看的。(4)经德不回:经德即

"常德",谓始终不变的品德。不回,谓不改变。(5)非以正行:不是为了证明自己的行为。(6)君子行法:朱熹注:"法者,天理之当然者也。君子行之,而吉凶祸福有所不计。"俟命:sì ~,听天由命。

【原文】34 孟子曰:"说大人,则藐之,勿视其巍巍然。[1]堂高数仞,榱题数尺,[2]我得志,弗为也。食前方丈,侍妾数百人,[3]我得志,弗为也。般乐饮,驱骋田猎,后车千乘,[4]我得志,弗为也。在彼者,皆我所不为也;在我者,皆古之制也,吾何畏彼哉?[5]"

【白话译文】

孟子说:"劝说大人采纳自己的意见,就要轻视他,不要看他那自我高大的样子。殿堂几仞高,出檐的椽子几尺长。我实现志愿了,不像这样干。面前菜肴挤满桌,周围侍妾几百人。我实现志愿了,不像这样干。作乐饮酒,驱使车马疾驰而打猎,跟随的车子千多辆,我实现志愿了,不像这样干。取决于他的,都是我所不为的;取决于我的,都符合古时的制度,我为何怕他呢?"

【英语译文】

Mencius said, "When you persuade a monarch to adopt your proposal, you should not care his air of superiority but contempt him. A hall is several *zhang* high but rafters out of eaves are several *chi* long. Since I realized my will I won't do like this. In front of me delicious dishes are placed on the table and many servants serve me. Since I realized my will I won't do like this. Drinking wine and seeking for pleasure, driving horses to go hunting one is followed by several thousand carts. Since I realized my will I won't do like this. What was decided by him isn't what I want to do. What was decided by me is obeying ancient rules. Why do I fear him?"

【注释】(1)说大人:shuì ~ ~,劝说大人听从自己的意见。藐:miǎo,轻视。巍巍然:高高大大的。(2)堂高数仞:殿堂几仞高。榱题:cuī ~,亦作"榱提"。指椽子的出檐部分。(3)食前方丈:吃饭时面前一丈见方的地方都摆满了食物,形容生活奢侈。(4)驱骋田猎:驱使车马疾驰而打猎。后车千乘:跟随的车子千多辆。(5)在彼者:取决于他的。

【原文】35 孟子曰:"养心莫善于寡欲。[1]其为人也寡欲,虽有不存焉者,寡矣;其为人也多欲,虽有存焉者,寡矣。"

【白话译文】

孟子说:“修养本心没有比节制欲望更好的了,做人处世接物少欲,纵使本心有所丧失,也不会多;做人处世接物多欲,纵使本心有所保存,也是很少的了。”

【英语译文】

Mencius said, “When cultivating original nature he should do nothing but restrain his desire. While conducting himself and getting along with people he should desire less. Even if there is a loss of original nature, it will be just a little bit. If he desires more while conducting himself and getting along with people, the original nature will remain less even if it has reservation.”

【注释】(1)欲:朱熹注:“欲,如口鼻耳目四支(肢)之欲,虽人之所不能无,然多而不节,未有不失其本心者,学者所当深戒也。程子曰:‘所欲不必沉溺,只有所向便是欲。’”

【原文】36 曾皙嗜羊枣,而曾子不忍食羊枣。[1]公孙丑问曰:“脍炙羊枣孰美?[2]”孟子曰:“脍炙哉!”公孙丑问曰:“然则曾子何为食脍炙而不食羊枣?”曰:“脍炙所同也,羊枣所独也。讳名不讳姓,[3]姓所同也,名所独也。”

【白话译文】

曾皙喜欢吃羊枣,曾子因而舍不得吃羊枣。公孙丑问道:“佳肴与羊枣哪一样好吃些?”孟子答道:“佳肴啊!”公孙丑又问道:“那么曾子为什么吃佳肴而不吃羊枣呢?”答道:“佳肴是大家都喜欢吃的,羊枣只是个别人喜欢吃的。好比父母的名应该避讳,姓却不避讳一样;姓是许多人相同的,名却是一个人所有的。”

【英语译文】

Zeng Xi loved eating sheep jujube and Zeng Zi was unwilling to eat it. Gongsun Chou asked, “Delicacy and sheep jujube, which is more delicious?” Mencius replied, “Delicacy.” Gongsun Chou asked once more, “Then why did Zeng Zi eat delicacy not sheep jujube?” Mencius answered, “Everyone loved eating delicacy but only a few loved eating sheep jujube. People’s parents given names are taboo but their surnames are not. Many people have the same surname but given name belongs to a specific person.”

【注释】(1)羊枣:亦称“羊矢枣”,果名,君迁子之实,长椭圆形,初生色黄,熟则黑,似羊矢,俗称“羊矢枣”。(2)脍炙:细切的肉和烤熟的肉,亦泛指佳肴。

【原文】37 万章问曰:“孔子在陈曰:‘盍归乎来!吾党之士狂简,进取,不忘其初。[1]’孔子在陈,何思鲁之狂士?[2]”孟子曰:“孔子‘不得中道而与之,[3]必也狂狷乎!狂者进取,狷者有所不为也。’孔子岂不欲中道哉?不可必得,故思其次也。[4]”“敢问何如斯可谓狂矣?[5]”曰:“如琴张、[6]曾皙、牧皮者[7],孔子之所谓狂矣。”[8]“何以谓之狂也?[9]”曰:“其志嘐嘐然,曰‘古之人,古之人’。夷考其行而不掩焉者也。[10]狂者又不可得,欲得不屑不洁之士而与之,是狷也,是又其次也。[11]孔子曰:‘过我门而不入我室,我不憾焉者,其惟乡原乎!乡原,德之贼也。’”曰:“何如斯可谓之乡原矣?[12]”曰:“‘何以是嘐嘐也?言不顾行,行不顾言,则曰:古之人,古之人。行何为踽踽凉凉?生斯世也,为斯世也,善斯可矣。’阉然媚于世也者,是乡原也。[13]”万子曰:“一乡皆称原人焉,无所往而不为原人,孔子以为德之贼,何哉?”曰:“非之无举也,刺之无刺也;同乎流俗,合乎污世;居之似忠信,行之似廉洁;众皆悦之,自以为是,而不可与入尧舜之道,故曰德之贼也。[14]孔子曰:‘恶似而非者:恶莠,恐其乱苗也;恶佞,恐其乱义也;恶利口,恐其乱信也;恶郑声,恐其乱乐也;恶紫,恐其乱朱也;恐乡原,恐其乱德也。[15]’君子反经而已矣。经正,则庶民兴;庶民兴,斯无邪慝矣。[16]”

【白话译文】

万章问道:“孔子在陈国说:‘何不回去呢!我那些学生们志大而略于事,追求高远,不能改其旧。’孔子在陈国为什么思念鲁国这些志大而略于事的人?”孟子答道:“孔子说过不能结交中行之士,就一定结识狂放之人和狷介之士罢。狂放之人,求望高远,狷介之士有所不为。孔子难道不想中行之士吗?不能一定得到所以只想次一点的了。”“请问,怎么样的人就可叫狂放的人?”答道:“像琴张、曾皙、牧皮这类人就是孔子所说的狂放的人,”“为什么说他们是狂放的人呢?”答道:“他们志向大也爱说大话。总是开口‘古人呀!古人呀!’考察他们的行为却和言语不对应相合。这种狂妄的人也得不到的话,便想同不屑于干坏事的人相交,这样的人便是狷介之士;这是又次一等的了。孔子说:‘从我家大门经过却不进我屋,我也不遗憾,这种人,只是好好先生罢。好好先生是戕害道德的贼人。’”问道:“那人的实际表现到底如何,就可叫好好先生了?”答道:“他批评狂放的人说,‘为什么志气这么高,谈吐这么夸张?言语不顾行为,行为不顾言语,来不来都是古人呀!古人呀!’他批评狷介之士说,‘为什么这样落落寡合呢?'他说,'生在这个世界上,为这个世界做事,只要过得去就行了。'八面玲珑,四方讨好的人,就是好好先生。"万章说:"全乡的人都说他是老好人他也到处表现出是一个老好人,孔子竟把他看作戕害道德的贼人。为什么呢?"答道:"这种人要非难他却又举不出什么大错误来,要讥刺他却也没有什么可讥刺,他只是同流合污,为人好像忠诚老实,行为好像清正廉洁,大家也都喜欢他,他自己也以为正确,但是不可同他进入尧舜之道,所以说他是戕害道德的贼人。孔子说过厌恶那种似是而非的东西;厌恶田间杂草,因为它把禾苗搞乱了;厌恶不正当的才智,因为它把义搞乱了;厌恶能言善辩,因为它把信实搞乱了;厌恶郑国的乐曲,因为它把雅乐搞乱了;厌恶紫色,因为它把大红色搞乱了;厌恶好好先生,因为它把道德搞乱了。君子使一切事物回到常规正道便行了。常规正道不被歪曲,老百姓就会兴奋积极;老百姓兴奋积极,就没有邪恶了。"

【英语译文】

Wan Zhang asked, "Confucius said while in Chen State 'Why not go home? My disciples cherish great ambition but don't do trivial things.' While in Chen State why did Confucius think of these men who cherished great ambition but didn't do trivial things?" Mencius replied, "If one cannot befriend men observing great Way, he surely befriends unrestrained men and upright men. An unrestrained man cherishes great ambition but an upright man doesn't do trivial things. Didn't Confucius want scholars who observed great Way? Since he couldn't, he just wanted less graded one." Wan Zhang asked, "What kind of person can be called unrestrained?" Mencius replied, "Qin Zhang, Zeng Xi, Mu Pi were what Confuciuscalled unrestrained men." Wan Zhang asked, "Why were they called unrestrained men?" Mencius said, "They cherished great ambition and also liked to boast. They always uttered 'Ancient men, O, ancient men!' If we checked them we found that their words didn't conform to their actions. If one cannot get such unrestrained men he just wants to befriend those who refuse to do trivial things. Such kind of men are called upright men and they are much less-graded. Confucius said, 'I don't feel pitiful if he doesn't enter my room while passing my house because they are just nice guys. A nice guy is a thief who does harm to morality." Wan Zhang asked, "To what degree can a man be called a nice guy?" Mencius replied, "He criticizes the unrestrained man saying 'Why are you so ambitious and boastful? While speaking, you don't care about actions. While acting you don't care about words.

You are always mentioning ancient men. O, ancient men!' He criticizes the upright men saying 'Why are you so much aloof from people?' He says 'While living in this world you do things for it, and it is alright if you have no fault.' A man being smooth and slick and pleasing all people is just a nice guy." Wan Zhang asked, "People in a village all think that he is a nice guy and he acts as a nice guy. However, Confucius regarded him as a thief doing harm to morality. Why?" Mencius replied, "If such kind of person is rebuked, one cannot find any big mistake. If such kind of person is satired, one can find nothing to satire. He just associates himself with undesirable trends and thinks himself honest and white-handed so that people all like him. He thinks himself right but other people cannot get the Way of Sage Yao and Great Shun if they befriend him. Therefore he is a thief who does harm to morality. Confucius said that he loathed things which appeared right but in fact wrong. People loathe grasses in field because they meddled crops. People loathe unjustifiable talent because it meddled righteousness. People loathe talkativeness because it meddled honesty. People loathe music of Zheng State because it meddled elegant music. People loathe pink because it meddled red color. People loathe a nice guy because he meddled morality. A moral man makes everything return to the right Way. If the right Way isn't digressed, the common people will be excited and active. If common people are excited and active, there aren't evils."

【注释】(1)盍:hé,何不。吾党之士:我的同乡士人。孔子对门人不以老师自居。士人,泛指知识层。狂简:谓志大而略于事。进取:谓求望高远。不忘其初:谓不能改其旧也。(2)狂士:指志向高远,勇于进取之士。(3)不得中道而与之:不能同行中正大道的人相交。(4)中道:赵岐注:"中正之大大道也。"(5)敢问:犹请问。敢,谦辞,犹冒昧。《贾公彦疏》:"敢,冒昧之辞者,凡言敢者,皆是以卑触尊不自明之意。"(6)琴张:未详。(7)牧皮:无考。(8)孔子之所谓狂矣:孔子所所说的一类狂人。(9)何以:为什么。(10)嘐嘐:xiāo ~,志大言大。夷考:考察。夷,发语词。其行而不掩焉者也:他的行为不能同言语对应相合。掩,关闭,合上。凡是关门闭户盖上有盖之物,必须双方对应相合。言行一致,才是可信的人。(11)不屑不洁之士:轻视污浊的士人,不同流合污的士人。(12)乡原:xiāngyuàn,指乡里中貌似谨厚而实与流俗合污的伪善者。原,同"愿"。朱熹注:"乡者,鄙俗之意,原与愿同……盖其同流合污,以媚于世故在乡人之中独以愿称。"(13)踽踽凉凉:jǔjǔ liángliáng,落落寡合的样子。阉然:yān ~,曲意逢迎的样子。(14)德之贼:破坏道德的人。(15)利口:能言善辩。(16)君子反经而已矣:君子恢复常道罢了。朱熹集注:"反,复也;经,常也,万世不易之常道也。"

【原文】38 孟子曰:"由尧舜至于汤,五百有余岁,若禹、皋陶,则见而知之;[1]若汤,则闻而知之。[2]由汤至于文王,五百有余岁,若伊尹、莱朱则见而知之;[3]若文王,则闻而知之。由文王至于孔子,五百有余岁,若太公望、散宜生,[4]则见而知之;若孔子则闻而知之。"由孔子而来至于今,百有余岁,去圣人之世,若此其未远;近圣人之居若此其甚也,然而无有乎尔,则亦无有乎尔。"

【白话译文】

孟子说:"从尧舜到汤,经历了五百多年,像禹、皋陶那些人便是亲自看见尧舜之道而知其道的;像汤,便是听传说而知尧舜之道的。从汤到文王,又有五百多年,像伊尹、莱朱那些人便是亲自看见延续的治道而知其道的。像文王,便是由听闻而知其道的。由文王到孔子,又有五百多年,像太公望、散宜生那些人便是亲自看见延续的治道而知其道的。像孔子,便只是听传说而知其道的。从孔子一直到今天,有一百多年了,离开圣人的年代如此不远,离开圣人的家乡这样近,但是没有承继的人,那就是没有承继的人了。"

【英语译文】

Mencius said, "There were more than five hundred years from the time of Sage Yao and Great Shun to that of King Tang. People like Yu and Gao Yao saw and understood personally the Way of Sage Yao and Great Shun . And Tang had heard and understood the Way indirectly. There were also more than five hundred years from the time of Tang to that of King Wen of Zhou Dynasty. People like Yi Yin and Lai Zhu personally saw the continuation of the Way and understood it. King Wen had heard and understood the Way indirectly. There were also more than five hundred years from the time of King Wen to that of Confucius. People like Tai Gong Wang and Sanyi Sheng personally saw the continuation of the Way and understood it. Confucius had heard and understood the Way indirectly. There are more than one hundred years from the time of Confucius till today. It's not far from the age of sage and it's so near to the hometown of the sage, however, there isn't anyone who inherits the Way. There isn't anyone who inherits the Way. "

【注释】(1)知之:朱熹注:"尹氏曰:'知,谓知其道也。'"(2)闻而知之:听传说而知尧舜之道。(3)莱朱:汤之贤臣。(4)散宜生:散氏,宜一说散宜氏;生,名。文王之贤臣。

参考文献

1. 杨伯峻．论语译注．北京:中华书局,1980.

2. 杨伯峻，杨逢彬．论语(国学基本丛书)．长沙:岳麓书社，2000.

3. 赵海燕．论语(儒家道家经典全释)．大连:大连出版社，1998.

4. 费孝通．关于“文化自觉”的一些自白．学术研究,2003(7).

5. 许渊冲．典籍英译,中国可算世界一流．中国外语,2006 (5).

6. 王宏印．开放视野系统开展典籍翻译事业．中国社会科学报,2011(8).

7. 王宏印．中国文化典籍翻译——概念、理论与技巧．大连大学学报，2010 (1).

8. 朱熹．四书章句集注．北京:中华书局，1983.

9. 董洪利．孟子研究．南京:江苏古籍出版社,1997.

10. 十三经注疏整理委员会．十三经注疏．北京:北京大学出版社，2000.

11. 杨伯峻．孟子译注．北京:中华书局，2005.

12. 唐君毅．中国哲学原论·导论篇．北京:中国社会科学出版社,2005.

13. 刘瑾辉．清代《孟子》学研究．北京:社会科学文献出版社，2007.

14. [清]戴震着 何文光整理．孟子字义疏证．北京:中华书局，2008.

15. 李峻岫．汉唐孟子学述论．济南:齐鲁书社,2010.

16. 王方路．诗经·国风白话英语双译探索．成都:四川大学出版社，2009.

17. 王方路．诗经·雅颂白话英语双译探索．上海:华东师范大学出版社，

2013.

18. Jakobson, Roman: On Linguistic Aspects of Translation [A], On Translation [C]. (ed.) Brower R. A. Cambridge . Mass: Harvard Univ. Press, 1959.